Salt Mackerel, Codfish, Fresh Lobster
Sold Direct to Families Through Mail Orders

"Heaving the Seine." Rowing desperately as the seine is payed out, the fishermen attempt to surround and capture the whole school of mackerel, which are swimming near the surface.

NOW READY FOR YOU ! Frank E. Davis' Own Pick of Newly Caught, Freshly Packed Ocean Fish

WHAT'S better, what's more delicious than a nice broiled mackerel—what's more tempting than well-browned codfish cakes—what's so sure to please as a dainty salad of lobster, pink-white and crisp in all its goodness? Yet these are only a few of the seafood treats that await your call for Fall and Winter meals. A glance through this folder will show you how easy it is to enjoy at your home table just as good fish as we folks here at the seashore have. I send, right to your door, all charges prepaid, the very choicest of the catches, packed to your order, and packed to keep. From my 37 years experience, serving families everywhere, I know my fish will more than please you. I guarantee your complete satisfaction or money refunded.

Send Your Fall Order Now

Everything is ready—freshly packed—in prime condition. Fall-caught mackerel, fat and juicy; new codfish, tender and white; fresh lobster; crabmeat; clams; shrimp—as good as though you had taken them from the shell yourself. Make your selection now while the list is complete. Stock your pantry or emergency shelf. Enjoy these good things while they are at their best. Choose from this list with full assurance that my definite guarantee removes all risk and protects you, absolutely.

Frank E. Davis

They're here! *First of the fat, tender, Autumn-caught* MACKEREL. *Try these at my risk*

Let me send you some of these new, Fall-caught mackerel. You'll actually be amazed to find that mackerel can taste so good. Plump, tender, thick-meated fish, they are wholesome, delicious and satisfying. Good for any meal; may be broiled, baked or boiled. We clean and trim the mackerel of heads and tails, and pack full net weight of clear fish in new brine. They keep perfectly in your home for weeks. Just freshen a fish and it is ready for cooking. Now, when the fish are at their best, is the time to get yours. Simply select the size you want, and send today.

NOTE: The large mackerel, because of extra fatness, are especially well-flavored, and are better value. Freshen a half or a whole fish for a meal, cut lengthwise or crosswise, as you prefer.

Delivered price:	6-lb. pail	10-lb. pail	15-lb. pail	20-lb. pail
Small Mackerel	$2.60	$3.90	$5.50	$ 6.95
These fish weigh one-half pound each. About 18 or 20 fish to a 10-lb. pail.				
Medium Mackerel	3.20	4.95	6.95	9.15
These weigh from 1¼ lbs. to 1½ lbs. each. About 6 or 7 fish to a 10-lb. pail.				
Large Mackerel	3.45	5.25	7.50	9.75
These weigh about 1½ lbs. each. About 6 fish to a 10-lb. pail.				
Extra Large Mackerel	3.60	5.50	7.85	10.25
These are fancy bloaters. About 5 fish to a 10-lb. pail.				

Right from the fishing boats to you

AMERICAN SEAFOOD

American Seafood

Heritage, Culture & Cookery
From Sea to Shining Sea

BARTON SEAVER

STERLING EPICURE
New York

STERLING EPICURE
New York

An Imprint of Sterling Publishing Co., Inc.
1166 Avenue of the Americas
New York, NY 10036

ISBN 978-1-4549-1940-7

Distributed in Canada by Sterling Publishing Co., Inc.
c/o Canadian Manda Group, 664 Annette Street
Toronto, Ontario, Canada M6S 2C8
Distributed in the United Kingdom by GMC Distribution Services
Castle Place, 166 High Street, Lewes, East Sussex, England BN7 1XU
Distributed in Australia by NewSouth Books
45 Beach Street, Coogee, NSW 2034, Australia

For information about custom editions, special sales, and premium
and corporate purchases, please contact Sterling Special Sales at
800-805-5489 or specialsales@sterlingpublishing.com.

Manufactured in China

2 4 6 8 10 9 7 5 3 1

sterlingpublishing.com

Design by Carrie Anne Seaver
For image credits, see page 506

To my babyfish, Alden

Contents

FISH SPECIES: A COMPLETE CATALOG OF AMERICAN SEAFOOD

Salt in Our Veins

THE STORY OF AMERICAN FISHERIES IS ONE OF American character—of our bravery, of our will, of our courage. Within this story lie channel markers leading to our history, our flavor, our cuisine. Fish stories tell of the people and the cultures implicated. They herald a brave time and a brave people who make up, in no small part, the backbone upon which this country was founded. The narratives that follow tell who we were and how we were fed. In our agrarian America, we sing songs of the fruited plain and the amber waves of grain— shouldn't we also sing songs of latitudes lost, long and lonely, where men and women of iron spirit toil?

Humans have been contemplating the oceans' dynamic personality since the beginning of time. To experience the shore is to witness the crucible of our two earthly systems attempting to share common space. This ebb and flow has been the inspiration for some of our species' greatest expressions, the muse of our creative selves. Artists such as Andrew Wyeth, Winslow Homer, and Edward Hopper have each in their unique way captured something hauntingly revealing about our relationship with the shore. In these artists' paintings, we find equal stage for exuberance and melancholy as their subjects, caught between nature and industry, seem to contemplate our human condition.

In the same way we revere and consider these artists' works, we should celebrate fishing communities and be thankful that by their efforts the sea comes to our tables. But we should also ponder how seafood reflects our relationship with the oceans. Explore the diversity of the species written about in this book and we will begin to appreciate the nuance and beauty of what we have too long seen as a commodity, ever the same. In reality, each season is different, each showing a different side of the unique personality of the ocean ecosystem. And when we answer to such a dynamic system with a static mindset, we fail to understand the oceans and find nothing in common with its nature or the people and communities whose lives respond to the tides.

RIGHT An old salt. Cape Ann, Massachusetts, c.1905.

OPPOSITE *The Fog Warning* by Winslow Homer, 1885.

When European immigrants first set foot upon American shores, settlement was made in the most bountiful places—on protected edges and coves and along bays and tributaries. These outposts on this "new continent" were isolated and provided for all the needs of the settlers. The success of each wave of immigrants depended upon what the ocean could provide. As our population grew, and our attentions turned westward, the economy of America as a maritime nation gave way to a more manifest destiny. A pillar of American values is based on the Jeffersonian belief in the yeoman farmer, that those who own and work the land are the surest form of prosperity and virtue. No one can own the oceans, and this lack of rootedness focused the inherent divide between an agrarian society and that of the hunter-gatherers that fishermen represent. As populations grew stable, settlements expanded and spread inland; our prosperity became the product of a larger, more diverse environment. As America grew into itself, as economies evolved and shifted by landownership and self-determination, these little fishing towns remained, their dependence on the sea unchanged. Some grew to tremendous size and power, becoming capitals of trade and culture, but most remained coastal outposts.

Along the way, lured by westward expansion and railroads, industry and capitalism, we lost familiarity with the fishing towns that were the foundation of this country; we became unmoored from this country's first industry. Despite all of our nostalgia for the Rockwellian character of these towns, we do not often cherish our maritime communities. We have forgotten them as we have drifted inward, and they have become somehow other. But it is upon those docks that the settlers carried the burden of the birth of this nation. When we stand on a dock gazing wistfully out at the wine-dark sea, we think of fisheries as a place beyond the gentle slope of the horizon. But to truly see a fishery, we must turn around. Among the houses and the schools and the roads, in the opportunities for a son or daughter to follow in their family's bootsteps—there we find a fishery. It is the sum of the efforts and aspirations of the brave men and women working in one of America's most dangerous professions. A fishery is our heritage.

While fishing may recall our nation's past, it also represents the future of this country. On and under the ocean we can create jobs. Through our exemplary fishery management, we can expand our leadership among nations and turn America's greatest blessing—our oceans—into the pillar of our economy, our health, and our stewardship of our world. And at the end of the day, we can serve our families healthful meals proudly produced right here.

I have spent two decades now in restaurants, in my home kitchen, aboard fishing vessels, and traveling the world exploring fisheries, and in that time, I have developed a focused awe of the oceans and the infinite variety of flavors that they provide. I have also cultivated a deep admiration for those who bring seafood to our tables. Seafood is not just a preference or a diet choice for me, it is a deeply-rooted and carefully studied passion for ingredients, stories, and the taste of place that each bite brings. And that is why I have written this book. We lack connection. Fishing communities provide for our families, create jobs, sustain heritage, and preserve opportunity. It's only right that when we consider them, we think of the food they provide as a vehicle for us to engage with and help sustain them.

Seafood is also a part of our culinary heritage, as it represents flavors, cooking methods, and recipes, some lost to time and others still celebrated. But many of us know very little about seafood, either the fish it comes from or the role it's played in our country and cuisine. In the pages that follow, I elucidate some of the biology of fish, a lot of the history we share with the species that grace our waters, and some of the delicious opportunities to be enjoyed from them.

What you hold in your hands is not a cookbook. It's not an Audubon-type guide, it's not an unbiased reference book, it's not specifically a history book, yet it's all of these things at once. It is the story of American seafood—the product, the people, and places. Just as we claim Grandma's recipes as part of our heritage, as we claim colorful tomatoes as treasured heirlooms, so too should we see seafood as providing for us the same fundamental values, both civic and emotional. I hope that in these pages you find inspiration to explore your relationship with our fishing communities and to read about and try "new" species of seafood. In doing so, you may realize how not new they actually are within the greater American experience. And how in the dishes they've inspired we taste the tale of immigrants coming to a land of unbelievable riches, which stretched from sea to shining sea.

The Character of Fishermen

"It's nae fish ye're buying, it's men's lives."

—SIR WALTER SCOTT

FISHING HAS ALWAYS BEEN A DEADLY OCCUPATION, in paradox to its purpose of sustaining those it feeds. To this day it remains among America's most dangerous jobs. Referring to the incredible number of lives lost, Jeffrey Bolster, in his brilliant book *The Mortal Sea,* described fishing communities as "seemingly at war with the seas." The architectural structure known as the *widow's walk,* first introduced as a feature of homes in New England coastal towns, is an example of how this sorrow has entered our culture's common lexicon. These railed perches atop houses offered views of the ocean for loved ones to spot returning ships, which all too often never reached safe harbor. In the town of Gloucester, Massachusetts, during a 25-year span in the late 1800s, 380 vessels never returned with the 2,450 lives they carried. There are memorials to fishermen all over this country, which not only mourn lost sailors but, more appropriately, celebrate their lives and contributions to their communities.

Most fishermen consider their work as a way of life. There is a deep connection to the ocean and the nature of the tasks required. I have seen the joy in an old fisherman's face, five decades on the water yet still made giddy by the tug at the end of a line. Though pious Pilgrims arrived on our shores in pursuit of religious freedom, successive waves of immigrants to America were drawn by cod and the incredible wealth to be mined from the sea. Some families became very wealthy, while others remained poor laborers within the perilous industry. The wealthy families became known as the "Codfish Aristocracy," and they largely populate the register of America's first families. These religious Pilgrims and entrepreneurs alike had found a new Eden, though the socioeconomic structures thought left behind in Europe were quickly established as the New World order.

There quickly rose an obvious dissemblance between the righteous Puritans and the salty mariners. Fishing laborers were characterized in early descriptions as undevout, independent, coarse men. The structure and seasonality of fishing work put it at odds with the Puritan tenet that work was pleasing to God only when performed in a regular and disciplined manner. The boom-bust cycles and alternation of frantic activity and idleness built into the nature of fisheries was seen as evidence of a moral failing of those involved. From the very beginning, this perceived division between fishermen and farmers placed fisheries at social and sometimes moral odds with the increasingly prevailing agrarian principles of America. As the decades went by and the industrial revolution took hold, generations of fishermen aged out of the industry, or made enough money to take a job inland in the factories and dissuaded their sons from working the fisheries. This is when itinerant workers began to step in, and immigrant waves from other regions of Europe began to greatly influence the culture of fisheries. In many locations, they took over various regional fleets. As fisheries grew, new workers were enlisted from among the successive waves of immigrants. Slavic, Italian, Portuguese, Greek, and Chinese immigrants, among others, all contributed to the ever-changing nature of the industry.

With the abolition of slavery, large populations of newly freed men and women found little opportunity in the South, outside of the antebellum order. Many took employment in regional fisheries that served the African American population, which by and large could not afford meat, thus making fisheries and the oceans a primary source of food. As reported in an 1880 survey of South Carolina fisheries, 94 percent of its participants were African American.

The cost of owning one's own boat and the prevailing ruling class of the Codfish Aristocracy ensured that most laborers in fisheries never had opportunity to amass any riches of their own. They were in a system in which they remained only laborers. These immigrant populations and their American-born descendants tended to maintain intimate communities that identified strongly with their cultural and religious heritage. Many of these populations came from Catholic backgrounds, and despite our foundations touting religious freedom, religious discrimination was deeply entrenched in early American society. Associating fish as a food of the Catholics, among other cultural and social shifts, led to seafood being seen as food of the poor and distrusted. As farm animal meat consumption soared, a further separation was created between maritime communities and the new American guard.

In America, we have always morally subsidized farming because we have understood and respected the hardships of its labors and its associated civic values. We deem farmers virtuous. But since our founding, we haven't understood the labors of fishermen and the role they play in our society and culture, and thus we have largely failed to comprehend the civic values they embody.

Fishermen brave dangerous and brutal conditions and spend extensive time away from home and family. It can be hard to see why people are drawn to the industry. From economic and community relations standpoints, fishermen face further pressures as the working waterfronts on which they depend are threatened by the constant advance of coastal development into summer homes and hotels.

These traditionally tight-knit communities, models of American self-reliance and independence, have become wary as they see themselves forgotten or viewed with indifference or even enmity by regulators and the general public. But at the core of fishermen's character is a deep understanding of nature, as well as great pride and joy that they provide food for our nation through their physical labors. Fishermen are bound together as a community by a profound respect for the ocean and a heritage of skill and work ethic.

And though fishing communities have become somewhat marginalized socially and economically, there is a great literary tradition of paying homage to the fortitude and character of these brave fishermen. From Melville and Kipling to London, Whitman, Audubon, Steinbeck, Hemingway, Warner, Hersey, and Matthiessen, so many have celebrated and immortalized American fishermen. And though the handsome sailor often stands in the shadow of our agrarian hero, we still reminisce and hold sacred these captains courageous. As Longfellow muses:

> *I ploughed the land with horses,*
>
> *But my heart was ill at ease,*
>
> *For the old sea-faring men*
>
> *Came to me now and then,*
>
> *With their sagas of the seas.*

THEY THAT GO
DOWN TO THE SEA
IN SHIPS
▲ ▲ ▲
1623 — 1923

Honoring Those Who Slipped Beneath the Sea

"The history of the Gloucester fishery has been written in tears."

—ANONYMOUS

NEARLY EVERY TOWN WITH A HISTORY OF FISHING has a memorial to those whose ships never sailed home. While in some cities these monuments are small and out of the way, in cities like Gloucester, pictured at left, and Juneau these tributes are carved directly into the heart of the town, never far from mind. And they are closer still in the hearts of every person who knew, worked with, prayed with, or was kin to the men and women whose names adorn those stoic markers.

Throughout New England, Newfoundland, and Nova Scotia, tributes honouring those who slipped beneath the surface of the sea are often similar in size and station to the monuments commemorating fallen soldiers. These statues are not only a way to remember a town's lost fishermen, they are also sacred spaces rooted in faith and draped in ritual. The community may gather around them to sing hymns, share remembrances, and pray for God's presence and protection.

In regions throughout the country, religious or faith leaders serving the fishermen's families captain local variations of a Blessing of the Fleet ceremony. From New England and throughout the South, to San Francisco, Seattle and north, various rituals and rites communicate humility toward the sea and entreat deities, saints, and angels from a number of faiths to look over those who navigate the waters. In some towns when the officiant has concluded his or her blessing, the gathered crowd falls into a serene hush (not unlike the ocean conditions for which they pray) and a wreath is lowered into the water in honor of all the fishermen and women whose final rest came far from shore. As the wreath slips solemnly into the waves, a growing rumble is heard. The normally dolorous exhale of foghorns is today a celebratory angel band praising the newly blessed fleet. The church bells peal as they do on Easter morning. And that's a pretty apt analogy—these communities always take care of each other, and they always rise again.

The day's not done. Like any hard-laboring community living in the intimate company of tragedy, fishermen know how to have a good time. After the foghorn's beckoning call quiets, the celebration begins. The community toasts the fleet and the year ahead. Spirits are high and optimism is renewed. Fishing boats costumed as mermaids, shrimp, and sea monsters compete in races around the harbor. There are shucking contests and dances and more food and beer than one might think holy.

But the monuments stand sentinel long after the festivities end. Haunting and beautiful, they attest to the lives lived in the crucible between safe harbor and tempestuous seas.

FULL RIGGED FISHING SCHOONER AND MODERN POWER FISHERMAN PUTTING OUT TO SEA, GLOUCESTER, MASS. 1107

The Hand of Man in a Dynamic Environment

"For all the development and pollution and privatization of our shores it is easy to lament good days passed, but let's not mourn best of times because we still live in them."

—EUELL GIBBONS

Shifting Baselines

America is a land of improbable riches. Explorers here found fish so legion as to be caught by lowering a bucket, soils so fertile they could feed billions, natural beauty that has inspired art ranked in the highest echelon of human expression, rivers that sparkled with gold, and land so vast as to be a physical manifestation of our political freedoms. With this wealth we achieved the single greatest victory in human history— the ability to choose our own path. Sterile seas and fruitless barrens pit humans against nature. Abundance allows us to choose how we want to interact with our environment. And this plays out especially clearly in our nation's fishing history.

The widespread adoption of the otter trawl over centuries, paired with the advent of gas-powered engines, did more to radically alter the industry than any other advance in history. The cone-shaped net was developed in western Michigan, where it was successfully used in Great Lakes fisheries for years, and later introduced into the New England fleet at the turn of the twentieth century. Sharp captains immediately made the investment. For almost all of history, using hand gathering, traps, weirs, lines, and the elegant Grand Bank's fleet, fishing was long limited by man-power and compassed under sail. The facility of the Banks' fisheries schooners was not hauling nets. They efficiently employed the traditional method of men in dories setting out from the mother ship to fish using hand lines, each baited with several hooks.

It was the introduction of the gasoline engine, followed soon after by the diesel that proved the watershed moment of transition in fisheries. Captains, now armed with enough power to quickly tow large nets, called trawls, inaugurated a series of changes that opened up the seas like never before. The legacy of this shift defines our relationship with the seas to this day.

Catches grew exponentially, dwarfing what had previously been considered normal. With the baseline of European resource depletion imprinted on the popular consciousness of this young nation's citizens, we were keenly aware of the destructive power that our efforts paired with technology could bring upon a resource.

While the otter trawl was at first vociferously rejected by traditionalists (a dismissive term for those who expressed a precautionary point of view), as catches soared, the traditional method lost its romantic appeal and suspicions were quickly forgotten. The enormous efficiency and capacity of the trawl fleet cemented the growing income gap between the laborer and the financier and changed the structure of the fisheries economy to aggregate wealth for those who could afford the technology to compete in a commodity market. This innovation marginalized small-scale fishers and represents one instance of the social and economic stratification in fisheries between the haves and have-nots. Until the trawl was introduced, every fish was caught by an individual or in a net, which was only as productive as the strength of those hauling it. There was real democracy in the equal opportunity offered by fishing. The industry had always preferentially profited the boat owners, the elitist Codfish Aristocracy who had amassed wealth by mining the Atlantic's fortune, but it was still for the most part an industry that rewarded the laborer's aspirations. Each fisherman was able to earn what he compelled his own hands to achieve. The introduction of trawl technology not only replaced much of the human labor required in fisheries—catching immense quantities of fish immediately altered the nature of the fishing economy. A man with a baited line of hooks would never again be the central figure in fisheries, and rapidly expanding markets would only marginalize him further, as he could not compete with the efficiencies of scale that crowded out the small producers. The introduction of such an impersonal technology was seen as immoral and antithetical to the working social order and brought upheaval to the community construct of fisheries.

The arguments offered by the laborer class were initially heard. Authorities made an effort to reconcile the cultural and economic schisms widening with every fishing trip. But this was America. The notion that a few individuals could introduce something new and in the process concoct a new reality from the comfortable dimensions of the status quo was not original.

ABOVE Unloading the catch, Astoria, Oregon, c. 1950.
OPPOSITE, LEFT Trawlers docked at Boston T-Wharf, 1947.
OPPOSITE, RIGHT Postcard showing changing technologies, c. 1910.

Schooner fishing fleet, Gloucester, Massachusetts, c. 1900.

We had declared independence and upended the political world order. The increasingly antiquated platform espoused by the traditional fleet conflicted with American ideals. This was the land of opportunity, and progress was part of its natural process.

Jeffrey Bolster in *The Mortal Sea* considered that at this cultural crossroads the concept of *tradition* was a fleeting tenet in America, as nearly every aspect of contemporary life was evolving. Equal opportunity was subjugated to innovation. Once an idea, technology, or movement takes form and reaches a tipping point, previous protestations were laid aside and the new normal was assimilated into our dogma. The theism of America was progress. Any debate against fisheries progress ceased when in 1915 a single boat landed 280,000 pounds of fish during a five-day trip. The very next month that same vessel landed 300,000 pounds. (A hand-line schooner averaged 200,000 pounds during a two-week trip at sea.) In light of such astounding volume, any contention was muted before the complaint could be registered.

But as Bolster is so keen to point out, there was another and perhaps even more damning advance that happened simultaneously as we institutionalized progress. When we fished by hand, we engaged the natural world through our wits and physical abilities (and limitations). Captains knew where the cod should be and would guide his crew to fertile waters. Once embarked in their dories, each fisherman was putting into practice hundreds of years of inherited knowledge, from the curve and size of the hook to the type of bait to the spacing of hooks on the line. These details and infinite others necessarily kept man an intimate part of the system that he was working to exploit. This was still an industry that could rightly be called fishing, as there was no guarantee of catching but for the skill of the individual. Fishermen had to find the cod. They had to do their best to lure them. They had to win the ensuing battle to land them.

It can be said that fishing under sail power was an important watershed development in fisheries, and indeed it was. But it didn't change the very disposition of fishing. Its contribution was access to an expanded area upon which we could apply established techniques, and from them expect similar results. With the advent of the engine-powered trawler, we no longer waited for the fish to bite. We now had the ability to chase them down, to find them where they were, and to take what we wanted when we wanted it.

When we set a baited hook, experience informed our expectation and control of the resulting catch. With a trawl drawn across the seabed we forfeited control over what we caught. Up came flounder and Haddock and monkfish and Sea Robins, and . . . and . . . and . . . (many of them small, unmarketable, dead). This newly available bounty timed well with a significant rise in the popularity of fresh seafood being enjoyed in America's increasingly populous urban centers. Flounder, a fish that was never before commercially targeted on a large scale, was among the most valuable and popular species within a decade of the otter trawl's introduction. Flounder would not take the large baited hooks designed to catch the much larger cod, and it's probable that fishermen who had plied those waters for 400 years had never known of the incredible abundance of these flatfish blanketing the sea floor beneath them.

Technology is constantly changing, and something new will always be competing for our attentions long before we have grown comfortable with, let alone mastered, the technology we previously delighted in. Progress and growth handicap our reasoning and are as powerful a drug as has ever enfranchised a people and influenced their ambitions. It reminds me of a quote from author Kurt Vonnegut: "Dear future generations: Please accept our apologies. We were rolling drunk on petroleum."

Historian Henry Adams captured this cultural submission to technology, calling it the age of the Dynamo and the Virgin. The Virgin did not stand a chance, as Adams wrote, "Newness and power became the sole measures of worth." We betrayed our faith in the precautionary principle. Our copies of Thoreau and Emerson gathered dust. Radical individualism and self-reliance gave way to "better living through science."

As technology evolves so, too, do our expectations, what can be called our *baselines*.

I have read many old fishery books and reports, their tales about shoals of fish as large as a city, or the frenzied feeding of Bluefish on menhaden, so violent as to unnerve observers, or storms that washed up piles of five-pound lobsters on Northeast beaches. It's not just that the accounts of abundance show woeful patterns of decline and negligence—the cultural mentality of living to fulfill our needs in a shared world is gone. Abundance makes us eager and greedy, and it can blind us, even as we witness what ecologist Garrett Hardin called "the tragedy of the commons."

Our vague awareness of declining resources, or our *commons* has been tempered by the underlying faith we place in science and technology. We believe a solution will soon be invented to solve any issue. The early accounts of explorers in America were ridiculed as outlandish because they were viewed through the lens of the European experience, which had witnessed the serial depletion of their own resources over the centuries. They simply could not relate their baseline to what was described along our shores, telling accounts of fish schools so dense as to seemingly allow man to walk on water. Early colonists thrived off this abundance yet brought with them concern, aware of the damage we could cause. At this country's outset, we put faith in a precautionary approach to using our resources, but as populations grew, abundance suffered by man's destruction of habitat and by the stress of fishing pressures. Our baselines began to shift in real time, responsive to what we saw in the present. Our short-term memories allow us to rationalize the present as an isolated event outside the scope of history, and we are apt to avidly defend that the current state of things is the normal state of things. With each shift in baselines, we afford the new normal the respect and protection that we feel morally obligated to provide. And we think well of ourselves for our conservation ethos. But to understand our natural world, we must not evaluate ecosystems by our current perception but relate our experience to the paradigm of history.

The contemporary character of our fisheries cannot be fully understood without this long view. When we see things through a historical perspective, we begin to understand how our current reality evolved and appreciate where we have come from and what we have gained and lost in the process.

It is a sacred tenet of the American dream that our sons and daughters will lead better lives than our own. But it's a losing argument that fishermen have it better now than their forebearers did. Our children are increasingly conscious that they are entering into a world that is managed for scarcity of resources rather than for abundance.

Though a decline in resources and opportunities has been noted by every generation, we've been able to convince ourselves that everything was just fine because as one fish stock declined, improved technology allowed us to catch even more. As one species disappeared, fisheries moved on to other species in other waters. And at the retail counter the consumer has been blinded to the declining abundance of our seas by the ever-present availability of our favorite foods. Globalized trade has very effectively hidden localized collapses.

The first step to solving a problem is often acknowledging that we have a problem. As early at 1871, the fishing industry asked the government to help mitigate the depletion of resources it was witnessing, and the United States Fish Commission was created. Its charge was to study and reverse declines in fish populations. The overarching goal was not to conserve resources, but rather to create agency to ensure resource availability for fisheries. In those heady times of manifesting our destiny, Americans considered the resources of land and sea to be theirs by constitutional and God-given right. The idea of limiting access was a bitter political and cultural pill. And so the U.S. Fish Commission initiated hatchery programs to artificially boost declining populations of economically important species. A Massachusetts fisheries scientist wrote, circa 1900, "The true solution lies not in limiting demand though prohibition of fishing effort, but rather in developing methods to secure an increase in supply of fish, to such as artificial propagation." This attitude, which reflected the pervasive philosophy that we could and should humanize the earth for our benefit, was foundational to our national ethos. The hubris that led to the notion that technology gives us dominion over nature and her systems was a far cry from our pious Puritan beginnings.

The concept of *shifting baselines* can be explained as the ever-changing denominator by which we measure the health of our environments. But there are also shifting social baselines. Now that we have become aware of how our industries have damaged the environments that sustain us, we think about the condition of the world that we are leaving for our children. And in our desire that they lead better lives than our own, we need to decide what we want the world to look like. The future we are building for our children will not mirror our experiences or those of our grandparents or the generations before them.

LEFT Dragging in the catch, Provincetown, Massachusetts, 1942. RIGHT Boats unloading at the Boston T-Wharf, c. 1920.

Our purpose is not to make the world a better place, but rather to find how we can better coexist within dynamic and ever-changing ecosystems in ways that allow us—and the oceans—to thrive. Bounty must no longer be measured by what we can take from the oceans, but rather by what the oceans can afford to give us. We must shift our priorities to focus not on desires but instead on needs. Desire is infinite; need is finite.

The impact that humans have levied on the oceans is not limited to overfishing or to pollution or to habitat destruction. What we choose to eat, and more importantly what we choose not to eat, is the source of a systemic shift in the biological order of the marine food chain. When we think of fisheries' decline, we think first of decreased populations. But our preferences as consumers have the power to alter populations, and that is the result of cultural bias. For tens of thousands of years, indigenous peoples lived sustainably in concert with ocean ecosystems. Even in relatively modern history (meaning the last 300 years), we've preferred shellfish and diverse and seasonal species of seafood. I'm pretty sure that is because a lot of those types of seafood can be harvested very near to shore or, in the case of herring and shad, actually swim toward us. I'm not saying our ancestors were lazy, but if making dinner meant waiting until low

tide to collect oysters, clams, mussels, and whatever happened to get trapped in a tide pool, what incentive did they have to expand their environment? Within the last century our preferences for seafood have shifted. Partially this is because we ate up most of the nearshore seafood. Technology has allowed us to expand our culinary repertoire to include the vast array of offshore species previously unavailable in the human diet. Studies have looked at restaurant menus spanning a century to document the species served in a given region, and they show evidence that the species we eat today are higher in the marine food chain. You won't find herring, once popular in restaurants across the country, on many menus today. In its place are halibut and tuna, which were rarely served in years past. Indeed, the guiding hand of natural selection is ours, and it is holding a fork.

This shift in culinary preference has had a measurable impact upon the function of ocean ecosystems. The marine food chain is an intricately woven drama of interdependent relationships, and the systems' resilience requires stability at all levels. When we remove apex predators from any system we create an imbalance, much like the eradication of coyotes and wolves has led to an ecologically damaging abundance of deer and other "prey species." Nature operates on her own momentum;

our responsibility now is not to reverse engineer its health, but rather to learn how to minimize our impacts while still sustaining ourselves. We must learn how to act in concert with nature rather than act upon her.

Our impacts are not always obvious. Sometimes there are subtle repercussions that manifest over such time as to blind us to their process. There is a particularly masculine motivation that humans often express: it's often the shiniest or newest or biggest of anything that most strikes our fancy. Our pursuit of the most impressive of the oceans' large predators has resulted in shifts in the genetic diversity of many species. If we remove all of the big fish, then there are no big fish to pass their big-fish genes on to the next generation. We have seen fish populations display a genetic shift over the course of decades. The photos on this page were all taken on the same dock at the same marina, and each captured the same moment as experienced by people over the course of decades. These are the trophy boards where charter boat parties hang the largest of their catch. It's a time-honored judgment that the best fish is the biggest fish. These proud anglers beam with the thrill of the catch, and the joy expressed in their faces doesn't change throughout the years. But the size of the fish certainly does. In the most recent photo, a successful angler went home as happy as could be having caught that 25-inch grouper. A hundred years ago, that 25-inch grouper may have been used as bait.

The function of marine ecosystems is not a simple arithmetic, but rather an incredibly complex calculus involving variables both within and beyond our influence. As science continues to explore how we impact ocean ecosystems, we need to equally invest in an exercise of self-reflection, to consider our personal baselines and expectations. If we are focused only on sustainable fishing, then we abdicate our responsibility to behave sustainably. It is not enough to demand sustainably produced seafood if we still expect to enjoy an all-you-can-eat seafood buffet. If we expect too much from the oceans, we forfeit balance. If we are only willing to eat certain species or fish of a certain size, then we make demands of the oceans and what they must provide. We need to shift our baseline to ask for only what the oceans can provide and to accept the diversity it offers as our normal.

Upstream Influences on Dinner

Sustainable fisheries are a construct that begins far inland. Though it is the action of the fishermen on the water that is most easily noted as the point of engagement, that is but a small portion of the entire biological system. When we consider our impact on fisheries, we have to look at the entire geography that influences life in the ocean. Essential to nearly every fish and shellfish we so savor from the mid-Atlantic throughout the Gulf of Mexico are the estuaries, bayous, brackish river deltas, and all manner and form of onshore and nearshore habitat. Without salt marshes, there would be no shrimp. Without the shallow waters of the Chesapeake Bay and its billowing tidal fields of eelgrass, there would be no Blue Crab or Striped Bass. Without the voluminous and mighty flow of rivers like the Damariscotta in Maine there would be no salmon or herring or Alewife or shad. It's not enough that we look only at our actions on the sea. We must also see how we affect the habitat vital to the very existence of these species. Draining marshlands for golf courses, polluting water quality in estuaries so that eelgrass cannot grow, allowing legacy dams left by long-obsolete industries to block essential river spawning grounds for marine life . . . all of these actions condemn our oceans to decline as much as, if not more than, fishing technology does.

OPPOSITE Lobstermen talking shop, c. 1935. ABOVE Mending nets, c. 1925.

Consumer Demand and Our Evolving Tastes

FROM THE EARLIEST DAYS OF AMERICA'S FOUNDING, this land of plenty's first economy was built upon fisheries. Yet we've mostly considered the eating of fish to be beneath our aspirations. Countless examples throughout the centuries point back to a bias against seafood as a top-quality food or even one fit to be served. As early as 1623, William Bradford, the governor of Plymouth Colony, wrote, "If ye land afford you bread, and ye sea yeeld you fish, rest you a while contented, God will one day afford you better fare."

It wasn't long before "better" fare was available due to the westward expansion of our young nation. Meat has long held a cultural significance as an aspirational foodstuff—families could mark their wealth by the amount of meat they served. In the European experience meat had been a limited luxury. On most small farms, animals were principally considered to be beasts of burden; their second purpose was as meat. Historically, the impediment to eating more meat had been the ability to dedicate huge swaths of fertile farmland to the production, not of human food but of silage. America's prairies offered seemingly limitless agricultural expansion. They were oceans of a different sort, oceans that rippled with the amber waves of grain.

The religious implications surrounding seafood in Europe followed and took root in the Protestant culture of early America. Seafood was associated as Catholic fare for the more than 150 calendar days that required the devout to abstain from meat. Salt cod was a commodity of trade, not often used for popular consumption in America, with only poor families and servants consuming it with any regularity. There are accounts of five-pound lobsters—blown in by a storm and piling up on the shore—getting tilled under as fertilizer for the fields. It was considered an embarrassing commentary upon a family's tastes and economic standing if lobster was served at their table. And even the great shad of the East Coast was at first considered to be "despised and rejected," and those who ate it were shamed.

Even knowing how to fillet the bony fish stereotyped one as being of crass character. This was in part born of the popularity of shad as a Native American food, and thus our overt disdain for Native Americans was transferred onto America's poor. From the very beginnings of this country, food has been a measure of status and wealth, both of which directly attributed to the judgment of the quality of one's character. Eating lobsters or shad in this new land of opportunity was considered proof of failure.

The early American fisheries scientist Fred Mather said, "We have often said that there is more good food wasted in the United States than in any other country, but as our population increases this will remedy itself. At present our people are too proud to buy anything but the choicest things in the market." Perhaps it was the immense bounty of America's natural resources and the wealth Americans made from them that created the mindset that we deserve to have whatever we want. Having more food than we could possibly eat, we were able to eat following our whims, choosing the foods we wanted from an uncommon volume and variety of goods. The irony is that this freedom to have whatever we want has led us to want fewer things in terms of diversity. While the expansion of farmlands into the west increased the amount of food available to us, it didn't necessarily increase our demand for a greater variety of foods.

According to USDA data first available from 1909, Americans were eating well over 150 pounds of beef, pork, and chicken per person per year but just 10 pounds of seafood. That amount of seafood has remained largely static, peaking at around 16 pounds in 1987 but hovering in the low teens for more than a century. In that same time frame, meat consumption has topped out at more than 200 pounds per person.

Since the time of Plymouth Colony, we have always been slow to adopt new ingredients or flavors. The Pilgrims endured years of struggle and hardship and terrible hunger. When a second wave of Pilgrims was greeted, Bradford wrote, "The best dish we could present them with is a lobster or a piece of fish without bread or anything else but a cup of fair spring water." The half naked, nearly starved Pilgrims must have been quite a sight. Looking back through the lens of history, we realize that so much of the bounty of this country was wasted or never even considered by European settlers, who brought with them such a narrow-minded view of the world. The only reason some

MRS. EVELENE SPENCER
Fish Cookery Expert, U. S. Bureau of Fisheries, Author of "Fish Cookery"

Says——

Eat more Fish for your health's sake.

Get acquainted with cheaper kinds and use more of them.

Use Smoked and Salt Fish for breakfast.

Use Frozen Fish when Fresh Fish is scarce or out of season.

Use more Shell-Fish—America produces finest in the world.

Separate Fish from Friday
—Make TUESDAY a Fish Day as well
EAT MORE FISH
—A Real Health Food

of them did not starve was that they begrudgingly ate from the sea. I understand that it is difficult for people to expand their comfort zone and embrace something new, but it seems unconscionable that anyone suffering from hunger should complain about food so abundant that it literally washed up on shore for them to gather.

Given that we have long relegated seafood to second-tier status, it's interesting to look back through old cookbooks and fishing industry reports to see how we have come to define the quality of seafood through the years. The standards by which we have judged a fish to be a preferred species or not is based on a complex blend of cultural and social forces that shaped our subjective viewpoints. In some of the earliest cookbooks to have widespread influence, seafood's easy digestibility became its chief selling point. Entire chapters were dedicated to dishes for the "infirm," and many of these were seafood dishes. One pamphlet from 1920 advising food choices offered this piece of advice: "Moreover fish is less stimulating as a food than meat, which is a matter of importance in these days of heavy nervous tension." The great Fannie Merrit Farmer wrote in her *Boston Cooking School Cookbook* that seafood was less nourishing than the meat of other animals, which she could forgive since it was considered easier on digestion. She goes on to recommend that white-fleshed fish is preferred for "sedentary people," but that fish categorically could not be recommended for "brain workers" on account of its inferiority to meat. It's funny that

now a diet rich in seafood is recommended for both optimal health and also for the development of our brains.

By the beginning of the twentieth century, fish gained a larger role in our culture when World War I broke out and food came to be recognized as one of our greatest weapons. Wartime campaigns to conserve the healthful and nourishing foods that would feed our boys abroad made dietary choices a matter not of subjective personal taste but one of patriotic duty. There are instructional books and pamphlets from that era developed by the government to teach Americans how to better incorporate underutilized seafood into their regular diet. But even the fervor of patriotism could not enhance seafood's standing or increase its long-term popularity. In 1898 icthyologist David Jordan wrote, "Our people are too well fed to take care for the coarse rank flesh of shark, however much its flavor may be disguised by the ingenious cook." One government pamphlet urged Americans to consider what was among the most abundant food sources, the Grayfish. It was touted to be the most affordable and accessible of any animal protein, and its culinary versatility was impressive. Whoever the author of this pamphlet was did a very good job being a cheerleader for what I can only assume he considered a lost cause. In the very last pages, it states, "in few things is [. . .] the public so steadfast and conservative as in the fish that it eats. This is particularly the case with the American, who, blessed beyond most peoples with a great variety of excellent food fishes, eat but few of them. Quality and price fix the economic character of a fish, but not until it has a name can it have a reputation, and without reputation, and a good one, the public will not eat it, however excellent it may be."

What I enjoy so much about this statement is the acknowledgment that name is so important. Grayfish was just the most recent attempt to rename the Mustel, which had been the Sea Bass, which had been Ocean Whitefish, as well as the Japanese Halibut, Harbor Halibut, Cape Shark, and Rock Salmon, all of which were short-lived market names for the Dogfish. We have always gotten on just fine with catfish, so I don't understand what the big deal is about calling it dogfish. But public spirit did expand the market for whatever you want to call it, though immediately after armistice—with the seasoning of patriotism removed—sales of dogfish collapsed.

Failure to grow market share for delicious cheap foods was not due to any fault or flaw with the product itself, but rather with our underlying cultural bias against seafood. Not only did seafood carry the cultural albatross of being the food of penance and fasting, war efforts on the home front had the unintended influence of promoting seafood as something we eat as a sacrifice for the good of the nation. This only served to cement its place in our culinary pantheon as a second-tier food. And directly following World War I, per capita seafood consumption declined as meat consumption continued its steady rise.

I think that the per capita seafood consumption figures of that era don't tell the full story of what was happening in America's rapidly evolving culture and growing diversity in its population. Between 1900 and the end of World War I, America's population grew by more than 30 million people. Many were immigrants arriving from countries such as Italy, Ireland, and Japan. These new Americans brought with them their traditional cuisines in which fish played a very prominent role, and as most of these immigrants formed communities in coastal cities they became a very important consumer base for the rapidly evolving American seafood industry. The gasoline engine and the highly efficient otter trawl were just becoming industry standard. As enormous quantities of fresh fish could now be landed, the focus on salted fish diminished. These densely populated urban areas allowed for fresh catch to be quickly sold and consumed, thereby allowing the fishing fleet to

realize efficiencies in a market now based on quick turnaround of product. At the same time, we were making great advances in the efficiencies of raising animals as farms began to consolidate and specialize. Around this time fish was incorporated as part of animal feed and synthetic fertilizer was introduced. As a result, animal growth rates accelerated and the cost of production dropped, making meat even more affordable and accessible to a broader population. My theory is that though seafood consumption per capita figures remained static, immigrant communities were eating a greater percentage of fish per capita than the established American communities of northern European origin, who had turned to meat for a greater portion of their diet.

OPPOSITE AND ABOVE Wartime poster encouraging seafood consumption. 1918–1943.

Save the
products of the Land

Eat more fish —
they feed themselves.

UNITED STATES FOOD ADMINISTRATION

PREVIOUS PAGES Grand banks schooners, 1907.
ABOVE Wartime poster, 1917.
OPPOSITE Fulton Fish Market, New York City, 1954.

If we look at restaurant menus from the time period, we discover the advent of fine dining in America as served in temples of gastronomy such as the Waldorf-Astoria Hotel and Delmonico's. Catering largely to an international crowd, these European-inspired establishments notably served a wide variety of seafood that, while familiar to much of their clientele, had long been considered trash or fertilizer in the United States. But when we look at the culinary texts of the era written for home cooks, all sense of seafood adventure is absent. These hotels and similar establishments created a secondary seafood market in New York City. The first market carried a small selection of mainstays—serving the tables of common households. The second fisheries market supplied the hotels with less common species.

But our tastes have changed over the course of many decades, and the seafoods that were most popular in the everyday market in the 1920s (and the species that were most economically important) are very different than those of the current day. Of course, some species endure, such as cod and Haddock, but in addition to these ever-popular fish were pollock, hake, Whiting, mackerel, Bluefish, weakfish, and Scup. Even the Bonito, now more often found in cat treats than at the fish market, made the list of 10 highest value fisheries. These species are still around, many of them in great abundance. But our interest in eating them, and cultural reference to them in cookbooks and on menus, has disappeared. As meat consumption continuously increased throughout the twentieth century, seafood's growth was negligable by comparison. When preferences and markets for seafood shifted, it was always a slow process by which one species traded vogue with another. The history of seafood consumption and America is not a story of increased demand but simply a slow shuffle of fish rotating through our culinary trends.

As technology in fisheries advanced, small regional multispecies fisheries became few and far between. In 1925, Clarence Birdseye introduced his revolutionary invention: the Quick Freeze Machine. With the advent of frozen seafood came decreased perishability and greater stability of supply. Seafood was now a global and commodified market that marginalized smaller -scale operators. At the same time, consumers developed a preference for convenience foods such as TV dinners and fish sticks. As we grew further separated from the source of our fish, with more and more fish caught on factory trawlers far from shore, many

20557 Buying Fish in the Market, Chinatown, San Francisco, Cal.
COPYRIGHT 1906 BY C. L. WASSON.

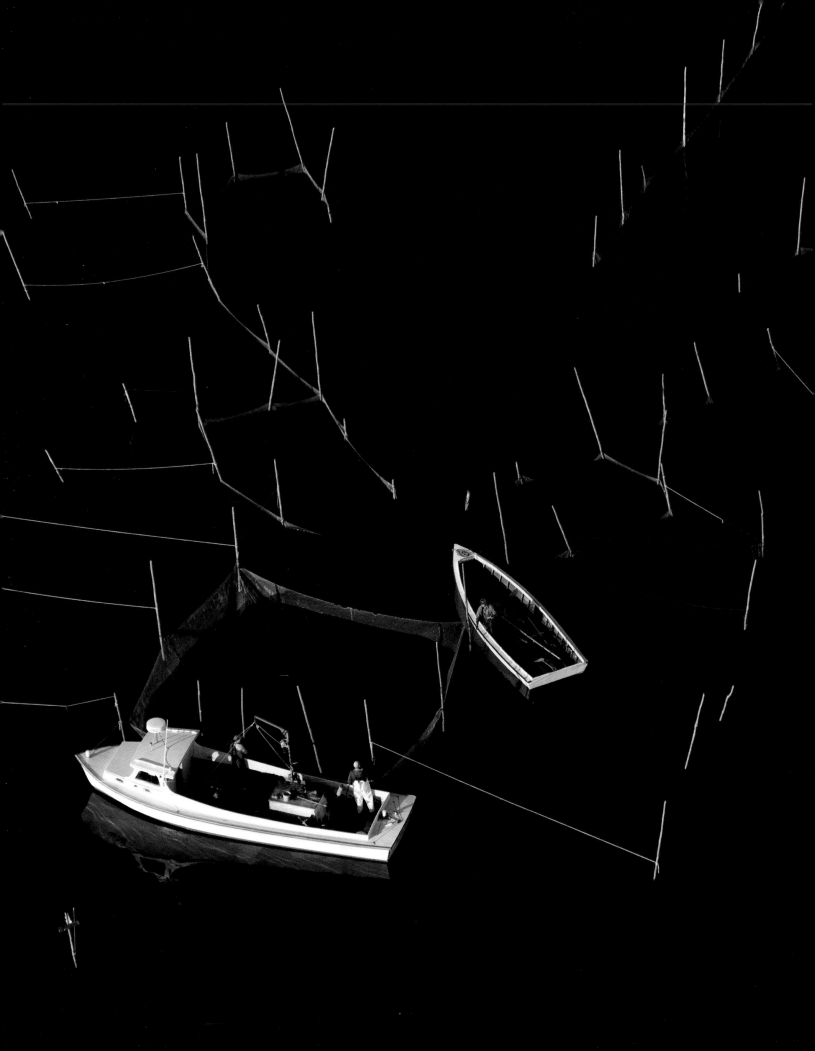

Fishing Methods Through the Centuries

FISHING EFFORTS HAVE BEEN EVOLVING CONSTANTLY throughout history. As fishermen respond to different environments, changing ocean dynamics, seasonal shifts in targeted species, and infinite variables unique to each fishing trip, the techniques they use have reflected their best efforts to adapt. Though these adjustments happen in real time, there are some consistencies that course through all fisheries and across eras. The methods explained below are a selection of those most commonly employed in modern fisheries. While certainly not exhaustive, this list gives a sense of the mechanical aspects of the term fishery.

DREDGES are sturdy metal baskets designed to dig into the sea floor to scoop up clusters of oysters, clams, and scallops, among others. The dredge been used in one form or another in fisheries along every coast of the United States, and we owe its inspiration to European tools of similar function. The mechanism's blunt actions can damage sea bottoms when they are dragged through sensitive habitat such as coral. These are typically used in shallower waters such as those in the Chesapeake or in the mid-Atlantic along sandy bottoms. Dredge fisheries have earned somewhat of a bad rap for this, as they can capture a number of untargeted species and disturb bottom habitat. Not all applications of the dredge have these impacts.

GILLNETTING uses a mesh net positioned like a curtain and held in place by a system of floats and weights to keep its broad side anchored toward the incoming fish. The netting is invisible to fish, and as they swim into it, the mesh openings are tailored to snare the fish by the gills. Once they've swum into the net, their gills prevent them from escaping backward. The mesh size and placement of the gear can be very selective in terms of what fish are caught and of what size. Gill nets are often used to catch sardines, salmon, and cod. Sometimes the nets are left to "soak" for days. But quality of gill-netted fish can be very high, as they are sometimes hauled on board within an hour after hitting the net, if not sooner. And because the fish have not struggled against the net or been crushed together, the fishermen are able to handle the fish carefully, making a top-quality product.

HARPOONING is the most direct way to catch the highest-quality large fish such as tuna and Swordfish. This method is only practiced by a legendary few, and to watch them at work is a marvel. Once a fish has been spotted (sometimes lolling on the surface to warm its body in the sun), the boat is positioned alongside the fish and, with incredible skill, a harpoon is thrown by hand. A clean strike ensures that there is no bycatch and the fish will struggle only a very short time. This results in very high-quality flesh, as the fish does not build up lactic acid during a prolonged fight. Since the fish are targeted one at a time, the fishermen are able to clean and chill the fish rapidly and with the utmost care.

LONG-LINING targets large, migratory species in the mid-water range such as Swordfish, Mahi Mahi, and tuna. This technique of stringing lines between buoys is also used to catch species such as halibut at the bottom of the water column near the ocean floor when it is called **DEMERSAL LONGLINING.** The lines are divided into branch sections with leaders of baited hooks. The depth of the hooks is determined by the interval of buoys placed along the main line, which can be up to 50 miles long and carry 3,000 baited hooks. After the gear is prepared, the crew, following the captain's intuition and knowledge, will cast out, or "soak," the line. Setting the line often takes several hours and can be retrieved after roughly four hours after the last hook has been set. It can take up to a day to haul in the line, which can lead to poor-quality fish if they have been left to struggle on the hook for a long time. This method is indiscriminate and can catch various unwanted species such as turtles, sharks, and juvenile fish. The introduction of the circle hook, which can only hook a fish in the cartilage of the mouth (rather than "deep hook" them in the throat or stomach), has significantly reduced this type of bycatch. It enables the release of unwanted species and can prevent some species from being hooked at all. Shark bycatch has been reduced with the application of magnets affixed to the lines. Sharks can sense electrical fields generated by the magnets and will be deterred from taking the bait. The technique of stringing multiple hooks from a main line has been used in fisheries for centuries. It was introduced in the cod fishery around 1850 when the method was called *trawling.*

OPPOSITE Pound net fishing on the Chesapeake Bay.

MID-WATER TRAWLING uses large nets that are towed through the water column at various depths. Sonar is used to locate schools of fish and to determine at what depth the nets should be placed. This method, used to catch species such as herring, squid, and shrimp, is selective and has little bycatch due, in part, to the introduction of turtle excluder devices (TEDs) and by varying the net's mesh size, which allows smaller fish to escape. This method can result in low-quality fish, as the fish are crammed into the "cod end," or back, of the net, and can be crushed by the weight of the subsequent catch.

POLE/TROLL is a very selective method that uses baited hooks cast from individual rods or poles and towed behind the boat. This method is used to target species near the surface such as Mahi Mahi, tuna, Bluefish, and mackerel. This is a particularly important method used in Alaskan salmon fisheries to catch Chinook Salmon and Coho Salmon. The fish are reeled in immediately after striking the line, and the resulting quality is very high. The scale of these fisheries is small but the increased quality commands a high price.

PURSE SEINING uses a very large weighted net to create a curtain around a school of fish or in an area where lots of fish tend to aggregate, such as just outside the mouth of a river. When a school of fish such as squid, herring, or salmon is spotted, a skiff boat is used to let out the net, which is then towed in a wide arc around the school. Once the fish are encircled, the bottom of the net is drawn together like a drawstring purse and hauled aboard. This can result in huge catches of fish of good quality, especially if they are taken ashore and processed quickly. This method is commonly used to catch tuna for the canning industry.

HAUL SEINE NETS are small curtains of weighted mesh that are laid out in shallow water, typically around a beach. The net is then drawn toward shore to herd and enclose fish that are then dragged onto the shore. This can be done by a few people by hand or with the aid of power winches. In early fisheries, horses were used to provide the additional power needed to pull in large catches. This method is typically used to catch Striped Bass, Bluefish, weakfish, mullet, and catfish.

TRAPS AND POTS are used to catch bottom-dwelling shellfish such as lobster, crab, and same species of shrimp. The design of these cages varies by region and targeted species. In the Alaskan king crab fishery, the traps are very large, whereas lobster traps are only a few feet in length. Most traps are wire mesh with openings lined with a funneled mesh. The trap is baited to entice the creatures to enter, after which they cannot pass back out due to the narrow opening of the mesh. In most fisheries, the traps are designed to allow undersized individuals to escape. When the traps are hauled aboard there is no mortality of the catch, and anything undersized is thrown back alive, making this a very low-impact fishing method. In the lobster and Dungeness Crab fisheries, minimum (and sometimes maximum) size limits are strictly followed. The traps are weighted to rest on the bottom and are attached to lines marked by buoys on the surface. Often several traps will be attached to a line and separated by a dozen feet or more. Traps are required to have escape hatches made of biodegradable mesh so if a trap is lost the material will break down, causing the trap to open and preventing it from capturing more fish.

POUND NET/WEIR FISHING uses a wall of netting to form a fence that blocks migrating fish and guides them into a funnel or trap. The fish aggregate in this area and do not swim back out, allowing fishermen to draw up a net at the bottom to bring the fish to the surface. They are then easily removed with a hand net and all unwanted species or juveniles set free with no mortality. These are built near shore and target Bluefish, Striped Bass, catfish, flounder, and schooling fish such as herring and menhaden.

BOTTOM TRAWLING uses wide-mouth nets of varying sizes but all share a similar design, which ends in a constricted "bag" that collects the catch in what's known as the "cod end." These nets are weighted in the front and spread open by an "otter" door. Often there is a chain along the bottom opening that also acts to stir up the sea floor directly ahead of the net, rousing fish and shuttling them into the mouth of the net. The size of the netting has a major impact on the sustainability and efficiency of the fishery. If the holes are too small, unmarketable juvenile fish are caught along with the large fish and are killed in the process. Larger mesh size allows smaller, non-targeted fish to swim out through the netting.

Mesh size of nets is regulated to avoid unnecessary destruction of non-targeted sea life. It can also be regulated to enable fishermen to target species for which they previously couldn't fish due to intermixing of species. All fish have particular behavioral traits that can be exploited for the benefit of the fishermen. For example, when startled, Haddock tend to swim up whereas cod and flounder swim down. Because cod is currently depleted, fishing limits are small and strict. The problem is that cod and Haddock often swim together, and fishermen weren't able to catch enough Haddock because they had already taken the limit of cod. The solution was to develop nets that responded to the cues the fish were giving us. Thus, large eight-foot holes were cut into the bottom side of the nets, which allow the cod to follow their instinctive escape route while capturing the Haddock above.

Bottom trawls are not without their controversy, as the process of dragging a weighted chain across the sea floor can damage the sea floor. When a trawl is dragged along a sandy, muddy, or gravelly bottom there is little to no damage inflicted. In fact, some scientists argue that trawling churns up the bottom and makes buried nutrients and food available, increasing productivity of the sea floor in the same way that agricultural plowing can increase the productivity of a field. But when a trawl is dragged across more fragile habitat it can leave an area lifeless. Delicate eelgrass provides protection for juveniles of countless species, and if the grass is torn out by its root the entire ecosystem is compromised. Trawls can also decimate formations of deepwater coral. These reef ecosystems take hundreds of years to grow. Where they exist, they are the foundation of the ecosystem, and destruction of a reef can eliminate most associated sea life.

But fishermen are always innovating, and advancements in the design of the otter door have led to significantly decreased environmental impacts from the gear. A large metal sheet resembling a door is placed on either side of the net, and when the net is dragged through the water, the precise angle of the "fold" creates drag that pushes the net to billow open and controls the depth at which the net travels. Some of the best designed gear is so precise that it keeps the net floating just a few inches off the ground, thus avoiding any bottom contact, though fishing is equally effective.

Gillnet fishing for Striped Bass.

Exploring Our Inland Fisheries

AS POPULATIONS OF AMERICANS GREW AND SPREAD westward, major fisheries were soon established in the Great Lakes, the Mississippi and Missouri rivers, and many of their tributaries. Initially, these inland industries were connected to eastern population centers via canal and river routes, and eventually by rail. Later, significant fisheries for lake herring, white fish, catfish, carp, bass, and various trout and salmon species were important food resources for the burgeoning industry towns of the Midwest, providing cheap food for the labor class. Many of these fish were initially preserved in salt and shipped in barrels to markets as far away as England. A good volume of fish were smoked and gained great popularity in the markets of major East Coast cities.

The large immigrant populations of far-northern European descent that settled in the Midwest brought with them a taste for fish that was readily supplied by these regional fisheries. Many of these immigrants had fishing experience, and some of the most important advances in fishing technology were developed in the Great Lakes, specifically the otter trawl, which was first used by Michigan fishermen who subsequently introduced it to Atlantic fisheries.

In the Mississippi River, there was a large fishery for river mussels, whose pearly shells were ground down to make buttons. These buttons were used by the major clothing and shoe industries in St. Louis, one of the towns on the western frontier that was an important trade hub, supplying many of the goods used by settlers as America further expanded to the west.

Important fisheries still remain, especially in the Great Lakes, for species such as smelt, perch, bass, pike, walleye, and carp. Many of the historic fisheries crashed due to overfishing and pollution, or were stressed by invasive or introduced species such as Asian Carp, Steelhead Trout, and lampreys, which were particularly devastating to large trout and salmon populations. A few products derived from freshwater fisheries remain culturally important on a national scale, especially smoked white fish and chubs. Trout from Idaho and catfish in the South are very important aquaculture industries, providing a high volume of product to national markets. But the vast majority of fish caught in inland fisheries remains in the region.

The great tradition of the Midwestern Fish Fry traces its roots back to large populations of German and Polish Catholics that settled in the area. As the Catholic faithful were forbidden from eating meat on Fridays, the fish fry became a cultural institution that to this day is regularly served on Fridays in many restaurants and supper clubs, Rotary Clubs, churches, and other community centers. The meal, which has become common to people of all religious backgrounds, consists of beer-battered fish, usually perch, pike, crappie, or catfish, along with coleslaw, potatoes, tartar sauce, and lots of beer.

Beyond this tasty tradition, Midwest populations traditionally shun seafood in favor of a meat-based diet, and thus a distinct regional cuisine using seafood never developed to the point that it has migrated to or influenced the cuisines of other regions.

OPPOSITE Yellow Perch.
FOLLOWING PAGES, LEFT Walker Evans photo, taken for the WPA, of a roadside stand near Birmingham, Alabama. Jefferson County, 1936.
FOLLOWING PAGES, RIGHT Scup fishing in Newport, Rhode Island. c. 1920.

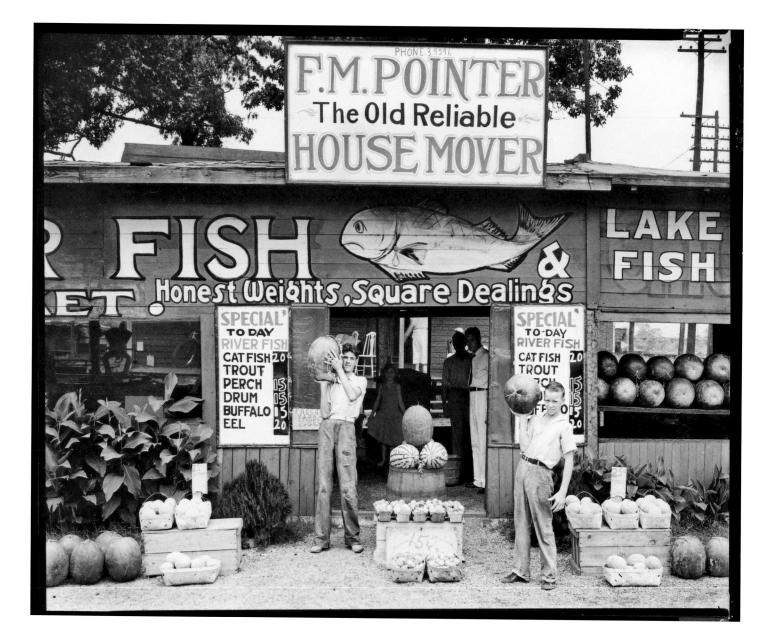

Farming Our Seas

THE TERM AQUACULTURE IS OFTEN USED TO BROADLY describe the farming of finfish, shellfish, seaweeds, and other aquatic animals in either fresh or salt water. As a part of our nation's food system, aquaculture is a subject deserving an entire book dedicated to exploring its role in the seafood economy and fisheries culture. As such I will be brief in my summary and further explain aquaculture's role through the narratives of the individual species that have been enhanced or developed by farming.

Aquaculture as a science has a very long history in America, having been adopted as a solution to declining fish stocks since the nineteenth century. Early on, colonists recognized that spawning runs of Alewife, herring, and Striped Bass were becoming depleted in coastal New England. Community leaders enacted fisheries conservation efforts with regulations regarding the capture of these fish and the erection of dams that might block their passage to spawning grounds. Soon after, scientists began traveling through the country, documenting the nation's resources with an eye toward transplanting and propagating species. Increasingly, the public began to demand action to restore traditional fisheries, and it was deemed easier, both politically and scientifically, to pursue the cultivation of species as a direct means to restore or enhance traditional fisheries, and even create new ones. Marine resources were considered only valuable as an opportunity for exploitation, and thus it was against the American way to limit demand or to prohibit access to a resource. It was believed that the real solution was to increase the supply of fish. The first artificial propagation of fish occurred in 1853, when Brook Trout were first hatched on a farm near Cleveland, Ohio. We were now armed with the ability to augment nature. Over the next hundred years, trout farming would slowly evolve to become one of the most important aquaculture industries in the country. By the late 1900s, the prevailing philosophy that fueled the Industrial Revolution posited that humans, because they could, *should* control nature. This is not far from the dominant agrarian thinking, which put forth that the hand of man can manipulate and alter nature for his purposes.

In 1871, the U.S. Fish Commission was founded with the charge of studying the reasons for the decline of various Atlantic and Great Lakes fish populations and to identify solutions for their restoration. In response to the growing outcry about declining stocks from industrialists involved in the salmon canning industry on the West Coast, the commission opened two salmon hatcheries in California to revive overfished populations. Early Fish Commission efforts also included campaigns to remove undesired fish that preyed upon targeted species. But in addition to making up for our mistakes in the past, the idea of growth and creation of fisheries quickly became a guiding principle, and non-native species were soon introduced into waterways all over the country in the hopes of establishing new populations for fisheries to target.

The species that generated the greatest enthusiasm was carp. By the late 1800s, wild carp had been established in the Hudson River after escaping from a pond owned by a German immigrant who had brought European carp to the United States. By the middle of the century, the government and individual citizens had imported various species from Europe and Asia to stock rivers throughout the Midwest and California. So great was the momentum behind carp that by the 1880s the government was distributing free juvenile carp to anyone who asked for them, in all sending fish to citizens in 1,478 counties across every state in America. The U.S. Congress even appropriated funds to build carp ponds on the grounds of the Washington Monument. Due to lack of demand as well as ready access to the rapidly expanding wild carp populations, carp farming never took off as a major industry. But that didn't prove a deterrent to aquaculture. Rather, it had proven our ability to alter ecosystems and furthered the belief that science and technology were capable of augmenting natural systems and ameliorating any man-made environmental decline.

In the 1880s, specially designed railcars were transporting juvenile shad and Striped Bass from the Atlantic across the country to stock West Coast rivers. Meanwhile, in the Atlantic, hundreds of millions of cod, flounder, Pollock, shad, and salmon were being reared in hatcheries and released into the wild to augment existing fisheries. In 1897, the Fish Commission published a manual containing detailed descriptions of techniques for rearing more than 40 species of seafood. Lobster was a species that had been propagated early

on and was thought to offer one of the biggest opportunities. From the early 1900s through the 1970s, lobster was often referred to as "ocean chicken" in aquaculture circles, as it was believed that vast additional quantities of this valuable species could be introduced through hatcheries.

Despite this knowledge and enthusiasm, until the 1960s commercial aquaculture was limited to hatchery-enhanced salmon fisheries on the West Coast and trout farms, which had taken root in every state but Hawaii and Alaska. It's estimated that around that time there were 1.6 million trout ponds in the United States, most for private use. But the advancements that took the trout industry a hundred years to achieve were being realized by other industries within a period of decades, quickly growing from the experimental stage to full-scale industry. Catfish farming in the American South, which began in the early 1960s, had reached by the 1980s reached a phase of exponential growth. It is now the largest finfish aquaculture industry in the United States.

In 1967, the first net pen for farming salmon was introduced in Washington State and salmon farming quickly took hold in Maine. Other species followed suit: crawfish in southern Louisiana and Hybrid Striped Bass in North Carolina, which later spread throughout the country. Tilapia and shrimp were introduced in the South, and farmed oysters, mussels and seaweed emerged as part of the New England and Pacific Northwest economies.

But even with all of this advancement, the United States is still lagging very far behind its potential. Though we are among the largest by volume consumers of farmed seafood, we produce just a small fraction of the global total. Within the U.S. exclusive economic zone (our sovreign territory that extends 200 miles offshore), more of America is underwater than above it. There is incredible opportunity to expand efforts and to use our resources to create jobs, bolster food security, and claim new opportunities to expand upon our marine heritage.

Aquaculture has not been without controversy. In the early years, bad ideas were propagated and fish were planted where they should not have been. In some cases we saw aquaculture as a means to undo the damage wild fisheries had on the oceans so that we could continue to behave in the same irresponsible ways. But the technology of aquaculture has evolved and addressed some of the early environmental issues associated with farming some species.

Aquaculture should not be thought of as a replacement for wild fisheries. It should not be considered as separate from the systems of nature. Rather, we must view it as complementary to the heritage and legacy of wild fisheries. It must be practiced in ways that are benign in their environmental impact, if not beneficial to the environment as are some species. If we want to see our marine heritage endure, we must support its evolution. There is a vast ocean of opportunity out there, and a huge chunk of that ocean is ours.

U.S. FISH HATCHERY.
NEAR MANCHESTER IA.
PHOTO BY HENSLEY

Fish hatchery near Manchester, Iowa. c. 1913.

The Taste of the Sea and All Things in It

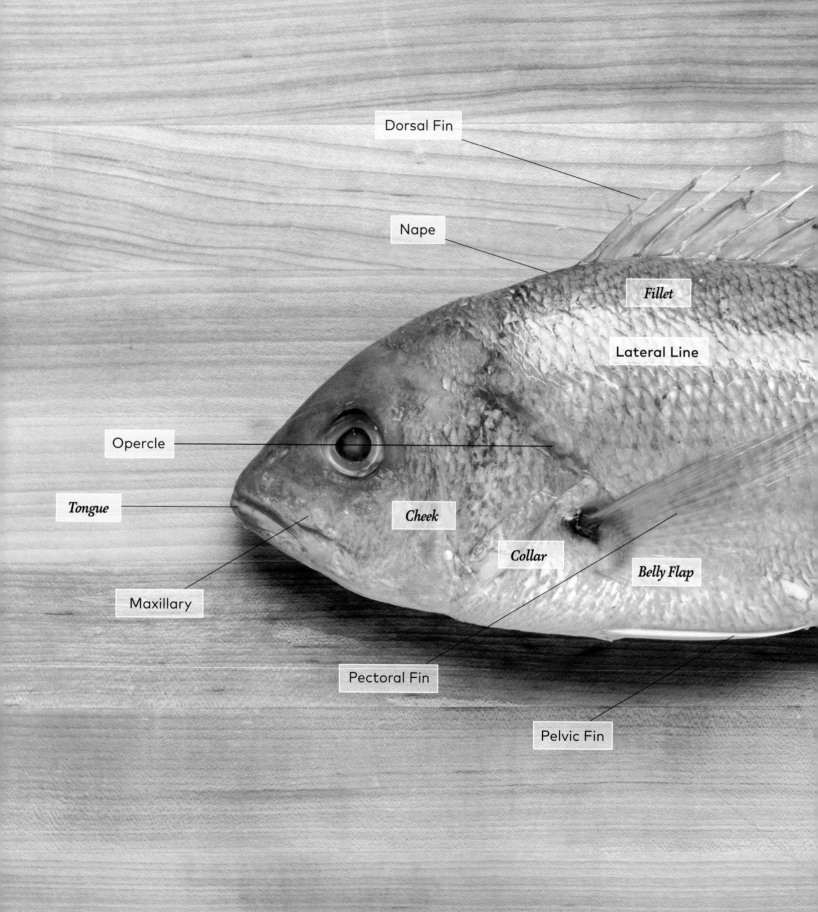

Dorsal Fin

Nape

Fillet

Lateral Line

Opercle

Tongue

Cheek

Collar

Belly Flap

Maxillary

Pectoral Fin

Pelvic Fin

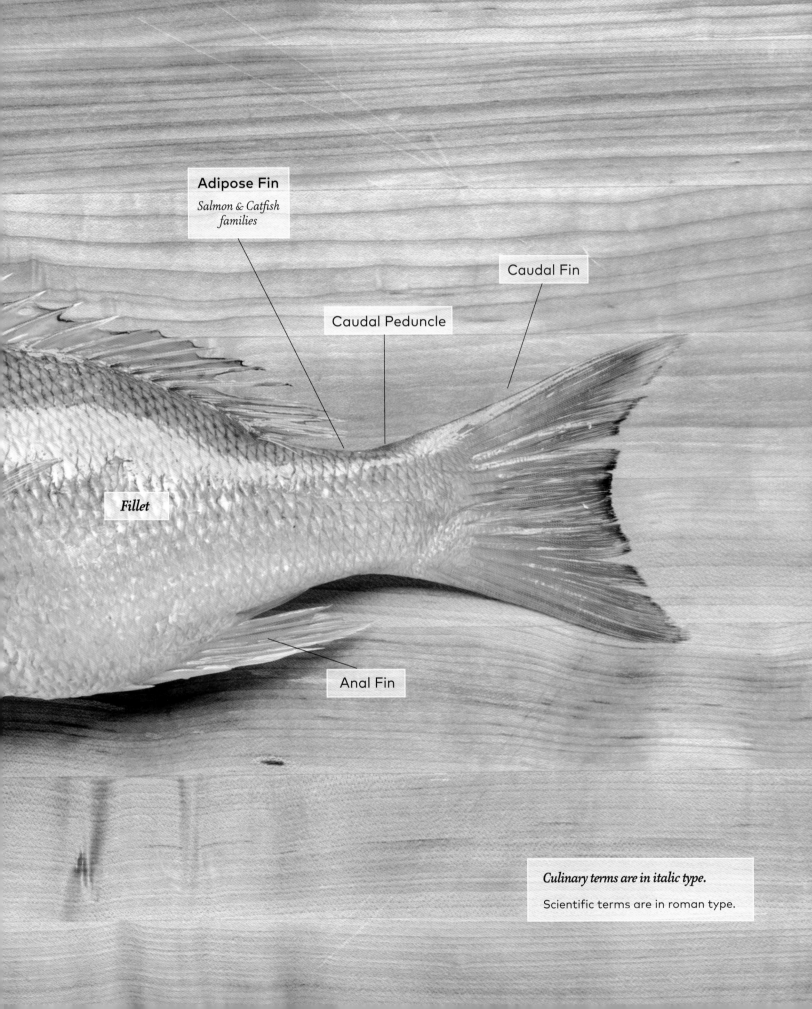

Adipose Fin
Salmon & Catfish families

Caudal Fin

Caudal Peduncle

Fillet

Anal Fin

Culinary terms are in italic type.

Scientific terms are in roman type.

Marine Trophic Scale

The oceans contain 95 percent of the livable space on this planet and are rich with an unimaginable diversity of life in many forms. Of the hundreds of thousands of sea life-forms that we know of, it is estimated that there are more than a million species we have yet to discover. But all life is governed by one fundamental rule: eat and be eaten. Sometimes in science (and in rules) we find a bit of poetry in the order of things. Function can be very elegant—take, for example, the way that a chess game is governed by rules designed around a series of ascending hierarchies. Likewise, the formula for the hierarchical relationship between all living things is called the *trophic scale*. This is a simple, well-defined organization of predators and prey, which helps to elucidate how energy transfers from the sun all the way to your dinner table.

The basis of all life, for our purposes, is the energy of the sun. In every ecosystem there are a host of organisms that capture this energy and from there it is transubstantiated through the diversity of life. From the Bible in the book of Isaiah comes the quote "All flesh is grass." There is great humility in recognizing that even the grandest and most charismatic species are but the sum of smaller things.

In the ocean, the entire food chain is based on microscopic organisms called *phytoplankton*. These photosynthetic entities absorb nutrients from the water and gather carbon, the common currency of life. These occupy the first level of the trophic scale and are known as *primary producers*. The diversity of plankton is seemingly infinite and depends on many environmental factors unique to location. This is also the basis of the flavor in all seafoods, providing evidence that the classic adage from Jean Anthelme Brillat-Savarin—"Tell me what you eat and I will tell you what you are"—is as true for fish as it is all others animals. The word *plankton* is derived from the Greek word meaning "to wander." This is a perfectly apt description, as these organisms live drifting in ocean's currents.

When we stare out at the ocean discerning its color, pondering its mood, we are indeed looking at a massive floating cloud of life, described by John Hersey "vast sea meadows." If all flesh is grass, then all seafood is plankton.

The trophic scale is organized into steps, each one representing a degree of separation from the primary producers. Sitting directly above primary producers are *primary consumers*. These herbivores include a huge diversity of zooplankton, tiny creatures that feed upon phytoplankton and other zooplankton species. The name *zooplankton*, also from Greek, means "animal wanderer."

From there, the ascending levels are all carnivorous. The first of three levels of distinction includes fish such as herring; the second, salmon, Bluefish and snapper; the third, large species such as tunas and Swordfish. The following level is unique in that it features the apex predators of the food chain such as orcas, large sharks, and polar bears, beasts that nothing else messes with.

Humans have inserted ourselves as a major part of the marine food chain, but the trophic scale is the result of billions of years of evolution fine-tuning complex interwoven relationships among sea life. Life in the ocean did not initially evolve with humans as part of the mix. When humans fish, we alter the calibration of nature. This is not necessarily a bad thing. But if not planned carefully, our efforts can radically shift the balance of a localized area or even vast ranges of ocean ecosystems.

Humans, as the true top predator, have extirpated more than 200 populations of salmon in various rivers. Though salmon as a larger species endures, those genetically distinct groups (a family is an easy way to understand it) are now extinct. In the Gulf of Maine, we have precipitated the collapse of populations of cod, which was once an important predator in the ecosystem. Though cod populations still limp along at a fraction of their original numbers, the system that evolved around them has quickly responded to their absence. Cod feed on many species including mussels, lobsters, crabs, and small fish such as herring, sand eels, and mackerel. With the stress of predation from cod gone, many of these species have exploded in abundance and other fish such as Haddock have become the most important top predators. Once changes like this manifest in an ecosystem, there can be either temporary or permanent distortions in the known order.

These are extreme examples of humans' influence over the environment. The goal of fisheries is to act upon the ecosystem with a light touch. While fishing certainly has an impact on any fish we target, sustainable fishing maintains fish stocks that are resilient and can endure the added stress of human engagement.

Another component of the trophic scale is the presence of *detritivores*. These are species such as sea cucumber and a variety of worms and slugs. Typically, detritivores are not considered food species for humans, but they play an important role in ecosystems by helping to decompose dead sea life and then, in turn, being eaten by predators, recycling nutrients back into the food chain.

Trophic levels are typically visualized as a pyramid, with the apex predators at the top and the descending orders occupying the larger slices of range. There's an interesting and inverse dynamic at play in the system. Primary producers require only nutrients and sunlight, and their populations are so prodigious as to darken the seas. But herbivores and midrange predators play the very important role of being eaten. The lower a fish measures on the trophic scale is a general indication of the fecundity of that species. For example, herring are quite an important food for so many fish; they have a very high mortality rate because of predation. In order for the species to survive it has to breed prolifically. The eggs of the herring are a favorite food of many fish, and once the surviving eggs hatch, the larval, juvenile, and brit stages of the herring life cycle are all subject to heavy predation. Of the 20,000 to 200,000 eggs typically laid by a mature herring, only a minute fraction will ever reach the age at which they will spawn. The biological survival mechanism of herring and other fish like it, such as menhaden and sardines, is that they are so prolific in reproduction that despite such predation the species survives. With each step up the trophic scale the fecundity generally decreases, as the pressure of predation upon these larger fish is less. At the very top level, predators such as sharks are very slow to reach maturity, breed irregularly, sometimes years apart, and have long gestation periods. Many high-level species give live birth to only small litters of pups, as they are known, with some others up to a hundred, but the survival rate is exponentially greater than that of a larval herring. This ecological balance of populations is also supported by typically longer life-spans associated with high-order predators. Correspondingly, smaller species of fish may live only one to three years but might spawn multiple times over the course of the season.

This balance, so intricately interdependent between species, is called *trophic efficiency*. The rule is that every step is based on a factor of 10. For example, to have one pound of herring the fish must have consumed 10 pounds of plankton. For every pound of cod it must have eaten 10 pounds of herring. And so up the chain this ratio applies. This is how energy is kept within the food system as it aggregates through the slow growth of large predatory species.

Anatomy of Fish

Because of the buoyancy of salt water, the muscular and skeletal structure of fish is very different from that of land animals. Because land animals must fight gravity, they have tightly bundled muscles that allow them to move under atmospheric pressure and bones that are much stronger and larger in proportion to their body. Fish don't have to work against gravity, so their muscles are far more delicately structured and have less connective tissue. Their bones are not nearly as dense and make up a smaller proportion of their body.

Fish have two kinds of muscle known as *fast-twitch* and *slow-twitch*. The composition of these muscles in different species depends on behavioral patterns of that fish. Slow-twitch muscles are designed for constant movement and are fueled by fat (typically around 20 percent), which is stored within the cells of the muscle fibers. Slow-twitch muscle also requires oxygen, just as our muscles do, which results in a darker-colored tissue due to the presence of oxygen-carrying myoglobin. Often known as *bloodline tissue*, it runs underneath the skin and concentrates along the midline of the fish. Fatty fish such as Bluefish, mackerel, tuna, and other highly migratory species have the highest concentrations of bloodline tissue to sustain their long-term and constant motion.

Sedentary fish, often known as white fish, don't require the same level of performance from their musculature. These fish, such as cod and flounder, attack their prey in very quick, short bursts of motion. This requires fast-twitch muscle, which is white in color. These muscles are fueled by carbohydrates and do not require oxygen. In sedentary fish the fat is mostly stored in the liver. The absence of fat (around 1 percent in cod) in the muscle is what gives white-fleshed fish its characteristic texture.

All fish muscle has four components: connective tissue, fat, water, and protein. The quantities of each range dramatically between species and are the basis of their individual character. The muscle fibers are short strands called *myotomes*. These are tightly bundled in segments, what we think of as flakes, that are held together by connective tissue called *myocommata*. It's this connective tissue that influences the texture of cooked fish. This is another way that fish tissue is different than that of land animals. In land animal meat, connective tissue initially toughens when heat is applied and then slowly breaks down throughout the cooking process. But because fish live in a much gentler environment, the connective tissue does not need to be as strong and so it breaks down at very low temperatures, quickly freeing moisture and fat from the cells to help baste and flavor the flesh. The connective tissue in fish is on average about 3 percent of its entire weight, while in land animals it's around 15 percent.

The largest component of muscle is water, usually accounting for 80+ percent of the weight of white fish and about 70+ percent of fatty fish. But these percentages can range significantly, depending on season, diet, and spawning events. A fish that has just spawned and is undernourished might have 90 percent water content whereas an extremely fat pre-spawn fish might have water content as low as 30 percent. The water within the muscles is very tightly bound to the proteins and is not readily expelled under pressure, allowing fish to occupy a range of depths and their associated pressures.

A traveling fish has more fat and bloodline tissue in its flesh than a sedentary one does, and thus activity means flavor. Just as the cells of these species are fed by the oxygen in the myoglobin, so too are the cells exposed to oxygen during cooking and thus the aromatic and flavor compounds of the fish oxidize, giving them a stronger presence. This is also why fatty fish spoil more quickly, as their high fat content and the associated oxygen interact and cause rancidity.

But fish are not just flesh. When alive, their skin is a marvel of color and radience, providing camouflage perfectly tailored to their environment. Fish such as halibut that live on the ocean floor have darkly pigmented skin on the top side and no pigment underneath. That makes them nearly invisible from above, and when one looks up at a halibut from below the fish blends into the water column. Some flounders can change their color, depending on the composition of the sea floor, allowing them to blend in with rocks, sand, or mud. Schools of small fish seem like a dizzy apparition of stars, twinkling and fading as they dart and dance about the water, confusing predators. A fish's coloration is a visual measure of its freshness, and one could argue that a fish's flashes of pigment express a part of its soul. A squid just from the water is a glowing, iridescent array of fantastic hues—blues and purplish gray and streaks of red. A Mahi Mahi just landed on the deck, hook still in its mouth, evokes a drug-induced hallucination as greens, oranges, and yellows shimmer in waves down the fish. But these colors are certainly not just for our benefit. They all perform or enable some biological function, whether it be for mating purposes, for camouflage, or to be as conspicuous as possible so as to intimidate potential predators.

What Makes a Fish a Food Fish?

"WE AMERICANS ARE SO VAIN, COCKY AND ARROGANT THAT WE think many great foods are inedible just because you can't buy them at the drugstore lunch counter. We think we know it all, but we missed an awful lot while the rest of the world goes right on enjoying itself," writes Howard Mitcham.

In this nearly bitter judgment is the truth that we have very limited parameters by which we define our preferences for seafood. I often hear people dismiss the idea of trying new fish. Bluefish was once the most popular fish in all of America, and now I regularly talk with fishermen who think it is best used to fertilize their lawns. Here's the simple truth about fish: almost anything you pull from the sea tastes good when treated the right way. Over the years I've tasted so many different species of seafood, and I have come to realize there are specific qualities by which I judged my appreciation of the fish.

General characteristics I look for:

- Its flavor reflects its orgin.

- It has an identifiable culinary personality—it doesn't have to be unique in flavor, but it has to have flavor.

- It has been properly handled from the boat to my plate (regardless of species).

- It has been properly eviscerated without puncturing the gallbladder.

- It has been chilled properly and quickly.

- Its surfaces are not dry by sight or by touch—fish should always have a slight sheen (the exception being scallops).

- It has not been immersed or washed in freshwater.

- It is easy to fillet; fillets are easy to handle.

- Non-fillet parts are edible (livers, cheeks, roe).

- It is resilient to cooking.

- Its flesh is not drying or chalky on the palate.

- It is able to stand alone without sauce.

- It is versatile and applicable to multiple cooking methods.

Flavor of Fish

The fine art of cooking seafood is really more the practiced skill of buying good ingredients. The circumstances that govern the flavor profile of any given fish are very complicated and are affected by a host of variables unique to season, diet, region, method of capture, and water temperature. In addition to the matter of salt water or freshwater, there are great differences in flavor between fatty fish and white fish.

The first thing that we think of when buying seafood is simply the word *fresh*. I think we've gotten into our heads the idea that seafood is either good or bad and that asking which fish is fresh is just a blunt but polite form of segregating quality. Fresh is really just a relative term and one that I'll show you doesn't always give any indication of the seafood's culinary qualities.

The word *fresh* itself defines a measure of time—the fresher the fish the more recently it came from the water. But that's no longer always a measure of quality, as deep-freezing technology allows for fish to be processed, their spoilage arrested, while it is in pristine condition, sometimes within an hour after capture. There's a good argument to be made that this frozen product is actually "fresher" than our normal consideration of the word. To me fresh is better thought of as a measure of wholesomeness—that the fish is unspoiled due to careful handling, proper chilling, lack of exposure to moisture and bacterial growth, and a host of other factors that influence our appreciation of it. And at the end of the day that's what we are after—something that we will enjoy.

M.F.K. Fisher, famed American food writer, in her enigmatic but always romantic way, wrote, "It is perhaps impossible to say what 'fresh' smells like, except that is smells right, not dubious. It smells like new cut grass, new mown hay, an innocent brook, or a child emerging from his bath, or almost any happy clean thing for that matter." What I like most about her sentiment is that she inspires confidence. The consumer doesn't need to know the complex biochemistry of the enzymatic processes at work upon fish. No, that something smells "right" is nearly as perfect an instruction for judging quality as could be.

People often remark upon their trepidation to eat seafood because they don't like "fishy flavor." And I don't blame them. Unfortunately the ugly descriptor "fishy" has come to define an entire category of fish, generally those that are on the fatty side. But such a generalization blinds us to an important consideration about seafood and its quality. Any seafood has an initial flavor and later expresses a developed flavor. Each of these stages have distinct characteristics with merits all their own.

Seafood has an incredible array of flavor compounds, most of them having names that are phonetically challenging and often include numbers, so we won't talk about those here. But these flavor compounds are either water soluble or fat soluble and accumulate in different species of fish in different formulas. Fatty fish, those too often described as "fishy," have a higher proportion of the fat-soluble compounds, but as their behaviors and muscle structures are very different from white fish, there are a number of factors that influence their flavor. For one, diet is very important in determining taste. Fatty fish are active, constantly swimming in search of prey, and typically feed on small oily fish and crustaceans, things that themselves are well-flavored, which is, in turn, reflected in the predator. These fish also have a dark bloodline, or red tissue, as their muscles are fed by oxygen that must be carried in myoglobin-rich tissues. When fatty fish are cooked, not only does the fat render and baste the fish, helping to keep it moist and to add aroma, there's also a chemical reaction happening. As the fish cooks and the fats are released, they are immediately exposed to the oxygen carried in the cells. In turn, the volatile compounds, those which give flavor, immediately oxidize, blooming their flavor and aroma, thus giving it a much greater impact. It is the same concept as swirling a glass of wine or pouring a dash of water into your scotch. What you smell from that wine after swirling was there before, and your scotch was just as complex, but these interactions help those complexities become accessible and expressive. When I eat a piece of fatty fish, especially my favorite Bluefish, just the heat of my mouth will melt some of the intramuscular fat, creating a dynamic flavor experience that evolves even as I'm eating it.

White fish, a descriptive term that includes fish like cod, Haddock, and flounder, has a very different personality. These fish carry very little fat in their cells and so lack the dynamic, lush, rounder flavors of their darker-fleshed kin. But they still have plenty of flavor, though it is more heavily dependent upon diet; they gain their personality through aggregation rather than anatomy. All fish, especially white fish, when first caught have a green melon or crushed leaf aroma and flavor. The flesh is notably acidic from the presence of lactic acid, though the tang is pleasant and reminds me of buttermilk.

The fish will soon enter rigor mortis, which sets in between 3 and 18 hours after death. This is the result of a continued contraction of muscles and often leads to a curved posture. Fish in this condition are sometimes called "stiff alive," as they still seem to have all the vitality of the fish in its prime. Rigor can last for up to two days, at which point the muscles again relax. This is known as having "resolved." It's very rare that you would ever find a fish in pre-rigor form, and if you did I'm not sure you'd enjoy it all that much, as it is very different from the softened, settled, matured flavor that results from the process. The constant contraction of the muscle pulls in opposite force to other muscles, thus putting great pressure on the structure of the fillets. If the fish is not properly handled, this will lead to gaping in the fillet and more rapid spoilage, as its volatile flavor compounds will be exposed to air and will additionally diminish their flavor impact. The acid present in freshly caught fish settles out. What was initially a rather sharp, metallic flavor gives way to a more malty aroma, possibly with a hint of potato or milk. This is particularly true of members of the cod family, known to be crisply metallic in flavor until they age and mature, at which point their flavor becomes sweet and almost nutty, like almonds. In my opinion, cod does not make for great eating if it's less than two or even three days old. In fact, many fish are this way. And this is why I gave pause when talking about the term *fresh*. Fresh may have happened today, but tasty has to wait until later in the week.

The texture of fish becomes more rigid post-rigor. This is the taut, slightly chewy flake that we're accustomed to with fish. Prior to rigor, the fish does not flake nearly as well, and its texture is a little more pliable, but it doesn't have that melting quality or display any of the slightly drying texture that comes from the tightly bundled muscles falling apart.

There's an old culinary method called *crimping* that can prevent some of the negative effects of rigor on the flesh. When a fish is just from the water, minutes after its last breath has left, several shallow gashes are sliced along each side of the fish, barely cutting through the skin. Tradition then calls for the fish to be soaked in salt water for five minutes (or up to 30 minutes for larger fish). When the skin and the thin layer of connective tissue beneath it are sliced, the muscles become less constricted and can contract with less pull exerted on the other muscles. Soaking in water accelerates the pace of the contractions, shortening the period of rigor and making for a far gentler process, leaving the texture moist and pliable and the meat relaxed yet still punctuated with the acidic tang. This technique works for just about any fish, though I've found it especially improves the already all-star qualities of mackerel, Bluefish, and snapper.

Salt Water vs. Fresh

When it comes to the environment in which a fish was caught, salinity plays a fundamental role in defining the culinary character of the fish. Freshwater species are not as flavorful as those living in salt water. For one, freshwater fish don't uptake salt into their flesh nor any of the many other micronutrients and minerals that affect flavor, such as potassium. Freshwater fish are different from their saltwater kin in that they hydrate by absorbing water through their skin, and thus the flavor of their flesh reflects the quality and flavor of the water. If the water is not flowing and clean, any stagnation in the environment can result in musty, green, and sometimes stale aromas and flavors in the fish. Freshwater fish also lack the acidic chemistry that punctuates flavor. Many freshwater species are perfectly delicious but, in my opinion, are not flattered when compared to saltwater species. It is a totally different flavor experience.

Saltwater species hydrate by taking in water through their digestive system and do not absorb flavors from the environment. They have a more complex biology in that they have to osmoregulate their systems, meaning they must continuously keep balance between their internal salt content and the salinity of the water surrounding them. On average, oceans are about 3 percent salt. Fish tend to have about 1 percent salt, and as salt must always be in equilibrium, the deficit in cell structure is filled with two amino acids, glycine and glutamate. Glycine is notably sweet while glutamate (like monosodium glutamate) is savory in nature. This pairing adds an incredible complexity of flavor that, in addition to the salt and minerals present in the flesh, endows saltwater fish with a more dynamic flavor profile. That doesn't necessarily mean it's better than your favorite freshwater fish, but there's a greater opportunity for diversity of flavor. Simply put, there's more going on.

Crimped skin of a Spanish Mackerel.

The aroma of saltwater fish is heavily characterized by bromophenols. These aromatic compounds are the result of naturally occurring bromide absorbed by algae and then accumulated up the food chain, giving seafood its charming smell of sweet sea breeze. It is in fact bromophenols that we are smelling when we stand on the beach, taking in a deep breath of salty air. As the waves churn, bromide is released into the air, perfuming the entire scene.

Another important flavor found only in saltwater fish is that of iodine. This naturally occurring element is abundant in seawater with salt concentrations between 15 and 30 parts per thousand. In low-salinity brackish and freshwaters, iodine is not available to be absorbed. Saltwater fish collect iodine from their diet, and in some cases the iodine levels can be significant enough as to impart a bitter and unpleasant taste. But in normal amounts, this slightly sweet-sour metallic accent can add a very distinguished quality to seafood. In some species it comes to be the identifying flavor, such as is the case with brown shrimp. In the amounts that are present in seafood, iodine poses no risk to us and in fact may provide benefit, as many people are iodine deficient.

Cold Water vs. Warm Water

The influence of water temperature on seafood flavor is a particularly divisive debate. As taste is a completely subjective exercise, adding a regional component to the argument ups the ante by pitting our hometown pride against anyone who would care to disagree. In short, I think that we prefer (and think superior) the products with which we grew up or with which we are most familiar. But there is a real difference, scientifically and objectively, in the flavor construct of fish from different waters. Warm waters are often crystal-clear. Phytoplankton, the basis of much of the marine food chain, requires nutrients and sunlight. While warmer climates certainly get enough sunlight, the water is often nutrient poor—it is a lack of phytoplankton that makes the waters clear. The life in warm waters is concentrated around coral reefs and the algae that live on them. There's far more intermixing of cold, oxygen- and nutrient-dense water with sun-warmed surface layers in the northern seas, which leads to explosions of life that give the sea its enigmatic color. Simply because of the diversity of available food, the flavor profiles of cold-water species are often more complex, but not necessarily better.

Warm-water denizens tend to breed more prolifically, eat more food, have quicker digestions, show accelerated growth, and lead shorter lives. There is greater diversity of life in warmer waters as opposed to the smaller number of species in the colder northern waters. Even though there isn't significant multiformity, the sheer volume of fish of those few northen species is usually greater than the total volume in southern waters.

Regardless of provenence, when properly handled, delicious fish can be found. Truly, all of it is good. And on the whole seafood is made more interesting by the diversity of flavors and textures to be discovered in each region.

Artisan Preservation Methods and Early Cuisine

THE PRESERVATION OF SEAFOOD WAS A SKILLED trade based on artisan techniques passed down through generations. In the days before refrigeration and powerful motors allowed fresh catch to be delivered promptly, the sea's bounty was only as useful as our ability to prolong its shelf life. Many of the techniques developed were based on efficiencies that allowed for the greatest amount of product to last the longest time. There was also market for higher-quality products that were the result of more delicate methods and techniques. Maybe it was the composition of the salt used, which produced either a silken or coarse texture in the flesh, or a particular chemistry, high in minerals that led to a reddish or brown coloration. These techniques evolved over hundreds of years and were designed for different markets and practiced in different fisheries in different regions all governed by different climates and conditions. In our modern world some variations of these antiquated techniques are still practiced, but now they are less purposed with preservation as they are with flavoring.

There's a parallel set of skills common to agricultural food systems: the development and perfection of charcuterie methods. On a subsistence or small family farm, a slaughtered animal provided far more meat than could be consumed in the immediate term and so means were developed to harness the beneficial aspects of bacteria, desiccation, pH, and salinity in order to make full use of the animal over a longer period of time. Another example is cheesemaking, which was once a determined attempt to ensure a lasting food supply and is now an art form judged in competitions that award gold medals. These were not developed as culinary techniques. These were survival skills.

Over time, what began simply as utilitarian industry now represents an entire discipline of culinary skills and a stage for creativity and talent. In contemporary cuisine, we appreciate and celebrate how simple raw ingredients can be transformed into completely different taste experiences through the knowledge and application of natural sciences. Our efforts to preserve the bounty of the land and sea became unnecessary as cold storage, rapid transit, and globalized markets served to even out the boom-bust cycles that are nature's hallmark. But for centuries, we knew the harvest principally in its preserved form. Salt cod was not only the food from which enormous wealth and power were drawn and upon which empires were built, it was the food that provided a foundation of the cuisines emerged throughout the world. Regional specialties, unique to small-scale fisheries, provided the building blocks of regional taste profiles, and their influence can still be savored in today's culinary preferences.

In the last few decades we have "rediscovered" the preservation techniques of charcuterie, cheesemaking, winemaking, pickling, and fermenting as elevated functions in cuisine. We use them to connect us to our past and intimately to the environments in which we live. Through these methods and the foods produced by them, we can read quite a bit about our past as we recognize flavors lost to time and to "progress" in the advancement of our food systems. Granted, there's great blessing and benefit in having a more secure and stable supply of safe food. It is a luxury that we can regard what were once staples of our survival as fanciful culinary experiments. It's an equal luxury that we can look backward and retrace some of the steps we took in the evolution of our cuisine.

The same opportunities exist with seafood. Though the world's culinary preferences have shifted to prefer fresh product, which is more a function of the food system than a cultural shift, the flavors of salt cod, smoked mullet, cured roe, preserved offal, and rendered oils are part of our heritage and are well worth remembering.

Of course not every product we preserved through the years deserves equal appreciation for its culinary merit, but all of these foods offer insight into early American life, the influence of immigrant communities, and the discovery and opulence of this land's profuse resources.

OPPOSITE Hot-smoking mackerel.

FOLLOWING PAGES, LEFT Smoking finnan haddie, c. 1890.

FOLLOWING PAGES, RIGHT Fisherman's Wharf postcard, San Francisco, 1930.

1432

67461

This chapter elucidates many of these antiquated arts used by every generation before the advent of our modern food system. As we are busy rediscovering the heirloom vegetables that grew in our elders' gardens and reevaluating the civic and social values that were the foundation of our food systems, let's also reacquaint ourselves with the industry upon which this country was founded and reclaim what I'll call "heritage seafood" that fed our young nation.

Seafood may be preserved by many methods, most of them involving salt, others with smoke, and still others by the seasonal conditions of regional environments. The northern European process of curing fish solely by air-drying (resulting in what's known as *stockfish*) was not widely practiced in the United States, as there are few localities where the necessary climatic conditions exist. One such industry originated near New Orleans in the late 1800s, when a Chinese community built platforms to sun-dry shrimp in the hot summer swelter. The dried product was crushed underfoot to break off the brittle shells, and the meats were packaged and shipped to China. These slightly fermented shrimp, which rehydrated to a condition and texture similar to fresh, also found local favor as part of the Creole classic gumbo.

Native tribes in the Northwest air-dried a number of species, including halibut, salmon, cod, Eulachon, and smelt, for subsistence consumption (not trade). Larger fish were preserved by cutting off the head and removing all but the last three inches of backbone in the tail section; thicker fillets would be sliced into strips, keeping everything attached at the tail. The fish would be hung from a pole with the flesh side out to dry, a process that took three to four weeks. These fish, which looked more like an octopus than the original finfish, were usually hung from the rigging of boats to dry over the course of several weeks, and arid air and wind served to dehydrate the fish as low temperatures prevented immediate spoilage.

The principal products of commerce and consumption came from large-scale fisheries such as those for cod and mackerel. Our ability to profit from their nutritious bounty was made possible by salt curing. The use of salt performs a two-fold function in curing fish: First, it eliminates spoilage-causing microorganisms by pulling water from the microbial cells through osmosis. As the unwanted bacteria decline, beneficial lactobacillus-type bacteria flourish and cause fermentation, lowering the surface pH, which further inhibits harmful bacterial growth. The quality of cured fish can be no better than the quality of the raw fish used and the quality and purity of the ingredients used to preserve it. Sea salt contains varying amounts of minerals such as magnesium chloride, magnesium sulfate, calcium sulfate, and potassium chloride, all of which have undesirable effects on curing. The preferred salts for curing came from various solar evaporation industries located around the world, the most popular being the salt flats of Trapani, on the west coast of Sicily.

In addition to cod and mackerel, other fish commonly cured were hake, Haddock, Cusk, pollock, and Ling (most members of the cod family and sold as salt cod) in the Northeast. In the Southeast and Gulf, mullet, shrimp, drum, grunts, and weakfish were staples. In the Pacific fisheries, the common fish in the south were barracuda, Bonito, Wahoo, and yellowtail, and other jacks. To the north, it was halibut, Pacific Cod, and salmon (also in Atlantic fisheries). In all regions, smaller fisheries' products were also cured or smoked, but the volumes were low and intended only for regional consumption.

The specific salting method depended upon the season, the fattiness and musculature of the fish, the length of the voyage, and the market for which it was destined. Salt cod was the mainstay of our maritime economy and provided food for poor Americans. High-quality product was traded throughout the Mediterranean, while the lowest-quality product was used to feed slaves on sugar plantations in the Caribbean. To this day, salt cod is a very popular part of island cuisine, a holdover from this terrible history. Salt cod was culled into four categories, ordered in terms of quality. *Merchantable* was the finest grade, based on texture and color. Nearly equal in quality to merchantable, the vast majority of salt cod produced was grade *Madeira,* which was bound for trade in Europe. *West India* fish was mainly the refuse from the production of Madeira quality. *Dun-fish,* also known as *broken fish*, was the last category and was not fit for trade due to a higher moisture content that could not withstand long voyages but was considered highest quality for local consumption.

In the cod fisheries, thousands of pounds of fish were hauled onto boats and processed immediately, due to the limited space. Though there were some variations, generally the fish

Kench method-cured halibut, Gloucester, Massachusetts, 1882.

was split either through the belly cavity or along the backbone. How the fish was split (and even what side of the backbone was left attached) and what cures were used all helped to identify the fishery's regional appelation. The head and viscera (except the liver) were discarded, the black membrane lining the stomach was scraped off, and the splayed fish was then soaked in salt water to remove any blood. The fish would then be packed with salt using one of two methods.

By one technique, known as *kenching, dry-salting,* or *slack-salting,* the salted fillets were stacked in piles, which allowed the liquid drawn out by the salt to run off, leaving the fish dry. This was the primary method used for cod and related species. On the Pacific coast, select salmon were dry-salted for higher-

end markets. The fish was split down the back and laid out flat, with the head and most of the backbone removed. Before salting, the flesh was smeared with the blood of the fish, giving the meat an intense ochre color that was highly valued.

In the other technique, the salted fillets were layered in large barrels to capture the brine exuded by the fish and left to soak there. Known as a *wet cure, brine pickle,* or *pickle cure* (not to be confused with an acid pickle preparation), this method allowed for the longest shelf life, as the fish would remain in the brine until needed. This brine method was also particularly applicable for fatty fish, such as mackerel, whose oils could oxidize and spoil rapidly. Keeping them submerged prevented air contact and thus delayed the oils from going rancid.

ABOVE Yellowtail in Pensacola cure. OPPOSITE Yellowtail tied for smoking.

Once the boats had returned to land, the kenched fish would be washed to remove excess salt before being laid out on flakes—large open-air drying racks—until dry enough for long-term storage. Brined fish would typically remain in the barrels until ready for sale, when it would be briefly air-dried on flakes.

A similar curing method commonly applied to mackerel called for splitting the fish, removing the head and entrails, and salting them, layered in pork or beef barrels (leftover hardware from another preservation industry). After several days the fish would be deemed "struck," meaning that the salt had completely penetrated the meat and the cure was complete. The fish were then drained and carefully packed in white pine barrels. The reserved brine was then boiled and strained of blood and particulates. Once chilled, the clarified brine was poured over the fish. Pickling oily fish with a clean brine removed the oils that separated and rose to the surface, not only increasing shelf life but also giving the fish a cleaner flavor and color.

Most New England states regulated the composition and size of the barrels in which pickled mackerel could be packed and the materials from which they were made. Maine required all barrels and casks to be made of sound, well-seasoned white oak, white ash, spruce, pine, chestnut, or poplar staves, with headings of the same kinds of wood. This not only provided consistent standards in trade but also added to the quality of the product by precluding faulty barrels that leaked air. And these barrels would have imparted some flavor to the aging fish just as they would to a wine.

Brine, a solution of salt dissolved in water, cures fish more quickly than a dry salt-cure as the liquid carries the salt evenly into the fish. Dry-salting is slower to penetrate the flesh and can be inconsistent, leaving some salt-burned areas where there was too much salt and other areas that did not get adequately cured. One reason for this is that on a typical fillet, there will be a higher ratio of fat toward the head (meaning a lower water content) and the opposite toward the thinner section of the tail. Being water soluble, salt would act more quickly on the higher-water-content areas.

Sugar was sometimes used to help reduce the salty character of cured products, and sometimes pickling spices were added to brines to tame stronger-flavored fish or enliven leaner fish such as catfish. Before cooking, salt-cured fish was soaked in fresh water to desalinate and partially rehydrate the flesh. Brine-cured fish, once refreshed, has a texture much closer to fresh fish, which is beneficial to some culinary uses.

Salt-cured fish has many different classifications depending on the length of cure, exposure to air, the amount of moisture loss, and its intended shelf life. Some product was meant for local consumption, as in select products from Maine-based fishing communities. Other product was cured until very dry in order to withstand long voyages at sea in the humid and often sweltering heat of the tropics.

Saltfish is very similar to salt cod except it is not dried after curing and so less moisture is removed, only 40 percent of its whole weight as opposed to 60 percent or more in other cures (fish is generally 80 percent water). This product has to be kept cold, as the moisture level is too high to fully preserve the fish. Saltfish, unlike salt cod, has maintained market presence, is still regularly available, and is often packaged in one-pound boxes or bags marketed as *boneless cod*. Its flavor is cleaner and less sour than other products. This is the product that gave rise to the popularity of New England fish cakes and fish hash.

Dun-fish were cod that had been kench-packed in salt and aged for two to three months in a dark room under a cover of saltgrass (a type of grass that thrives in salt water or heavily salted soils) to develop an attractive reddish color thought to be the highest quality and most complex flavored. The term *dun-fish,* and its equivalent *mud-fish,* were confusingly also used to describe low-quality fish that had discolored due to poor quality salt.

Green-fish was cod pickled and left in casks of brine. As it was not laid out to dry on flakes, it maintained the pure white color of the flesh, adding market appeal. It had the added benefit that it would refresh faster than products cured by other methods.

An important industry in Southern California in the 1800s cured almost 500,000 pounds a year of barracuda, Bonito, and various species of jacks. After the fish were split down the belly with the backbone left in, they were heavily salted in kenches. The cure struck in two or three days, and when the weather turned favorable (dry and warm with a slight wind), the fish were washed and spread on drying flakes. When properly cured, the barracuda made a very popular product that had a desirable white flesh with an excellent flavor said to be the best of any fish on the West Coast.

OPPOSITE A small portion of a record catch of dogfish taken by the *Albatross IV,* c. 1965. FOLLOWING PAGE Dressing and salting mackerel in Gloucester Harbor. c. 1882.

Dressing Halibut
Mackerel on board
vessel Gloucester Harbor

Located throughout the South but focused in Florida, the large mullet fishery had the benefit of being executed in nearshore waters and in rivers. This allowed for the very oily fish to be processed quickly, key to preventing spoilage in the area's hot weather and humidity. The fresh fish were eviscerated and soaked for two hours in salt water to bleed the fillets and to remove excess slime from the exterior. Then the head was removed, the fish split down the back, and the backbone removed. Several slices were made in the flesh to ensure even curing in the fillets before they were kench-packed for one week until the cure struck. They were then washed of excess salt and remaining slime and suspended in the shade, where they dried for six weeks. The dried but still fatty fish were sprinkled with a light coating of salt, individually wrapped in waxed paper to protect the oils, and suspended in a well-ventilated room to age for several months before being sold.

A variation on the brine pickle was a technique called a *blood pickle.* It's surely not an appealing term, but fish cured by this method could have an incredible complexity and character. The only detail that makes this different than the regular brine pickle is that the fish were not bled, and sometimes not fully eviscerated, before being salted and put into barrel. The color and flavor imparted to the fish by the blood was important in developing the unique character of these products. Some cultures (mostly of Mediteranean descent) would cure mackerel in blood pickle to ripen and develop the flavor of the fish's thick band of red muscle tissue, imparting a rusty color and deeply savory flavor.

In a rapid version of this method, corned Alewives or herring were brined for less than a day, and sometimes lightly smoked, before being sold "fresh" to be fried up for breakfast. In a longer version that is applied to sardines and anchovies, the fish are headed and gutted then layered in barrels with salt. The fillets, which begin the process as white or light gray in color, turn pink after about three months and dark red after six months. This is the typical cure time for what we know as tinned anchovies. Mackerel was sometimes cured in this same manner.

Smoked seafoods are a step beyond kenching or pickling. Seafood that is to be smoked is treated by either of these methods, pickle traditionally being best for lean fish such as Haddock or cod, and kenching historically for fattier fish such as salmon. Small silver fish such as herring are very commonly smoked and are known by a variety of names to describe the exact method. For instance, kippers are fat herring that have been split and brined for 12 hours. The fish are then air-dried for several hours, then cold-smoked for several days, after which they are sold to be eaten fresh within a couple of weeks. (Confusingly, the term *kipper* or *kippered* has been appropriated and commonly refers to any brined and hot-smoked fish.)

The process of drying is very important in determining the quality of the final smoked product. When seafood is cured or brined, water-soluble proteins are drawn from within the flesh toward the surface. When these dry they form a tacky film called a *pellicle* that allows for the adherence of smoke to the fish and also serves to protect the fish from moisture loss.

Cold-smoking is a process used to flavor seafood and also in preparing them for long-term preservation. Cured seafood is hung in a smokehouse and smoked in a low-heat environment in which the temperature does not exceed 90°F. It could be more generally defined as smoking at a temperature below which the fish cooks. This also has the effect of drying the fish slowly and in this way is used to help preserve fish, though it can take several weeks for this process to be completed.

Hot-smoking is executed at temperatures ranging from 100°F, up to 180°F. More generally, hot-smoking is purposed with attaining an internal temperature of 140°F for a fully cooked product. Many products are initially cold-smoked for many hours, if not days, to help dry and flavor the fish before higher temperatures are later applied to finish cooking. While smoke primarily adds flavor and sometimes color, its compounds deposited on the surface have some preservative effects.

Traditional smokehouses required incredible skill to operate, given the immense number of variables involved, from the type of fuel and external temperature to the humidity, volume and distance of product from the fire, smoke intensity, seasonal variations in the qualities of the fish, and the degree of heat applied. Adding to the complexity of the process, commercial smokehouses were typically very large structures that could process tens of thousands of fish at a time.

In Europe, it was common to use peat or soft woods such as pine or birch for the smoke source, whereas American smokehouses typically used hardwoods such as oak, maple, and orchard woods. Oftentimes green wood—freshly cut, uncured wood—was used, as this gave off a more flavorful and resinous smoke. Because it is still moist, green wood burns at lower temperatures with a heavier smoke. Other times, cured or dried wood, as one would use in a fireplace, was called for. Wood chips or small logs produce heat and a more sharply flavored smoke and are best for hot smoking. Sawdust is best for cold-smoking, as it gives off a lot of light, aromatic smoke and smolders slowly at low heat. Sometimes the smoke source is more unique to a region such as with the traditional Florida preparation of split and salted mullet smoked over eucalyptus or sweet bay laurel wood or dried palmetto roots. In the Pacific Northwest, salmon was sometimes cold-smoked over green juniper or balsam fir.

Mostly the wood varieties were similar to those used today: alder, maple, oak, hickory, apple, and other orchard woods. The heat and duration of the smoke process is described as light to hard. Light smoke gave foods a slight coloration and elegant, smooth flavor. Hard-smoked meant that the foods were aggressively smoked over a longer period, which resulted in dryer products with a robust smoke flavor and coloration. A few of the classic smoked preparations are still popular in some form, though they have often been adapted to modern tastes, such as the ones that follow.

Finnan haddie is a split Haddock, brined for 15 minutes and hung to dry for a day before being cold-smoked for flavor. The resulting fillets have a pale gold or blond color that is a marker of quality. Originally produced in Findon, Scotland, where they were smoked with peat, the product soon became very popular in America, and several smokehouses began producing it using native woods and a yellow dye to give it the traditional color.

Mackerel was smoked by many different methods and forms. Sometimes it was left whole or eviscerated and hot-smoked. Split, brined, and smoked mackerel was a common form that was a very popular breakfast food and was simply broiled and served with melted butter. Mackerel destined for canning was not cured but just quickly charred over a charcoal grill to render some of the fat and give it a light smoky flavor. Mackerel

is one of the most beautiful fish when smoked, as it retains the striking iridescent markings on its skin and takes on a rich golden hue from a long and moderate smoke. The slow cooking causes the skin to slightly wrinkle and allows the meat to fall easily away from the bones.

Bloaters are made from large, fatty, whole herring, dry-salted overnight. They are then cold-smoked in a dense smoke for one to two days. The fish takes on a gamy taste from its viscera as natural enzymes and fermentation get to work. The long, heavy smoke gives it the balance of flavors needed to complement the acidic tang. These are not fully preserved and are meant to be eaten within a short time frame.

Red Herring are whole herring cured in brine, refreshed in water, dried for several days, then cold-smoked for several weeks until they are dry. The resulting product can be held at room temperature for a very long time and was a principal product shipped to inland markets.

Pickled herring were important for export trade and were made by brine pickling the fish and then further processing them with the addition of vinegar, sugar, spices, onions, sour cream, or any combination thereof. Pickled herring were also made by the method more common today, which was to brine pickle them with the addition of vinegar, which results in softer flesh but a weaker cure that requires refrigeration. The vinegar also serves to soften the bones of the fish, making them easier to eat.

Salmon has long been one of the most important of the species commonly smoked. It comes in many different forms and was an important product of both Atlantic and Pacific fisheries. In the Pacific, the fish tend to be hot-smoked, as they are particularly susceptible to a parasitic nematode once they enter freshwater, where a significant number are caught. Since a dry-cure or cold-smoking does not kill the parasite, the fish must be cooked in order to render the product safe. Several styles of salmon are as follows.

Lox were originally kenched Atlantic Salmon fillets that were refreshed in water before serving and sometimes brushed with brandy for flavor. Modern preparations cure the fish less and often cold-smoke the fillets, giving them a gentle smoke

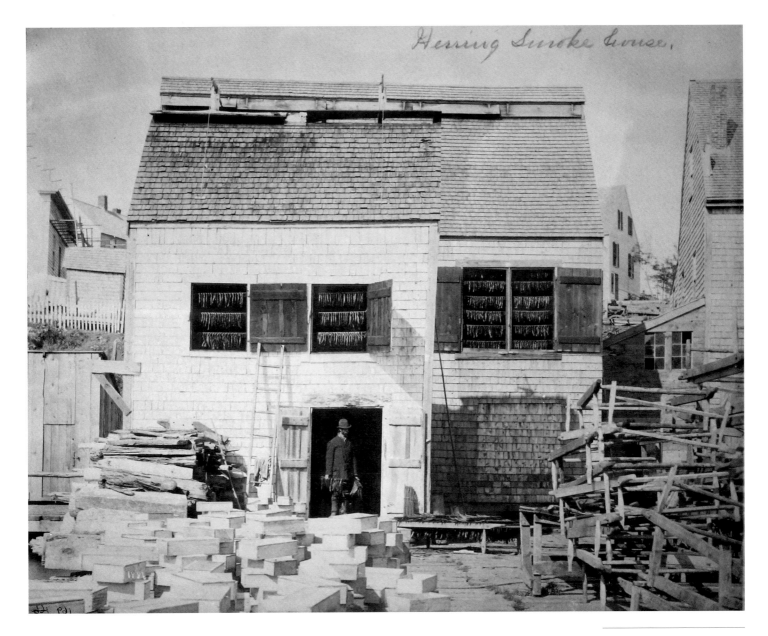

Herring smokehouse, c. 1890.

flavor. This modern approach makes them equivalent to the historical method called *Nova salmon* or *Nova lox,* as referred to in Nova Scotia, Canada. This is different than gravlax, or gravadlax, which is a two- to three-day marinade of salt, sugar, and herbs used to flavor the salmon and dry its flesh, giving it a silken texture. The fish is weighted after the application of the marinade to help push out moisture, and the fillets are turned halfway through the process to ensure an even cure. Historically gravlax was considered a raw product, whereas lox was cured. This is no longer the case, as now both are raw. This distinction was made by the length and strength of cure and the resulting moisture content. Nova lox and gravlax preparations were not common before refrigeration, as they did not extend the shelf life of the product by more than a few days and needed to be kept cold throughout the process.

European-style smoked salmon is another more modern product in which fillets are cured for a short time using salt and sugar mixed with spices, often mace and onion powder. A common rule for this method is that the duration under cure is equal to one hour per every pound that the whole fish weighed. The fish are washed of the cure, dried to form a pellicle, then cold-smoked for several hours. Besides the application of smoke, the main difference between this style and nova lox or (modern) lox is the character imparted by flavors in the cure.

Northwest-style, or *kippered*, salmon is brined for several hours and then hot-smoked over alder wood. As the fish will not hold together when cooked, the smoking process requires the fish to be laid on racks rather than hung. Sockeye and Coho Salmon are most commonly used for this method, as they have brilliant color and a fairly uniform size. This product must stay cold, and it only extends the shelf life by a few days and is not intended for long-term preservation. Recent advances in packaging allow this product to be vacuum sealed, thus increasing the shelf life and allowing it to be held at room temperature.

In Alaska, the common long-term preservation method uses a very strong brine of salt and brown sugar, sometimes mixed with pickling spices. Salmon fillets are cut into thin strips and brined for 15 to 30 minutes and then hung to dry in cold-smoke for several days before a brief hot-smoke to finish the process. This is a fully preserved product that will last throughout the year in the predominately cooler climate. When the strips are cut from the fatty belly portion of King or Coho Salmon it is referred to as "salmon candy."

Indian cure, or salmon jerky, is made from strips of meat that are heavily salted until nearly dry. The strips are cold-smoked for several days, then hot-smoked to finish, resulting in a salty, hard, and chewy meat that's very durable.

Salted salmon, or pickled salmon, was produced by curing fillets by the brine pickle method. This differed from lox, which was cured by the kench method. Salted salmon was mainly an Atlantic industry, though there was a small production of Pacific product. The Pacific industry began salting only the bellies, as the fish were so plentiful that it was feasible to cure only this most valuable section and throw away the rest. The government ended this wasteful practice in 1906 when it regulated that the entire fillet of the fish must be used for "economic purposes." The mild cure (thus intermediate shelf life) gave the fish a unique flavor. In addition to its use as lox, there was a market for the product in Hawaii and Japan, where it was refreshed and grilled or chopped and made into the classic Hawaiian dish, lomi lomi, a tartare-like preparation that was mixed with tomatoes and onions. The salted salmon industry in the Pacific was eventually replaced by canning, which was a far more cost-effective and efficient method of preserving the incredibly abundant catches.

Around the country, several dozens of other species of fish were commonly salted and/or smoked, but the quantities produced limited trade to regional markets. Among these were sturgeon, Swordfish, Albacore, and several freshwater species such as white fish, catfish, and Cisco.

Large quantities of shellfish were smoked and jarred, and this product remains somewhat popular today. Oysters were the predominant shellfish in the market, though mussels and clams were also used. The shellfish were first steamed to open the shell and set the meats. Once removed from the shells they were dipped into a medium-strength brine and dried on oiled racks for several hours before being hot-smoked for no more than 30 minutes. They were packed in vegetable oil and heat-processed in glass jars. These were particularly popular for use in chowders and stews.

Pre-Salting Fish

Almost all fish benefit from salting prior to cooking, and there are several different methods for doing this generally known as *green salting* or *slack salting.* There is the straightforward sprinkling of salt just before cooking or serving raw. Time is an important factor, as it allows the salt to penetrate and to draw out moisture. For thin fillets, just a dusting of salt 10 minutes ahead of time is enough to firm the texture and focus flavors. For thicker fillets, sprinkle a moderate amount of salt on about 15 to 20 minutes before cooking. For fatty fish, it's best to heavily salt for 10 to 15 minutes and then gently wash in lightly salted water before preparing.

This practice is sometimes used in the preparation of sushi to help "clean" the flavors of the fish by drawing out some of the more distinct odors and tastes. Similar results can be achieved by soaking the fish in a medium-strength brine made of salt and sugar for the same times given above. This method will give the fillets a sheen on the surface and quicken browning. This also helps to strengthen the integrity of the fillets of delicate fish for preparations such as grilling.

If the fish is pre-salted for a longer period of time, six hours to overnight, the process is called *corning* and was traditionally applied to fish such as hake and mackerel. The result was a texture that was considerably firmer and chewier. The flavor would be more pronounced but not nearly as strong as in a fully salt-cured product. Corned hake was traditionally boiled with potatoes and pork fatback and served with the melted pork fat drizzled on top. Corned mackerel would often be baked in milk with peppercorns and bay leaf, the milk then thickened with egg yolk to make a sauce.

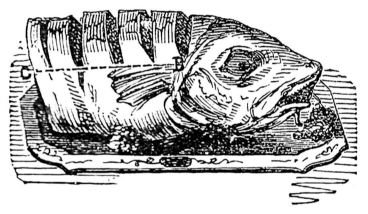

Cod's Head.

TOP Grilled tuna collar.
BOTTOM Woodcut illustration of a roasted cod's head.

Everything Else: The Offcuts

Consumers used to eat more of each fish than is currently in vogue. Species such as cod and salmon are over 90 percent edible; the gallbladder and the contents of the stomach were the only portions avoided. Some "offcuts"—meaning anything but the fillets—were quite valuable, such as the sounds (or air bladders) of hake, which were processed to make a clarifying agent called *isinglass* used in the production of beer.

Certain muscles, such as the cheeks and chin (known as the *tongue*), from larger species like cod and halibut were often used in various dishes and typically eaten within the fishing communities that had access to large quantities of them. Fish bones have long been used as the basis for making flavorful broths, rich in nutrients and gelatin. In years past, the heads of fish were often simmered into soups or roasted whole over a bed of herbs. These would yield not only a flavorful broth but also multiple bits of meat too small to remove raw as whole muscles but perfect to be picked out from various nooks and crannies when cooked. Salmon head soup and roasted cod heads were particularly noted dishes. In John Smith's accounts of his explorations of America, he recounts catching Striped Bass in such abundance that his men prepared only the heads, thinking them the choicest part, and put up the "lesser" fillets in salt. This is completely the opposite of today's preferences. Smith also wrote of huge halibut being caught in abundance and used only for their fins and the fatty, collagen-rich connective tissue just beneath. The rest of the halibut was discarded, as it did not preserve as well as the other fish. And though halibut fillet is among our most preferred seafood today, I, like Smith's men, would choose the fatty fins and cartilage over the fillet any day. I think they are particularly excellent brined and slowly smoked, the fat remaining in the tissue yielding a dish that is slightly crisp, slightly greasy, and pleasantly smoky, offering a pleasure not dissimilar to that of eating bacon.

Of the internal organs, the livers of many fish have long been valued, most notably those of the cod family. Historically, these have been an important additional value realized by the fisheries, as they would be cut from the fish and left in barrels, exposed to the sun, gently heating them enough to render the fat. This process produced a powerful stench that was called "the devil's perfume." It's by this slow rendering process that the oils remain stable and retain their nutrients. The oil of cod family fish is particularly high in vitamin D, which can be lacking in northern populations not exposed to as much sunlight as our southern kin. Another rendering method calls for simmering the livers very slowly in water and skimming the oil from the surface. If oil is exposed to direct heat, its molecular structure breaks down and oxidizes, rapidly increasing its rate of spoilage.

Sharks, particularly dogfish, were also valued for the high levels of vitamin A in their livers, though the market for shark liver oil collapsed in 1941, when scientists created a synthetic version of vitamin A that could be produced much more cheaply and efficiently. Monkfish liver has gained popularity for its similar qualities to foie gras in shape, appearance, and culinary character (though its flavor is distinctly marine). Salmon livers are delicious when lightly salted for a few minutes to firm their texture, then sautéed in butter or bacon grease. By this method they are akin to chicken livers and can be eaten as is with a sprinkle of lemon juice, or puréed into a pâté. Lobster's tomalley, or the hepatopancreas that functions as both liver and pancreas, is a greenish-gray paste found in the head. This has a particularly robust flavor, heavily redolent of iodine. Known variably as "the lady" or "old lady," it is sometimes eaten as an accompaniment to the meat of a steamed lobster, or it can be whipped with butter to make a compound butter or whisked into sauces to flavor and thicken them.

Fish oils, along with those of marine mammals, especially whales and seals, were for centuries rendered and used as lamp oil, industrial lubricant, and in rare instances, as sauce. The blubber-rich mammals, needing the layers of fat to maintain their warm blood, were hunted almost exclusively for this purpose. Whale meat was generally unavailable, as the fisheries were often conducted very far from shore, and voyages could last two years or more. The relatively small quantity of whale meat that was taken near shore was often salted and used in stews or as a substitute for items such as corned beef. As late as the 1920s, whale meat was used in the production of pet food.

Some species of fish were also targeted for their oil, rendered from the fatty tissue in the head, eyes, fins, and belly. A notable example is Bluefin Tuna from which several barrels of oil would be extracted from a single large fish. The oil from the eyes was particularly prized and in Mediterranean cuisines was used as a sauce drizzled over grilled tuna steaks and also used in the canning of tuna meat. Oily fish such as mackerel and sardines were in some regions water-rendered for their oil to be used as a sauce. In modern cuisine, avant-garde chefs use the proteins in fish eyes to thicken sauces and soups, as they act much like chicken eggs in their binding qualities.

The vertebrae of large species such as tuna, Mahi Mahi, and marlin can be split, revealing a gelatin-like translucent marrow. The spines can be roasted and then cracked and the marrow eaten like beef marrow with a garnish of herbs and lemon juice or whipped with butter and used to flavor and thicken soups and sauces. In sturgeon, there is a long elastic band of tissue within the cartilaginous spine called the *notochord*. This was dried and pulverized and made into soup or used as a seasoning when mixed with salt.

A few species of fish have as part of their digestive system thick, muscular stomachs in their throat known as *gizzards* (just as in chickens). Most common of these species is the mullet. The gizzards are easily removed and can be preserved in salt and then stewed into hearty and well-flavored chowders. When fresh, they can be ground for use in chowders or sautéed in butter and garnished with herbs as quite a unique snack.

The blood of various fish is used in many ways. In lobster it is found as the white gel-like substance that coagulates around the meat. This is well flavored and should always be eaten with the meat or reserved to be mixed into risottos, soups, or butters. With salmon, the blood was brushed over fillets to enrich the color when salted for preservation.

The most recognizable "offcut" is roe, meaning the eggs, and is a common food product from a myriad of species. The eggs of sturgeon are famously cured and sold as caviar. But the roes of many other species have different culinary applications. The most famous in America is the shad roe. These large skeins, or egg sacks, are taken from the female fish as they migrate upstream to spawn. The roe is found in what is known as a pair, meaning two skeins, that together can weigh over half a pound. The shad run has long been considered a harbinger of spring, and the fish's roe a great delicacy.

There are many methods of cooking shad roe and the roes of other fish that are similar, such as those from mullet, Mahi Mahi, drum, and others. Some chefs will briefly poach them in acidulated court bouillon before sautéing or roasting them. In other recipes, they will be poached until fully cooked.

The roe of some species, particularly mullet, Mahi Mahi, barracuda, hake, Ling, herring, and tuna, are traditionally used in a Mediterranean preparation called *bottarga*. The roe can be brined and dried for a brief period while pressed under boards, or it may be heavily salted for several days and then dried for up to a week in the open air. Grated as a seasoning or sliced as part of a salad, the cured bottarga of each fish has a unique flavor, though as a category they are very similar, giving dishes a fermented and intensely salty punctuation. The heart of Bluefin Tuna can be cured in the same way, resulting in a product very similar to bottarga though its flavor is stronger and rich in iron. It does not have the same delicacy of texture and must be grated or sliced razor thin.

The roe of cod and herring were traditionally salted and smoked and would typically be puréed into a pâté and spread on toast or used to flavor and thicken soups. Both roes can also be used fresh, simply sautéed in butter. Herring roe, and those of the closely related Alewife, were briefly salted, poached, and marinated in a light pickle with onion and dill.

Another kind of "roe," but one that comes from the opposite sex, is the sperm, known by many different names, including *milt, soft roe, or buck roe.* These soft sacks were typically either lightly salted and fried or pounded with butter and used to thicken soups and sauces. A specialty in Mediterranean cuisines, the buck roe of tuna was pressed and cured, resulting in a product similar to bottarga known as *lattum* or *lattume.*

In crustaceans, the roe is commonly referred to as the *coral* and was often cooked, dried, and grated into a powder to season various dishes and sauces.

The roes of many fish are cured in the same manner as caviar, though they are not technically caviar, and can vary greatly in quality and character. Other species are cured in such a manner, and if sold as caviar, FDA rules require that the species be listed in addition to the word *caviar,* such as

"Lumpfish caviar." To cure roe for such a purpose, the eggs, individually known as *berries*, are removed from the skein and separated from the connective tissue. Typically, they are gently rubbed against a mesh screen, allowing the berries to pass into a brine, where they soak for 15 to 30 minutes, depending on the desired product. When cured, proteins in the skin of the berries coagulate, giving them a jelly-like texture and a snappy bite, which is a marker of the quality of cured roes. Typically the roe is then left to air-dry for up to 12 hours to further develop this tacky quality.

Salmon roe is quite different from other roes that are cured, simply because of their size. These bright orange eggs are very popular in sushi and are used as garnish in modern cuisine. They can be made from the eggs of any of the wild salmon, but those from the Chum Salmon are considered the best. Among the non-sturgeon caviars, some of the most popular come from Paddlefish, a relative of the sturgeon, which has a large berry with a grayish black color. Capelin and Flying Fish both have very small berries and are heavily brined, yielding a very snappy, crunchy texture. In Japan, these are known as *masago* and *tobiko* respectively and are used in sushi and as garnish. These are often flavored with ingredients such as wasabi. The roe of Bowfin, a freshwater species that swims in the southern waters of the United States, is quickly gaining favor under the trade name Choupiquet Royale. And white fish from the Great Lakes yields a crunchy, golden-hued roe that is commonly used in spreads and is sometimes flavored.

The queen of the category is the true caviar, that which comes from sturgeon. Caviar is now considered the epitome of luxury, but it is only since the advent of refrigeration that it has become the product we know today. Historically it was very heavily salted, needing to be more than 10 percent salt in order to preserve it. The caviar we know of today has a much lighter cure, known as *malossol*, with a salt content between 3 and 5 percent. *Malossol* is a Russian word meaning "little salt." High-quality caviar should have a slight crunch and a nutty flavor, and the palate presence of the salt should really be an afterthought. Caviar should be kept at 26°F, and though this is below the freezing point of water, the salt content of the eggs prevents crystallization of the water inside the cells that would otherwise rupture their walls. Caviar with a higher salt content is sold as pressed caviar and is used as a spread, since the berries are usually broken due to swelling from the added salt.

The Atlantic Sturgeon was a favorite food of eastern Native American tribes, though it was largely ignored in popular cuisine until efforts were made to popularize it as a food source in the 1800s. Sturgeons are long-lived fish, with some species living more than a hundred years. They are slow to reproduce and are easily susceptible to overfishing. The fishery began in earnest in the Hudson River, where it was called "Albany Beef" because it was so plentiful and its texture is more like beef than fish. Hudson River caviar was so common that it was served free in bars as a salty snack to encourage drinking. The sturgeon industry lasted only a couple of decades, as greed and overfishing decimated the population. Another great sturgeon habitat, the Delaware Bay and the Delaware River, produced, at its peak, more than 270,000 tons of caviar in a single year. The Delaware population also was victim to overfishing and was soon closed. Commercial fisheries in the West, most notably on the Columbia River, began exploiting the species in 1888. In 1892, six million pounds of sturgeon were taken from the Columbia River. Ten years later, the total catch was only 100,000 pounds. Sturgeon is now being successfully farmed in the Pacific Northwest and in Florida, for both meat and caviar production.

When buying caviar, look closely—the eggs should glisten and be luminous, almost emitting light. They should appear consistent in color and size and their texture should be taut. When serving caviar, use spoons or utensils made of bone or mother-of-pearl, as metal affects the flavor of caviar, giving it a "tinny" taste. To taste caviar, inhale the aroma, then take the caviar and push it against the top of your mouth to crush the eggs, releasing their flavor. On the finish, there should be only a slight brininess and a lingering coppery nuance that fills your palate. Farming American Sturgeon is a young industry that's really come into its own. The caviar of American Sturgeon has very small, firm beads with a very lively pop and a pronounced aroma of toasted almonds, subtly flavored of the sea. The color is quite striking, with violet hues streaming out of the overall midnight black to gray color, along with hints of cream and gold.

Please Post Conspicuously

DEPARTMENT OF COMMERCE
U. S. BUREAU OF FISHERIES
WASHINGTON

FISH ROE AND BUCKROE

Appetizing delicacies.

Rich in tissue-building protein.

Contain as much fat as fishes, and more of an important food constituent, organic phosphorus.

Comparable to hens' eggs in food qualities and may be prepared for the table in as many different ways.

The roe of sturgeon, shad, and spoonbill cat is the most highly-prized part of the fish.

The roe of many other fishes is fully as good for food.

The buckroe or milt roe is an equally palatable and delicate fish food and lends itself to preparation in all the ways in which sweetbreads and brains are served.

Large quantities of these good foods are wasted annually.

Considerable quantities are now marketed; the amount will increase with the demand.

Therefore eat fish roe and buckroe.

Use the fresh products when available.

Can them in time of plenty for future use.

Order the canned goods from your dealer.

Cook them carefully and intelligently.

Ask your dealer for Government cook book (Economic Circular No. 36) or write for it to—

U. S. BUREAU OF FISHERIES, DIVISION F, WASHINGTON, D. C.

Seafood Nomenclature

WHAT WE CALL THINGS MAKES A DIFFERENCE. In science, names help distinguish some fish from others that are similar, both identifying individuals as part of a larger whole and making note that they are worthy of individual distinction. But names are equally important in a cultural context, as they demonstrate a link to the people, places, cultures, and history from which that product comes. Through names, we celebrate the rich diversity of immigration, cultures, language, and histories that are the backbone.

Fishing has always been a profession taught by practice, imbued with the character, values, charm, and colloquialisms of its distinct regions. Each region—each port even—often had descriptive language and naming conventions wholly unique to that community. Sometimes the colloquial names are funny or biting. For example, consider United States Commissioner for Fish and Fisheries George Goode's comments on the Baptist Flounder: "Caught in abundance but thrown back; it goes bad shortly after coming out of the water, whence its name." Looking back and studying the history of a particular fish like the menhaden, it's daunting to wade through the dozens of names that are used in reference to this one fish. Engaging through a common lexicon was one of the great challenges and charges of early fisheries management. Over the past century or more, we have whittled down long lists of names, eventually arriving to the point where we have strict regulation and legal enforcement on exactly what a fish can and cannot be called. But this betrays some of our culinary aptitude. Just as all red wines cannot be taken as the same—for example, the name Cabernet communicates different personalities when in the context of Napa or Bordeaux—so too do we fail to truly describe salmon when we lump species all together in a single culinary category. Such broad qualitative judgments and associations are inept, though by name are scientifically accurate.

It is undeniable that fisheries' science and regulation, as well as our understanding of ecosystems, have benefited from a scientific lexicon. But there has been a great loss associated with this process. A *fish* may rightfully be claimed by science and defined by its strict parameters through which to communicate the biological aspects of fisheries. But *seafood* is part of a more biographical story, one that includes the culture of fishing communities, and cannot be defined by strict parameters. Rather it reflects part of a unique heritage that defines a community and that helps us to better understand our history as a people and as a nation.

Regional names for seafood are often very colorful, drawing inspiration from long-since-irrelevant happenstance or honoring an era or person. I grew up spending time on the Chesapeake Bay, where the Striped Bass is iconic. But don't you dare call it Striped Bass! It is Rockfish and always has been Rockfish. And to me, it always will be. That name is a part of my past and part of my identity. That I call it Rockfish identifies a bit of who I am to the rest of the world. You can tell an awful lot about a person by the name he or she uses for menhaden. You know that old song lyric "tomato, tomahto"? Well, this is the same thing.

In historical texts, I have found mention of Horse Mackerel, a little-used though abundant fish not often eaten that was documented more as a curiosity, and an inconvenient one at that. You are likely familiar with the Horse Mackerel, as today we call it Bluefin Tuna. But these monster fish, sometimes weighing over 700 pounds, were not so useful to a fisherman in a boat the same size as that tuna and who lacked a refrigerator or any proper way to cool it. But it's not just Horse Mackerel—it's also known as "Tunny," "Great Albacore," and very often, just "tuna."

The preeminent scientists and ichthyologists whose legendary work advanced our understanding of the oceans were working from offices, examining preserved samples of fish. Other times, they were out in the field walking through markets and catching fish themselves, and busy writing letters to their colleagues in an attempt to accurately describe their experiences. The challenge was for this group to coalesce around any universal result of such disparate research. While there was certainly rigorous scientific method involved, it's also incredibly difficult to capture the poetry, beauty, and temporal existence of the details in nature. It is hard to describe in a letter a sound made by a fish or to breathe life back into the soulful colors of its skin after it's been pulled from the water, its physical character fading as the fish loses vitality moment by moment. How does

one describe in writing the color of a wave, or the ripple and flex of a muscle, the smell of the sea itself flopping from a net? That's what these scientists were up against, and without the benefit of iPhones.

Adding to this artistic and intellectual difficulty was the sheer exponential diversity of life that they were discovering every day. And while I find it a bit frustrating to read hundreds of books and still come away slightly confused and unsure if I'm communicating to you the right name, it has also been an incredible reminder of just how magical, mysterious, and enigmatic the sea and all its creatures are.

There's a deeper and more meaningful moral issue at stake here. White colonists arriving on America's shores found advanced cultures of indigenous tribes that had been living off this land for eons and that survived through a deeply ingrained understanding of the systems of which they were a part. These tribes had their own languages—beautiful expressions that communicated information about their world and also gave voice to the faith, wonderment, and curiosity that became

their mythology. That we choose to call a fish a Weakfish robs all of us of the culture and experiences discerned through its native name. A Weakfish is just a fish, but a Squeteague is a part of culture. And it is the right of all people to engage the world around them by familiar monikers that connect them to it. And while this argument holds less emotion when we consider how you and I might disagree over Rockfish versus Striped Bass, it is still just as valid and necessary we understand that words, and especially names, are instruments of our relationship with the natural world.

We also create barriers to experience through language that reduces nature to classifications and orders. The Linnaeic system for naming our living world limits us to a singularity of learning. We should, of course, have standardized means of communicating within the sciences, but we must also honor our cultural relationship to our seas, use creative language to help us engage with nature on our own terms, and have personal mythologies and curiosities born of our own witness. Because in the words of Euell Gibbons, "When there is little we see in nature as ours, nature soon becomes damnably boring."

A Short List of Fellow Fish Lovers

Though my research for this book included well over 100,000 pages of reading from old newspaper articles, government pamphlets, scientific studies, to multivolume texts on ichthyology and industry, I regularly quote or reference the authors below throughout the text and consider them very important in the creation of this book. A selected bibliography of other sources used in writing this book follows on page 504.

James Beard (1903–1985)

A legendary cook and educator to whom we owe a great deal regarding our understanding of taste in America, James Beard was a man of very strong opinions. His book *James Beard's Fish Cookery* (1954) offers great insight into the culinary inspiration for well-known dishes and documents the great shift that occurred in American cuisine between the 1950s and 1980s. It also provides many laughs.

Henry Bryant Bigelow (1879–1967)

Henry Bryant Bigelow was a visionary oceanographer and marine biologist. His book *Fishes of the Gulf of Maine* (with William C. Schroeder, 1953), now in its third edition, is both an important history of New England fisheries and a reference of the changes that have occurred in both industry and ecology.

W. Jeffrey Bolster (b. 1954)

Jeffrey Bolster is a professor at the University of New Hampshire who was awarded the 2013 Bancroft Prize for his book *The Mortal Sea: Fishing the Atlantic in the Age of Sail*. I relied on this book heavily, especially for the front sections of this work. Bolster's brilliant account of early fisheries the economies based on them, and their impacts on ecological health is a truly masterful tale, one that speaks as much about our character as our history.

Alan Davidson (1924–2003)

This British diplomat and historian was an extremely influential food writer, having penned *The Oxford Companion to Food* (1999). He also wrote several tomes on seafood, including *North Atlantic Seafood* (1980). While the fisheries and cuisines of Europe are its main subject, that book touches quite a bit on the Americas, too. It provided a wonderful resource for understanding the cuisines of many of our immigrant populations.

Euell Gibbons (1911–1975)

Euell Gibbons was a homesteader and naturalist whose love of wild foods prompted him to write several books documenting the edible riches of our coasts and wildlands. In his 1964 book *Stalking the Blue-Eyed Scallop,* he delights the reader with tales of encountering many species absent from the common culinary lexicon. This work provides not only some great thinking about our relationship with nature but is also an important record of the foods found underfoot and under waves—and what delicious opportunities we were missing.

George Brown Goode (1851–1896)

An ichthyologist by training, Goode ran the fish research program of the U.S. Fish Commission and the Smithsonian Institution, prior to being named the U.S. Commissioner for Fish and Fisheries. A prolific writer, Goode authored more than a hundred scientific reports, notes, and books in the late 1800s, documenting and curating knowledge of this burgeoning nation's marine resources. He was a truly legendary scientist and hero in terms of his codification of the riches in our seas. In researching this book, I relied heavily on his multivolume *The Fisheries and Fishery Industries of the United States.*

Paul Greenberg (b. 1967)

Paul Greenberg is the finest voice chronicling the current state of our nation's and world's fisheries. His award-winning books *Four Fish: The Future of the Last Wild Food* (2010) and *American Catch: The Fight for Our Local Seafood* (2014) are essential commentaries that have significantly influenced my thinking about the historical and continuing importance of fisheries in America. He is also an excellent fisherman and campmate.

Jane Grigson (1928–1990)

An English food writer and long-time columnist for *The Observer*, Grigson's 1973 book *Fish Cookery*, with its charming wit and detours, was very useful as a historical account of seafood cuisine in both America and Europe. It also speaks of the shifts occurring in the mid-to-late twentieth century that provided the foundation of our modern cuisine.

David Starr Jordan (1851–1931)
and Barton Warren Evermann (1853–1932)

The U.S. Fish Commission funded these two ichthyologists to write several important works, illustrating the discovery of many species and early fisheries for highly regionalized products. Of their many works, I relied most heavily on several commission bulletins and reports, especially *American Food and Game Fishes* (1902).

Val Kells

Kells illustrated and co-authored two amazing guides to the fishes of our waters: *A Field Guide to Coastal Fishes: From Maine to Texas* (with Kent Carpenter, 2011) and *A Field Guide to Coastal Fishes: From Alaska to California* (with Luiz Rocha and Larry Allen, 2016). Though I do not quote from these directly, they are vitally important in that I referenced them for every species entry in this book. They offer concise, easy to understand information on thousands of species, and their illustrations proved indispensable for identifying many of the species that do not have popular renown on our tables or in our fisheries but are nonetheless important to our understanding of the diversity of regional fisheries and the culinary opportunities therein.

A.J. McClane (1922–1991)

A.J. McClane wrote the book that largely informed the nature of this one. Though his focus was mostly on sport fish, I credit McClane's *Encyclopedia of Fish Cookery* (1977) with enabling my deep dive into seafood and fisheries. McClane was a famous sportsman and angler, a celebrated author on the topic, and the longtime editor of *Field and Stream* magazine. Of all the people passed whom I'd like to invite to dinner, he is near the top of that list.

Howard Mitcham (1917–1996)

Mitcham was a poet, artist, and chef who spent his career in two of the best seafood towns in America: Provincetown, Massachusetts, for the summers and New Orleans, Louisiana, for the winters. He published several witty and engaging books on the subject of his craft. His books—*Provincetown Seafood Cookbook; Recipes and Reminiscences of Forty Years Among the Shellfish: Clams, Mussels, Oysters, Scallops and Snails;* and *Creole Gumbo* and *All That Jazz*—give a personal and flavorful account of their respective regions and subjects.

FISH SPECIES

A COMPLETE CATALOG OF AMERICAN SEAFOOD

*With comments upon their
social, historical, and culinary qualities*

Abalone

Until the 1970s, abalone (sometimes pronounced ABBA-lone, like a lonely member of the Swedish band, though it technically rhymes with bologna) was a booming fishery on the Pacific coast. Archeological evidence shows that, before westward expansion, native tribes fished extensively for abalone. Commercial fishing began in the 1850s, with Chinese Americans harvesting mostly **Green Abalone** and **Black Abalone** from the intertidal zones. The fishery, centered mostly around San Francisco, peaked in 1879, with landings of four million pounds, but by 1900, shallow waters were closed to fishing due to overharvest. The Japanese-American community later fished for abalone in the subtidal zone, both by free-diving and with breathing gear. This fishery was basically stopped during World War II when, in one of the ugliest chapters of American history, thousands of Japanese Americans were forced into internment camps. After the war, the industry revived with landings of more than four million pounds a year, but the bounty didn't last. In 1949, due to years of overharvesting commercial fishing was banned from San Francisco County north to the Oregon border. Fishing continued to the south, but catches declined rapidly until 1997, when fisheries managers stepped in to protect the last of the decimated population and abalone fishing was closed in California.

More than 15 species of abalone have been harvested commercially. The most common was the **Red Abalone**, which is now farmed in California and Mexico. Due to overfishing, disease, and loss of habitat, several species are now listed as endangered, with several others in the species of concern program. There remains a recreational fishery of Red Abalone, with a limit of 18 per year, with size limitations. The abalone you now find on the market is all coming from farmed sources that are raising a consistently high-quality product that delivers an unforgettable flavor prized to such an extent that we almost lost it completely.

The abalones, members of the *Haliotidae* family, live in intertidal zones ranging down through the subtidal zone to depths of 200 feet. They are so named for the Greek meaning "sea ear," which describes its shape well. The curved, hard shell's exterior camouflages easily against an ocean's rocky bottom, but inside, beneath its meat, hides a truly gorgeous jewel-like patina. The brilliantly lustrous shells are whittled down into mother-of-pearl spoons used for caviar service, a stronger association for many chefs than the culinary use of abalone meat. Certainly many Americans are more familiar with the colorful shell, once commonly used as ashtrays, than they are with the edible portion of the animal.

The animal consists of a large shell and a strong muscle that firmly grasps rocks. The tough edible portion known as the foot must be tenderized and sliced before eating. Once the meat has been removed from the shell the stomach must be removed from the side that was attached to the shell; the dark mantle around the edges as well as the dark skin from the bottom of the foot must also be trimmed. These trimmings are great used in chowders or minced and added to fritters. Canned abalone was at one point one of the most important markets for the harvests, and the meat was used in similar fashion to fresh, with its canning liquid making a good addition to soups or sauces.

The preparation of abalone is all about timing—do not get distracted. Once the abalone steak has been removed from the shell, slice it about a third of an inch thick across the grain. Tenderize the steaks by pounding them with a bottle or wooden mallet. Some prefer to slash the edges of the steak just a bit, which helps prevent curling. Dip the slices in egg and water or milk and then in breadcrumbs before pan-frying in butter.

OPPOSITE The pearlescent shells of abalone.   ABOVE Acadian Redfish.

They should cook for no more than one minute per side. The goal is to achieve a chestnut color on one side before turning to the next. Sometimes the pan is flamed with sherry before serving. The flavor of abalone is very mild, so avoid strong sauces, which may overpower the meat's delicately nutty nuances and sea-brine flavor.

The abalone can also be brined, slowly hot-smoked, and then sun-dried, a preservation process that reduces the meat by 80 to 90 percent of its weight while intensifying its flavor. The resulting leather-like discs are packed with umami flavor and used either very finely shredded or powdered to accent pastas, risottos, or sauces.

Acadian and Golden Redfish

The two Atlantic representatives of the *Sebastes* family, to which the Pacific Rockfish also belong, are the **Acadian Redfish** and the very closely related **Golden Redfish**. Redfish are also known as **Rosefish** or its most common market name **Ocean Perch**, but should not be confused with the Red Drum, which may also be referred to as redfish. Primarily fished in the Gulf of Maine to northern Labrador, these were very important species in the North Atlantic in the early 1930s: as much as 151 million pounds were caught by American trawlers per year, most of which was exported for the frozen food trade or the fillets processed into fish sticks. By the 1950s the populations had begun to decline, and by the 1980s the fishery was no longer viable and fishing effort ceased. The stocks have since rebounded and now the fishery is trying to recapture a place in the market. The historic average was six to eight pounds for the Golden Redfish and three to five pounds for the smaller Acadian Redfish.

Due to overharvesting, those that are caught today are significantly smaller, ranging just up to two pounds, with larger fish being quite rare. (For more information, see "Our Changing Oceans," page 12.)

The fish have a moderate edible yield of about 50 percent, yielding thin, roseate-shaded white fillets with a scarlet-orange skin similar to snapper. The mild-flavored flesh cooks up pearly white and has been referred to as "snapper lite." The thin skin does not crisp well, especially given the thinness of the fillets, which are prone to drying out. When overcooked, the fillets lose any charisma they had, and their briny-sweet ocean flavor gives way to a cardboard-like aroma and very coarse grain. Its clean flavor makes it popular in Midwest markets, where skinless fillets with the bloodline removed are often sold as a substitute for perch. On the East Coast they are most often sold eviscerated but otherwise whole, what's knowin as "in the round," though there is increasing demand for fillets. With their sweet, lean, and very mild flavor paired with a traditional fish texture, redfish have gained their popularity and appeal from being an unchallenging fish.

Because these fish are caught at great depths, they often appear distended, with their eyes and/or air bladders bulging due to barotrauma, an effect of rapid change in pressure when they are hauled from fathoms below. This unattractive, bug-eyed presentation may hinder curb appeal, but it is not a representation of quality. Most of the U.S. catch comes from the Gulf of Maine and around the deeper waters off the Grand Banks. The racks, or the carcasses of the filleted fish, are now commonly salted for use as lobster bait.

The **Blackbelly Rosefish**, a scorpionfish related to the *Sebastes* family, is very similar to the fish mentioned above. These fish, while found in northern waters, are most abundant throughout the South and Gulf, where they are regarded as a second-class sport fish. Its flesh, however, is nearly identical to that of the Acadian and Golden Redfish and should command equal respect. But given the depths at which it is caught, there is only a small amount landed as bycatch in commercial fisheries, making it unlikely to find popular menu appeal. The fish earned its name for a pretty logical reason: when cut open, the lining of the belly cavity is black. Sometimes fishermen have fantastical tales about the fish's moniker, and sometimes they just tell it like it is.

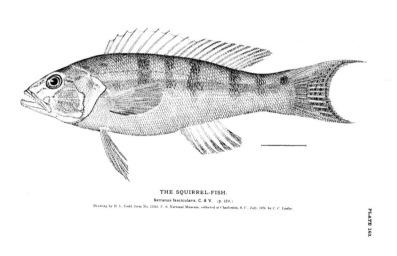

THE SQUIRREL-FISH.
Serranus fascicularis, C. & V. (p. 410.)
Drawing by H. L. Todd, from No. 21544. U. S. National Museum, collected at Charleston, S. C. July, 1878 by C. C. Leslie.

PLATE 163.

TOP A large catch of Acadian Redfish, 1942.

Alfonso Squirrelfishes

Three commercial fish families hail from this order, each of them presenting different culinary qualities, though they inhabit similar waters and are all taken as bycatch of deepwater fisheries, mostly in the Gulf of Mexico. The widely ranging **Big Roughy** and its smaller cousin the **Silver Roughy** are nearly indistinguishable from the Orange Roughy of the southern oceans, which gained such popularity in recent decades as to be nearly nonexistent today. These grow between 8 and 15 inches and are most always served as fillets. Their flesh has a moderately firm texture and very mild flavor.

The **Splendid Alfonsino** takes rank as the highest-quality relation. These slender fish, scarlet-stained along their dorsal ridge fading to pink and silver toward the belly, are often confused with the Mediterranean delicacy Red Bream, to which it is equal in character and quality but completely unrelated. The flesh, lush in oil, is often served in sushi preparations. Some chefs suggest softening the skin of the fillets by dousing it with boiling water to match the consistency of the elegantly flavored flesh. Like all members of this group, the Splendid Alfonsino feeds on crustaceans, cephalopods, and small fish, a diet that its flavor reflects.

The largest family in this order is the **Squirrelfishes**, usually taken as bycatch from Vermilion Snapper fisheries. Most of these species grow no larger then six to eight inches, the exceptions being the **Longspine Squirrelfish** and the **Squirrelfish**, both growing up to a foot or more. Given their relatively small size, these fish are often grilled whole or the fillets are used in stews such as a court bouillon or bouillabaisse. Their firm texture and moderate flavor lends itself to a wide variety of preparations and flavor combinations. While all these fish mentioned are relatively abundant, they are a rare find in the market, as they are not a target species and their size does not recommend them to high demand.

Anchovy

Though they've never supported an important food fishery in America, anchovies have long been an important part of our culture and cuisine. Swimming at the top of the water column, the 16 species of anchovies are active filter feeders, meaning they sieve the water as they swim in search of their prey. Like fellow filter feeder the sedentary oyster, anchovies feed on phytoplankton and zoo plankton and thus play an important role as a keystone species that helps regulate the quality of water in the entire ecosystem.

Anchovies are very short-lived creatures, with 45 to 55 percent of the entire population dying of natural attrition yearly. Their purpose is not only to help filter waterways but to feed other fish that swim in them. As such, they make up a very important bait fishery. They are also often taken as bycatch in other fisheries, such as Gulf and Southeast Atlantic shrimp fisheries.

One of the most common fish in the Gulf of Mexico is the **Bay Anchovy**, commonly known as the **Glass Minnow**. Though there is no directed fishery, at certain times of the year they are caught in shrimp nets, but only when the fish are abundant in the brackish nearshore waters and large enough to not slip through the netting.

While commonly caught for animal feed and in small-scale bait fisheries all over the United States, mostly for the recreational fishing trade, anchovies are often taken in a mixture of species, including the young green fry of herring with which they swim. Culinarily, these are most often incorporated into a dish known as "white bait." Though this term in Europe refers to a certain fish, in this country it refers to a preparation in which small whole fish are breaded and fried, often served with tartar sauce.

Preserved anchovies have long occupied a ubiquitous role in cookery, mostly in the Mediterranean, from Roman times onward, but they act as a flavoring agent, never a star—a dependable foundation upon which dishes can be built. What we consider the anchovy is really any one of 20 species of fish marketed as such, in the salted, oil-packed fillet form that we are so used to. Known as a "red cure," this method calls for layering headed and gutted whole fish with sea salt in 60-gallon drums, then letting the fish cure for six months at around 40°F, until the flesh turns that bold russet hue. Much of this

production is based in Japan, Morocco, the Mediterranean, and especially Peru. It's also about the only major foodstuff that's regularly sold in a tube, just like toothpaste. But to me that is a mark of sustainability, as it's merely creating a market for less-than-perfect beautiful fillets that have likely been crushed at the bottom of the salt barrel.

Though a salt anchovy cannery has not existed in this country as far as I know, we do have 16 species of anchovies in our waters. The **Northern Anchovy** is the most important, with more than 23 million pounds landed, mostly for bait and industrial uses, though there is a small commercial food fishery in the Pacific Northwest.

One rarely finds fresh anchovies at the market, and it's not hard to understand why they are not taken seriously as a food fish. Their skin and scales are very thin and easily damaged. Their low value and high volume of capture tend to make them impossible to care for on an individual level. Plus, like most small silver fishes, their soft bellies tear easily and they are very often delivered in less-than-peak condition.

Cured anchovies have a pungent and boldly salty flavor, while fresh specimens have a very mild flavor, light and briny, with an almost fluffy texture. Their oily flesh pairs well with fresh herbs and lemon juice, as well as good-quality extra-virgin olive oil. Fresh cured anchovies are a thing of beauty and to salt your own does not require six months. Simply rinse the fish in a bit of seawater or brine, then layer them, stacked head to tail, with a healthy dose of sea salt between. After just a few weeks in the refrigerator, you will note that their flavor takes on a very distinct shift, going from fresh salt breeze to a mildly funky aroma. Anchovies are ready after 10 days to bring all of their culinary wallop to the plate, but they can continue to mature over the course of a few weeks. The benefit of curing them yourself is you also gain the salty pickle, or the juice that comes off of them. If left to ferment in the warm sun this liquid becomes *garum*, the fish sauce of Roman fame, though it is also known as *liquamen*, *colatura*, or, simply, *fish sauce*. Rich in umami, this seasoning is used in cuisines around the world, especially in East-Asian cooking.

Salt-packed anchovies can be used just as oil-packed fillets, though they must first be soaked in cool water. This may take as long as 12 hours, depending on how salty you want them to be. After soaking, the fillets are easily removed from the bones by peeling them off from the tail toward the head. The bones can be deep-fried into a delicious and crunchy snack. The salt from the cans can be dried in a low oven and used as you would regular salt but with an added potent tang.

Anchovies smoke exceedingly well, adding another layer of depth to their flavor. After a quick bath in brine, either cold-smoke the anchovies until delicately flavored or hot-smoke them until nearly dry. I often use smoked (or regular) anchovies mashed with olive oil as a bold and beautiful way to start any vegetable dish, braise, or pan sauce. When making seafood stew, you can pull together a quick stock by sautéing a few tins of anchovies, a couple of stalks of celery, and a bulb of fennel in a good glug of olive oil for a few minutes before adding a couple of quarts of water and bringing to just under a boil.

Recipes for meat pâtés in early cookbooks often call for the addition of anchovy paste to add another layer of flavor. Traditional sauce making often uses anchovies as a base for flavor, as in Caesar and Green Goddess dressings, and many classic compound butters of French cuisine. Indeed, though the fish themselves are tiny, their contribution to cuisine has been outsized.

Barnacles

Of all the tenants of the tide pool, the various species of barnacle too often escape our culinary attentions. The **Gooseneck Barnacle**, also known as the **Leaf Barnacle** in British Columbia, confused the ancients, who were unsure whether it was a plant, bird, fruit, or mollusk. According to Euell Gibbons, the most ridiculous of these bygone theories was that the Goose Barnacle, from which its modern name is derived, was the young of an arctic goose that wintered in Britain and whose mating habits were subject to a great deal of mystery. English biologist Thomas Huxley ended this confusion when he surmised that "a barnacle may be said to be a crustacean, fixed by its head and kicking food into its mouth by its legs."

OPPOSITE Fresh anchovies.

FOLLOWING PAGES A cluster of Gooseneck Barnacles.

Once cleaned, smaller fish can be slashed with ½-inch-deep cuts along the side of the fish and heavily seasoned with salt all over the outside with a small amount of pepper rubbed inside the cavity. Grilled or broiled whole, the fish picks up a sexy rustic smoke flavor while still showing its fresh briny qualities and offers an impressive presentation.

The fillets themselves are perfect diced and puckered with citrus and spice for ceviche. Cleaned and dressed whole fish can be cut into thick steaks and slow roasted at 230°F to 250°F; gentle cooking develops and matures the flavors of the fish while preserving all of its moisture and fat.

James Beard wrote that barracuda is "an exceptional fish when smoked," and I could not agree more. A very quick cold-smoke flavors the fillets without cooking them—a perfect way to condition the fish before sautéeing or broiling it with a pat of butter. The skin becomes crisp, while the fish, butter, and smoke all blend seductively.

I feel that hot-smoked barracuda holds its own against some of the true classics, such as mullet, Bluefish, and salmon. Prior to hot-smoking, it's best to slowly brine the fillets in a moderate salt and sugar solution for four to six hours. After drying the fillets and brushing them with rum or Pernod, I smoke them over gentle heat (+/−100°F) for four to six hours before I stoke the fire to about 140°F. From that point, I will smoke another two to three hours. Given that I first encountered the fish in the South, I like to play up that Southern personality and cook it using peach wood, the queen of all smoking woods, blended with sweet pecan shells and the gentle spice of oak.

Historically, the fish were salted and sun-dried. Old preservation texts suggest that these fish were most often split along the belly cavity past the backbone and up to the dorsal ridge, leaving the fillets attached by a thin band of flesh and skin. As they are mostly caught in warm weather climates, the curing process had to be more aggressive than northerly methods were. High humidity quickly spoils the flesh, and high heat can bake the meat and render off the fat. To avoid this, the fish were very heavily salted and dried on racks during the cool evening and overnight hours, then collected and taken out, of the direct sun during the day. Under normal conditions, the fish were sufficiently dry after about two weeks of this process.

Any excess salt was then brushed off, and then the fish was rubbed with a small amount of fresh salt before being sent to market. Unlike most salt-cured fish, salt-cured barracuda was best used quickly rather than stored for long periods. Old recipes called for fillets to be soaked for one to two days before being broiled and basted with a pat of butter. Other dishes saw soaked fillets simmered into chowders and stews and even cooked with beans as you would normally use a bit of salt pork.

Barracudas sometimes contain beautiful plump roes. If I'm lucky enough to come across such treasure I sauté them slowly in butter, adding a smashed clove of garlic and a stick of cinnamon to the pan. Fresh woodsy herbs like thyme or rosemary add a gentle perfume to the rich and pleasantly coarse-textured roe. I find barracuda roe to be similar to shad roe but with a more elegant flavor. It can also be cured as for bottarga (see page 76 for more). The resulting salted and dried roe is equal to that of a mullet and presents a vibrant ocean scent and sassy tang, a perfect culinary incarnation of the barracuda's personality.

Barrelfish and Black Driftfish

Little is known about these species, and to this point they have never been observed underwater though they are infrequently caught in deep water as a bycatch of longline grouper fisheries. These two rarities are closely related and interchangeable in the kitchen, as little distinction is made between them on the lucky occasions they show up at market. That said, an average of 16 metric tons of these fish are landed every year, so there is reasonable chance that one or the other might cross your path.

The **Barrelfish** swims as far north as Nova Scotia, while the **Black Driftfish**'s familiar latitudes don't extend north of Florida. Together, they are commonly referred to as **Barrel Grouper**, not because they are of any relation to grouper but because of similar eating qualities. They are closely related to the very highly prized Blue Nose Bass of the southern ocean. Both Barrelfish and Black Driftfish range in size from 4 to 30 pounds, but average around 20 pounds. Their flesh is firm and tense but also rich in fat, giving it a delightful and moist flake. Like their southern cousin, they share a mild flavor that is meaty like bass but finishes with a hint of shellfish. They should be cooked gently; high heat can cause the meat to seize and become rubbery, making it difficult to cook through evenly. Both fish smoke exceedingly well, and the resulting product is wonderful flaked over salad or in chowders.

Other fish in our waters that are closely related but are not recorded in any landing data are the **Medusa Fish**, **Black Ruff**, and **Brown Ruff**, all of which are members of the Medusa Fish family. Should you ever come across the chance to taste one, it seems their culinary qualities would be similar to Barrel Grouper, given the habitat and features of these fish.

Bigeyes

Of the five species of bigeye, four swim in Atlantic and Gulf waters and one in the Pacific. All are identical in culinary terms. Most of their abundance occurs in the Gulf, but they swim as far north as Massachusetts in the east and Oregon in the west. Commercially these are mostly taken as bycatch of snapper fisheries. They are nocturnal fish, hiding in caves and crevices during the day and emerging and gathering in schools at night to eat crabs, shrimp, and little fish. Though they are not prized in the United States, there is an export market to Japan, where their elegant, buttery-smooth texture and unmistakable crab-sweet flavor commands good money. Their fillets are thin, which makes cleaning smaller fish a chore. Larger fish reward your effort, as the fillets are perfect for pan-searing, poaching, and steaming. The whole fish roasts very well.

Size is really the only deciding quality factor when it comes to eating these delicious fish. The lone Pacific species, the **Popeye Catalufa** (what a great name!), tops out at one foot in length. In the Atlantic, the **Bigeye**, **Short Bigeye**, **Bulleye**, and the **Glasseye Snapper** grow to maximum sizes between one and two feet. The Glasseye Snapper is not a snapper at all, but it is the only domestic species of any culinary renown, especially in the recreational fishing community. The Bigeye is often mistaken for the Glasseye Snapper, and about six tons of the two species are landed every year. These brick red–colored fish are all pleasingly shaped, like a bass, and share the family trait of enormous eyes, hence the name. But this look is not quite flattering, as they appear in a permanent state of paranoia.

Bulleye.

Billfish

Most of us know the majestic billfishes through the lore of fish stories, most famously the spirited contention of Hemingway's old fisherman, Santiago, with a Marlin, and in turn with the sea itself. In this family are several species of marlin and their cousins the **Spearfish** and **Sailfish**. None of the species ever gained much footing in the tradition of American cuisine, and they are still largely considered a sport fish, a highly valuable industry that releases the vast majority of fish caught back into the ocean alive. Though the fish are delicious, commercial fisheries never expanded beyond a cottage industry due to the fact that billfish are oceanic species that swim far from shore, requiring a great deal of labor and danger to catch. It made little sense to chase after these elegant creatures when there were so many other species readily caught and in high demand. Today, all commercial billfish fisheries are limited to Hawaiian waters, where they are both targeted and taken as bycatch of the longline Swordfish fishery. There is no commercial fishery in the Atlantic.

The Sailfish and Spearfish are singular fish, while three species of marlin are landed—the **Striped Marlin**, **Blue Marlin**, and **Black Marlin**. They can grow as long as 16 feet, though any length provides ample canvas for their skin's beautiful shades of blue, as varied in tone as the swatches at a paint store. These fish start life as microscopic larvae and over their lifetime can increase in size by a millionfold. Females can grow up to four times the size of males, and nearly one-fifth of the fish's length is the bill. These bony spears known as *rostra*, are the defining characteristic of the billfish and Swordfish families. On Swordfish this weapon of prey is flat, more like a true sword, while on billfish they are round like a spear. They use these to slash through schools of fish to injure them for easy eating. All billfish have a distinguished dorsal fin that only accentuates their formidable mien. On marlin, the fin is a punk rock mohawk, tall in the front and tapering down toward the tail. The Sailfish fin outsizes its body by threefold and has an irregular edge on top, giving it an unkempt look, like an early 1990s' Andre Agassi hairdo.

The flavors of billfish are equally excellent, delicate with subtle sweetness and pleasing hints of iodine paired with a lingering nutty character. They have the sour tang associated with sharks and the earthy flavor of Swordfish, which makes for an overall very complex and nuanced taste. These fish average 11 feet and so must be cut into sections to enable transport. The meat is sectioned into loins like tuna, and portions are cut as cross sections. These tend to have a fair amount of connective tissue, so when purchasing, ask for pieces cut from the middle section nearest the spine where the muscles are more contiguous. If possible, avoid both the tail and areas near the skin, which can be marked by a fair amount of sinew. If you are adventurous, ask for the collars, the bony plate just behind the gills. These long curved bones have a delicious steak-like chop of meat attached to them that is incredibly tasty when marinated and grilled or broiled, offering a variety of textures and a perfectly Flintstonian presentation.

All billfish may be prepared using the same methods as when cooking Swordfish, but because they are generally leaner they are less forgiving to overcooking, I recommend moderate heat and keeping your attention turned to the fish. Another trick is to constantly baste the fish with butter or oil as it cooks, helping it to retain moisture.

My favorite preparation is to marinate them in a mild salt brine heavily spiked with vinegar and herbs for at least one day and up to three days. This permeates the fish with intense flavor while tenderizing the meat, making it perfect for slow roasting large chunks to a perfect medium doneness over a charcoal or wood fire. All species of marlin are favored for sushi preparations both in Japan and increasingly in Hawaii. Blue Marlin and Black Marlin have darker flesh that can be rust hued or even colored as dark as walnut. The Black Marlin interestingly is often used to make fish sausage. The Striped Marlin flesh is pale to pink in color, has a lighter and more delicate flavor, and is the most tender, making it the top choice for raw preparations.

All billfish are equally beautiful when smoked. It is best to give them a long soak in a weak brine, then cold-smoke the fish for 12 hours before increasing the temperature to around 160°F to finish the smoking process, about 24 hours total.

I rarely get to eat billfish, but I fully appreciate the experience when I do. When I am preparing it, I am aware of the majesty of the animal. I shy away from using strong flavors, careful not to mask or challenge the fish. Billfish retain in death their boldness and raw power expressed in life, and in each bite I taste that spirit.

Ernest Hemingway posing with a marlin, Havana Harbor, Cuba. July 1934.

Bluefish

The **Bluefish** is a curiosity in the canon of American seafood cuisine. For centuries it was considered among the most important, most appreciated, and most valued of all fish, keeping company with mackerel and pompano in the highest culinary echelon. In more recent times, Bluefish has gone from being a fish that fed millions to a hugely popular recreational fishery that largely ignores its qualities at the table. I've had guests in restaurants belittle me for daring to serve them fertilizer. "Oh, I go out and catch dozens at a time," one guest said with likely no exaggeration, "and it's only good for tilling into the yard." Such a response illustrates the ignorance that surrounds this august fish.

The mysterious Bluefish has been prone to periods of extreme abundance followed by spells of near total absence. Early Colonial American histories recount Bluefish being extremely abundant, but by 1764 they had totally disappeared and mention of them in texts ceased. It was not until 1810 that a few fish began to show up again. In 1817 their numbers began increasing, and by 1825 they were again abundant, peaking in 1841 when massive schools began arriving along the New Jersey coast. There is not much scientific consensus as to why this happens, but the historical evidence validates Bluefish's cryptic singularity.

When abundant, they have been a blessing for the poor, as they are easily caught near shore. In the hard years during the Great Depression, the Long Island Railroad ran "Fishermen's Special" trains out to Montauk, returning at day's end with men and sacks of Bluefish packed together as tight as sardines in a can. As recently as the 1990s, Bluefish provided important sustenance for many poor families in the mid-Atlantic and New York regions.

These are transient fish, with migration patterns that span the entire Atlantic coast. The Bluefish congregate in schools of incredible size, once recounted as covering an area equal to 10,000 football fields. Within schools, the fish are roughly of similar size, a good idea as the famously voracious blues are cannibalistic, so they've figured out it's best to stay away from larger kin. Baby Bluefish just about one year in age are known as *Tailors* or *Choppers*. Juveniles earn the name *Snappers*, as when in the deranged fury of a feeding frenzy their jaws click with the sound of castanets. As they grow larger, about three to five pounds, the names *Harbor Blues* or the less-flattering *Rats* apply. Large blues, weighing 10 pounds or more, are here on out known as *Horse Blues*.

Despite being the only member of its family and its historically esteemed presence in our cuisine it is also known by myriad regional and colloquial names: **Yellow Mackerel**, **Horse Mackerel**, **Skipjack**, **Green Fish**, **Snapping Mackerel**, **Blue Snapper**, **Skip Mackerel**, and for reasons I cannot conceive, when caught in the Hudson River above New York City, they were known as **Whitefish**. "Call them sir, by whatever name we please . . . They are all the same *Pomatomus saltatrix* still, and deal out destruction and death to other species in all the localities they visit," said Hon. N. E. Atwood, representative of the Cape District 1870, in official testimony to describe the calamitous personality of these fish.

They have been likened to animated chopping machines—no deeper purposed than to cut or otherwise destroy as many fish as possible. Of all the fish in the ocean it seems somewhat incongruous that the Bluefish, with all its vicious vice, should be the subject of such romantic and rapturous writing. There are marvelous poems in honor of this sage-green, sea-blue, white-bellied, stub-nosed fish. One of the most beautiful books ever written on man's relationship with the sea, *Blues* by John Hersey, explores our place in this world through our pursuit of food. This narrative confesses sacred reverence for the vigor and immense power of Bluefish, which Hersey describes as "possessed of pin-sharp teeth and murderous little underslung jaws." As they corral prey, the conflict tempestuously boils the waters in what's known as a "Bluefish blitz." The sea turns a frothy red as Bluefish busy themselves chopping and consuming anything that fits between their jaws. Viscous oil stains map the geography of the killing. Once upon a school of prey such as menhaden, it is their nature to be so covetous of any fish left alive that even when fully satiated the Bluefish will disgorge themselves in order to continue killing. Not even sharks in their most hysteric frenzy come close to the blind and frantic energy that Hersey describes when the "blues strike like blacksmith's hammers." Despite their pleasant name, these violent vandals are as lurid in demeanor as they are siren in savor.

At their peak, Bluefish fisheries landed well over 120 million pounds per year, though just 10 percent of this was product of a commercial fishery. Blues have always been an important species for the recreational industry, second only to the Striped Bass with which it is commonly found. Unfortunately, blues are sought mostly for thrill and are landed without much regard for the quality of meat. For Bluefish to reflect its true potential, it must be immediately bled, flushed with salt water, and eviscerated, then iced. Only such care will proffer fillets having any chance to impress once on the plate. I think too many people first experience Bluefish as the result of a long day's derby: dozens of fish landed, not properly tended to before being relegated to a freezer or unenthusiastically cooked by a fisherman whose ambitions were for a Striped Bass dinner. Given such an experience, I sympathize with the distrusting gentleman in my restaurant who thought I was selling him Bluefish as a tailor once sold an emperor new clothes.

Despite the vast quantity of Bluefish sold in markets in New York and Boston, and even the very popular trade carrying Bluefish into the interior of our early nation, there remained a distaste for the fish in Washington, D.C., and points south along the coast, where it was considered unfit for human consumption. There are two important populations of blues: one remaining in the Gulf, the other migratory along the East Coast. In the Gulf, Bluefish are ignored and even disdained as a nuisance. Fisheries in the Gulf land only a couple dozen tons. Of the Eastern Seaboard Blues, as these fish grow larger they develop a tendency to stay further north, and thus the average size of southern-caught blues tends to be a bit smaller than the average northern catch.

I do believe that fish caught in northern waters tend to be bolder in flavor, in part because the principal food in the north is potent menhaden while in the south they feed upon mullet, anchovy, and other small fish that are slightly more demure in personality. But I feel there are some other factors at work, including the chill of the northern waters, which may help sculpt the flavor into something more keen and resolute. While I certainly admire and would never turn down quality Bluefish from any shore, the northern late-summer-fat blues are lusty and brighter than their southern counterparts, which can taste slack, or uninspired.

Young Bluefish, tailors or snappers, lack the coarser texture common to larger Blues, and their sweeter flavor reflects their diet, which consists of crustaceans and smaller fish. By nearly every account, it is considered that these smaller fish, those being two to three pounds, are more versatile in culinary applications and are superior in flavor. Fish that weigh eight pounds or less are considered fine eating but are best for the grill or broiler, as these high-heat methods will render out some of the copious fat, resulting in a charred but moist dish. Fish larger than 10 pounds are thought best for smoking, as they are often quite high in fat

and can be robust in flavor to the point that they overwhelm other preparations. One notable exception is the *Fannie Farmer Cookbook*, which states that larger fish offer the best quality. It further advises that when fresh Bluefish is unavailable, frozen is the best option. I am a great proponent of quality frozen seafood, but Bluefish simply does not freeze well. Period.

I find larger blues perfect for chowder. The flesh should be coated in salt for an hour or two, then rinsed before using— this tames its flavor and firms the flesh, otherwise the meat will soften and flake apart. The old *Gourmet Cookbook* has an unlikely declaration that the head and bones of Bluefish are ideal for making fumet, or stock. This runs counter to nearly all recommendations that stocks be made only from bones of neutral flavored lean fish such as cod or halibut. But, indeed the old masters are correct. When the Blue is simmered very slowly with lots of white wine and onions, the strength of this robust fish is tempered and the resulting broth is gelatinous, brightly aromatic, and sweetly flavored.

Because Bluefish are in constant motion, a pelagic species ever on the hunt, they develop a large amount of dark muscle tissue laminated thickly beneath the skin.

When fresh, this tissue is well-flavored and bright red. Though it may be too intense for some tastes, I think it provides a nice contrast in flavor to the gunmetal- to beige-colored fillets. There is the misconception that Bluefish is a "fishy" fish, but that is just an old sunburned day-trippers' tale that deflects blame. There is no "fishy" or bad Bluefish, only once glorious Bluefish that was poorly handled.

James Beard called its flavor "delicate," so much so that he recommended avoiding heavy seasonings that might mask its nuance. The flesh is relatively firm with an easy flake that reveals moist musculature. Fresh fillets will have an animated aroma and an energetic flavor, but that's because it's sharp, not strong. Its excellent taste is smart, well balanced, and highly aromatic, with notes of herb, citrus, and brine. It is also somewhat gamey in flavor like Sockeye Salmon and is punctuated by a slight sourness. The brine flavor fades into a lingering malty or creamy aftertaste that is tart with a touch of natural smokiness. Though Blues have a quite acidic flavor, they are still best paired with tangy ingredients such as vinegar, citrus, mustard, or tart fruit like sour apples. It is complemented beautifully by fresh basil, as the two summery flavors provide equal match for each other.

Bluefish is one of my favorite fish for pickled preparations, this being the only example of the fish gaining quality as it ages and becomes infused with piquant vinegar and floral spices like juniper and fennel seed. But Blues really reach their culinary summit when smoked, especially over orchard woods. Stronger woods work well, but they give the meat a sharp edge that can be challenging. The fillets can also be cured like gravlax, burying the fish for three days in a mixture of salt and sugar with tarragon and orange slices. After this cure, the fillet will be delicately textured. It will not hold together as well as salmon, but slicing it thinly on a sharp angle toward the tail end will yield silky slices that are an equal replacement for salmon in any canapé or appetizer preparation.

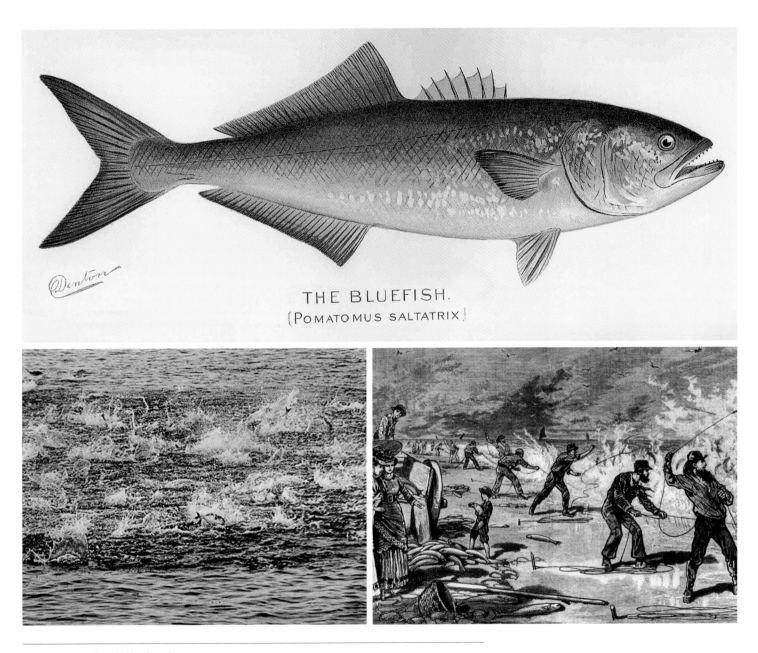

THE BLUEFISH.
(POMATOMUS SALTATRIX)

BOTTOM, LEFT Bluefish feeding frenzy.
BOTTOM, RIGHT Catching Blue Fish from Syasconset Beach in Nantucket, 1879, artist unknown.
FOLLOWING PAGES Shrimp boat marooned by Hurricane Katrina in Empire, Louisiana.

Bowfin

The **American Bowfin** is one of our more interesting freshwater species. Though not historically esteemed at the table, it is nonetheless quickly becoming a Southern delicacy. Its range spans throughout the eastern states, southern Canada, and the Great Lakes spreading south into the Mississippi basin, sometimes ranging into brackish waters. These are primitive fish, literally, in that they retain the morphological characteristics of their early ancestors. These unattractive fish look very similar to the invasive northern snakehead, and like their doppleganger, they are able to breathe both air and water and have been recorded as having traveled as far as a quarter-mile between bodies of water. They feed on crawfish, freshwater mussels, small fish, and just about anything else. They are distinguished by a continuous dorsal fin that runs the length of the fish, which averages 20 to 30 inches.

The flesh has been commonly dismissed as soft and insipid, but if treated properly it can be firm and well suited as a pan-fry fish, shredded for making fish balls, or as a fillet layered into a Pine Bark Stew. Its mild flavor takes well to heavy seasonings, especially Southern classics like blackening and Creole spices. It is also a good fish for smoking, as a dense brine firms the fish and hearty oak wood smoke adds depth and balance, bringing its character into focus. The fish should be "crimped" when first captured; that is, just after death shallow incisions should be made along the lateral line running the length of the fish. This will temper the mollescent result of rigor mortis and help to maintain the density of the flesh.

As this fish has been around far longer than any spoken language, it makes sense that it should have a host of names, all of them appropriate to say in polite company, though none of them are particularly flattering. Among many others, **Mudfish** and **Shoepick** are the most common vernacular names in the South. Shoepick being a bastardization of either the Choctaw name *Shupik* or the Cajun name *Choupique*. Both are beautiful names but just pretty ways of saying Mudfish.

Bowfin are caught throughout the South, but are both wild captured and farmed in Louisiana. Leave it to Southern gentility to attempt to elevate a fish long burdened with a negative reputation, lending it grace and a bit of romance. While the meat itself slowly gains in popularity, the caviar made from its roe is the real driver of the recent surge in interest. Treated with a traditional *malossol* cure, the processed roe is marketed under several names such as "Cajun Caviar," "Black Caviar," and the trademarked "Choupiquet Royale."

It is said to have a similar nutty, woodsy, even ashy flavor common to some of the far more expensive caviars. I find the notion of caviar disrobed of its elitism and injected with good ol' Cajun spirit of "rougarou-in'" to be so satisfying.

Otranto Pine Bark Stew

Though its origin is debated, Pine Bark Stew is widely recognized as a part of Lowcountry cuisine, or that of the area surrounding Charleston, South Carolina. "It proved to be a fish chowder, highly spiced, and stewed over a pine bark fire sufficiently long to get some of the flavor of the pine into the decoction," the *New York Times* declared of this freshwater fish stew in a 1909 story. This recipe, from the 1950 cookbook *Charleston Receipts* by the Charleston Junior League illustrates the basic structure of the dish. While this recipe originally calls for bass, I have more often than not seen it served with catfish, a far more accessible species:

Place a large deep iron saucepan over the fire and fry one pound of bacon. Remove bacon and leave grease in bottom of saucepan. Place a layer of sliced potatoes and then a layer of sliced onion in saucepan (using ⅓ of potatoes and ⅓ of onions). Cover with boiling salted water. Let simmer for 10 minutes, then place a layer of whole fish on top. Sprinkle about 1 tablespoon curry powder on fish. Then place a second layer of potatoes, onion and fish and add boiling salted water to cover. Top with third layer of potatoes and onions. Place top on saucepan and cook very slowly all morning. It is done when the top layer of potatoes is soft.

Sauce

Melt ½ pound of butter in saucepan. Add about ½ bottle of Worcestershire sauce, ½ bottle tomato catsup, 1 tablespoon curry powder, ½ teaspoon red pepper, and ½ teaspoon black pepper. Add to this several cups of the extract from stew and mix well. Pour sauce over Pine Bark Stew and place bacon on top and serve with rice. Serves 12. —Louis Y. Dawson, Jr. (President of Otranto Club)

Boxfish

Native to both our oceans, the boxfish family is truly unique as fish go. Their "skin" is made up of bony plates that encase the body with a hard, shell-like carapace. Only the fins, eyes, and mouth move. Some say they look like a beechnut crossed with a turtle, improbably both triangular and square in shape. These fish have an additional defense mechanism: when scared, they secrete a toxic substance into the surrounding water that kills any nearby fish—and sometimes the boxfish itself.

Boxfish are bestowed with names as colorful the fish themselves, including **Moa** or **Pahu** in Hawaii, **Honeycomb** and **Scrawled Cowfishes**, various modifications of **Trunkfish**, and more regional vernacular sobriquets such as **Cuckold** and **Buffalo**. Smaller boxfish are popular in the aquarium trade. When fully grown, species range between 12 to 18 inches, making them a great fish for the table.

Despite being a culinary turn-off, the boxfish's toxin does not preclude us eating its flesh, as it is not embedded in the body as with puffer fish. In fact, they make for a particularly fine food fish, though they are not popular beyond Hawaii, where they are caught in a small directed fishery and as bycatch. Often found swimming near coral reefs or sea grass, boxfish eat crabs, urchins, and bivalves, and their flavor is aptly delicate and the meat soft with a fine flake. A lengthy muscle grain adds texture and a pleasant chewiness. The meat is relatively boneless, as the fish lack both a pelvic structure and a dorsal fin. By some accounts the liver of this fish is very delicious, but my instinct is to avoid the organs for the sake of safety.

Boxfish are best gutted and grilled whole over a charcoal fire. The plates harden when cooking, sealing the meat inside to steam in its own juices, a result not unlike cooking lobster.

Butterfish

James Beard called **butterfish** "among the most delicately meated and thoroughly pleasing fish in the sea," and I would agree. Buttery and tender, it deserves its name, which, according to dockside legend, was bestowed by fishermen from whose hands this slippery fish would regularly escape. These are small, very thin fish, averaging six to seven inches (though they may grow up to a foot in length), with a very deep body that reminds me of a CD. Smaller butterfish are best cooked as whitebait, a dish of small fish battered and fried whole. Larger ones, those five inches or more, are best used as panfish. To prepare these as a panfish, typically separate the head and twist it at the spine and then twist downward, pulling it away from the body and taking with it the viscera. At this point the fish is pan-dressed and ready to cook and needs little adornment—pan-frying the whole bone-in fish then eating it with your hands, picking the meat from the bones with your teeth, is a joy. It's like the chicken wing of the sea.

Butterfish.

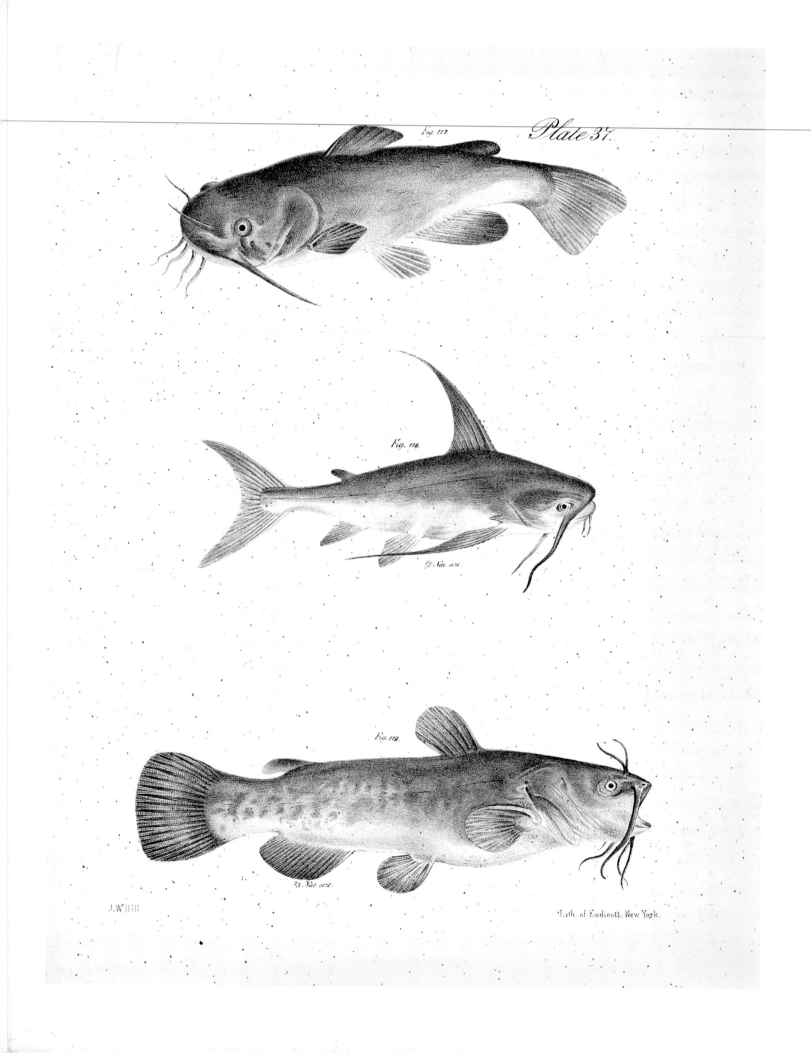

Fig. 117

Plate 37.

Fig. 118.

⅓ Nat. size

Fig. 119.

⅔ Nat. size

J. W. Hill

Lith. of Endicott, New York.

Catfish

Catfish is one of America's most familiar and favorite seafoods. Though it is not considered to have a particularly high culinary pedigree, it so often just seems to fit the bill, whether it's a fried catfish po'boy, smoked catfish chowder, or catfish tacos. It has certainly moved past its Southern soul food roots and has quietly become a mainstay in the American seafood repertoire and a bright spot in our seafood industry. There are numerous species of catfish that swim wild or are farmed in our waters, fresh, brackish, and salt. They populate just about every river system and lake east of the Rockies, which I think has something to do with our acceptance of them—they've always been so close. They are also easy to catch and are often an entry point for young anglers. Even Mark Twain muses about catching the big old lazy catfish in *Huckleberry Finn.*

There's nothing attractive about catfish. They come in an assortment of dark colorations, with long wispy chin barbels. Their scaleless bodies are somehow sneaky looking. Some catfish, particularly river-dwelling species, are active predators, feeding on crustaceans and small fish. Most catfish are omnivorous, spending their days rooting around the bottom for bits of food, be it plants, insects, or shellfish. This behavior has given them somewhat of a tarnished reputation, as "bottom-feeder" has no positive connotations, and catfish's meat often elicits complaints of a musky, muddy, or earthy aroma or flavor. Freshwater fish absorb water through their skin, and because these are resilient fish, able to live in marginal habitats where the water is stale for lack of oxygen, this process makes catfish even more susceptible to taking on off flavors. But I've always thought that if catfish can absorb off aromas, couldn't they be farmed in, say, a nice Chablis? Why can't we raise flavor-added catfish?

From a culinary standpoint, one incredible benefit to catfish is their resilience. They can stay alive for days out of water and are most often delivered to processors shortly after capture, sometimes in their live state. Whole fish have a thin layer of a viscous protective coating on their skin, and an easy way to divine the freshness of catfish is to check it—when old, this coating will appear dried out. Catfish have a very simple bone structure, making the work of filleting them quite easy. However, their skin is thick and chewy, not appropriate for eating. It is easiest to remove the skin before cooking. However,

when slowly cooked with the skin on, as braised dishes or soups, the skin breaks down and adds a rich, gelatinous texture to the dish. And once cooked it can be simply scraped off with a butter knife. But few cooks will encounter catfish in their whole form, especially because boneless, skinless fillets are readily available in almost every grocery store, and the quality is most often impeccable.

Raw fillets have a translucent quality to them; when cooked, they become pearly white and opaque. The texture, though it varies among species slightly, is often described as having a dense and meaty flake with a short, snappy texture that doesn't fall apart during cooking, making them great options for chowders, gumbos, and fried preparations. The medium-firm flesh is somewhat innocuous in flavor, and when properly farmed or prepared, they can exhibit a very delicate, charming and elegant flavor that would surprise anyone hesitant to try catfish.

Most cooks prefer fillets of smaller fish, those weighing less than three pounds, with the majority of product available coming from 1½- to 2-pound fish. These younger fish have a more tender texture to them and can be noticeably sweeter, especially when it comes to wild catfish.

The vast majority of catfish we eat in this country is farmed, much of it produced here in America. Indeed, catfish farming is the largest aquaculture industry in the United States. This great success story started in the 1960s in Arkansas and quickly spread throughout the southern states, especially in the Mississippi delta, Alabama, and Louisiana. The industry has developed and employs a number of different tactics that have led to production of a very consistent, clean-flavored fish. As the taste of catfish is a reflection of the water it is grown in, most catfish are raised in environmentally sustainable, closed-system tanks or ponds that allow farmers to control and correct water quality. As the quality of domestic catfish improved over the last few decades it also grew in popularity and gained significant market share. In 1994, the United States resumed trade agreements with Vietnam, which had a very well-developed and large-scale aquaculture industry raising several different species of fish that were very similar to the American catfish. Basa and Swai (or Tra), both species of **Pangasius**, flooded into the American market labeled as "catfish." These species are all in the catfish family; however, they did not represent the quality and characteristics that consumers had come to identify with American catfish. The lower-priced Vietnamese product cut into domestic catfish sales significantly, prompting American catfish farmers to lobby for trade protections for the unique qualities of their product. In 2002, the Farm Security and Rural Investment Act became law and included a mandate that only designated species, those commonly caught and farmed in America, could be labeled and sold as catfish. The industry has rebounded and has certainly succeeded in setting themselves apart by the quality of their product. But the imported species had already garnered a loyal customer base and, at the time of this writing, still exceed the per capita consumption of the domestically raised product. However, if you count imported and domestic species together, "catfish" is the sixth most popular seafood in America in terms of per capita consumption.

On the wild side, there are six species that represent the vast majority of fisheries. The **Brown Bullhead**, also known as **Mud Cat**, is the smallest of the fisheries by volume. These rather sluggish freshwater fish are very common in the Midwest, where they are appreciated for their pink- to reddish-tinged flesh that is moderately rich, with a meaty texture and sweet flavor that is particularly well suited to smoking or pan-frying.

The **Flathead Catfish** inhabit the river systems from the Great Lakes through Texas, where they are popular sport fish. They are predatory, preferring live bait. Their flesh is quite firm and smoother than most catfish and has been compared to lobster when simply cooked and dipped in melted butter. (I'm not sure the folks championing that position have ever tasted Maine lobster.) These can grow to be quite large, and though smaller fish are preferred for their culinary qualities, larger fish have cheek meat that is a popular delicacy, considered the finest tasting and textured part of the fish. As both the Brown Bullhead and Flathead catfish can be somewhat muddy in flavor, there is an old tradition in the Midwest of boys bringing home their catch and letting it swim in the bathtub for a few days to purge the fish and clean their flavor. I can't imagine Mom and Dad cared too much for this.

In the southern states, there are significant fisheries for **Channel Catfish** and **Blue Catfish**, both of which are found in swift-moving rivers. The constant exercise results in a more muscular and flavorful meat. Channel "cats" are described as being mild flavored with a firm flesh that can range from somewhat yellow to pink. The meat of the channel cats is noted for retaining moisture when cooked, giving the lean fish a richer mouthfeel. The Blue cats appear very similar to channel cats and are quite similar in culinary qualities as well. They do, however, have a more distinctive flavor, as they store more fat than other catfish, which imparts a fuller taste and more luscious texture. Both the Blue and the Channel Catfish are the species that are farmed in the United States, though the channel cat is utilized to a much greater extent. Given these qualities, blue cats are the most versatile when it comes to cooking. In recent decades, the blue cat has been found in areas outside of its traditional territory, where it is causing havoc for native catfish and other species. The Chesapeake Bay is one of the areas blue cats have invaded, and it is there that they are doing the most damage, but opportunistic fishermen and chefs in the region have taken to fighting the invaders by putting them on the menu.

In brackish waters and the open ocean along the East Coast and throughout the Gulf, there are a number of **Sea Catfish** that find their way onto our tables. The **Gafftopsail Catfish** is by far the most popular and commercially sought species. These are sleeker and more elegant in shape than other catfish, and their name is derived from an attractive sail-like dorsal fin. But don't let its beauty charm you too much, as it has venomous spines that can give a rather stinging wound to a wayward hand, though there's no lasting damage nor is the fish's flesh affected in any way. These are mostly caught in the Gulf, in river deltas and estuaries, where they are targeted and are also a bycatch of white shrimp trawls. These three- to five-pound fish have all the sweetness and typical catfish flavor, with an added briny tang boosting its personality. Their size makes them perfect for broiled or grilled preparations, and they are particularly great when smoked.

With Americans urged to incorporate more seafood into their diets, catfish, both farmed and wild caught, provides a perfect gateway fish that will gently welcome newly minted fish eaters while also pleasing those with a more curious palate. American catfish also has a great story. It's been a part of our fishing and culinary folklore in nearly every region, both north of the Mason-Dixon—where in early Philadelphia, catfish and waffles was a particularly popular dish—and south of the line, where catfish has always been part of the great tradition of Southern cooking.

Clams

Often mentioned in culinary texts and the earliest accounts of America's shores, both the history of the clam and its culture are well documented, but I think Howard Mitcham said it best when he wrote, "Clams are for happy people." There are few things I find more pleasant than looking out my bedroom window through the early morning mist and seeing the tidal flats pockmarked with small mounds, evidence of the exploratory pitchfork prospecting of clammers. These scars represent the clammers' path, a visual record of their trial and error, but it's only a matter of time before this presence is obscured and healed as tidal waters, right on schedule, flush back into the coves and inlets. Equal to a factory's whistle, the shifting salt breeze signals the day's work done, and in unison, the clammers turn and make their muddy slog toward shore. This tell-tale scene of New England shore life compelled one of the greatest American mythologists, Walt Whitman, to write in *Song of Myself*: "The boatman and clam-diggers arose early and stopt for me, / I tuck'd my trouser-ends in my boots and went and had a good time; / You should have been with us that day round the chowder-kettle."

Dozens of clam species are harvested along our coasts, and they have long been popular in our regional cuisines, particularly on the East Coast, where they are featured in a majority of historical culinary texts. These cuisines are based primarily on the **Hard Clam**, or the **Quahaug/Quahog**, corrupted from the Indian name *Poquahok*. This tradition dates back long before the presence of white settlers, as evidenced by acres-wide middens covering large swaths of what is now known as Cape Cod, the largest near Pilgrim Spring. (Shouldn't it be called Native Spring?) The genus name of the quahog was once the *Venus mercenaria*, meaning "loving, money conscious," though it's now classified simply as *Mercenaria mercenaria*, the redundancy of "money conscious" referencing the lustrous purple part of the clam's inner shell that was made into *Suckanhoc*, or black money. This currency was worth twice the value of *wampum* or white money, made from white shells or conch, and was long used in trade along the East Coast and stretching far into the Plains, having been found in circulation among the Sioux and Chippewa tribes. The **Butter Clam** of the West Coast, a staple in the diet of Indians native to the Puget Sound area, is also known by the common name **Money Shell** for its numismatic use in trade.

America's love affair with clams is among our most democratic, being popular among all classes, and varied culinary relationships. American restaurant critic and cookbook author Craig Claiborne described the clambake, one of the few American Indian food rituals assimilated into modern American culture, as "the most colorful, joyous and festive of American feasts." In her *Mrs. Lincoln's Boston Cookbook* from 1884, Mary Bailey describes a genuine clambake as including Bluefish, lobsters, crab, potatoes, and corn steamed over clams, thus imbuing them with all those delicious flavors. Any which way a clambake is undertaken, the secret is that the food is arranged with the longest-cooking items on the bottom and the shortest on top, with layers of seaweed between each.

There are different schools of thought about when clams are at their best, but now that a significant amount are farmed, they have become consistent in quality year-round. In some older New England culinary texts, clams are celebrated as the oyster lover's salve in summer months—those without the letter *r*—when oysters were once rightly considered unfit to eat. To further this still-honored idea of seasonality, Florence Fabricant of the *New York Times* writes that "oysters call for black tie, but with clams, jeans or shorts are fine." In short, clams epitomize casual, summer fare.

Clams are sold most often alive in their shells, though they are also found shucked in canned form, breaded and frozen, smoked, and pickled, and their liquor is bottled in many forms, straight from the shell as clam "juice," slightly diluted as "broth," and slightly reduced as "nectar."

Some species of clam have long been considered bait, rather than fine table fare, but nearly all are worthy of our culinary intentions. Perhaps the most useful tool for distinguishing them into categories is whether they are good raw on the half shell or if they are best cooked.

The Quahog and Butter Clam are considered the apogee for serving on the half shell, especially when smaller in size. When eaten raw, these have a viscous liquor that carries with it, as author A.J. McClane wrote, a "salt fragrant glory" and cucumber scent. Their texture is somewhat crunchy, and their distinctly mild flavor is consistent from beginning to end.

Little Neck is a market term in the New York region that refers to all Quahogs, as Little Neck Bay on Long Island was once the center of the Quahog industry. This can be confusing, as "little neck" is also one of the size designations under which Quahogs are sold. Further, there is a Pacific clam known as the **Littleneck** (one word) that is a different species entirely. Little neck as a size designation means 6 to 10 per pound. The next size up is the **Cherrystone** at four to six per pound. These are named after the Cherrystone Creek area of Virginia, another historically important industry home. **Topneck** or **Countneck** are the next size up, at four per pound, and **Chowders** the largest, with three or less per pound.

These clams are sometimes referred to as **Northern Quahogs**, as their range extends north from North Carolina, and are related to the **Southern Quahog**, a separate species occurring from Virginia through the Gulf of Mexico. These differ from their northern relation in that their shell is thicker, they are more strongly flavored, and the texture of the meat makes raw and quick-cook methods such as steaming unviable, as the meat is very chewy. They are fabulous in braises, ground in fritters, or long-cooked into chowders.

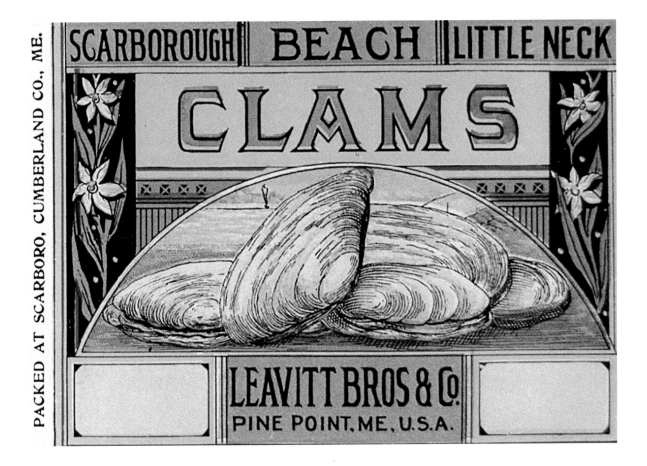

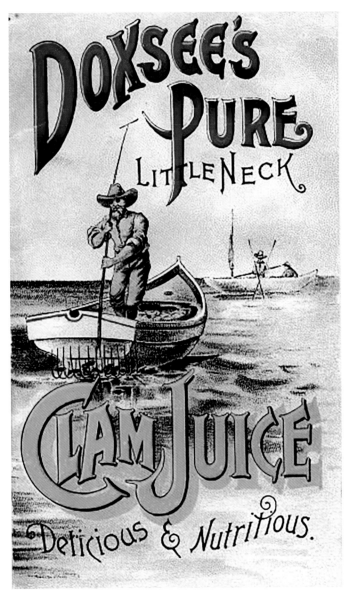

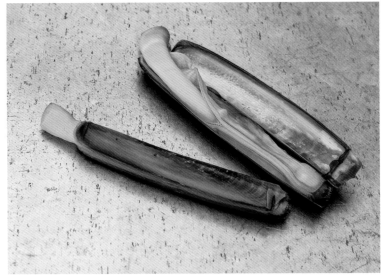

OPPOSITE Shucking Soft-Shell Clams.

CLOCKWISE FROM TOP LEFT Old advertisement; Razor Clams; mud-dug steamers; Manila Clams.

The **Ocean Quahog**, a deepwater northern catch, is often sold as **Mahogany Clam**, though it is more commonly known as the **Black Clam**. These very long-lived species attain ages nearly triple the life expectancy of a human. The oldest known specimen, found off the coast of Iceland, was born around the time of the Ming Dynasty in China; it died at the age of 507. Often these clams are fairly large, and they are best steamed open and bathed in butter. They have a thin mantle and a small stomach. Their supersalty brine is all in the liquor, as the meat is surprisingly crunchy and sweet, with aromas of honeydew and seaweed. They can have quite a heavy iodine flavor, which can be somewhat mitigated by removing the dark stomach and liver.

The **Atlantic Surf Clam** is the largest in volume and size of all the Eastern wild capture fisheries, growing to be more than eight inches long. They are also known as **Bar Clams** or **Skimmer Clams**. The meat of these clams can be very sandy. They are mostly ground or chopped for pasta sauces, fritters, and chowders and are sliced and used to make breaded clam strips. The clam's red tinged foot is commonly used in sushi, as it is very crunchy with a slight radish flavor. The adductor muscles, the two white discs that keep the shells closed, are very tender and delicious when picked out and served raw. According to McClane, they also can be cooked like scallops. This clam is also the source of bottled clam liquor products. Its fishery is focused in the mid-Atlantic, where clams are caught far offshore with dredges.

The **Soft-Shell Clam**, also known as **Steamer** or **Piss Clam**, is *the* clam north of Cape Cod, as it is an iconic part of the cuisine from the North Shore through Maine, though its range extends as far south as North Carolina. These clams are also found in the Pacific Northwest, as they were transplanted there in hopes of building a new fishery for them. They are more oval in shape and very thin with a fragile shell that doesn't fully close. They have a black siphon, which extends from the shell, through which they feed. These are caught in the tidal and nearshore zones in sandy and mud bottoms, and a distinction is made between these two origins at market. It is said that sand clams tend to be sweeter, though more difficult to clean than their mud counterparts.

The Soft-Shell Clam has quite a history, being enjoyed by Native Americans through our modern day. They were considered a

Steamer Clam in Cape Cod.

regional specialty until a gentleman named Howard Johnson introduced "sweet as a nut" fried clams on the menu of his eponymous restaurants. Coinciding with the dawn of America's interstate highways, Howard Johnson's restaurants proliferated across the country, bringing the breaded and fried soft clam to national attention and admiration. Subsequently, the soft clam was replaced by a cheaper alternative—frozen surf clam strips, a lesser-quality product that, at least in my mother's opinion, marked the end times of this once mighty chain. Proper shucking and removal of the thin membrane around the siphon is a careful task, to put it best. When shucked correctly and lightly breaded or battered and deep-fried, the clams are one of the very best reasons to visit New England.

Their regional name, Steamers, comes from another common preparation in which they are steamed simply with a bit of water and sometimes a chunk of celery, and then served piping hot with lemon, drawn butter, and a cup of steaming clam broth. They are also sometimes, but rarely, used for chowder preparations.

In New England, these clams have been devastated periodically by the invasive Asian Green Crab, which by some accounts first appeared in the Gulf of Maine around 1830. These voracious predators burrow into mudbanks in search of the Soft-Shell Clams that they easily devour, not only diminishing clam populations but causing the habitat to erode. Around 1950, a Chesapeake waterman named Fletcher Hanks heard of the decline in New England stocks due to the Green Crab and innovated a way to harvest the Chesapeake's abundant soft clam population. In 1951 he patented the Hydro-escalator, a system of high pressure jets and pumps that pushed soft clams from the submerged mud and onto an escalator which carried them to the surface. According to William Warner, in 1952, 95 percent of the U.S. Soft-Shell Clam production was taken in New England. By 1960, 70 percent of the production came from the Chesapeake Bay.

A very different form of clam, of which multiple species are found along all coasts, is commonly referred to as the **Razor Clam**. Though Razor Clams range in size and shape according to geography and are of different genera, they all share common culinary characteristics. They can be somewhat difficult to catch, as they can burrow into the sand several feet down almost as quickly as anyone can dig. Their thin, long, narrow shells are shaped like old straight razors; hence their name. They all share beige-colored meats that are quite full in the shell. They are too chewy to be eaten raw, though are excellent when steamed and served with butter, griddled and covered with a garlic, herb, and olive oil marinade, used in fritters, or fried, as they most often are on the West Coast. Razor Clams are a very popular bait used by recreational fishermen, and a significant portion of the catch is directed to the anglers.

The **Blood Clam**, a member of the **Arc Clam** family, is common to waters all over the world and is a particularly unique species. All clams have blood, though it is almost always clear, and when the animal is shucked, the blood mixes with brine as to become indistinguishable. The Blood Clam, however, carries hemoglobin in its system, thus giving its blood the same iron-rich red tone as our own. Once you get past this rather alarming presentation, they are in fact quite delicate in flavor, with a mildly salty brine and crisp texture. They can be served raw on the half shell, or steamed, roasted, or grilled. When prepared for sushi, quite a bit of trimming is done to remove the stomach and all discolored material covering the body. Once trimmed, it has a beautiful sculptured appearance, and its crisp texture and distinctive nutty flavor, almost like that of brown rice, are elevated.

In the southern Atlantic and Gulf of Mexico, a very tiny specimen known as the **Coquina**, or **Bean Clam**, can be found in great quantities. No bigger than a periwinkle, these are quite limited in their culinary uses, though it is said that of all clams they make the best and sweetest broth. They can also be eaten just like periwinkles—steamed open and their meats removed with a toothpick and dipped in butter.

The **Sunray Venus Clam** is a species most abundantly found in Florida. These have a porcelain-like shell that's smooth and slightly pink to multi-colored. Their creamy or light-colored meats are quite plump and taste of sweet brine and seaweed. They can grow up to six inches. They were first commercially harvested in Florida, particularly in the 1960s and 1970s, though in recent decades they have been introduced as a farmed species. This uniquely Southern product is worth seeking out.

The West Coast is prolific with its own coterie of unique species. The succulent Butter Clam is very versatile. It has a finely textured, smooth shell. When small, they are delightful eaten raw, though when they grow larger they become tougher and are best for cooked preparations. These have historically been important as a canned product, though they are enjoying increased popularity in their fresh state. To my opinion, these are the best of the Pacific clams for smoking.

Two species that are relatively the same when it comes to culinary use are the **Horse Clam**, also known as the **Gaper Clam**, and the **Geoduck**. They are the two largest clam species caught in American waters, Geoduck (pronounced gooey-duck) being the larger with its shell growing over 10 inches and its weight achieving upwards of five pounds. These are

Digging for Steamers in Cape Cod.

both defined by their very large siphon, which in the Geoduck can extend more than three feet beyond the shell. According to cookbook authror Helen Evans Brown, these preposterous animals were described as such: "Their necks, thus relaxed, are such a grotesque sight that ladies of an earlier day stayed at a discreet distance when their men went hunting them." Both of these clams are delicious, with a taste similarly sweet to abalone, and very versatile, as they have multiple types of meat within, each having particular textures and uses. To clean these clams, they can be briefly plunged into boiling water, not more than a minute, until the shell opens. The skin of the siphon must be removed by gently peeling it from the meat. The stomach and skin are both discarded. The body can be ground and used in fritters. The siphon can be sliced thinly on a bias and used for sushi or thicker slices can be pounded and sautéed as a stand-in for abalone. I think that these species are particularly well suited to smoking. I brine the siphons either whole or butterflied before gently hot-smoking them over alder wood.

The tiny and radially grooved shell of the **Manila Clam** holds within it one of my favorite of all shellfish. Their meat is very sweet, firm, and plump. It fills much of the shell, leaving little room for liquor. Best eaten when they are about one inch in size, these are equally great on the half shell dripped with lime juice as they are served in pastas or stews. They came to the Pacific Northwest via oyster shells transplanted there and have taken up permanent residence. These days almost all Manila Clams sold are farm raised.

Though similar in shape, the **Pacific Littleneck** is not related to the eastern little neck Quahog. It is found throughout California and Alaska. I don't find them suitable for raw preparation and like them best steamed and served with butter or simmered into a cioppino or other fish stew.

Several species of **Cockle** are caught and used on the Pacific coast, ranging all the way north through Alaska. Tender in texture, these quarter-size clams are perfect for incorporating into pastas and stews or steamed and served with their broth and butter.

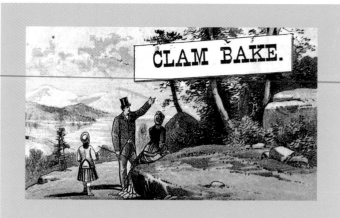

The Clambake

A traditional low-tide event held along the shores of New England and replicated in many ways and forms, the clambake became quite the pastime for large groups to gather, either in friendship or as part of a political event or fundraiser. It involved a large party digging clams and gathering mussels from the rocks, as well as Bluefish, lobsters, potatoes, and corn. A shallow hole would be dug in the sand and lined with rocks, over which a large fire of driftwood would be lit. When the fire had burned down to embers, the rocks, now white hot, were covered with seaweed and then the copious amounts of gathered foods were layered in, according to their cooking time. More seaweed was thrown over to cover the food, and the hole was then covered with fabric to capture the heat. The hissing steam and aroma of the seaweed and the juices from the clams and lobsters would perfume the other foods. Once all layers of clams were cooked, the entire meal would be revealed and guests helped themselves to whatever their pleasure. Accompanied by only drawn butter, sometimes vinegar, this was a somewhat raucous departure from the gentile norms of polite society, as the food was eaten by hand while feet were barefoot in the surf.

Chowder Red and White

When it comes to chowder, there are few culinary arguments more ferocious than that surrounding Manhattan or New England. This feud between red and white, tomatoes or milk, is as bitter as that between the Capulets and Montegues. Chowder is so integral to New England cuisine that in *Moby Dick* Herman Melville describes his protagonist's first encounter with the dish at the Tri Potts Inn on Nantucket as "Oh! sweet friends, harken to me. It was made of small juicy clams, scarcely bigger than hazel nuts, mixed with pounded ship biscuits, and salted pork cut up into little flakes; the whole enriched with butter." Indeed, this is a dish that has entered our cultural canon. But the red-style Manhattan and Rhode Island versions are equally great, just of a different origin.

Manhattan Clam Chowder

According to the Long Island Seafood Cookbook, *Bob Matthews, a long-time resident of Long Island, is quoted as the source of the original "Manhattan" clam chowder. This recipe is adapted from that book by J. George Frederick.*

½ pound salt pork, diced

48 hardshell clams, chopped

2 cups celery, chopped

2 onions, chopped

5 large fresh tomatoes, coarsely chopped

Salt and freshly ground black pepper

Start out 12 or 24 hours before eating to make this chowder. Heat the kettle (preferably an iron one) in which the chowder is to be cooked, then put in the salt pork, and fry out. Then put in the clams, chopped, and all the clam liquor. Add to this the celery, onions, tomatoes, and seasoning. Put on a very slow fire, never let come to a boil, and let simmer all day long (or at least six or seven hours), stirring occasionally. Then take the pot off the fire, and let cool in the open air. Then reheat (but never boil) when ready to serve.

New England Clam Chowder

Who better to turn to than the master of New England seafood, chef Jasper White, who describes chowder as "a one pot dish, more stew than soup. It should be thick but not thickened, except by the starch released from the potatoes during the cooking." This recipe is adapted from Jasper White's Cooking from New England.

5 pounds quahogs in the shell

¼ pound smoked bacon or salt pork,
cut in small ¼-inch dice

1 medium onion, diced

1 bay leaf

1 sprig fresh thyme

1 tablespoon butter

½ pound new potatoes, cut into ½-inch pieces

1 cup heavy cream

Freshly ground pepper

Scrub the clams and place in a large pan with 1 cup water. Cover and cook over high heat until the clams are steamed completely open. Pour off the liquid and reserve. Remove the clams from their shells and cut into ½-inch pieces. Strain the clam broth through a fine mesh strainer.

Slowly render the bacon in a soup pot until crisp. Add the onions, bay leaf, thyme, and butter. When the onions are translucent, add the potatoes and reserved clam broth, and simmer until the potatoes are cooked. Add the clams and cream, and simmer 5 minutes more. Season with pepper, and ladle into soup plates. Serve with common crackers.

LEFT Crab boat heads out at dawn. Chesapeake Bay, 1981. RIGHT Chesapeake Bay oyster skipjack, c. 1985.

Cobia

The first time I had the opportunity to cook **Cobia** I had no idea what to do with it, which is funny because of all fish it ranks as one of the most versatile. You can cook this fish by almost any method including not cooking it all and preparing it as sushi.

The **Cobia** is known by very many different names, which is a bit surprising given that it has never been widely important as a food fish. Historically, it was very well regarded in Maryland and Virginia and supported a large fishery for local consumption. In the Chesapeake region it was known as the **Crab-eater**, though **Sergeant Fish**, **Coal Fish**, and **Bonito** (confusingly the name of an unrelated tuna species) were all used interchangeably. In the Gulf of Mexico it has long been an important recreational species, and the name Crab-eater is also applied here, though it is most often referred to as **Lemon Fish**. Additionally it's known as **Ling** (though it bears no relation to the true ling) and **Blob** (for reasons I cannot imagine), and in older texts the closely spelled **Cabio** is used. Adding to its list of names are **Black Kingfish**, **Black Salmon**, **Black Bonito**, and my favorite, **Prodigal Son** (really?). I think that this abundance of names is proof of how versatile this fish is as it can be whatever you want it to be in the kitchen.

Cobia are pelagic fish and swim near to shore. They are caught using rod and reel, though the commercial fishery is very limited. It has a growing fan base, as it has become an important species in aquaculture for which it is particularly well suited, given its rapid growth rate, value, and fitness for thriving in farming conditions. I find that the farmed product is superior to the wild in terms of consistency of quality, and the flavor is more cosmopolitan than the sometimes unrefined and brassy flavor of the wild product.

These fish do not share relation with any other fish. Their shape is similar to that of a small shark, with which it is sometimes confused, muscular and long with a sharp nose. Its dense round body with long tapered snout and forked tail makes it an attractive fish. The dark green coloration on its back grows lighter on its sides, and stripes extend from head to tail making it look as though it were harnessed for a race. It is these stripes that may have earned it the name Sergeant Fish, as the stripes appear like military epaulets.

Its raw flesh is pinkish-white with a hint of tan and resembles well-marbled pork. It is firm with moderate to high fat content, and it retains its moisture during cooking. Though it can easily be overcooked, its richness of flesh is similar to that of a salmon and as such provides some resiliency to error. Cobia feeds on crustaceans and squid, their favorite food being crabs (hence the name Crab-eater, though also for its meaty crab-like flavor). Its texture is firm but flaky, with just a hint of squeak that is well suited to frying, broiling, steaming, and especially to grilling, when its texture evolves into a wonderful chewy bite equal to Swordfish. When raw, it is juicy and flavorful in sushi and sashimi, and it makes for a wonderful ceviche fish. A word of caution: wild Cobia are subject to parasites, so be sure that the fillets were deep-frozen prior to serving raw.

The musculature is very consistent, enabling it to be portioned in specialized cuts for different preparations, for example loin cuts for grilling and broiling, belly fillets for steaming and sautéing, and thin bias-cut "sheets" perfect for a quick pan-fry. These fish maintain a consistent texture at any size. Farmed cobia are often 10 pounds or under, while most wild fish landed weigh between 12 and 50 pounds, with an average being 25 pounds. The collar of these fish, a succulent portion of meat attached to the bone just behind the gill plate, makes fabulous and fun eating. Those coming from larger fish are substantial enough to be entrée sized, whereas smaller fish yield appetizer-sized "lollipops."

Of all of the uses for which Cobia is outstanding, making stock from its bones does not make the list. The resulting broth, though sweet and aromatic, also has a muddy brackish quality to it that is not at all desirable. Like many fatty fish, Cobia is a perfect candidate for smoking. In this regard it is somewhat unique, as it is equally show-stopping cold- or hot-smoked. When hot-smoked for 24 hours over spicy and stoic woods like hickory and oak, its tender but dense flake suggests smoked sturgeon. When dry-cured and cold-smoked, it yields silken texture equal to the finest quality smoked salmon and deserves equal praise.

With such qualities and charisma, Cobia is quickly emerging as a regular offering at the seafood counter and is a very welcome addition to our culinary repertoire.

OPPOSITE Poster urging consumption of more fish to help the war effort, from the Office of War Information, 1941.

Unloading and processing a catch at South Boston fish pier, c. 1930.

Cod

"Cod may not yet be regarded as an epicure's delight, but as the fish of human martyrdom, of tragedy of lost lives, it does have a splendid novel to itself," wrote Jane Grigson. That splendid novel tells a story no less than the discovery and founding of this nation. As Mark Kurlansky aptly argues in his delightful book *Cod*, it is indeed the fish that changed the world.

Long before Columbus set to sea, the fishing fleets of Spain, France, and Portugal were voyaging the Atlantic to fish upon the virgin stocks of cod found in such plenitude. Early accounts from a host of explorers documented a wealth of fish so great as over time it would come to be equal to the value of all the gold mined from South America. And as Europe had depleted her stocks of cod, the underwater riches to be had along American coasts provided food that for centuries fueled empires and ultimately became an international currency that provided the first stepping stone for the American colonies to gain freedom.

When the early explorer Gosnold, in his quest for a new source of spices, rounded the great hook of land called Cape St. James in 1602, the richness of its waters inspired him to rechristen the land Cape Cod. It was not the sterile and bare rocky coast that drew the first settlers to the new world. It was the **Cod**, known as *Panganaut Tamwock* in the Narragansett language, meaning "that which comes a little before Spring." And so it was upon the backs of cod that New England and this country was built, leading John Adams to declare, "[Cod was] to us as wool was to England, or tobacco to Virginia—the great staple that became the basis of power and wealth." And in honor of the economic cornerstone of the "new world" a gilded effigy of the Sacred Cod hangs above the State House in Massachusetts.

The cod industry as an American institution was first ventured in Gloucester, at the time of the town's settlement in 1623. Early efforts failed to gain traction, and the fishery was largely stalled until it was revived and found enormous success in 1628. By 1640, Gloucester was producing more than 300,000 dried codfish for the market per year, and the stage was set for it to become the most important fishing port

in the world for the next several centuries. The opportunity was siezed for economic freedom by entrepreneurial colonists, who soon took their first minor step toward independence from the British rule. The cod fishery was so productive that the British were forced to allow colonial merchants to bypass British merchants and trade directly with the Mediterranean and Carribean markets. This began the slow creep toward freedom from the Crown as wealth and power began to accumulate in American families, but at the same time it bound the foundling economy of this nation to the vicious slave trade. The triangular trade routes carried high-quality salt cod from New England to Spain and Portugal. The ships then loaded slaves in Africa and headed for the Carribean, where the ship's stores were filled with sugar cane to be shipped to New England and distilled into America's favorite spirit, rum. This commerce was not in keeping with the puritanical mores of the Pilgrim settlers and was representative of the rift in values that to this day haunts the American character.

The families that early capitalized on the abundance of natural resources and trade opportunities were derisively termed the "Codfish Aristocracy," a contemptuous commentary on the new elite that amassed great wealth in this country. The pioneer spirit that prevailed in this new country meant that a man's wealth could be the direct result of how hard he was willing to work. This was (and is) the promise that called so many to our shores. But quickly the same exclusionary economic systems of Europe came to govern the American social order, as was illustrated in a celebration in the early 1900s, roasting two of the most important of New England's dynasties: "Here's to dear old Boston, the home of the bean and the cod, where Lowells speak only to Cabots, and Cabots speak only to God."

The New England groundfish fishery is a complex of 35 different species of which cod was by far the dominant population. Included in this intermingled web of species are the Acadian Redfish, skate, dogfish, various relatives of cod, flatfish, and others. But in the early days of the fishery it was the cod, and only the cod, that was of any value. As the fishery evolved with a growing number of fishermen and advancing technology, cod stocks were found in many different areas, each with a different term to denote its origin. **Rock Cod,** aka **Native Cod**, were those fish caught in nearshore waters among red coral reefs and ledges. These fish had a tendency toward dark coloration, with a reddish tinge due to pigments in the prey they sought. According to *The Fannie Farmer Cookbook*, these tended to be wormy and were considered lesser to cod taken from other waters. Another class of cod was the **Shore Cod**, or **Inshore Cod**, which lacked the red hue, as they were not found near the reefs. **Deepwater Cod**, or **Bank Cod**, coming from the offshore waters of the Grand Banks and George's Bank, were considered the finest. Other fish were labeled by regional names that identified them by the environment or by the predominant seasonal prey they sought. In southeastern Maine they were known as the **Herring Cod** and the charming name **Pine Tree Cod**. Off Nantucket were found the **Squid School of Cod**, so named reflecting their preferred prey. Swimming along the vast stretches of sandy bottom off New Jersey were the **Pasture Cod**. These names were not representative of different species so much as they were a result of the keen observations and deeply rooted local knowledge of fishermen. However, centuries later it has been acknowledged that there are indeed different stocks, or tribes to describe it another way, that are found in different areas along the coast. Though fish from these different stocks may intermingle during feeding season, they segregate into different populations when it comes time to spawn. This is responsible for some of the noted differences in the qualities of cod, but it has also contributed to the difficulties in managing the sustainability of catch for these different stocks.

Another attribute that led to the American fisheries' dominance of world cod markets was that in Europe cod were caught only in the summer months, while in New England the fishery was productive year-round, thus creating a lucrative opportunity to supply markets during off-season in Europe.

In the early years of the cod fishery, the trade was plied from skiffs or shallops, stout and heavy single-mast boats designed for inshore use. The fish were hand-lined, and the vessels were not capable of carrying huge volumes or traveling far out to sea. As cod fishing pitted man against the angry and tempestuous North Atlantic, the industry has always been dangerous, and the feats of these brave men have been immortalized in poetry and literature such as Rudyard Kipling's *Captains Courageous*. The danger increased as fishing pressure grew and nearshore populations were depleted. Fishermen were drawn farther from shore and safe harbor, and the boats to carry them evolved with the prevailing economic pressures. Soon, great schooners, marvels of beauty and design, were carrying fishermen to the Grand Banks off the continental shelf, where they would cast out from the main ship in dories to fish. This marked a great improvement in the efficiency of catch, as hundreds of baited hooks were attached to a single line, called "trawl lines," to be set then hauled in by two-man teams. Following the trawl lines came the introduction of purse seining, and then gillnetting. These all required the fishers to separate from the main boat in small rowboats, dramatically increasing the dangers of the trade. The principal fishing grounds were subject to incredibly dynamic and unpredictable conditions as the warm Gulf Stream current mixed with cold waters brought by the Labrador Return Current and forced upward from the depths by the suddenly shallow banks. It was precisely this collision of opposites that made the Banks verdant grounds. But these natural forces also brought with them clashing personalities that could rapidly bed the area under dense fog, causing the satellite fishers to lose orientation toward the mothership, many forever lost to the open ocean. Storms could rise up with terrifying speed, catching all off guard. Furthermore, the schooners, already designed more for maximizing economic return than for stability in the swirling currents on the Banks, were more and more tailored for speed. With the advent of artificial ice production and a general market shift from salt cod to fresh product, this demand for expediency led to shorter trips at sea, as the catch needed to be delivered as fresh as could be. But speed was gained at the sacrifice of stability, leaving in its wake many tragedies, widows, and orphans. It is said that "the history of the Gloucester fishery has been written in tears." As author Jeffery Bolster recounts: "It was as if fishing ports' populations were constantly at war at Sea, with news of casualties trickling in year-round." Between 1866 and 1890, the community of Gloucester had a population of 15,000 to 16,000 and grieved for more than 380 vessels and 2,450 men who were lost to the deep. Captains Courageous indeed.

FOG

Over the oily swell it heaved, it rolled,
Like some foul creature, filmy, nebulous.
It pushed out streaming tentacles, took clammy hold,
Swaddled the spars, wrapped us in damp and cold,
Blotted the sun, crept round and over us.

Day long, night long, it hid us from the sky
Hid us from the sun and stars as in a tomb.
Shrouded in mist a berg went groaning by.
Far and forlorn we heard the blind ships cry,
Like lost souls wailing in a hopeless gloom.

Like a bell-wether clanging from the fold,
A codder called her dories. With scared breath
The steamer syrens shrieked; and mad bells tolled.
Through time eternal in the dark we rolled
Playing a game of Blind-Man's Bluff with Death.

—CROSBIE GARSTIN, from *The Vagabond Verses*

It was the introduction of the otter trawl in 1905 that marked the single greatest revolution in the fishery. Large nets, spread open by metal doors, were dragged along the bottom by powerful boats. Fishing could now be executed more efficiently with less risk to the fishermen. This advancement certainly saved many lives, but it also forever changed the nature of fishing. As Jeffrey Bolster summarizes, for all of history fishermen had waited for the fish to come to them. They knew which bait to use and where to find the fish. But it was still fishing. With the introduction of the otter trawl the dynamic of the relationship between fish and fishermen was flipped from fishing to catching. Fishermen were now able to chase the fish by dragging a net through the fish's habitat and indiscriminently taking everything in its swath, including the physical character of habitat such as reefs.

Soon after the introduction of the otter trawl came the advent of engine-powered vessels. Freed from the limitations of sail power and the vagaries of weather and wind, catches rose dramatically. In 1904, 1.4 million pounds of cod were landed. By 1908 much of the fleet had converted to gas power otter trawls and catches topped seven million pounds.

Militarization during World War II subsequently armed the fishing fleet with technologies such as radar, sonar, and polyester fiber, which made fishing nets more durable. In 1954 the world's first factory freezer ship, named the *Fairtry*, capable of catching, processing, and freezing huge volumes of fish, arrived on the Grand Banks. Two more vessels followed shortly thereafter, the *Fairtry II* and *Fairtry III*.

Cod stocks had been in decline for centuries, which led to the watershed moment when these freezer factory trawlers precipitated their eventual collapse. In the decades prior to 1955, total landings ranged around 250,000 metric tons. With the ascension of these floating factories, landings jumped to 600,000 metric tons in 1960 and 800,000 metric tons in 1968. With few outlying years, catches have been in decline ever since.

It is within our photographic history that cod weighing 175 pounds or more and measuring over six feet in length were not uncommon. In present-day fisheries, a 20-pound fish is an outlier. What is most odd to me about this tale of decline is that we never celebrated the cod from a culinary perspective. Described by Kurlansky as "the default setting from which all other fish species vary," cod was considered, like herring, to be too cheap to be fashionable. When it was so common we found reason to discriminate against it, loath to eat this commoner's food. The demand for salt cod has its roots in the church calendar, which had over 150 fast days when consumption of meat was forbidden. As a result, salt cod was considered a common food and became associated with sacrifice and penance. The French chef Escoffier in his legendary and influential tome on French cuisine lists among the thousands of recipes only 10 recipes for cod. Compare that to the hundreds of recipes included for sole (oddly enough, sole was not well esteemed in America). The codfish is often conspicuously absent in classic American culinary texts and rarely discussed in relation to other fish. Some of this is due to the nature of culinary texts as documents that celebrate foods outside of the everyday repertoire. Now that it has become a rarity, we are rekindling our love for its gentle-textured and succulent convex flake. The moral of this story? William Bell sums it up well in his classic soul ballad: "You don't miss your water till your well runs dry."

FOLLOWING PAGES Fish sellers on the waterfront, 1939–1940.

The history of cod in cuisine is that of salt cod. Its preeminence as a global commodity was made possible by the trait that it cured well, thus providing a durable food for long voyages at sea and a safe and affordable protein source before the advent of refrigeration. At times called "turkey of the sea," or "Cape Cod turkey," cod and many of its relatives display an impressive culinary versatility. Nearly the entirety of the fish—97 percent—was used in some form. The body of the fish was split, salted, and left to cure in the open air on racks called flakes. There were a number of different styles of cure that depended on the type of salt used and the length of the cure and air-drying, all of which determined the character of the final product. (For more on the specific cures, see page 59.) Regardless of the cure, preparing salt cod first required soaking it in a succession of freshwater baths. Once desalinated and moistened to near original texture, the fillets would then be used in chowders, shredded and used in cakes (known as cod balls), or topped with butter and broiled. Other variations I've come across in classic culinary texts call for the soaked fillets to be slowly poached in a kettle of water mixed with molasses hung over the fireplace. The smoky-sweet-salty combo is very intriguing. Refreshed salt cod can be sliced very thin and layered on a platter to be served in a carpaccio style, drizzled with olive oil and a sprinkling of mace and fresh chopped mint.

Cod tongues, the gelatinous flesh from the underside of the head between the jawbones, were historically removed from each fish, a reasonable effort when the fish were quite large. The tongues were then salted and later prepared in the same manner as the fillets. There was also a practical aspect to this, as it provided a way for individual fishermen to keep count of how many fish they had caught and what they had earned. I particularly like this cut, though I always use them fresh. The meat is rich with a silky gelatin that, when sautéed in olive oil with chopped garlic and a splash of white wine or sherry, makes for a palate-coating sauce that perfectly flatters the meltingly tender meat. Served over toasted bread, this easy preparation is worth every bit of trouble you might endure in trying to find cod tongues. The cheeks, or jowls, of the fish are an equal delicacy, and I often mix them in with the tongues.

The Portuguese, the world's most enthusiastic cod lovers, are said to have a different cod dish for every day of the year. As generations of Portuguese immigrants have made their home in many of the fishing communities of Massachusetts, especially along the South Shore area, their richly passionate yet humble cuisine has permeated New England cooking. The bold flavors and bright acidity so often punctuating these dishes are inspiration for some of the very best seafood cooking anywhere.

Fresh cod jawbones make for a delicious rustic chowder, the bones adding body while also holding the tongue and cheek meat to be eaten like a chicken wing. The whole jawbones are also fabulous when marinated in vinegar and garlic, then lightly floured and deep-fried.

And my favorite of all cod dishes is a whole cod head roasted over aromatics and herbs. In classic culinary texts I have found recipes calling for heads to be stuck liberally with cloves, coated in a mixture of lemon peel, horseradish, nutmeg, and pepper, before being baked on a bed of sliced onions. I prefer to rub the cod head with butter mixed with anchovy and horseradish (anchovy being the perfect partner for the shyly flavored cod) and roast it over a bed of celery. Either way, serve with a side of melted butter and no expectations of decorum.

Cod fillets are often sold under the categories of Capt'n's Cut (the first two thirds of the fillet) and Mate's Cut (the remaining third or tail section). The skin crisps nicely with beautiful golden brown coloration, and the flesh of cod is described by the great French chef Alain Senderens as "white, delicate, resilient." I find its character to be low intensity, having a baked potato flavor, slight sourness, and a biscuit-like aroma. As the fish are mostly sedentary and thus the fat is stored in the fish's liver rather than between the muscle, the large and generous flake of the flesh is very lean (see page 48 for more on muscle structure). I think that fresh cod benefits from a light salting a couple of hours before cooking, as this firms the flesh and unlocks its more subtle nuances. I also think that a few days of aging improves the flesh; when superfresh, the fish can be mouth-drying, almost tannic, like a muscular red wine. Aged over a couple of days, the flesh oxidizes and its flavor matures, but the window is short. Formaldehyde created by enzymatic breakdown in the flesh accelerates the denaturation of proteins, thus causing it to oxidize rapidly. If too fresh, this can present as a slightly bitter flavor. If aged too long, it expresses a woodsy or cardboard aroma and has an increasingly metallic or tinny flavor. When past its prime, cod does not taste spoiled but rather it's simply flat, pallid, and stale.

Processing whiting at a plant in Gloucester, Massachusetts, 1955.

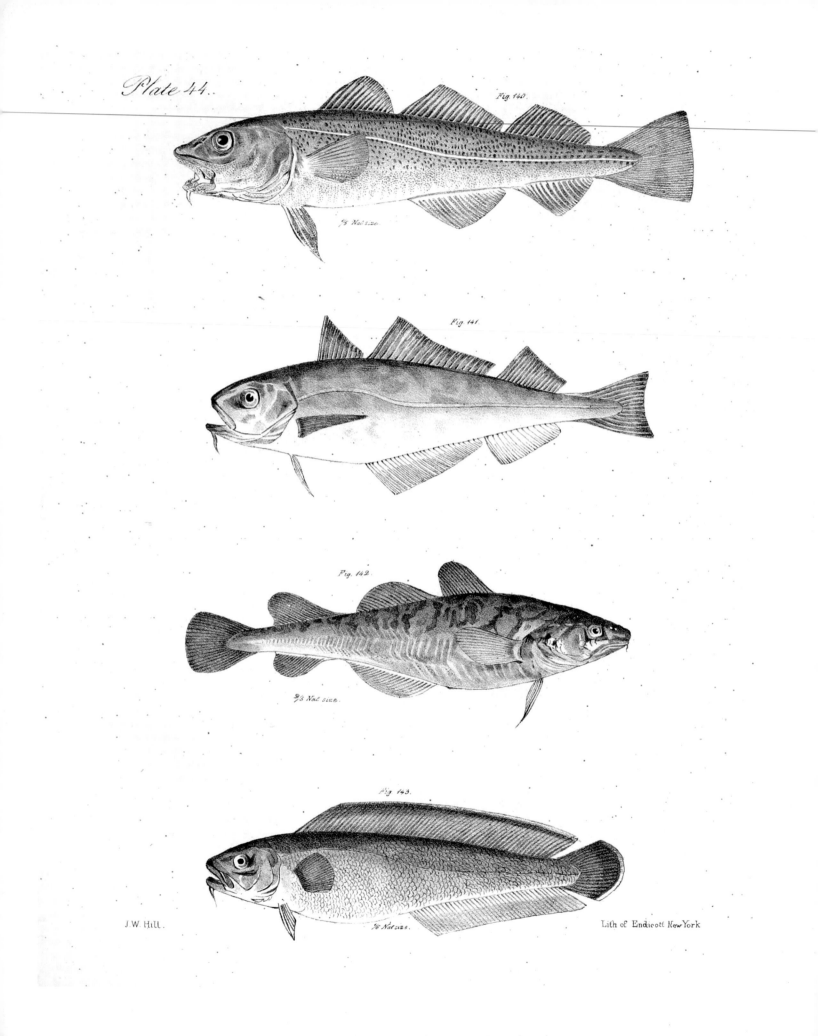

Plate 44.

Fig. 140.

⅓ Nat size.

Fig. 141.

Fig. 142.

⅔ Nat size.

Fig. 143.

J.W. Hill.

⅙ Nat size.

Lith of Endicott New York

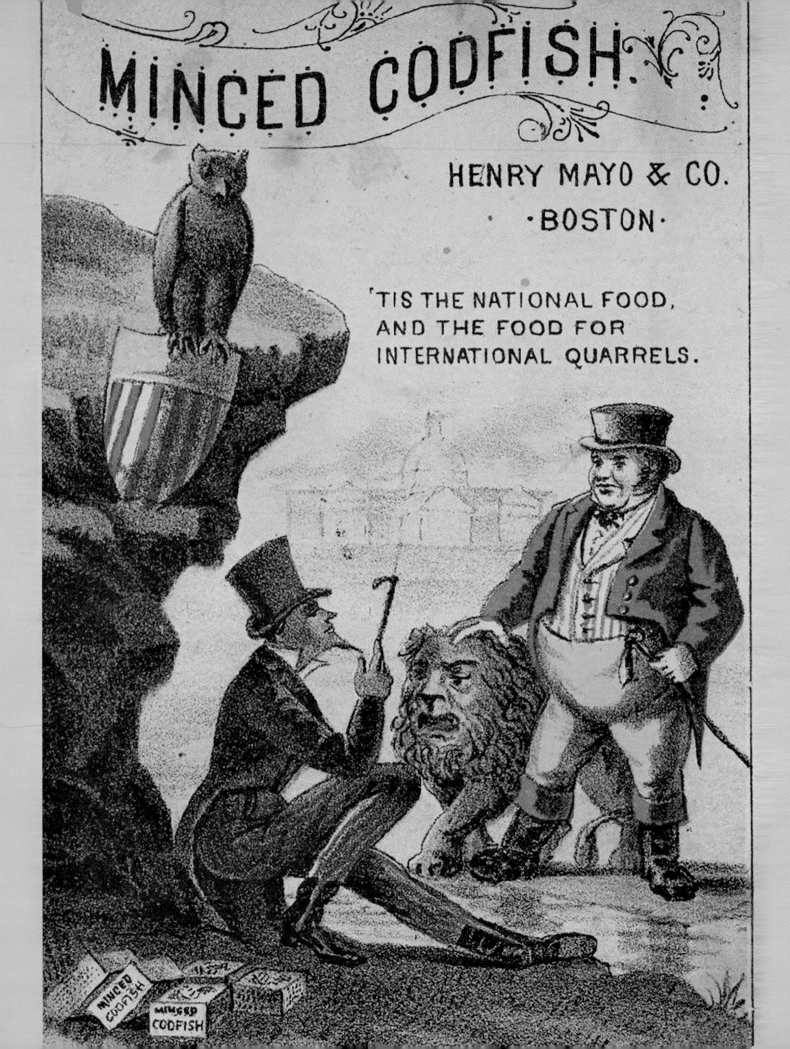

On average, this one fishery accounts for about 30 percent of the entire U.S. catch by weight. This is the currently world's largest fishery, and for years now, the largest for food fish. The Peruvian anchoveta is sometimes caught in greater volume but has almost exclusively industrial uses.

So why don't we hear about Alaska Pollock all the time and see it everywhere? It was rarely marketed directly to consumers because it's the fish behind the brands. This is the fish that goes into making frozen, breaded products. It is the McDonald's Filet-O-Fish® and the fish on many other fast-food menus. It is the fish that is processed into *Surimi*, better known in America as imitation crabmeat, or the recently coined "crab-flavored seafood."

The other reason why we don't see this fish is that the fishery is centered in Dutch Harbor, Alaska, and remote outposts along the Aleutian chain. The industry is highly mechanized, operating on state-of-the-art vessels that catch, process, freeze, and package the fish. They now also process the trim into fish meal and oil, making full use of the animal.

Alaska Pollock fillets that have been carefully handled, cut, and frozen are of a quality that rivals most of the more popular white-fleshed fish, such as flounder, tilapia, catfish, and others. It is versatile though not very assertive, making it a good fish to carry other flavors in a dish, but the fish itself is not particularly notable in flavor.

Atlantic Tomcod and its western twin, the **Pacific Tomcod**, were once regarded very highly as a food fish in the Northeast and Pacific Northwest, and they still have loyal fans in certain parts; however, there is no longer any directed fishery. Not much larger than a foot long, these are shallow-water fish that live near the mouths of rivers in brackish estuaries. They have the rare ability to produce proteins that act as an antifreeze, allowing them to ascend near-frozen rivers in the dead of winter to spawn. They are now mostly taken in recreational fisheries or as an incidental catch. If you're lucky enough to come across one, it makes great eating. Spawning season is November to February, and that is when they are chiefly taken. They are also aptly known as **Frostfish** and **Winter Cod**. Historically, they were sold as **London Trout** when they were fished commercially.

One member of the cod family that you are unfortunately unlikely to meet outside of fishing communities is the **Cusk**, sometimes called **Tusk**. This is a deepwater-dwelling species that looks like a cod crossed with an eel, and its culinary qualities are rather well explained by that crossing. They eat sea urchins, clams, and crustaceans, a diet that is well reflected in its flavor. Cusk has the highest amount of fat of all the cod family and takes very well to marinades. It is well suited for broiling, kebabs, and grilling. Its texture is admirable, as it has the generous, large flake of cod with the pleasant firmness of monkfish. It is easy to cook and is resilient to drying out. Cusk is one of the very best fish to eat as leftovers, as its flavor, once the fish is cooked, matures and gets better if left overnight. Lightly dressed with a vinaigrette and placed atop bitter greens, it makes for a great meal. It is no longer a targeted species, but it is still caught in some quantity as bycatch of other groundfish fisheries. The head of the cusk is very large (and unattractive), so any time the fish is landed, it will have its head removed to save space in the ship's hold. Fillets should be pearly white, moist, and glistening, with no hint of yellowing around the edges, which is a sign of age.

Though there was never much consideration of Cusk as a market species, those that were landed in the early cod fisheries were salted in the same manner and likely as not sold as salt cod. The one difficulty presented by this fish is its row of pin bones, which runs nearly three-quarters down the length of the fillet. They are easily removed by slicing on either side and removing the entire strip. But this leaves a difficult-to-portion fillet. One workaround is to cut it into chunks for kebabs or use it in a stew or chowder, as it holds its texture well. Salt Cusk is a great variation when added to a classic dish such as a cassoulet.

A species that is very similar to Cusk though it is not related to the cod family is the **Bearded Brotula**. It has a large flake like the Cusk and a meaty flavor similar to grouper, and in fact is often referred to as "poor man's grouper." Like most cod kin, its flavor is somewhat muted and needs the tang of citrus or vinegar in a marinade or sauce to bring its character to the fore. It is not a targeted species but is caught as bycatch in snapper fisheries in the Gulf of Mexico and is erroneously sold as **Kingclip**.

Burbot is the only freshwater member of the cod family that is very similar to cusk and is often compared to lobster in flavor and texture. They are found in the Chesapeake, throughout the Great Lakes, and rarely in western rivers such as the Columbia. They can grow up to 60 pounds, though that size is quite rare. Also known as **Lawyer**, **Coney-fish**, and **Bubbot**, they are eel-like in shape and have very few bones. The fish's firm white flesh gives it away as a relative of cod, and it shows well in nearly any recipe as a substitute for its far more famous relative. It is slightly more fatty than cod or Haddock, giving it a unique richness not often associated with freshwater fish. Its liver is about 10 percent of its body weight, and the oil from it is higher in vitamin D than that of cod.

Whiting is a common name applied to all the hake species, though it is also a specific name referring to the **Silver Hake**. These fish, often around 15 inches long, have an extended silvery-gray body, a very pointy head, and a particularly vicious look. Their flavor is mild and the flesh is very soft, prone to gaping, and does not age well. Even when pristinely fresh, these fish appear limp. But when at peak quality, whiting are fabulous eating, especially when fried whole or when filleted and used to add body and flavor to chowder. To serve them whole, I will snip off the fins along the belly but leave the tail and dorsal fins, which crisp nicely once fried. Their skin is very thin and should be left on, as it lends structural integrity to the fillet. The tiny scales can easily be removed by scraping gently with the back of a knife. My favorite preparation for whiting is flouring and frying the fillets and then marinating them in the Italian style of *en saor*. These fish can be deboned quite easily by chopping off the head, then, with the belly down, pressing along the dorsal ridge to flatten toward the belly. The spine and most of the pin bones can be simply lifted out and any remaining pin bones removed with tweezers. These are labor-intensive little fish, but they make up for it with their bargain price. There are those who voice derision for these fish. Ruth Spear, author of *Cooking Fish and Shellfish: A Complete Guide*, comments that they are an "inelegant fish" with a flavor that runs from "delicate and oceanic to lean, unassertive and downright insipid." To bolster her point there is very little mention, if any, of this fish in classic culinary texts. Mentions of whiting that I do come across are always for Kingcroaker, a member of the drum family, colloquially known as whiting. There is a peculiar history of true whiting being very popular

in fried fish shops in St. Louis in the 1920s, which became the primary (really the only) market for these fish until a lucrative fishery was developed in the 1930s to supply whiting to the rapidly expanding poultry-feed industry.

PREVIOUS PAGES Unloading in Gloucester, Massachusetts, 1942. ABOVE Whiting.

Drying Hake Sound at wharf of.
S. Smith Gloucester
1882.

SMITH

The **Pacific Whiting**, also known as **Pacific Hake**, is one of the more important West Coast fisheries. They have a fine flake, and their flesh is the white so typical of members of the cod family. Its flavor is a bit stronger than most of its kin, best equated to the Pollock of the East Coast. There are three different stocks of this fish ranging from Baja, California, all the way north through Alaska. These differ in size and in seasonal availability, though they are all equal in culinary character and no differentiation is made at market. These fish are subject to a unique enzymatic reaction that causes the flesh to soften when cooked. Recent developments recognizing methods of proper handling on the boat have negated this issue, and now high-quality fillets are available in frozen form. They are particularly popular in the Midwest, where the name **Jack Salmon** has been prevalent. These are a perfect stand-in for any other cod family member, but be aware that its delicate texture requires a gentle touch and that it should be cooked with the skin on. These fish are also used in the production of surimi.

Of the several species of hake swimming off the Atlantic coast, several are, or have been, subject to important fisheries, while others are bycatch or are generally too small to be of value. The two most important species are the **White Hake** and **Red Hake**, also known as the **Squirrel Hake**. In early cod fisheries, hake were often landed as bycatch and salted and sold as salt cod. The livers of these fish are particularly appreciated, as they were good for rendering oil and also sautéed in butter (as chicken livers are) with hard herbs such as thyme. But it was the sounds, or air bladders, of hake that were most valuable. They were used in the production of isinglass, a fining agent used to clarify beer and wine. Aboard the schooners it was generally part of the cook's duties to remove the sounds, and then preserve them in salt for eventual sale to market. They are delicious as a food item—the salted sounds are soaked in water and then simmered in milk lightly thickened with flour and butter. The sounds were also pickled and, according to cookbook author Evelene Spencer, were among "the most favorite articles of food." The flesh of hake has a characteristic off-white or beige "stitching" running down the centerline of the interior of its fillet, as though someone hemmed the fillet. There is a row of pin bones that extends about three-fifths of the fillet's length and causes some yield loss. White Hake has the finest flake of any of the cod family and must be treated very delicately, though it is almost always cooked with the skin off due to the small and firmly attached scales. But the care is worth every bit of effort as, when at its peak of quality, hake's bright, briny clam and cucumber aroma is harmonious and balanced with just a hint of sweet and sour. Because of this, hake has long been a favorite among fishermen. On the other hand, hake does not age well, as it develops a dishrag aroma that is quite offputting.

James Beard was very fond of hake: "To me, a cold hake is one of the most delicate and delightful dishes." His preferred preparation was to poach fillets in court bouillon and cool the fish in the liquid, then remove the fillets and serve them with mayonnaise. Like most cod kin, hake benefits from pre-salting for a few hours in a process known as *green salting* or *slack salting*. These terms imply that the cure is not meant to preseve the fish but to firm the texture and punctuate the flavor while maintaining the fresh, or "green," character of the flesh. One of my favorite preparations for hake is to cure fillets for two days under a light dusting of sea salt. I then rinse and air-dry them for a day, then smoke the stiffened fillets slowly over pinecones or hickory nuts, echoing the flavors of a traditional mid-Atlantic preparation.

Hake have a long history in the fisheries of New England. Captain John Smith wrote in 1616: "Hake you may have when the cod failes in summer." Through the 1960s, the Red Hake were intensively fished by the Russian fleet, but since their important fishing areas were nationalized no significant U.S. effort has been made to build upon the opportunity. Hakes are generally smaller than cod, though they have longer and thinner bodies. Large hakes range up to 10 pounds, with larger specimens known as *sows*.

Additional species of hake range throughout the southern Atlantic and Gulf of Mexico. And while all have similar characteristics, it is only the **Gulf Hake** that grows large enough and is abundant enough to potentially support a fishery. This shares all the same culinary characteristics as the Red and White Hake; however, it lacks the characteristic stitching. Another cod relative, the **Grenadier** of both the Atlantic and Pacific, is covered in a separate entry (see page 226).

While all of the species in the cod family are comparable, the story of cod itself is as outsized as America. Cod, and increasingly its relatives, swim through the channels of American history, offering us a compass toward understanding critical social, economic, cultural, and culinary changes this country has witnessed. Most fisheries in America are enduring tales with shifting plots and players as fish stocks ebb and flow and ascend into and fall from our culinary graces. But the story of cod, at least as we knew it, is not enduring. This riches-to-rags drama tells of a once outlandishly profuse resource that has been eroded to a handicapped state. The American economy that was inaugurated on the salted flesh of fish and the centuries-old traditions and communities that exemplify the American dream have atrophied before our very eyes. The mighty cod no longer rules the western Atlantic. It is a classic case of the "tragedy of the commons" and example of our prentice understanding of nature. But fishermen, a resilient and artful species, are enterprising new opportunities and continue their labors to put food on America's tables. The splendid tale of this fish of human martyrdom is a splendid tale that may be over. But the fishermen, at least, endure.

Salt Fish Dinner

This New England classic is basically a chowder without the milk. While traditional recipes call for the salt fish and potatoes to be cooked separately, I find it is better to cook them together so that the potatoes absorb the flavor and seasoning from the salt fish. The gravy of pork fat and crispy bits of fatback is quite a generous, maybe even a gratuitous, use of calories for anyone not involved in heavy labor such as fishing. But remember, those hardy folks were forever battling a challenging climate, and a little extra fuel was always welcome.

Soak salt fish for one hour in warm water with the skin side up so that the crystals of salt may fall away from the fillet. Put new potatoes on to boil. When halfway cooked, add the salt cod and simmer for 15 minutes. Cut up 1 pound of salt pork into tiny cubes, and fry until nicely browned. Serve the salt fish and potatoes together with the salt pork and rendered fat on the side as a gravy to drizzle over the dish.

Conch and Whelk

Conchs and whelks are large marine snails called *gastropods*; the Greek origin translates to "stomach and feet." And that's a pretty accurate description of them. True Conch has always been well regarded in the cuisines of Florida and throughout the Caribbean. Though **Whelk** and **Conch** are similar in appearance, they differ in that whelks are a carnivorous species that use their curved shells to wedge open bivalves such as oysters and clams and then extract the meat. Conchs are less active, as their vegetarian diet of sea grasses and floating algae doesn't require much hunting.

The **Queen Conch** was the most popular of the bunch. Unfortunately, these creatures are particularly sensitive to overfishing as they move as slow as a, well, a snail, and their large beautiful shells are sought after collectors' items, adorning beach houses everywhere. There is a long history of a hand fishery for them, as they are easily plucked from the bottom by divers, with or without the use of underwater diving gear. Though they are as intricate as any sculpture in the Louvre, and sometimes as large a football, this "tummy on hoof" is surprisingly mobile, and they migrate constantly throughout the tidal zone and deeper waters near shore. The gorgeous and intricate helix-designed shells have been used as everything from trumpets to doorstops to mantlepiece fixtures to bathroom candles—even ear trumpets offering a direct line to the sea. Perhaps the only seafood home accessory more common is the abalone ashtray.

Whelks caught throughout New England were a sought-after ingredient in various ethnic markets along the East Coast region. Most often caught in specialized pots or by dredging, they are sometimes captured as uninvited guests in lobster and crab traps. Most of the northern fishery is executed with lobster pots redesigned to specifically target whelks. These emerging fisheries are becoming more profitable and more important throughout New England. The vast majority of the catch comes from Virginia, where there is a large dredge fishery. Confusingly, Whelks are often called Conch, and some states report separate landings data for conch and whelk, though they are in most cases one and the same.

FOLLOWING PAGES Frozen mackerel, Haddock, and Swordfish, c. 1940.

The **Waved Whelk** (aka **Common Whelk**), **Knobbed Whelk**, and the **Channeled Whelk** are the most common on the East Coast and are typically found in Italian markets, where they are sold as *Scungilli*. This market term often includes the conch species, but the true translation infers only the whelk, which has different culinary qualities. Of these species the Waved Whelk is the smallest, growing to about four inches, with the other two species growing up to nine inches. On our Pacific coast there are several species of marine snail, but only the **Killet's Whelk**, aka **California Conch**, is of equal size and culinary consideration as the Atlantic varieties mentioned.

There are numerous ways of preparing whelks and conch, though the first step is always to remove it from the shell. This can be done most invasively by drilling a hole at the top and then using a paring knife to cut the operculum, the thin bone-like disc that covers the meat at the opening of the shell, and pulling the live animal from its helical shell. The hammer method, on the other hand, works pretty well, and you can probably figure that one out for yourself. They can also be removed by boiling in salted water for just a few minutes until they release from their shell and can be plucked out. From a culinary standpoint, once the meat has been removed, they are similar to squid in that they should either be cooked very quickly or braised for long periods of time, as any intermediate duration of cooking makes them unpalatably chewy.

The flavor of whelks and conchs is distinctly briny, with a nutty, mushroom-like aroma. Whelks have an additional layer of flavor, slightly more complex and reminiscent of oysters. When prepared correctly, the meat of both conch and whelk has a natural sweetness bound by the sea. According to food writer R.W. Apple, Jr., the meat "tastes like an exotic version of the New England Quahog." When quickly boiled and dipped in garlic and herb-infused butter, they are springy and pleasantly chewy, but I prefer to braise them slowly in a flavorful broth of vegetables and herbs. The remaining broth can be reduced and fortified with sherry and olive oil, lending richness to this now tender, yet chewy dish. Whelk and conch are sometimes ground and made into burgers or sliced and featured in a ceviche-style dish, marinated in spices and lime. Most people's first experience with conch or whelk has been Bahamian-style conch fritters. Rarely, you may find very large whelks that have a muscle almost as big as a pork tenderloin in width. Should you ever cross paths with such a creature, the great champion of underutilized and underfoot seafood Euell Gibbons recommends slicing them about ½-inch thick, pounding them, and sautéing as you would a cutlet. Whelks are related to two other species of gastropods, the limpets and periwinkle, which are covered in separate entries (see pages 253 and 330, respectively).

Crab

In 1939, Gustav Brown invented the flavor of my youth. The classic Baltimore spice Old Bay®, redolent with celery salt, chile, and other spices, recalls via Proustian memory my summers crabbing on the Chesapeake Bay. The **Blue Crab**, with which that seasoning is so closely associated and upon which is so liberally showered, is an icon in and of itself. I regularly see decals of the outline of the crab colored with the patterning of the Maryland flag. It has become part of the identity of an entire region—and rightfully so.

Blue Crabs, a type of swimming crab, are "beautiful swimmers" (the title of the fabulous book by William W. Warner). They use their flattened back legs, known as *swimmerettes*, as paddles, propulsing their diamond-shaped bodies sideways through the water with improbable celerity. When these crabs swim just under the surface, their shells catch the sunlight and manifest a beautiful collage of sage green, cerulean blue, and dusky heather. The Blue Crab's scientific name, *Callinectes sapidus*—from the Greek *calli* for "beautiful," *nectes* for "swimmer," and the Latin *sapidus* for "savory"—could not be more apt. But their handsomeness masks the creature's bellicose nature. Their belligerence is such a part of their identity that the word *crab* shares root with the name of the world's most vicious disease, *cancer*, both derived from the Latin *cancer* and Greek *karkinos*.

Native Americans had been harvesting Blue Crab along the shallow eastern shores of the Chesapeake for centuries. As the area became populated by small towns of immigrants and freed slaves, a commercial fishery was slow to develop because these communities remained isolated both geographically and culturally. In the era before refrigeration, two days in the shade

OPPOSITE Channeled Whelk.

FOLLOWING PAGES Blue Crab, Delcambre, Louisiana.

was as best you could hope for to get live crab from the lower reaches of the Bay to the metropolises of the North. Despite the booming oyster trade running between the Chesapeake's rich estuarine environment and New York City, the steam vessels never made room for the bulky and perishable crab.

In 1866 a politician by the name of John Woodland Crisfield struck a deal with the railroad company and created the "Iron Avenue" linking Annemessex, Maryland, to Baltimore, forever changing the economy of the Chesapeake Bay. With the introduction of the icebox and the artificial ice machine, rail shipments laden with crab were departing regularly for Baltimore, Philadelphia, and beyond.

On the Bay's western shore, the first crabmeat cannery was opened in Norfolk, Virginia, in 1878. Packing houses quickly became a mainstay of the coastal economies and were an important source of employment for women. In the 1920s the invention of the crab pot increased the efficiency of crab fishing, and by 1929 pots had largely replaced historically prevalent fishing practices. But in this region of closely guarded traditions, many watermen still use time-honored methods, hand-harvesting with trotlines and dip nets. These artisans rise long before the break of day to tend their lines, a simple apparatus consisting of buoys strung with a couple of hundred feet of strong rope, from which every few feet extends another line tethering a fish head or, more commonly, a chicken neck. With the boat puttering just above an idle, the rope is slowly drawn from the depths, and the greedy and altogether distracted crabs clinging tightly to the bait are deftly netted just before breaking the surface of the water. With one hand on the wheel and periodic glances at the path ahead, the waterman swiftly scoops and deposits each crab into bushel baskets. This idyllic and timeless method has withstood the advance of technology.

The Chesapeake crab season begins toward the end of spring, when water temperatures shed their winter chill. With nature's perfect fluency, the coming summer's whisper stirs the crabs from their deepwater winter hibernation, and hundreds of millions of them surge back into the bay. Come fall, the process reverses itself, as temperatures slide lower, signaling first the females and then the males to prowl deeper and southward.

Female Blue Crabs spend the winter burrowed into the sand just at the mouth of the Chesapeake Bay by Norfolk. The males venture farther on to the deeper waters off Virginia and North Carolina. Unfortunately, a small but woefully destructive winter dredge fishery (since closed for the past several years) targeted this breeding population of females, tilling them from their hiberation. And while the modest catch of the dredges kept the picking houses operating through the lean season, the crabs were themselves lean, their fat stores depleted from having not eaten for months, and their meat far from showing its full charm. Blue Crabs live about three years, and the fishery targeting breeding-age females significantly impacted the sustainability of the populations.

The Chesapeake is America's largest estuarine environment and one of the most productive bodies of water on the planet. Its watershed begins as far north as Upstate New York and Pennsylvania, and into its vascular system gathers every drop of water in the mid-Atlantic region from Appalachia through southern Virginia. As development spread throughout the watershed, tributaries flushed nutrients that ran off from farms and cities into the Bay. That runoff, compounded with the loss of the oyster population that once filtered the waters, led to the deterioration of water clarity, which in turn led to the destruction of eelgrass beds, an essential habitat for juvenile crabs and just about every other species living in the bay. By the 1990s the Blue Crab, the "Pride of the Chesapeake"—once the embodiment of the bold spirit of the men and women of the Bay—was in serious decline. Reduced production opened the door for cheap imported crab from the Philippines or Venezuela to gain market share. What little product came from the Chesapeake region was often caught elsewhere in the United States and sent there to be picked.

Blue Crabs have only a 15 percent edible yield, but they have several different types of meat of varying quality. The best meat is the jumbo lump and lump—large single muscle sections from the back of the crab that power its beautiful swimming legs, also known as *sculling legs*. Additional grades are backfin, special, claw meat, claw fingers, and paste. Each of these has its own unique flavor—jumbo lump and lump are the suave sweet acme of seafood experience; backfin and special taste of brine and butter; claw has the fullest, almost gamey, flavor; and paste—an extraction of the remaining

LEFT King Crab. RIGHT Box Crab.

edible parts—is very potent in flavor (small amounts are used to season bold dishes such as gumbo). One of the very best parts of crab that's often discarded is the soft yellow or brown fat scraped from the corners inside the shell. Another is the liver or hepatopancreas, the creamy yellow substance found in the middle of the crab, which is very acidic, a quality that adds great complexity to the flavor of the meat or any dish it is added to. The hepatopancreas is also known as the *mustard*, due to its peppery bite and full flavor.

The Blue Crab has been significantly fished in the many waters of the mid-Atlantic from Long Island to the Delaware and Raritan bays. It has long supported significant fisheries throughout the Carolinas and into the Gulf, especially in the New Orleans region, with Lake Pontchartrain and Lake Borgne being very productive and considered the source of some of the highest-quality Blue Crab. The Gulf region has a particularly wonderful culinary relationship to the Blue Crabs, especially in gumbos and as a stuffing for fish.

In the 1850s, crabbers realized that they could capture Blue Crabs just as they were about to molt, the process by which they shed their shells in order to grow. Male crabs molt, on average, 21 to 23 times in their lives, while females molt 18 to 20 times. This offers plenty of opportunity for keen-eyed fishermen to notice the signs of an impending molt and keep those crabs in a special pen until they shed. Thus was born the soft-shell crab industry. Soft-shell crabs are particularly fragile and must be attended to nearly 24 hours a day before they are shipped quickly to market. These delicacies are entirely edible except for the face, the leathery apron underneath known as the *tablier*, and the lungs, called *dead man's fingers* or *devil's fingers*. As this is such a labor-intensive industry, operations are inherently small and the product commands a premium price.

Just as molting crabs require exacting care, the lexicon describing them is precise and intricately descriptive, beginning with the scientific term for the process of molting known as *ecdysis*. But scientists have reportedly shied away from using this term ever since the great American writer H.L. Mencken penned a description of a bawdy showgirl named Gypsy Rose Lee, whose leisurely and witty decampment from her clothes led him to coin the word *ecdysiast* as a term superior to *stripper*.

By examining the faint bands of color on the next-to-last segment of the rear or swimming leg, fishermen can tell when a crab is likely to molt. "White signs" will shed in two weeks or less. "Pink signs" will shed in less than a week; "red signs" will shed within just a few days; and "rank" is just hours from molting. A crab in the process of molting is known as a *buster*. The molting process can take place within the course of just a few hours. If left in the water, a newly molted crab begins to stiffen its new shell within 12 hours, becoming known as a *paper shell*. Within 24 hours, they are crinkly hard *buckrams*, and by 72 hours, their shells have fully hardened.

The Blue Crab is the only crab we eat as a soft shell, though there is another species that could support a market for such a product—the invasive **Green Crab**. This small crab, rarely measuring more than three inches, has been wreaking havoc on our ecosystems since it invaded the shores of Cape Cod in the 1800s. Native to Asia and parts of Europe, they found their Eden on our East Coast, and populations have boomed. Their favorite food is the soft-shell clam, one of the mainstays of the New England fisheries economy. A single Green Crab can eat up to 15 clams a day. Furthermore, the crabs burrow into the mudbanks of the shoreline, exposing the roots of tidal grasses, which leads to very troubling erosion. The Green Crab population seems to be cyclical, though we don't have enough history with them to say for sure. In the late 1950s, the booming crab population was largely killed off by a long stretch of cold winters. Recent periods of prolonged warmer weather and gentle winters in line with global trends has coincided with a dramatic increase in the population. Efforts to eradicate the Green Crab have included investigation into using them as lobster bait, fertilizer, and animal feed, but no solution has been found that is economically feasible. So maybe we should look to the Venetians, who have in their lagoon a nearly identical crab that is among their most prized delicacies. They harvest the crabs just prior to molting, and they are commonly found on menus as *moleche*, dipped in flour and deep-fried until crispy. Green Crabs also make a surprisingly good stock with a clean, sweet, ocean flavor. Jasper White is a proponent of using crabs with their carapace removed, the bodies simmered in water with aromatic vegetables and wine for an hour. It makes a perfect base for seafood stews or soups. And maybe, just maybe, if we eat enough of these Green Crabs, we can have some clams for an appetizer.

The **Jonah Crab** and Atlantic **Rock Crab** of New England waters are so similar as to be indiscernible to the amateur and are nearly always sold intermixed. Unless you live on the coast of northern New England, you are unlikely to find these crabs live. They were long considered a nuisance species by the lobster industry, as they would get into the traps and take their fill of bait. Traditionally, women in lobstering communities would perform the laborious task of picking the meat from these crabs, but it did not command high value and so rarely made it past localized markets. The meat is finer in texture and slightly stringy compared to the larger lumped meat of Blue Crab, but it has a sweet, briny flavor and flakiness that has earned it recognition as a desired product. Increasingly the picked crabmeat is becoming available outside of New England. And much of the success has to do with one man, Rod Mitchell, a vendor to some of the nation's finest restaurants who, in the 1980s, coined the term "**Peeky-Toe Crab**." This moniker is based on regional fishermen's patois, an abbreviated form of "Picked Toe," picked being a Maine colloquialism meaning "curved inward" as are the legs of the crab. This just proves that you can take an underappreciated regional product, dress it up with a fun cosmopolitan name, and the world will realize what it's been missing. Peeky-Toe's meat, like that of most crabs, is incredibly versatile, equally at home in risottos, soups, or as I prefer simply dressed with mayonnaise and piled into a buttered potato bun.

Both the Jonah and the Atlantic Rock Crab fall under the common name **Rock Crab**, which consists of many species, including the famed **Dungeness Crab** of the West Coast. Every hometown has its hero, and the Dungeness Crab is the pride of Alaska down through Southern California. The fishery for Dungeness Crabs began in the San Francisco area in 1848, and the entire production was marketed on the Pacific coast until 1957, when live and frozen "dressed" crabs were first shipped outside of the region. The crab gets its name from the small fishing village of Dungeness, Washington, home of another early commercial fishery, but its culinary fame lives in San Francisco, immortalized in a dish called *cioppino*. The crabs have a satisfyingly high-edible yield around 25 percent. Paul Johnson, a legendary fish authority, prefers Dungeness Crab prepared "live-backed." By this method the carapace and all viscera are removed before cooking, as it is thought that the viscera impart a bitter flavor to the meat. Plus, as Johnson points out rather practically, "You can fit more in a pot."

In California, there is a rock crab fishery that targets three species, the **Yellow Rock Crab**, the **Brown Rock Crab**, and the Red Rock Crab, collectively known simply as Rock Crab, which are caught through the southern reaches of California. Rock Crab claws have a greater proportion of meat than do those of the Dungeness Crab, and in this way they are more similar to the Florida Stone Crab. These rock crabs have very hard shells, and their meat is stringy and a bit hard to remove. But they are worth the effort, as their briny, iodine-tinged flavor is delicious—perfect for flavoring pastas and risottos.

Another southern Pacific species that is truly unique is the **Box Crab**. This particularly warty creature won't win any beauty contests, but its sweet, butter-rich meat, well endowed with fat, is possibly the best of any crab. Its large sections of leg meat resemble that of a Dungeness Crab. The apron, an appendage that folds along the underside of the crab, contains a delicious bit of meat known as the *crab tail*. Box Crabs absorb quite a bit of water when boiled, and thus steaming is the preferred method. The only drawback is that their edible yield is very low, and if the crab is not superfresh and vigorously alive, the meat can become watery and taste bland. All things considered, it's one of the easiest crabs I've ever worked with, and certainly one of the most delicious. There is no significant fishery directed for the Box Crab at this time.

The biggest crab fishery on the Pacific coast is for **Alaskan King Crab**, which includes four different species: **Golden King Crab**, **Blue King Crab**, the smaller and least valuable **Scarlett King Crab**, and the most desired, the **Red King Crab**. Not only is this one of the most valuable crabs, it is certainly the most famous, as it is the subject of the TV show *The Deadliest Catch*, so named for the vicious seas and weather braved by captain and crew. These giant crabs can grow to have a leg span of up to six feet and weigh well over 20 pounds. U.S. fisheries are relatively new, as prior to World War II, Japanese and Russian fleets heavily fished Alaskan waters, processing the crab and canning it. Americans bought about 10 million pounds of this crab a year until 1950, when our domestic fleets increased efforts. The catch went from about 700 tons, spiking in the mid-1960s at over 70,000 tons and a peak of 84,000 tons in 1980, before decades of decline leading to current catches under 10,000 tons. The fleet works waters far away from consumers, limiting availability of live or fresh product, thus necessitating that nearly every pound of king crab is sold having been boiled and frozen. And frankly, that's a damn good

PREVIOUS PAGES Crab pots at the Bay Bridge, Annapolis, Maryland. OPPOSITE Picking crab at Pontchartrain Blues in Louisiana. FOLLOWING PAGES, LEFT Jonah Crab claw. FOLLOWING PAGES, RIGHT Maryland waterman.

The live-backing technique also can be used with Blue Crabs and East Coast Rock Crabs. Live-backed crabs absorb marinades well and are good for grilling or pan-roasting. If boiling whole Dungeness Crabs, it's important to drop them into the boiling salted water upside-down, so the crab will fold its legs against its shell, giving an elegant presentation while ensuring even cooking. The **Red Rock Crab** is very similar to and caught in the same manner as the Dungeness Crab. It is, in my opinion, equal in culinary quality, though it has a significantly lower edible yield. These crabs are caught on rocky bottoms, whereas Dungeness Crabs prefer less textured environments.

thing. Their long slender legs are flush with generous sections of meat that are easily extracted, and preparing them is as easy as steaming them until warmed through. The meat is wonderful simply dipped in butter or pulled from the shell, marinated, and served in a salad. My favorite preparation is to grill the whole legs—the shell chars and perfumes the meat with a smoky flavor and slight bitterness, which balances the sweetness of the crab. Though their price tag is high, they have the highest edible yield of any crab, at about 32 percent of the total weight, but as we buy just the legs, the yield is higher. Each crab has six walking legs and two slightly shorter claw legs. I prefer the meat from the giant center claws, as it has a slightly more developed flavor and chewier texture. Aside from the leg and claw meat, the fleshy apron underneath the carapace, known as the *crab tail*, makes a wonderful little delicacy that is becoming more available as a few top chefs have made them vogue. I first encountered these while sitting at a bar in Dillingham, Alaska. Several beers in, and I went for it. These little flaps of meat are wonderful when salted and marinated, then grilled or broiled. But as my first experience attests, pickled as a salty bar snack might be their highest calling.

King crab became so economically important that little attempt was made to exploit the abundant populations of other crab species. Even when a large scallop population was discovered, no fishery was initiated, because the king crab fishery would have been affected by the new activity. It was only when king crab populations declined in late 1960s that the industry had incentive to diversify and begin targeting **Snow Crab**.

There are multiple species of crab sold as snow crab; two are caught in U.S. waters. The common market name is the catchall Snow Crab, sometimes **Alaska Snow Crab**, but these go by other names, including **Opilio Crab,** also known as **Queen Crab** or **Spider Crab**, and **Bairdi Crab,** also known as **Tanner Crab**. These are significantly smaller than king crabs, but have eight walking legs on each side and two claws. While not on par with the quality of king crab, they are certainly a delight in their own. The Bairdi Crab is the larger of the two, growing up to four pounds. The more common Opilio Crab reaches a maximum of 2½ pounds. The Opilio Crab is also found on the East Coast, where it is known as spider crab. A small fishery off the coast of northern New England has long targeted the species, but not in significant quantity.

An Atlantic species, the **Red Crab** was first discovered when fishermen were experimenting with deepwater lobster gear in 1879. This type of crab has a bright red, smooth shell, and its pink-tinged meat is similar in flavor to that of the king crab, but it is significantly smaller, growing to only about two pounds. Despite Red Crabs' incredible abundance, they have never gained popularity in the market, likely due to fishermen's lack of equipment and desire to fish such deep waters far from shore. It has only been within the last decade that companies have invested in gear to target this crab, found from Nova Scotia all the way through Florida. A very closely related species, the deep-sea **Golden Crab**, found in the coldest depths of the Gulf of Mexico is equally abundant and underutilized.

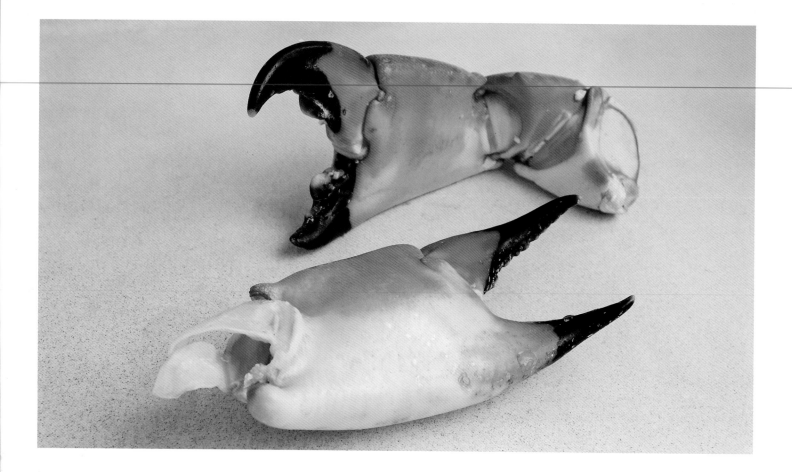

The hometown hero of the South is the **Stone Crab**. Mostly fished in Florida and throughout the Keys with small landings in other Gulf states, this is a unique fishery and a unique crab. Food author Mark Bittman refers to them as the "recyclable crab," because when they are caught in traps all females by law are thrown back whole while a single claw is removed from the males. The living crab is returned to the water, where it will regenerate its lost limb. To prevent deterioration, the claws are cooked within a few hours of capture. The shells are incredibly firm, requiring some effort to crack them, and so are often sold already split. The claws have a beautiful, porcelain-like texture, oval in shape, with orange stripes and black tips. They have a delicious flaky and very sweet meat and are typically adorned with nothing more than butter or a classic mustard sauce.

Another Florida crab, now only a historical footnote, is the **Land Crab**, a species still found throughout the Keys and Caribbean, though not nearly as abundantly as they once were. It is said that in the 1950s the streets would become overrun at night with these crabs making their rounds. Somehow a marauding army of nightwalking crabs in Key West fits perfectly with that place's wonderful weirdness. There is a recreational fishery for Land Crabs, and their meat is similar to Blue Crab.

Throughout the southeastern Atlantic and Gulf of Mexico, the diminutive **Lady Crab**, though having a rather classy name, is known to be the antagonistic culprit nipping at bathers' toes. Having beautiful yellow and white mottled shells with bright red and purple spots, these quite elegant creatures are also known as **Calico Crabs**. They only grow about three inches across and so making a meal of them proves laborious, and thus there is not much demand for them. But they are, in fact, very sweet and flavorful, and the shells make an excellent broth. My favorite use is to split them and braise them into gumbo or pound them into a paste that I sauté with tomatoes, smoked paprika, and lots of butter before adding white wine and water to simmer for an hour. Strained and finished with a touch of cream, it makes for a delightful crab bisque.

Of the dozens of species of crabs in Hawaii, the **Kona Crab** is the one of most significance. Caught in pots from depths of about a hundred feet, Kona Crabs average five inches across and a pound in weight. The meat is highly esteemed as a local delicacy and rarely makes it beyond high-end restaurant kitchens on the islands.

Ever since my childhood days along the Chesapeake, one of the things I've always loved about crabs is that (their price not considered) they are best enjoyed as part of a feast. This tactile experience requires patience, camaraderie, and lots of beer; it forces us to put away our copy of *Miss Manners*.

But some crabs fall outside this tradition. The **Oyster Crab**, part of the pea crab family, are tiny little creatures no larger than a penny that live inside the shells of oysters. The crabs do not hurt the oysters in any way but coexist with them and were once a product of great value and esteem, commanding top dollar from the best chefs and the fanciest hotels in New York and Boston. These were not a crab to make a meal of, but rather were fried as a garnish or floated in an oyster stew. The Oyster Crab has since been relegated to history, not because of any event or issue with the crab itself, but because we eat less than 1 percent of the oysters that we used to consume. Historically, wild oysters provided the bulk of our consumption, with many of them coming from warmer southern waters where crab cohabitation was more likely. Now with many of our oysters being farmed, a good number of them in northern waters, Oyster Crabs are simply not seen in any quantity to be of relevance in today's cuisine.

Among the oddest of all crabs is the **Horseshoe Crab**. And anyone who's ambled along an East Coast beach has likely seen the alien-like shell of this prehistoric creature. They were a source of food for Native Americans, who also used them for fertilizer and cleverly repurposed the hard-pointed tail as a tip for hunting spears. Early settlers in America widely used these crabs as feed for hogs and poultry and fertilizer in the fields. Aside from a few Asian cultures, which use the delicate leg meat in their cuisines, Horseshoe Crabs are largely avoided as food because they can carry some rather nasty toxins. Populations of the Horseshoe Crab are concentrated in the Delaware Bay and in the Gulf of Maine, though they are found along the shallow waters of the entire Atlantic coast. Their populations were once so abundant that they were a keystone species in the health of entire ecosystems, as when they scuttled onto the sandy beaches to mate, their spawn was so prolific that it provided a food source for myriad predators under the water, on the land, and in the sky. In modern days, they are still fished, but only for use as bait and fertilizer. But they also support another very lucrative business, providing blood for pharmaceutical industry testing. This involves transporting live crabs to a lab to draw blood with a needle before releasing them back into the wild, usually 36 to 72 hours later, while they are still alive. The blood, baby blue in color, is used to test the sterility of medical equipment and drugs. The blood can also be used as a thickener for sauces to coat the delicious bits of meat extracted from the legs, for those who are so brave as to eat it.

OPPOSITE Stone Crab claws.
FOLLOWING PAGES Dungeness Crab at Pikes Place Market in Seattle.

Crabcakes

The first printed record of crabcakes comes from 1939 in Crosby Gaige's New York World's Fair Cookbook, *in which they were called "Baltimore Crabcakes." Because of the extreme abundance of crab in the Chesapeake Bay, the dish has long been culturally associated with the region, though it is commonly found throughout the southeastern Atlantic and Gulf of Mexico. Though crabcakes can be made from any type of crab, Blue Crab is the historical basis of the dish. Some people believe that the crabcake is an emulation of the New England codcake, substituting the cheap and plentiful crab, which was popular with immigrant and poor African American populations post-slavery. By the late 1860s, Baltimore was the center of oyster and crab canning, and as such became synonomous with the crab. Though there are as many variations on the crabcake as there are cooks, the true classic calls for jumbo lump crabmeat, just enough binder, such as mayonnaise, to barely hold it together, a spoonful or two of breadcrumbs, and in more recent decades, Old Bay seasoning. Among those who carry on the proud legacy of the great crabcake tradition, few are more renowned than Faidley's. This family-owned business started in 1886 and is still in its original location, at Baltimore's world famous Lexington Market. Though their recipe eschews the Old Bay, they make up for it with the addition of Worcestershire sauce, mustard, and Tabasco. This recipe is adapted from their original recipe, as reported to* Southern Living *magazine.*

- ½ cup mayonnaise
- 1 large egg, lightly beaten
- 1 tablespoon Dijon mustard
- 2 tablespoons Worcestershire sauce
- 1 teaspoon Tabasco
- 1 cup crushed saltines (about 20 crackers)
- 1 pound jumbo lump crabmeat
- 4 tablespoons butter

Gently mix all ingredients and shape into four patties, and chill for 1 hour.

Place a pat of butter on each patty. Crisp under the broiler until golden brown and heated through.

Crab Feast

Heading north along the Atlantic coast, as shrimp territory gives way to the shallow reaches of Pamlico Sound and the Chesapeake, you will come to the heart of Blue Crab country. And there you will find the Crab Feast. Note that it is not called a "boil," as the cooking method involves steaming the crabs over water or beer. And the spice used to generously coat the steaming crabs is the iconic Old Bay seasoning. The Blue Crab does not consign its reward without patient and careful work by those gathered. These feasts last for hours and offer no immediate gratification but slow satiation in the company of friends and family all invested in mining their meal from within the spice-laden shells.

Crawfish

Skimming across the swamps of Henderson, Louisiana, with the town's mayor, Sherbin Collette, we're in Crawfish Country. We venture deep into inscrutable swamplands, cypress loom apparitional, Spanish moss woven between. Nailed to a tree a sheet of plywood painted with an esoteric folk art depiction of the last supper marks the mayor's favorite station. Here, in the Atchafalaya Basin, the country's largest wetland, is found the largest resource of wild **Crawfish**. Harvesting these small lobster-like creatures is a chance to witness centuries of heritage. Long before European settlers populated the area, Houma Indians ate crawfish and adopted its image as their tribal symbol. As cultural influences of Colonial powers spread, crawfish (variably known as **Crayfish,** in the North, whereas Crawfish is the preferred name in the South, also **Crawdads**, and **Mudbugs**) earned prominence in the evolving cusines of the region.

In 1959, the town of Breaux Bridge, Louisiana, celebrated its centennial and was honored by the state with the title *La capitale Mondiale de l'ecrevisse,* or the "Crawfish Capital of the World." The town, located in the heart of

Cajun country, puts on a wild celebration at the annual crawfish festival. The season begins in early winter when the crawfish first emerge from the mud, hungry after hibernation and so lean that it can take up to 30 of them to make a pound. The season continues through Mardi Gras and into early summer. It's just around Mardi Gras that I, and many others, think crawfish are at their peak. Fattened up from feeding on rice stalks and lily pad roots, their size has increased to 13 to 18 per pound. Their bodies are full of rich sienna-colored fat or butter, tucked between the tail and head, and females are heavily laden with colorful roe.

Crawfish are both farmed and caught in wild-capture fisheries (rudimentary mesh bags baited and hung from groves of cypress trees). Farming crawfish dates back to the late 1800s, and ever since then the industry has grown. Now most crawfish are farmed, largely in Lousiana, which alone accounts for roughly 90 percent of domestic production. Of the Louisiana product, nearly 90 percent is for live market.

The **Red Swamp Crawfish** is native to the Mississippi delta. In northern Louisiana, the **White River Crawfish** is the primary species. **Green Pacific Crawfish** are harvested in the Pacific Northwest and California, where they are especially prevalent around the Columbia River. Small fisheries exist from Wisconsin across our northern border to Maine and south into New York and Connecticut. These target a range of species, which can vary in color from yellow and beige to deep maroon, red, and black, though all are sold simply as crawfish and all shells become a familiar red once cooked.

Historically, New York City was the biggest market for crawfish, as caterers and fancy hotels, following French culinary traditions, used them extensively as garnish for intricately plated food. The New York culinary elite considered crawfish caught near Milwaukee to be the highest quality. In 1877, a canning operation started in Santa Barbara, California, though the enterprise did not last long due to low demand.

Today, crawfish sustain an important export trade to Nordic countries, where traditional celebrations, legendary for aquavit-and-schnapps-fueled intemperance, feature crawfish boiled in salt water with dill. Recently China has begun exporting processed or picked crawfish tail meat.

The edible yield of crawfish ranges from 10 to 24 percent, depending on size and season, meaning roughly three pounds of crawfish are needed to yield a half pound of meat. Before cooking, they must be washed or purged to remove sand or grit and to relieve them of any muddy flavor. When you are cooking a traditional boil, the pot should be twice as big as the amount of crawfish. Season the water with boil spice and vegetables, such as onions, garlic, potatoes, corn, and even artichokes. When the liquid is at a rapid boil, add a few beers to it and then put in the crawfish. Return to a boil, then kill the heat, and let the crawfish steep for 15 to 25 minutes so they absorb the flavorful spicy juices. Drain and pile onto a table. Open a lot of beers and dig in.

Beyond the classic boil, crawfish adapt well in many dishes like étouffée (Breaux Bridge, Louisiana, claims credit for inventing this Southern classic), sherry-spiked bisques, and creamy pastas. The crawfish's orange fat, or hepatopancreas, is integral to these recipes, adding its distinct flavor and creamy richness. Like other crustaceans, the crawfish grow by molting and can be eaten like soft-shell crabs when in their new shell, often deep-fried, as popularized in the late 1980s by legendary chef Paul Prudhomme. Though crawfish are earning more widespread appreciation, their cultural identity, like the Cypress tree, is firmly rooted in the enchanted and shallow waters of Cajun Country. As folklorist and American country musician Hank Williams famously related: "Jambalaya and a crawfish pie and filé gumbo. . . Son-of-a-gun, we'll have big fun on the bayou."

FOLLOWING PAGES Dorchester County, Maryland.

Mayor Sherbin Colette on the Atchafalaya in Louisiana.

A Louisiana Crawfish Boil

Crawfish boils are a part of the lore and legend of the Louisiana coast's jubilant cuisine. While crawfish are caught in many regions of the country, it is here that Creole charm seduces the best character from these "mudbugs." Breaux Bridge, centered in the swamps of the Atchafalaya basin, is the crawfish capital of the world, and as sure as you'll hear the zydeco thumping, you'll smell the highly spiced broth of a traditional crawfish boil. You will also see a crowd of people gathered, as these events are social affairs and typically involve an extended community of friends and family.

Every coast has its own version of a "boil" that makes use of the regional bounty. From the Dungeness Crabs of the Pacific Northwest to the lobster and clambakes of New England, each is distinct to the culture of its community. The crawfish boil, not surprisingly, tops the list as the steamiest, spiciest, most raucous affair. Large pots of water are seasoned with "boil spice," be it Zatarain's® or Rex's®, handfuls of garlic, lemons, lots of cayenne pepper, wine or beer, and whatever else the cook deems appropriate. It is recommended that each guest place their face over the pot and take in 10 deep breaths (through the nose!) to cleanse their spirits. As these events often feed dozens, if not a hundred or more, it is customary to cook in batches. The crawfish are washed of any mud and soaked in salt water to purge them. Once the seasoned water is at a boil, the cleaned crawfish, along with potatoes and corn, are put into a pillowcase and submerged in the flavorful broth for 10 to 12 minutes. Proper technique calls for ice to be added to the cooking liquid, allowing the crawfish to "galvanize," or soak up the flavorful juices, before being served. And no boil of any sort is complete without too much ice-cold beer and a clear schedule the following day.

Cutlassfish

The **Atlantic Cutlassfish** and **Pacific Cutlassfish**, also known as **Largehead Hairtail Beltfish**, **Saberfish**, and **Scabbardfish**, show that this unique fish is known regionally by a host of fairly accurate, descriptive names, all of which fall under the catchall **Cutlassfish**. Cutlassfish has a body iridescent with silvery, almost steely blue hues and a dusky yellow dorsal fin. Alan Davidson describes it well as "having a villainous appearance." The same species swims along all three U.S. coasts, though they are only moderately abundant. The name Cutlassfish and its aliases take their cue from the fish's long, thin, tapered body shaped like a sword. Its general structure is similar to ribbon fishes, an unrelated family with which it is sometimes confused. These fish grow up to four feet but are so lean as to weigh little more than three pounds.

In winter they gather in large schools off the coast of Florida, but because there is no culinary tradition or market for the fish, it remains underutilized. They migrate between shallow coastal waters and deep water and are often taken as bycatch in other fisheries. Fishermen have come to resent these fish for their razor-sharp teeth that slice through nets. Instead of scales, their bodies are sheathed in a thin silver membrane that

TOP Cutlassfish.

sloughs off with handling, and their soft flesh bruises easily due to their lack of a robust skeletal structure. When shopping for Cutlassfish, look for those that appear pliable with unblemished skin. To prepare the fish, its head should be discarded and the fish eviscerated. The belly cavity is a third the length of the fish; thus the belly flaps should be removed, as they are thin and unusable. Snip the dorsal fin with kitchen shears. The thinness of the fish can make portioning a challenge. I generally discard the tail section, where it becomes more bone than flesh, and cut the remaining body into two-inch sections, which are quite versatile in their uses. It's not necessary to remove the skin, and there are but a few pin bones.

When raw, the flesh is soft textured, but tightens when cooked, resulting in a small flake with notable firmness and a pleasant mouthfeel. The flavor is delicate; I describe it as tidal with a baked potato aroma. I've found that even superfresh fish doesn't necessarily taste "fresh." In other words, the flavor lacks vibrancy. Whole fish or large sections are great when first marinated, then grilled or broiled. The thin skin singes and sizzles, and the meat pairs well with the slight burnt taste.

Once cut, it's well suited to stir-frying, paired with onion, ginger, and peanuts to lend texture and flavor. The sections of fish can also be simply breaded and fried. When filleted, the cuts are too thin to effectively sauté but can be rolled and poached. To this day my favorite preparation remains the way I first encountered this fish, the traditional Portuguese style of escabeche in which the breaded and fried fish is marinated in vinegar with aromatic vegetables and spices. The **Dealfish** and **Ribbonfish**, both unrelated to the **Cutlassfish**, are similar in body shape and in their culinary qualities.

Dogfish

Dogfish are well represented in most of our coastal waters. The **Atlantic Spiny Dogfish** and the **Pacific Spiny Dogfish** are found in their respective waters and the **Smooth Dogfish** in the Gulf and East Coast. The dogfish have an impressive collection of interchangeable aliases, including **Cape Shark**, **Gray Shark**, **Dog Shark**, and **Spur Dog**. Regardless of name they all share culinary qualities akin to a cross between the chewy flake of cod and the richer, fattier salmon. When the fish are properly treated they are as good as flounder or halibut or other standard food fish, and for nearly all purposes dogfish are interchangeable in the kitchen with the aforementioned species.

These small sharks have long exasperated fishermen, as they are aggressive, abundant (but for a few decades when they were overfished), and capable of ripping fishing nets. Dogfish, so named by fishermen for their habit of hunting in packs, eat just about anything but seem particularly fond of any fish caught on a line or struggling against a net, the stress of these fish being an irresistible encouragement to attack. Additionally, they crowd out or chase off valuable target species such as cod. Once on board, the Spiny Dogfish is gratuitously menacing, having a sharp dorsal spine that can inflict vicious abuse on a heedless hand or foot. Dogfish have always been denounced as food, and thus fishermen, unable to avoid them, have good reason to loathe them.

If we as consumers, however, were to entertain judgment of their culinary merit, we would quickly rescind our centuries of censure of these delicious fish. But consumers are often easier to convince than fishermen. In my experience, I've met some fishermen who would court handsome profits if dogfish were to come to find favor but who are vindictive and defiant against any kind word spoken of this fish and obstinate believers that dogfish are a stain upon creation.

During World War I, the U.S. government began a vigorous campaign to increase the popularity of dogfish as part of its effort to diversify the country's food resources and make more meat available to ship to our troops. Its first act was to replace the disparaging name, and thus the **Grayfish** or **Gray Fish** was born. Very old fisheries texts make reference to dogfish as **Harbor Halibut**, and I'm not sure why that very flattering name wasn't used. The government also made some advances in the market by providing samples to hotels under the name **Japanese Halibut**, and in both Maine and Halifax large quantities were canned under the name **Ocean Whitefish**, as well as **Seabass**. In the South it was called **Mustel**. Aside from Grayfish and its Southern moniker Mustel, all of the marketing names (and a few not mentioned here) are inaccurate, as the dogfish has no relation to any of the fish whose names it appropriated. All of this naming confusion aside, I'm still perplexed as to why

dogfish isn't good enough, as we eat plenty of catfish in this country without complaint.

In a 1916 fisheries bulletin, much is made of the availability of canned dogfish, which is heralded as "one of the lowest priced fishery products on the market." A 14-ounce can cost 10 cents at the time. Interest in this fish dropped dramatically after World War I as consumers returned to their traditional and more familiar foods. It was the advent and growth of a market for dogfish liver oil, a rich source of vitamin A, that returned dogfish fillets to popularity. Because the livers were so profitable, the fillets could be sold at very low prices and became a staple on the tables of poor families. In 1941 the invention of synthetic vitamin A dealt an immediate and crippling blow to shark liver oil fisheries, and thus the dogfish fell from our graces once again.

Dogfish.

As with all sharks, if not bled and iced immediately, the flesh of dogfish develops a strong and sour smell of ammonia, as the fish lack a urinary tract, excreting urea through their skin. This unpleasant-sounding characteristic is not a deal breaker, for, when treated properly, the meat will be free of any taint. Dogfish are also a very low-yield fish, having small loin-like fillets similar to that of a monkfish. Under their thick skin lies an attractive pearly white flesh, but a pinkish slimy film covers the fillets. None of this is particularly good marketing for a species, though if given appropriate effort, the fish proves to be worthwhile. The firm and meaty flesh of dogfish, forgiving in cooking as it maintains its moisture well, has a rich flavor more savory-briny than sweet, and is basically a better version of halibut.

When fresh, dogfish is always sold and served as skinless fillets, and oftentimes the thin purplish-pink membrane will have been trimmed. This membrane is very similar to that found on monkfish, and while it has no negative edibility properties, it curls when it cooks and becomes an unattractive dark gray. (Maybe this is why it was called Grayfish?) Though its flavor and appearance are very similar to that of many white fish, the dogfish does not flake easily, and in that way is again reminiscent of monkfish, though it is not nearly as dense. Its long, thin body makes for fillets that are, on average, about the diameter of a half dollar at the thickest part before tapering significantly toward the tail. To gain any reasonable yield the entire fillet must be used, and thus it is somewhat difficult to cook, given the range of thickness.

For the past few decades, dogfish have been subject of a small export fishery, as they are popular in the United Kingdom in both fresh and salted form. There they are known as **Rock Salmon** and are the main fish used for fish-and-chips preparations.

Dogfish is fabulous in chowders or stews. Its semisoft, cartilaginous skeleton makes for a delightfully aromatic yet richly textured broth, and in stews especially, it adds a gelatinous depth of body and structure without an overwhelming flavor. Dogfish exhibits a character that author Jane Grigson notes is reminiscent of the finest veal. It takes as well to the grill and broiler as to the pan. My favorite method is to poach it, and I think it reaches its culinary halcyon when

poached, allowed to chill in the cooking liquid overnight, and then marinated with a vinaigrette made from the liquid. The great cookbook author Evelene Spencer states that when so prepared it is "so firm and so finely textured that it can be cut into cubes like chicken breast." She goes on to state that "unless you wish the credit of serving a novelty, the salad will pass muster as a fancy, well flavored chicken salad, and will cost about ⅓ of the price of chicken." Please, don't do that.

Historically the product was preserved using a nearly identical method as salt cod. By many reports, enormous amounts of salt dogfish were labeled and sold as salt cod, with no record of any observation to the wiser. I find salt dogfish to have a better flavor and more delicate texture than salt cod, and I actually prefer it when preparing traditional salt cod recipes such as creamed or curried dishes.

OPPOSITE A catch of dogfish aboard the *Albatross*, Alaska, 1966.
ABOVE Dogfish fillets.

One way to replicate the flavor without the months-long curing process is to remove the head of a whole dogfish and split it down the spine, leaving the belly cavity intact. Coat with salt and lay it on a rack in the refrigerator. This technique is not to preserve the fish so much as to focus its flavor. Salting the fish for just one to three days is all you need to introduce the deep flavors and matured character common to salt-cured products. This method also adds days to the fish's shelf life, though it is still a perishable product. The next step is desalting it in slightly acidulated water before throwing it over a wood-fired grill or under the broiler, topped with a healthy pat of butter.

Dogfish take beautifully to smoking, whether dry-cured in salt or brined. Each method results in equally good outcomes, though dry-salting and smoking is best if you want to alter the fish's flavor with spices or aromatics like citrus. Brining and smoking is best for enhancing the natural flavors in the fish, though any aromatics can be added to lend subtle nuances. When hot-smoked over the course of several hours, if not a day, the smoke permeates the flesh and mixes well with the fattiness of the flesh, yielding a product that is, in my opinion, near equal to that of fine smoked salmon.

The skins of dogfish have long been used to make faux-leather products. The livers can be used like those of monkfish, seared like foie gras, salted and poached or smoked, then pounded with butter and herbs to make a uniquely flavored compound butter. I also like to pound raw livers with a mortar and pestle, keeping them very cold. When fully smooth, I season the paste with salt and lemon juice and then use it as I would butter, either to mount sauces or whisk into a soup or seafood chowder as a finishing touch.

Evelene Spencer mentions a fascinating use of immature dogfish eggs that I had never considered. She states that prior to fertilization, the dogfish eggs are nearly identical to those of a chicken and are a perfect stand-in for such when used to make puddings and pancakes. I can't imagine any baker eagerly seeking out dogfish eggs for an angel food cake, but as I have never tried it I must reserve comment. If you give it a shot, let me know how it turns out.

Dory

The John Dory ranks in the very highest echelon of European seafood cuisine. Though that fish does not swim in U.S. waters, we are blessed with the **Buckler Dory**, also known as **Silver Dory** and formerly as **American John Dory**. The **Mirror Dory**, a Pacific species, is practically identical to the Buckler Dory in terms of culinary qualities, and so I will treat them as equals herein. The Dory is a fish of great quality but sadly is not abundant in either European or American waters. Due to its rarity and very low edible yield, it has never supported an important fishery in the United States. Because it does not command much value, there is little incentive to develop a bigger market presence. The moral of the story is that when you see a Dory at the market, make sure it goes home with you!

In addition to the Buckler Dory there is a **Red Dory**, which is too scarce and small to be of any culinary use, and aside from these kin the Dory shares no relation with other fish. It is a unique-looking fish that would be pitied if not for the outstanding quality of its fillet. Its head, comprising a large percentage of it body, is mostly mouth and made up of a collection of small bones that when called to action extend forward and open nearly as wide as the fish is tall. This truly strange mechanism is a curiosity you might expect to find in an *Inspector Gadget* cartoon, and the rest of the body follows suit. Its extremely thin spade-shaped body is topped with 10 long Mohawk-like spines shooting straight out of the dorsal ridge, which itself is lined with plated armor, or scutes, running the length of the fish.

The leathery, paper-thin skin has microscopic scales and the look and tender texture of kid gloves. Its most distinguishing feature is a dark black spot behind its gill plate. Its base color is a faded silverleaf overlaid with shades of olive green, while its scales lend a nearly imperceptible golden sheen. Some people think it is this golden luster that inspired the original name of Dory—an appropriation of the French word *doreé*. The "John" was added later by the Brits (though the story is not relevant to the U.S. species).

Esteem of the Dory dates back to Roman era, when it was believed to have divine connections as the sacred fish of the god Zeus. It is from this legend that its scientific name of *Zeus faber* was derived. As time and empires passed, and people placed faith in anotherdeity, the Dory became part of a new

Buckler Dory.

legend. As is written in the Bible book of Matthew, Jesus instructed Peter to cast his line and from the first fish he caught pull a coin from its mouth. As the story of this miracle was told through the ages, the black mark on the Dory came to symbolize St. Peter's thumbprint etched forever on the spot where he held the fish. From this legend the name **St. Peter's Fish** became an oft-used alias of the Dory and one that has translated into all the various languages of the Mediterranean and northern Europe. I think it's no coincidence that St. Peter is also the patron saint of fishermen. Biologists interpret the mark differently, positing that it is a defense mechanism—its resemblance to a large eye may discourage predators, as well as confuse the fish and squid upon which it preys.

A fish of divine provenance, this agent of gods has a lot to live up to at the table. And deliver it does. Grigson complements it as "one of the most desirable of the creatures of the sea." Its very thin fillets resemble those of flounder, having an off-white color and a firm texture with fine flakes. It has a very shallow belly cavity and remarkably few bones, which are easily removed. When cooked, the texture remains firm and the color brightens to pearly white. It has a very shallow strip of dark muscle tissue with a more developed flavor that balances nicely and provides contrast to the mild and floral taste of the meat. The scales are extremely small and require no attention, and the skin augments the texture and taste while providing structural integrity to the fillet. The Dory fillets are somewhat unique in that they naturally separate into

three pieces; one being the belly flap, the others sectioned along a distinct line in the top loin. Prior to cooking, you must score the skin to prevent the fillet from curling away from the heat. The skin is delicious and has a gelatinous richness. Though the skin can be crisped beautifully, the amount of heat required to do so can diminish the nuance and character of the meat, and so I prefer methods such as poaching, slow roasting, and, my favorite, slowly sautéing it in a small amount of fat, cooking it through from the skin side up. This method gains the flavor that permeates into the meat from the skin while preserving moisture in the fillet. The skin can easily be removed after cooking by scraping it off with a knife, and this allows for interesting presentations when the pieces of fillet are stacked upon each other.

The Dory does not have a distinguished culinary history in the United States, so we must look to the great cuisines of the Mediterranean for inspiration. In the Venetian *pesce bolito*, the whole fish is very gently poached, and then the cooking liquid is fortified with gelatin, combined with mayonnaise and chopped fresh herbs, and spread over the fish. Served cooled, the coated fish makes for a truly elegant if antiquated delicacy. Generally speaking, the moderately lean and subtle flavor of this fish is best flattered by bright, fresh herbs such as tarragon and sharp accents of vinegar and citrus. The Dory is very well suited for soups and stews and in classic Provençal cuisine is one of the stars of a traditional bouillabaisse.

The average size of Dory at market is 12 to 18 inches and two to four pounds, though there is record of them reaching up to 20 pounds or more. Regardless of size the amount of edible meat on the fish is very low, about 30 percent of its whole weight. The upside to this is that the bones and head make a truly excellent stock. A whole Dory makes an impressive presentation when flattered by smoke; it needs a lengthy soak in a mild brine before smoking for up to two days over a low, sweet orchard wood fire.

Drum

The drum family includes some of our most esteemed food fish. The **Red Drum** of New Orleans fame, the **White Sea Bass**, **Atlantic Croaker**, and **Spotfin Croaker**, as well as **Seatrout** and **Weakfish**, combine to form an all-star team of fish species. Most drums are highly sought after by both recreational and commercial fisherman, and in many cases the majority of fish is landed by sport fishermen.

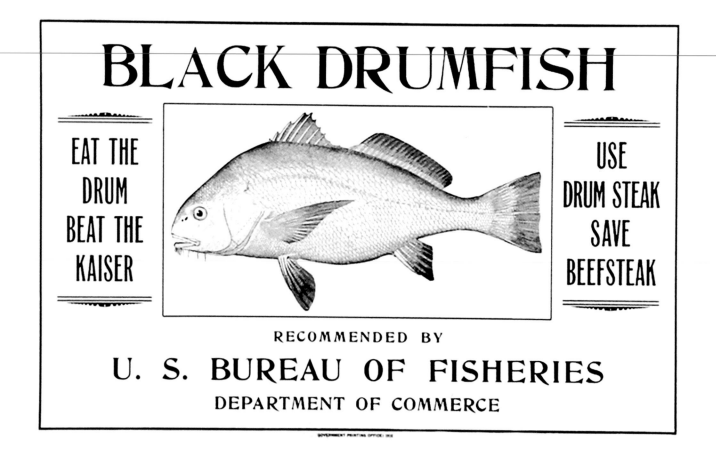

BLACK DRUMFISH

EAT THE
DRUM
BEAT THE
KAISER

USE
DRUM STEAK
SAVE
BEEFSTEAK

RECOMMENDED BY

U. S. BUREAU OF FISHERIES

DEPARTMENT OF COMMERCE

The drum family is so named because of the percussive-like sound these fish can make (by flexing a set of muscles) that is then amplified by the air bladder. When standing on land, it's possible to hear the sound of a single fish, so you can imagine that the chorus can seem positively otherworldly when a large school of drum swims by. The croakers are part of the drum family, and these fish are distinguished only by the nature of the sound they make—croakers croak, and drums drum.

An incredible diversity of species and a very wide geographical distribution exist within the drum family, and so its members represent many different culinary personalities. One common characteristic is that they tend to be rather staid in their appearance, many having a moping overbite look. The drums, both Red Drum and **Black Drum,** have important culinary and cultural histories associated with them. And the croakers, usually caught weighing an average of one to two pounds, are one of the most popular panfish and have a long history as subject of an important fishery.

The Red Drum is a fish of legend, thanks to chef Paul Prudhomme, who introduced the world to blackened Redfish in the early 1980s at his restaurant K-Paul's in New Orleans. Blackened redfish became the signature of K-Paul's and drew attention from gourmets and food writers all over the country, including Craig Claiborne, who declared the dish one "of the greatest inventions in this country." The glorification of blackened redfish coincided with (or helped fuel) the moment that New Orleans emerged onto the global culinary stage. The Red Drum is venerated in that city as few other seafoods are elsewhere.

While the label Red Drum is most commonly used along the Atlantic Seaboard, along the Gulf coast it's known as **Redfish**, **Spottail Bass**, or **Channel Bass**. Though the Red Drum can grow to be quite large, 75 pounds or more, much smaller fish are the norm. Most chefs, myself included, prefer the flavor and texture of fish under 10 pounds. These smaller fish are known as **Puppy Drum** and, more coarsely, **Rat Reds**. Larger fish, sometimes referred to as **Bull Reds**, are particularly popular with chefs along the Carolina coast for use in chowders and stews. The fish are covered in a thick layer of iridescent scales that, in the right light, cast a copper/bronze glow; hence, the name. The large scales are firmly attached but reveal beautifully patterned skin underneath.

As with many things in the South, a meal just isn't complete without a great story to accompany it. And so it goes that in the story of loaves and fishes, it is said that it was Redfish that Christ served to the multitudes. To forever remind us of that miracle, the thumbprint of Jesus was left upon the tail of the fish. That round black spot at the base of its tail fin is often the easiest and quickest way to identify it. (You'll notice many fish in this book lay claim to being Jesus' miracle muse.)

Despite Redfish's abiding popularity in the South, I've never felt that it possessed a unique flavor that set it far above other species. It is a fine food fish, at its peak in the late fall when it is full of meaty flavor, like Striped Bass, and having a soft texture but firm flake, like a perch. The fish's bloodline is compact and easy to remove but should be left in, as its mild flavor complements that of the fillet. The skin can be somewhat thick, especially on larger fish, and quite tough unless cooked properly, but it does crisp well. A healthy layer of subcutaneous fat both bastes the skin and moistens the flesh. Grilling unscaled fillets of Redfish or snapper is a classic Southern preparation known as "on the half shell." The scales protect the meat from the fire and add a unique perfume to the flesh as they char.

The layer of fat that lies along the dorsal ridge is a true delicacy and should be left on when filleting and included when preparing a dish such as court bouillon or chowder. The bones of the drum family all make good stock; the head and shoulders of Red Drum are particularly prized and make a fantastic dish in themselves when split, seasoned, and broiled till crisp.

Red Drum has long been an important species in the Gulf of Mexico, both as a sport fish and a commercial fishery.

After its blackened debut and meteoric rise in popularity, Red Drum was severely overharvested, and the populations were depleted. At the writing of this book, there are still restrictions and even moratoriums on wild capture, in fact most Redfish found on menus these days is a farmed product.

Red and Black drums are voracious predators of sweet-tasting, bottom-dwelling organisms—crab, shrimp, and mostly oysters. Drums can do incredible damage to oyster beds, wiping out entire areas in just hours. One of the great sights of the southern shores is to see the drums feeding in shallow waters, their tails sticking several inches into the air. As bottom-feeders, most drum family members are susceptible to parasites. Though the parasites are rarely harmful to humans, these fish should not be used for raw preparations.

Historically, the Black Drum was not favored, as its flesh was considered coarse, dry, and tasteless. Early fisheries for the Black Drum focused on salting the product, which added greatly to its flavor, or the fish were used for compost. Smaller Black Drum, those weighing less than 10 pounds, have a far more desirable flavor and texture. Tastes have changed, and Black Drum is now more widely appreciated (the disappearance of Red Drum helped open that door). The roe of any, especially that of Black Drum, is worth getting your hands on. They are delicious fresh, and sautéed as you would cook shad roe. When salted and air-dried, they also make one of the finer-tasting bottargas.

The Black Drum is the subject of a rather strange tale of Old World meets New. Dutch colonists settling on the island of New York in the early seventeenth century named the drum—a fish unknown in their homeland—*Dertien*, as referenced in a poem by Jacob Steendam. In singing the praises of Manhattan's rich environment, he refers to many species, including the shad (*Elft*) and the bass (*Twalft*). It is believed that Dutch colonists previously only knew 10 species of fish and, as they encountered new ones, simply named them by number—*elf* is 11, *twaalf* is 12, and *dertien* means 13. The Dutch have always been a practical lot.

The **Star Drum**, found along the Atlantic, Gulf, and Pacific coasts, rarely grows larger than eight inches. Though it is not

valued as a market fish, it is wonderful when smoked or cooked as a panfish (it's also blessed with a kickass nickname, the **American Star**). The **Sand Drum** of the East Coast, which grows to 14 inches, is a delicious fish sometimes landed as bycatch and is considered similar in quality to croaker.

Three species of **Kingfish,** a group of drums, are caught in the Atlantic and are defined by their geographical territories. The **Gulf Kingfish**, is also known as the **Sea Mullet**, overlaps somewhat with the **Southern Kingfish**, also known as **Southern King Croaker.** And holding down the northern territory is the **Northern Kingfish**. All of the kingfish are often confused with king mackerel, to which they have no relation. These fish are considered so similar in culinary qualities as to bear no distinction in the marketplace. They have a mild nuanced flavor and fine texture that encourages cooking methods such as poaching or steaming. Likely due to their moderate size (they rarely grow larger than two feet), these have never gained significant market importance, though there were popular fisheries for them in Long Island and the Chesapeake, where they've long been considered excellent food fish. A fourth kingfish, found in the waters of Southern California into the Gulf of California, is known as **California Corbina**. Almost always taken by sport fishermen, it is similar in qualities to the kingfish of the Atlantic. Note that this is not the same fish as **Corvina**, another drum, which is a popular food fish, due to its similarities to the Red Drum, caught throughout Southern California.

There are a few other drum species of commercial importance in the Pacific, one being the **White Sea Bass**. Also known as the **White Weakfish**, it is one of the larger members of the drum family. Though they can grow up to a hundred pounds and six feet in length, the minimum legal length is 28 inches, and the average fish weighs 10 to 15 pounds. In the early 1900s, this fish was reported to be the most important species in California. Its flesh is opalescent and glistening with fat. The texture is firm and dense, and its diet of crustaceans and fish add sweetness to its savory flavor. Its bloodline makes a sharp red contrast to the white flesh. According to Paul Johnson, the tender fillets can be gently grilled but are best suited to braising or steaming. He also notes that the skin is quite strongly flavored; I choose to remove it after cooking, as I like the flavor it imparts. These fish also have a uniquely large otolith, or ear bone, that was long used as wampum in Native American trade.

Though a member of the drum family, the **Spot** is singular in its qualities. These small fish (the largest growing to 1½ pounds) resemble a cross between butterfish and croaker. When I was a child, I wasn't a very versatile fisherman because I could never catch anything but Spot, as they are abundant, aggressive, and prevalent in the Chesapeake Bay where I fished. Historically, these fish are subject to cycles of fluctuating abundance, the cause of which remains unknown. They may be very scarce for years on end, then return so profuse as to cause trouble, as they did in 1925, when New York harbor was so overrun with Spot that they clogged the condenser pumps of the Brooklyn Edison Company, causing a blackout across the city. In an earlier instance, a sudden abundance coincided with the arrival of General Lafayette, on his 1834 visit to the country. Since then, they have carried the moniker **Lafayette Fish**. In the Carolinas, where they are also abundant, they were somewhat derisively called **Old-Wife Croaker**.

Spot's merit as a food fish has always been subject to debate. Some argue, me included, that Spot caught in more southerly waters lack flavor, while those taken in the north have a delicate and noble taste. Spot has historically been a very important food fishery, especially in the Chesapeake where, at its peak, nine million pounds were landed, though a large amount has also been used as fertilizer. As a food fishery it largely fed the poor, especially communities of freed slaves who moved north after the Civil War. In recent years the total domestic catch has fallen to less than six million pounds. Spot are best in the early fall, just prior to spawning, when their flesh is taut and fat. A good indication of their quality is the color of their belly: a pale-gold, butter color suggests the flesh is at its peak. These playful little discs of fish are covered in a dull silver skin with vertical brownish markings, seasonal and regional markings, and a single spot just behind the gillplate.

OPPOSITE Red Drum in search of oysters.

As Spot deteriorate quickly, they must be well cared for and iced immediately. These small fish are best prepared simply as panfish; the skin is well flavored and crisps beautifully. Dusted lightly with Wondra® flour or cornmeal, cooked in butter, and served with lemon, it makes a truly elegant dish that is easiest to eat with your hands like an ear of corn. When very fresh, they should smell sweet, with a hint of melon. Though they have a stronger flavor than most panfish, it is not overly assertive, similar to butterfish. I love to hot-smoke whole Spot over the course of 24 hours; this method retains all of the fish's fat and moisture while integrating the rustic flavor of a campfire. Spot caught north of Cape Hatteras tend to be larger than their southerly relations. Once a very important food fishery centered in the Chesapeake, these fish were so abundant as to glut the markets, with landings peaking in the 1940s at 57 million pounds, largely sold to inland markets. By 2014, total landings had decreased to eight million pounds.

The croakers, so-called for their plaintive moaning sounds, are another significant branch of the drum family. Present along all our coasts, some croakers grow over two feet long, though the vast majority of those caught are pan size. The most common, the **Atlantic Croaker**, known as **Hardhead Croaker** or **Golden Croaker**, as they turn autumn-hued near spawning, flood into nearshore waters in the spring and remain there through the fall, when they reach prime quality, having fattened and grown sweet during the summer's feeding. They are found along the Atlantic Coast, reaching into Texas waters, where it has traditionally not been targeted, though a trawl fishery has developed in recent years, which has greatly increased their presence and popularity in regional markets. Croakers' skin is thin but durable and crisps nicely. The meat is what I think to be the perfect white fish: mild, but with a slight tang and good texture and having moderate fat content, making them easy to cook, pleasant for beginners, and interesting for seafood lovers. Whole fish take beautifully to the grill but are also commonly steamed or pan-dressed and sautéed. In addition to the growing domestic market, they have been increasingly exported to Japan to make a fish paste called *Kamaboko*.

The remaining drums, a variety of modest-sized fish averaging just under a foot in length, include **Banded Drum**, **Reef Croaker**, and **Blue Croaker** caught mainly in Florida throughout the Keys, and the **Silver Perch** (which, despite its name, it is not a perch), also known as **Striped Croaker**. These abundant fish have each been important in various regional fisheries. Given that the drum family occupies a large geographic range, it is expected that they would have romantic regional names, such as in Florida, where the Atlantic Croaker is known as **Mademoiselle**. In Texas near the Mexican border, they are known as **Roncador**, which, in Spanish, means "snorer."

There are a number of croaker species in the Pacific, including the **Spotfin**, one of the larger species of the bunch, which grows up to nine pounds and is considered the finest in flavor and texture. Additionally there is the **Queenfish**, also known as **Herring Croaker**, the **Yellowfin** or **Catalina Croaker**, and the most northerly ranging **White Croaker**, a fish whose diet consists mainly of squid, octopus, shrimp, and crabs, which yields a pretty tasty fillet. Like the Atlantic, these are all very similar in being easy-to-use, easy-to-like fish. Pacific croaker tend to be at their best in late summer and fall.

There is a single member of the drum family found in freshwater, and it supports a fairly important fishery based in the Mississippi River system and Lake Erie. Though it has a number of common, mostly erroneous names, its only acceptable market name is **Freshwater Drum**, though it is known in the South as **Gasper Goo** or **Gaspergou**. Lacking the briny tang of its saltwater relations, it is otherwise quite comparable to weakfish in culinary quality.

Given the diversity of culinary qualities, physical characteristics, geographical range, and historic availability and prominence, the drum family seems an unlikely grouping, but the singular commonality is that its members all have something to say.

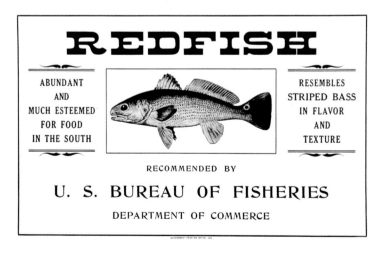

Blackened Redfish

With his amiable and outsized personality, Paul Prudhomme became the unofficial ambassador of Cajun cooking in the early 1980s. Best known to national audiences through his television shows, Prudhomme is widely credited, along with chef John Folse, for bringing one of America's most distinctive regional cuisines to the world's attention. In his restaurant K-Paul's, located in the French Quarter of New Orleans, Prudhomme introduced what was to become among the most recognized and celebrated dishes of the Cajun repertoire: the blackened Redfish. The dish was wildly popular and copied in restaurant kitchens all over the country. Demand for Redfish exploded, such that by 1987, due to depletion, a commercial ban was placed on fishing for them. Since then, the dish has morphed into a technique equally applied to just about any fish, and even now chicken and steak.

The technique for Prudhomme's simple dish calls for dipping fillets of native Red Drum in melted butter then coating them in a spirited blend of herbs and spices. The mixture includes paprika, cayenne, garlic powder, onion powder, thyme, and oregano, as well as white, black, and red peppers. The coated fish are placed in a screaming-hot cast-iron pan (by Prudhomme's instructions, the pan can never be too hot for this preparation) and then drizzled with a teaspoon of melted butter per each fillet. These are cooked for one to two minutes then flipped, and the process repeated on the opposite side. As you can imagine, the charred spices add a very special smoky perfume to the fish.

Eel

The **American Eel** is a unique fish made more so by its unbelievable life story. It is one of two freshwater eel species that live inland from the Atlantic. The other is the closely related European eel, and centuries of culinary and scientific intrigue have shown the two species are quite intertwined. Ancients were confounded by the reproduction of the eel, and theories of varying hilarity were posited by some of history's greatest minds. Aristotle mused that these "sexless creatures" must spontaneously emerge from the "earth's guts." Others speculated that they animated from certain drops of dew on specific days. As a young medical student, even Sigmund Freud published his first scientific paper reporting his efforts to find sperm or eggs in the thousands of eels he dissected. (There must be a joke in that.) I like how my friend James Prosek observes the Delphic eel as the "greatest beauty . . . the idea of a creature whose very beginnings can elude humans, and the potential that idea holds for our imaginations."

Of all the animal migrations on earth, that of the eel is among the most heroic, impressive, and improbable. All American and European eels begin their lives in the same place: the Sargasso Sea. There, in the swirling congregation, both American and European eels spawn, often overlapping, even interbreeding. The resulting offspring, translucent and thin as a wisp of hair, begin a journey from this remote saltwater sea toward their freshwater homes. The American eels self-navigate, laboring for about a year to reach their destination rivers that range from the Carolinas to the St. Lawrence. European eels have an even more implausible path to blaze, taking more than two years to navigate nearly a quarter of the circumference of the planet to reach the noble European rivers they'll call home. As for those E.U./U.S. hybrid eels, well, it only makes sense that they'd end up precisely in the middle, in Iceland. Eels on average will spend the next 9 to 25 years in their home waters before making the return trip to the Sargasso to spawn and die. This behavior—spawning in salt water and living in freshwater—is what defines a catadromous fish (the opposite is an anadromous fish, such as salmon).

Young eels, called **Glass Eels**, now one year old and wiser for their journey, make their continental arrival in early spring and begin ascending into the rivers. When they enter freshwater they begin to develop pigments to adapt to new environments and are now called **Elvers**.

In recent years they have become the subject of a fishery with lotto-like instant riches to be netted. While there is no domestic appreciation for them, these tiny creatures, numbering about one thousand per pound, are netted and sold live to Japanese and Chinese buyers at rates that approach the price of gold. Reared to full size, the eels are a staple in the cuisines of both cultures. The incredible wealth to be made has brewed a strange and unique fishery that resembles the madness of the Gold Rush, complete with its own culture of frontier justice. Fine mesh nets are strung across river passages, and weirs are built to trap the very small fish. Fishing sites are fiercely guarded areas, which can lead to sometimes violent confrontations. There has been great friction with environmental groups, regulators, and Native American tribes who (rightfully) assert their rights to the resource. Unfortunately the fishery has an associated carnival of social impacts resulting from the sudden influx of wealth in poor rural communities. I've heard tell of regions with no reasonable access to a doctor but which sustain a good business for several plastic surgeons, and there are more severe issues involving opioid use and the cancer of drug culture that takes over.

Glass Eels are considered a delicacy in Spain, where they are traditionally tossed into bubbling olive oil with chile and garlic, then served in the traditional *cazuela* (a stone or earthenware pot), the sauce finished with brandy and herbs. I had the opportunity to eat this dish when traveling through Barcelona, and while I may never again be able to afford such a luxury, it was so unique in taste that I will never forget it.

Those eels that make it past the initial gauntlet of mesh nets are identified by their colorations. **Yellow Eels** are those still ascending and beginning to grow. The designation **Bronze Eels** refers to those that have settled in and begun to mature. Years on, when they are ready for their final return journey to the birthplace, they are called **Silvers** or **Silver Eels**. The differing appearances offer no insight to the culinary character. Though they are interchangeable in most recipes, size may recommend one age of eel over another, depending on the intended use. The Silvers are considered the highest quality, as they have fattened up to endure travel to the Sargasso. They begin heading downstream in late fall, starting on a journey that might take up to a year. As part of this process, their physiology changes so that they no longer absorb water through their skin, as do freshwater fish, but begin to hydrate by drinking salt water through their gills and stomachs. This helps to purge any stagnant or off-flavors accumulated from surrounding waters.

Eel was an ingredient of distinction in America's early cuisine. In an impressive display, Squanto taught the Pilgrims how to catch eels from creeks and riverbeds, digging the fish out with his feet and catching them with his bare hands; in a few hours, he had as many as he could lift. To the hungry Pilgrims, the eels were a delicacy. A visitor two years later described them as "passing sweet, fat and wholesome, having no taste at all of the mud." Many settlers found comfort replicating their traditional meals using the bounty found teeming in America's rivers and streams. In the seventeenth and eighteenth centuries, eel was a staple food item found in such early American dishes as jellied eel, eel pie, and the rather nondescript and curious eel mash.

There has never been a consistent market for eels in the United States. The biggest demand is around the Christmas holiday, when many immigrant-American cultures celebrate with lavish meals brimful with myriad seafood, Silver Eel among the most anticipated and essential indulgences. Beyond this seasonal use, American eels have largely fallen from our graces and off our menus. In an era of formless foods with no obvious relation to their provenance, I can understand why the eel intimidates. They look like snakes, are often sold live, and stay alive for days. Though their tenacious vigor is a measure of quality, it also makes them a pain in the ass to kill and skin.

When cleaning an eel, you'll quickly know that they are covered with a layer of slime, which can make it hard to hold the thing. The easiest way to kill an eel and to get rid of the slime is to heavily coat the whole eel with salt and let it sit for two to three hours before scraping off both the slime and the skin. A more dramatic and humane method is to place the eel's head on a board that can be secured to a countertop or wall. Drive a sturdy nail directly through the middle of the head and into the board. Yes, the eel is killed instantly, but be warned: it will thrash around a lot and for a while. After either method of dispatching the eel, the skin can be removed by making a shallow incision around the neck just below the small finlets. Think of it just like removing the foil from a bottle of wine. Then using a pair (or two) of pliers, grasp the skin at the incision point and pull it toward the tail in a single quick motion. Remove the head and viscera, washing the cavity clear of any blood. You are now ready to cut it into whatever size or form your inspiration calls for.

Now that I've explained the less-pleasant aspects, here's why eels are so great.

While the American Eel ranges greatly in size due to age, an average specimen is usually two to three feet in length and weighs three to five pounds. The skin is often quite tough and distracting in texture, so it is usually removed (though it can add incredible richness and velvety texture to braised dishes). The meat of eel is fine-grained in texture and silken with moisture and fat, making it quite resilient to high heat. When cooked, the delicately flavored meat wilts away from the uncomplicated bone structure as would finely cooked pork spare ribs.

Eel is rich enough to be seared in its own rendered fat, and that fattiness is a perfect partner to acidic and bright ingredients. As eels are best flavored in the autumn, it is only proper that we celebrate them with other seasonal ingredients. Consider slowly stewing eel for hours with wine, vinegar, woodsy rosemary, bay leaf, and the sweetness of root vegetables.

I find that the flavor of eel improves if left to cool in the braising liquid to room temperature before serving, and I recommend allowing it to rest as long as overnight to then be served the next day. James Beard suggests this interesting combination: lightly pound the eel and coat it in sugar and cinnamon before breading it and broiling it until crisp.

My favorite preparation involves turning whole skin-on eels over a smoky wood fire, charring the outer membrane and allowing the rich flesh to baste itself with its own fat as it renders and drips. Smoke and eel are best of friends, and once the eels are cooked and removed from the heat, I bathe them in a vinaigrette of fried garlic and sage leaves tossed with pine nuts, orange zest, and a bitingly strong vinegar like Banyuls or sherry.

Smoked eel can be found in international markets and delis. The process to smoke them is similar to that used on most fish—the skinned bodies are filleted to remove the thin bones and soaked four to six hours in a heavy brine. After patting the fillets dry, I glisten them with Pernod or bourbon for flavor and to help dry out the surface of the meat (alcohol lowers the evaporation temperature of water) before slowly smoking them for 12 to 15 hours over orchard wood. At this point, it is ready to flake over a salad or, even better, get stashed into the broth of a simmering chowder, pea soup, or minestrone, where its smoky, buttery personality adds a haunting and deviant twist.

Though eel can be filleted, for home cooking it's often cut into small sections of three inches or so. These skinless (or skin-on, if stewing) barrels can be pan-sautéed, stewed, or seasoned and broiled or grilled. When you cook on the stovetop, I recommend that you use a very small amount of olive oil to help initially render the eel's fat. The acidic and spicy aromas of the oil fortify the confident, bold flavor of the eel and highlight its robust and macho personality. Cooking in butter is, of course, tasty, but the two ingredients are so similar as to diminish their charm as a couple.

Though the culinary character of American Eel stands alone, in the fish case it shares the company of many charlatans. The conger eels, a large family of churlish-looking creatures, deliver remarkably delicious fillets, despite appearances. Three species swim in U.S. waters, but only the **Conger Eel** and **Yellow Conger Eel** are relevant to the cook. Their gruff look has

OPPOSITE AND ABOVE Venice, Louisiana.

ASSORTING ENGLISH SOLE   BCF 784-25A
PHOTO BY BOB WILLIAMS
DATE: OCT.1969
LOCALITY: ABOARD THE LEMES   784 -25-A
          EVERETT, WASHINGTON

PREVIOUS PAGES, LEFT Hmong fisherman in Empire, Louisiana.　ABOVE Flounder fillets.

It is generally true that the flatfish of commercial and culinary value have similar flavor qualities, though their textures can be quite diverse. In most species, the fillets give slight resistance on the surface, with a firm, small, and yielding flake throughout. Size does matter (to flavor at least), and even within a single species size can range dramatically, and the flavor often differs in direct relation, for better or worse.

The fillets from the top, or colored side, of the fish are roughly 30 percent thicker than those from the underside. All flatfish benefit from what I call pre-conditioning, meaning salting the fillets lightly for 30 to 40 minutes before continuing with the preparation. This firms the flesh, making it easier to handle, and focuses the flavor. The skin of all flatfish has tiny scales that must be removed if you choose to serve it skin-on, though in most species only the scales of the top section need to be bothered with. The roes, milts, and livers of all flatfish are delicious and can be used in a variety of ways. In spring, pale orange flounder roes and the snow-white roe of soles can weigh up to a quarter of the weight of the whole fish. Evelene Spencer wrote that "the epicure might well consider a pair of flounder or sole roe equal in delicacy to a pair of sweetbreads." The livers are best dusted in flour, fried in butter, and finished with a squeeze of lemon or a dash of sherry. I often mash them with butter to mount into sauces or stir into fish soups or stews.

Across the board the flavor of flatfish is elegant, though by no means strong. Their flavors tend to be flat (pun intended), with a mineral and herbal character, but various species have different personalities. Though all species have distinguishing aspects, it is because of the widely shared similarities that they are recommended more as equals than as a category we seek for surprise and excitement. As such, they present a versatile canvas for other flavors and are ideally suited to pair with elaborate sauces. This tradition was born in French cuisine and exemplified by the popularity of the sole for which the great chef Auguste Escoffier wrote 180 recipes in his tome *Le guide culinaire*. That said, American flatfish, even those called soles, deserve nowhere near the esteem of the quality of the famed Dover Sole, turbot, or brill of European seas.

The **Arctic Flounder** and **Starry Flounder** of the Pacific coast are sometimes dismissed as only of fair quality, but as the great seafood writer Jay Harlow comments, "They have a distinctive, slightly grassy aroma and flavor, which is intensified if the fish is cooked with the skin on." These two fish tend to be slightly coarser in texture and have thicker fillets than most other Pacific flatfish. The Starry Flounder grows to as much as three feet, but the Arctic Flounder attains just half that size. Traditionally, indigenous tribes fished for these flounder and commonly ate them raw when on voyages.

The **Arrowtooth Flounder**, the largest fishery by volume of the Pacific flatfish, is a very distinct-looking fish with dark purple skin. It has an elongated head; sharp, protruding teeth; and very soft, pinkish-gray flesh. There has been little appreciation for these fish in the United States, as their already-soft flesh is further degraded upon death by a proteolytic enzyme released from a parasite within the fish. The fishery has served an export market to Russia and Japan, though recently food-grade additives that successfully inhibit the enzymatic breakdown have enabled production of fish sticks for sale in the United States.

The stars of the Pacific flatfish are the **Petrale Sole** and its similar relation, the **Rex Sole**. These have the firmest texture of the family and a charming floral aroma. They share a flavor that is nutty-sweet with hints of minerality, like a good Sancerre wine. The **English Sole** is similar to the Petrale Sole in texture and flavor, with the addition of a slight tang of iodine. It is also a far smaller fishery than the others, making the fish a find at market.

The **Pacific Dover Sole**, a sad imitation of the true Dover Sole of Europe, is a fish that's hard to like. Though it supports an important fishery on the Pacific coast, it is quite lacking in flavor and its texture is soft, best described as floppy. These fish are very difficult to fillet, as they wear a heavy coat of thick slime; hence, their moniker **Slime Sole**. As Harlow writes, "I wish I could find a way to like this fish."

The **Southern Rock Sole** and **Northern Rock Sole**, both economically important, yield only a fair-quality flesh that has limited uses due to its soft texture. The **Butter Sole** doesn't live up to its appealing name, as it is comparable in quality to the Rock Soles. The best preparation for these fish is poaching.

Curlfin Sole, the **Spotted Turbot**, and **Thornyhead Turbot** are considered excellent in quality, with an appreciably firm and fine-grained texture. They are more round in shape and have broad fillets of good thickness. While these fish are very much esteemed, none are taken in sufficient quantity to make them more than a minor market item.

The **Sand Sole, Flathead Sole, Yellowfin Sole,** and **Bering Flounder** are all major commercial species of parallel quality. They are good eating fish, but by no means standouts, as they have low-intensity flavor. Large quantities are landed, with most of the catch exported to Asian markets, where they are sold as frozen fillets.

Another group of flatfish, the sand flounders, includes the California Halibut (see page 233), and one of the most revered regional specialities, the diminutive **Pacific Sanddab** and **Longfin Sanddab** of San Francisco culinary fame. Though they can grow to two pounds, fish of these varieties are rarely landed that weigh more than a half pound. Given their small size there is but one way to cook them: on the bone, which helps to amplify their flavor. Fish expert Paul Johnson allays the trepidations of ichthyoanginaphobics—those with a fear of choking on fish bones—noting that once the fish are cooked the bones can be removed very easily. The fish must be eviscerated, trimmed of their fins, and scaled before preparation. James Beard wrote of them, "I can think of no other fish that is so delicately, subtly flavored." Italian immigrants likely deserve credit for elevating the Sanddab to culinary prominence with their traditional preparation of salting the fish before sautéing them in olive oil with slices of lemon and a copious amount of garlic.

In Atlantic waters, there are again a huge variety of flatfish species; most are caught in volume, many of them lumped together under **Flatfish** or **Righteye Flounder** in landing data. Of the commercially important species, leading in volume is the **Summer Flounder** and its close relations the **Southern Flounder** and **Gulf Flounder**. Together these are commonly known as **Fluke**, the name likely held over from the old Norse word *floke*, meaning "flat." These range in size from an average of three to five pounds up to 15 to 20 pounds, at which size they are known as **Doormats**. When large they have very thick fillets, and the whole fish are sometimes cut crosswise into steaks. Their flavor is more intense than other flatfish and considered

OPPOSITE Fresh flounder catch. ABOVE Deep-fried flounder.

to be one of the highest quality of all Atlantic fish species. These are the most versatile of the flatfish, equally good served raw, as sashimi or crudo, or trimmed and grilled over charcoal. They are well suited to almost any preparation, and they pair well with myriad flavors and cuisines. The name Summer Flounder comes from their habit of aggregating in nearshore waters in the summer, when they are easily caught in abundance. The Southern and Gulf flounders are both targeted species as well as significant bycatch of shrimp trawling.

The **Windowpane Flounder**, once considered unfit for human consumption, is so named because the flesh is thin enough to be translucent if held up to the light. Any culinary slight was in error, as this is a choice fish, among the sweetest of the flounders, though it must be cooked on the bone because to fillet it would yield pitiful strips of meat.

Winter Flounder, so named as it dwells near shore in the winter months, has many regional monikers that can be quite confusing, though they are used to designate size. Their flesh is very sweet and versatile, with a distinct shellfish flavor and a succulent texture. When under two pounds, their average size, they are often referred to as **Dabs** or **Blackbacks**, and it is best to cook them whole, roasted, grilled, or deep-fried. When more than three pounds, they are known as **Lemon Sole**; over five pounds, they are known as **Sea Flounder**. When they grow larger than six pounds, they are **Snowshoes**, which is exactly what they look like. Lemon Sole has gained market acceptance and so it's not uncommon for larger fish to be sold as Lemon Sole. As they grow larger, their flavor does not change, but their texture does become noticeably firmer. These are the only flatfish, other than halibut, that I find to be well suited for smoking. I like to smoke them whole, after scoring them deeply through the skin down to the bone. After four hours in a moderately intense brine, I cold-smoke them over orchard wood for 8 to 10 hours, then hot-smoke them for 45 minutes. The resulting meat is chewy and sweet with the fruity aroma of the smoke.

Witch Flounder, also known as **Grey Sole** or **Gray Sole**, is narrower than its cousins. The fillets of these fish are quite thin and delicate in texture, with a silver-gray hue. These are fragile when cooked and can be hard to handle. Recommended methods are cooking *en papillote*, rolled and poached, or steamed over spicy aromatics. The flavor is mild and slightly acidic but with the expected delicate flavor and sweetness of flatfish.

American Plaice, also confusingly called **Dabs**, are an increasingly important species in the New England ground fishery. Though they grow nearly three feet and up to 12 pounds, they average two to three pounds. They are a targeted species, but are also taken as bycatch in Haddock and cod trawls. Historically, flatfish other than halibut were shunned and in some locales, such as Boston, seen as unfit for consumption. While the flounders did not come into culinary vogue until the early 1900s, when the use of bottom trawls became prevalent, the American Plaice had always enjoyed comfortable distinction. Fishermen in Connecticut were known to hang the fish for two days to "dry," thus concentrating their reserved flavor. Their texture is snappier than most flatfish, thus making it a good option for a fish-and-chips preparation. Because of this quality, most of the U.S. catch is exported to the United Kingdom.

The **Yellowtail Flounder**, a very popular sport fish, is venerated for its eating qualities. Its texture is considered by some the standard to which other flatfish are held. A significant amount is landed in commercial fisheries from which this leanest of the common flounders are often filleted and sold regionally or frozen as breaded products. Other less-common flounders make irregular but memorable appearances at market, including the **Fourspot Flounder**, very similar to the Yellowtail Flounder. One of my favorites is the **Smooth Flounder**, also known by the name **Christmas Flounder**, because this fish would appear at Christmastime around Salem, Massachusetts, and in Casco Bay near Portland, Maine, and were not to be seen elsewhere or in other seasons.

The only true soles to swim in American waters are found in the southern reaches of our Atlantic coast. While none of these are valued as food, one species, the **Hogchoker Flounder,** historically enjoyed some regard at the table. It also earned a dubious reputation, as its very rough skin would choke hogs when farmers used the fish as feed.

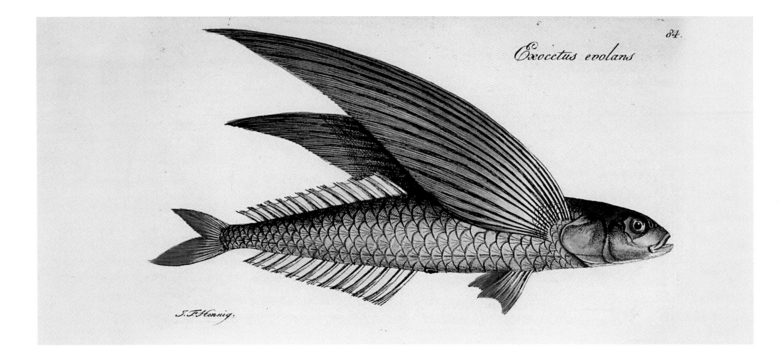

Exocetus evolans 84.

Flying Fish

In every family there's always at least one relative that's just a little different. In the fish family, it's the **Flying Fish**. Yes, fish with wings that employ spectacular bi-worldly gymnastics as means to escape predators, such a Mahi Mahi and tunas. They dart very fast just below the surface, then shoot upward, spreading their wing-like pectoral fins, to skim just above the water. Then, beating their tails back and forth across the water, they gain enough speed to attain liftoff and extend their ventral fins to "fly" higher. Flying fish have been recorded as covering more than 1,000 feet, though shorter travels soaring above the water for a few dozen feet are more common. This is truly one of the most delightful sights to be seen on the ocean. I was part of an expedition sailing from Portugal to Brazil becalmed for days upon days at sea with nothing but the horizon for company. Our oceanic meditation was broken periodically by the sudden, sporadic, and wholly improbable airborne appearance of these fish. This talent makes them difficult to capture on a large-scale commercial basis but entertainingly easy on a small scale.

Flying fish are attracted to light and at night sometimes launch themselves onto ships and through open portholes. Fishermen take advantage of this and attract them with lanterns to capture them in baskets once they land on deck. Gill nets are also used to snare the fish underwater.

A dozen species of these herring-like species are distributed throughout our oceans. They range from Massachusetts down through the Caribbean and up along the California coast into Oregon. They are schooling fish and highly migratory. Despite the vast geography they cover, they are remarkably parallel in flavor and use. They feed on phytoplankton and small crustaceans. Depending on the species, they range in size from 6 to 18 inches, and though there is not much commercial demand for the meat, some species are targeted for their roe. Their bright orange eggs are distinctively crunchy and are cured for use in sushi, known as *tobiko*. At one point there was a small commercial fishery for them in California that has since gone dormant. The only factor in determining quality of the meat is the size of the fish. Small ones are tasty too, but bigger ones are a lot easier to eat.

Their flesh ranges from white to light pink, with nice, firm flakes. It has a slightly cured taste with a somewhat sour, citrus aroma. It is not as oily as mackerel, but richer than a typical white fish. Given the strength and structure that their fins need for flight, these fish are bony, but they can be filleted and the bones sliced out with relative ease. They take well to any preparation for a small oily fish such as a herring or sardine, especially when marinated with citrus and fresh herbs, and they are perfectly paired with the smoke of a charcoal fire.

FOLLOWING PAGES Oyster skipjacks on the Chesapeake.

These fish are generally small in size, with Atlantic species, the **Yellow Goatfish**, **Red Goatfish**, and **Spotted Goatfish**, ranging just over a foot and weighing a couple of pounds. In Hawaii, several species, known collectively as **Weke**, are considered among the most popular fish. Some species, such as the **Kūmū**, grow up to 20 inches and five pounds, with other species growing near this range or slightly below. Smaller weke are sometimes salted for a few minutes before eaten raw or allowed to cure until dry. Another popular traditional Hawaiian preparation is to wrap the whole fish in tea leaves before broiling over hot coals.

One species swims along our Pacific coast, but its northernmost range is Southern California, and so it is not a common nor sought-after species.

I think goatfish's relative lack of popularity in the Atlantic is due to the availability of other abundant reef fish that are similar in taste and quality but are much larger, which creates a disincentive to market goatfish, as they are less profitable and attractive to fishermen.

Greenlings

Nine species of culinarily diverse greenlings swim in the Pacific, with populations mostly centered in the Pacific Northwest and Alaska. All are very colorful. Some are bottom-dwelling fish, and others swim farther up in the water column, taking refuge among kelp forests. Much like sculpin, they have oversized fan-like pectoral fins and enormous heads built upon intimidating jaws with menacing teeth. The fish's skin often mimics its environment and tends to be thick and rough, with a distressed leather look.

Greenlings have long been popular food and game fish on the West Coast. Historic records indicate that particular species were favored foods of First Nation peoples, as well as subject of important fisheries among Italian and Portuguese immigrant communities. From a cook's perspective, these fish are, with one exception, very similar to Pacific Rockfish, having dense, white flesh with large flakes.

Kelp Greenling is an important currently targeted species; it grows to a respectable size of just under two feet long. These were very popular among the Portuguese fishermen of Monterey Bay who called them **Bodieron**. The **Whitespotted Greenling**, which averages a foot and half in size, was favored by the early Italian community in the Puget Sound area, where they called the fish **Boregata**, and by Portuguese fishermen who called it **Mérou**.

The **Rock Greenling**, **Masked Greenling**, and the **Painted Greenling**, aka **Convict Fish**, are rarely caught and, when they are, die immediately once taken from the water. They do not keep particularly well; the meat becomes curt and rigid, and once cut, its flavor quickly oxidizes, developing a wet newspaper aroma.

The **Longspine Combfish** and **Shortspine Combfish**, the two being nearly identical, differ greatly from other relatives. These grow to only one foot in length, and while they're not a common food fish currently, First Nations peoples once prized their tender, sweet cream–scented white flesh.

The most popular of the greenlings is the **Lingcod**, which confusingly is neither a Ling nor a cod. These bottom-dwelling fish have white meat similar to that of cod and an elongated shape typified by the European Ling, which led unimaginative early biologists to combine both names, and it has stuck ever since. The Greek name for this fish, *Ophidon elongatus,* well details its likeness—*ophis* means "snake" or "serpent," and *odons* means "teeth."

Despite this fish having a significant presence in the diets of First Nation tribes, it was known in the native language as **Cultus**, a Chinook word meaning "little worth." When settlers of European origin arrived and identified their new surroundings by relating them to what they knew, cod was added to the name, thus the inception of the still-current moniker **Cultus Cod**. Any cook willing to see past this mashup name will find considerable qualities to recommend it. These are the largest of the greenlings, averaging 15 to 20 pounds, though they can grow up to 130 pounds. These tremendously strong fish live both close to shore and out in depths of more than 1,500 feet. They are voracious predators and will feed on almost anything, including

OPPOSITE Fishing the banks.

shrimp, squid, herring, and even salmon. Cultus Cod partisans consider it better than just about any fish of similar character. I agree. Similar to gar and Cabezon, their flesh is often greenish tinged, sometimes dramatically so (ichthyologist David Starr Jordan described it as "livid blue"—by livid did he mean angry or purple?), though it cooks pure white. Its very large flake makes it good for fish-and-chips, and its firm texture is well suited to grilling and broiling. Larger fish are often cut into steaks. I find that the flesh is best if lightly salted for an hour, then washed and dried before any preparation. That focuses the flavor and produces a more uniform texture and even cooking. Though these are relatively lean fish, they take well to light smoking; there is a tradition of Lingcod prepared in the "kippered style."

The Lingcod's large head and bones make a very rich and especially delicious stock. From larger fish, the heads either poached or roasted over thyme make an interesting meal, as they contain many different bits and textures of meat, including the well-developed cheeks, tongues and chins, collars, and the thin strips of fatty flesh that run along the top of the head between the eyes. The air bladders and tongues were traditionally salted, the cured product then soaked and sautéed with aromatics such as fennel seed, garlic, white wine, and herbs.

Medium-sized and smaller fish work well for whole roasted preparations. I stuff the body cavity with a mix of citrus wedges, olives, wine or table grapes, and croutons, all tossed with a healthy portion of olive oil. I make shallow slashes every few inches along the sides, then press rosemary or lavender into the fissures; I regularly baste the fish with a mix of butter and olive oil as it slowly roasts at 300°F.

Though the Lingcod supports an important fishery, it is dwarfed by the largest of the greenling fisheries, that of the **Atka Mackerel**. This fish is not related to a mackerel but earned its name due to similar culinary qualities, especially when salted. Though their range extends into Southern California waters, these fish are primarily taken in the Bering Sea and take the first part of their name from the island of Atka in the Aleutian Islands chain. They have long been extensively fished in American waters, mostly by foreign fleets, and they have never been especially popular or valuable in the United States. When our fisheries were nationalized, the American fleet took advantage of a ready market in Japan and, to this day, almost all of the catch is exported there. The Atka Mackerel is nearly identical to another member of this family, the beautifully named Arabesque Greenling, native to the waters of Japan and known as *hokke*. The most common preparation is to soak the salt-dried fish in a mixture of water and sake for several hours and then broil it. The salted fish make an excellent addition to chowder, providing a serious dose of umami. When fresh, the Atka Mackeral has a deliciously juicy texture and bright flavor that works well with smoke off the grill or char from the broiler. It takes well to marinades, especially ones with acidic ingredients and fresh herbs like mint and tarragon. Jordan complimented this fish as among the most handsome and flavorful of the Pacific coast. Despite his earnest and superlative-laced editorial, his prophecy that it would one day become the most popular fish sadly never came true. But it did become subject of a valuable and important fishery for the export market.

Grenadier

The nightmarish **Grenadiers** are fish we have little experience with. These derelict kin of cod are distinctively sharped with a very large head and oversized eyes, leading to the old nickname **Onion-eye**. The remaining body seems an afterthought, flaring backward from the head and ending in a whisper-thin rattail. There are several species of grenadier, also referred to as **Rattails**, swimming in the Atlantic and Pacific oceans. The **Marlin-spike**, a foot-long fish only caught as bycatch in trawls, is the only one of note in the Atlantic. In the Pacific, the **Pacific Grenadier** is the dominant species and accounts for about 90 percent of the catch. This fishery began in the early 1990s as these very deepwater-dwelling species had previously been beyond the reach of fishermen and conventional gear. Decline in other fisheries forced fishermen to target new species and develop new gear. In the early 1990s only a few fish were landed, but by the middle of the decade, the **Pacific Grenadier** was the fifth-highest-volume fishery in California. Landings have since plummeted, with fewer than 3 percent of peak catch landed in recent years. The five-foot **Giant Grenadier**, most common in Alaska waters, though very abundant, is not sought, as is the case with the more moderately sized **Popeye Grenadier**, **Shoulderspot Grenadier**, and **California Grenadier**. Many of their nicknames, such as **Pacific Roughy** and **Black Snapper**, are erroneous, however flattering, but Rattail, the most common nickname, aptly describes the fish's appearance.

In the Pacific, many species of grenadier are caught as bycatch of sablefish longlines. They were until recently used for surimi (imitation crabmeat made from fish paste) and fertilizer, which is a shame, as their diet of shrimp and crustaceans gives them a flavor worth celebrating. Low yields, averaging around 20 percent edible meat, further discourage use of this fish, as do its scales, which are so thick and dense they require mechanical removal. The flesh is fine-grained with a neutral intensity, iodine tang, and a shrimp-like sweetness. They have been appearing on more restaurant tables over the past few years as chefs have taken note of the quality and low price. Fisheries scientists are still trying to determine the number of these fish; while exact figures are debated, it is thought that the grenadiers are among the most abundant of all fish. Given that they are legion, tasty, and cheap, grenadier are likely to soon overshadow their famous cousin, cod, and become a household name.

Grouper

The **Groupers** are among the most likeable of fish. Their troupe casts a diverse range of characters, from the 700-plus-pound **Goliath Grouper** to others that only grow to pan size, such as the **Coney**. These relatives of sea basses are distributed along the Eastern Seaboard and throughout the Gulf of Mexico, with a few species swimming along our Pacific shores. Many groupers are protogynous hermaphrodites, meaning they are born male but change to female later in their life. They are incredibly intelligent, often loners and experts in camouflage.

As a sub-family, groupers are classified as Epinephelinae, from the Greek meaning "having clouds on it," which in a very Bob Ross way describes the beautifully patterned fish that are characteristically plump in shape, with very heavy bodies; their overall look can be best described as friendly.

The best-eating groupers tend to be smaller fish, as they can become fibrous in texture as they grow. Depending on where they live, larger groupers can accumulate a dangerous amount of ciguatoxin, a neurotoxin found in reef environments.

This is mostly a concern with some large fish caught south of the United States, as ciguatoxin is not present along continental U.S. coasts.

Groupers are, in my opinion, all-purpose fish, as their pearly white meat cooperates with just about any flavors and methods of preparation. There is nothing challenging about grouper's flavor, color, or bones that would put off an apprehensive fish eater. Their bone structure is relatively simple, making them easy to fillet. Their skin is oftentimes very bitter and should be removed before cooking, as it can influence the flavor of the flesh. The meat tends to be lean, exceptionally firm, and snappy textured. It is prone to drying out and becoming coarse if cooked over high heat. Better preparations include pan-roasting, deep-frying, poaching, and gentle sautéing. Grouper is particularly good in chowders, soups, stews, and braises.

Their firm white fillets have what is best described as heft in their thickness, a trait that is mirrored in its hearty culinary character. Each of the individual species has unique qualities and culinary characteristics, but all groupers are similar enough that the best type for any recipe will be the freshest-looking specimen. When fresh, they have a mild ocean-breeze aroma with a moderate flavor that is initially sweet-briny followed by a sharp and sometimes sour tang and a lingering flavor similar to clams. Their bones and heads make for a particularly resonant and well-flavored stock that adds fullness to chowders or stews.

The vast majority of grouper is caught in the Gulf of Mexico, though there are significant fisheries in the Carolinas and throughout the Southeast. Pacific fisheries are relatively low volume, except in in Hawaii, where the fish are highly valued and important in the traditional cuisine.

Historically, these have been difficult fisheries to manage, as multiple species are caught in the same areas along with many other species such as snapper, tilefish, and a host of others. In the 1970s and 1980s, fisheries were significantly depleted, and that pattern continued into the 1900s until a new fisheries management program was implemented; since then stocks have recovered remarkably. Some species such as the **Goliath Grouper**, aka the **Jewfish**, have been fished to levels where they remain significantly depleted. This is true for

SPECIAL TODAY

GROUPER

Recommended by

United States Bureau of Fisheries

some of the smaller species as well, and it's worth referencing a sustainability guide before purchasing any grouper.

Red Grouper is the most common and accounts for the majority of landings, sometimes nearly 70 percent. There's a significant history and love for these in the Carolinas, but the vast majority of them are landed in Florida, which is the epicenter of the grouper industry. The Red Grouper can grow up to three feet, but the average size tends to be half that. Though they are called Red Grouper their color is more rusty or mottled brown, or as sport fish expert A.J. McClane describes it, "a somber coloration." Groupers are known to be very tenacious in clinging to life, staying alive for hours on the hot deck of a boat. This vigor made them a perfect fish to develop as an export trade, when they were abundant but not in demand locally. Smacks, or well boats, would load up with live fish and ship them from Florida to Havana, where demand was high, and prices were too. Red Grouper is leaner and softer in texture than other groupers but is very similar in flavor to **Black Grouper** and **Gag Grouper** (often misidentified and sold as a Black Gouper). These are larger than the Red, growing up to 40 pounds, though at that size their meat becomes coarse and tough. Smaller fish, those under 10 pounds, are considered the best.

The **Yellowedge Grouper** ranks second in landings to Red Grouper and supports important commercial fisheries. The

ones typically caught weigh 5 to 10 pounds. The Yellowedge Grouper has a more compact and flaky flesh than that of the Red or Black grouper, more akin to snapper, and is one of the most prized fish in the Gulf.

The species considered the very best grouper, which is the standard to which all other groupers are held, is the **Scamp**. Averaging three to five pounds (though sometimes as large as 20 pounds), these are the best tasting and most versatile of the family. Their flavor is a bit more pronounced, with greater sweetness and an uncommon vibrancy. And unlike many other groupers, the crab-like flavor and texture of the Scamp is of equal quality at any size.

Another important commercial species is the **Snowy Grouper.** In size and texture it is equal to the Black Grouper, but it has a slightly more pronounced shellfish flavor.

Some of the most abundant and smallest groupers are the Coney, **Sand Perch**, and **Graysby**. Usually less than a foot in length, these all make excellent panfish. My favorite preparation is to braise them whole in a white wine broth seasoned with woodsy thyme and lemon. Unlike other groupers, the skin of these fish is neutrally flavored and thin enough to serve. Despite their abundance, these are not fished to any significant extent. On the Pacific coast the confusingly named **Gulf Coney** is far larger, growing up to four feet; it is likened to the Black Grouper. Though rarely seen at market, it is considered a premium fish and demands an equally premium price.

Of the many other species of grouper the **Yellowmouth, Western Comb**, **Tiger**, **Nassau**, **Misty**, **Yellowfin**, and **Marbled Groupers**, as well as the **Spotted Cabrilla**, a Pacific species, are all fished at moderate to low levels or not at all due to their scarcity or endangered status. Though I have not tried all of them, they are generally equal in size and culinary character, and they are all considered to be excellent food fish.

The **Warsaw Grouper** is a very deepwater species that can attain weights of 450 pounds or more, though average size of this fish at market is only 20 to 50 pounds. These are the fattiest of all the groupers, making them the only species I've found suitable for grilling. Despite their large size, their flesh is still elegant in texture with an oppulant butter-crab-cream flavor.

Another three groupers known as the **Hinds** are the most visually expressive of the family, having equally charismatic culinary personalities. Unfortunately, they are rarely found at market outside of Florida and the Carolinas. All of the hinds are more popularly known by alternate but accurately descriptive names. The **Rock Hind** is known as **Calico Grouper**. Thanks to its bright sunset-red body dotted with red and orange spots, the **Red Hind** is also known as **Strawberry Grouper**. My very favorite eating of the grouper family is the **Speckled Hind**, which is also known as **Kitty Mitchell**. The story behind this name is as colorful as a Bahama shirt worn in the Florida Keys, where legend has it that a lady of the night named Kitty Mitchell was so fond of this particular fish that she was known to trade her services for a meal of it.

Another fish with a great name is the **Star-Studded Grouper** of the Pacific coast. Though not commercially sought, it is a bycatch of shrimp trawls and is taken in minor quantities in subsistence and recreational fisheries. The **Broomtail Grouper** also swims the Pacific coast from San Francisco on south and supports a minor commercial fishery.

The **Atlantic Creolefish** and **Pacific Creolefish** are schooling fish that swim closer to the surface than most groupers, which mostly dwell near the bottom. The two fish are virtually identical, average about one pound in weight, and have a coloration and body shape similar to that of a snapper. Their flavor is equal in quality to snapper, though its texture is denser, with a brisk bite like that of triggerfish. Only a minor amount of these fish are landed, usually as bycatch of snapper fisheries. Given the abundance of creolefish, there is great potential to develop a targeted fishery. They are perfect panfish and great for whole roasting. The only drawback is their tiny scales, which are so firmly attached that the skin must be removed before serving.

The **Hawaiian Grouper,** locally known as **Hapu'upu'u,** is a very popular fish on the Islands, where 5- to 30-pound specimens are targeted or taken as bycatch of snapper fisheries. It has the most delicate texture of all groupers and is particularly well suited to steaming, slow roasting, and poaching. Hawaiian grouper are also very popular in soups, as the heads and bodies make a clear and excellently flavored broth.

Kitty Mitchell.

Though the grouper fisheries have been around far longer than modern refrigeration, they were always eaten as a fresh or market fish, as they are not particularly well suited for salt preserving or smoking.

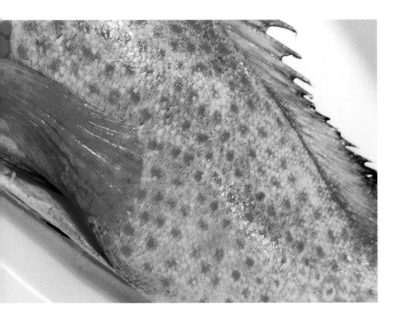

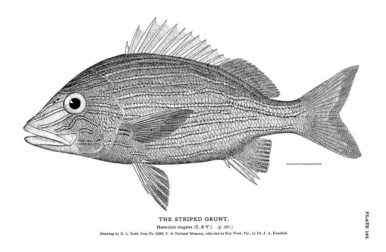

THE STRIPED GRUNT.
Hæmulon elegans (C. & V.). (p. 397.)
Drawing by H. L. Todd, from No. 32002, U. S. National Museum, collected at Key West, Fla., by Dr. J. A. Henshall.

PLATE 145.

TOP Strawberry Grouper.

Grunt

The Grunt family proliferates around the globe with more than 150 species. In our waters, the only species that are both abundant and large enough to be of any commercial or culinary value are found in the Atlantic.

Grunts are related to snapper and are considered by many to be the miniature cognant to that culinary icon. They earned their name, as they habitually grind their pharyngeal teeth, the sound of which amplifies off the swim bladder into a surprisingly audible bellow. It's a sound that has long been described as, well, a grunting noise.

Among the 15 species of commercial significance in America, all are colorful and ornately patterned fish.

Nearly every grunt is adorned with beautiful stripes—some with Caribbean blue overlaying a brassy yellow body, another patterned with vertical stripes of wavy yellow and scales with a silvery blue center and bronze margin. My favorite is the **Cottonwick**, which has a pearly white and silver body with lanes of bronze paving its length. The dorsal fin is jet-black but bleached nearly colorless at its edges. The black of the dorsal ridge spills onto the silver body, leaving a thick stripe continuing to the forked tail.

For all culinary purposes grunts are interchangeable as long as they are of similar size. The **Spanish Grunt, Caesar, Thick Lip, Porkfish, Pigfish** and its derivative **Piggy, Harlequin Grunt, Flannelmouth, Redmouth,** and **Sailor's Choice** (so named because any sailor, if given a choice of fish, would likely select this one) are but a few of the delightful names. Many of them are not accepted market terms but nonetheless provide an interstice revealing these fishes' storied past.

The two largest grunts, the **Black Margate** and **Margate,** are as timidly costumed as this family gets, having glowing silver sides marked with dusky bands and black fins. When fresh from the water they are something to behold, though their bright silver quickly dulls to amber brown.

Many species are categorized and used as panfish, as their average size is generally no more than one to three pounds. By some histories, these were considered the most esteemed food species along our southern coasts. Since their heyday in the mid-1800s their popularity and presence at market has decreased significantly. Despite this, grunts have remained relevant and in our modern day they bear a multitude of historical names as ornamented as the coloration of the fish themselves.

These fish were never widely targeted nor caught in quantities sufficient enough to supply national markets. I've seen historical reports stating that the pompano, mackerel, and Bluefish all rank a distant second to the grunt. I suspect it to be a reflection of local traditions rather than relevence to national consumer preferences, and this is supported by figures of volume and value of fish landed, including where they were sold.

But in those regions where grunts were popular, especially in the South, they have been enshrined as part of the area's culinary and cultural legacy. For example, when H.M. Flagler began the impressive task of constructing a railroad connecting mainland Florida to Key West in 1905, the vast teams of laborers hired to lay tracks were fed from the abundance taken from local waters. The daily menu was not a diverse one, and the dish "grits and grunts" was ubiquitous. But over time, this begrudged staple has become a celebrated classic. In our present lexicon, this dish, and even the expression "grits and grunts," recalls a bygone era of Southern history imbued with the charm and idyll of the region.

Grunts have a moderately bony structure, making them somewhat tough to fillet. As they are related to the snapper, it's not surprising that their flavor is comparable to that fish. All grunts have clean, white flesh with a small flake and a pleasant and delicate texture. Their flavor, especially that of the most esteemed members—the Porkfish, Pigfish, and **White Grunt**, earns high praise for its sweetness, a result of a crustacean-heavy diet. There are those in gastronomic circles who'd argue a grunt at its finest makes better eating than a snapper of equal freshness. The texture of grunt is not as firm as that of its more popular cousin, but this greater delicacy is favorable for grilling whole fish after an acidic herb marinade. A.J. McClane recommends deep-frying them until crisp, then gnawing them from the bone as you would a chicken leg. The grunt's distinguishing sweetness is magnified by baking the fish in a salt crust. And they are particularly good cut into steaks,

then stewed as part of a New Orleans–style court bouillon or bouillabaisse. As a panfish it excels, either dressed or as fillets, and when lightly dusted with cornmeal and then fried in bacon grease or lard, it hearkens back to those railroad days—a celebration of a fish that made the South proud.

Halibut

Of all the flatfish, the easiest category to describe is that of the halibut, in which there are four in our waters. The **Atlantic Halibut** and the **Pacific Halibut** are the largest of all flatfish, sometimes weighing 700 pounds and measuring nine feet in length, but the majority of these fish are 30 to 80 pounds. Smaller **Chicken Halibut** (either an Atlantic Halibut or a Pacific Halibut), as they are known in the marketplace, weigh from 2 to 20 pounds and have long been considered the finest representation of the species, if not among the finest of all fishes. The flesh of halibut is lean with large, curved flakes and makes exceptionally thick fillets. Sometimes it is opaque white; other times, a glassy, translucent white with a touch of sea green. Distinguishing between Atlantic Halibut and Pacific Halibut is more a matter of the individual fish than the ocean it swims in, as they are so similar that most experts would be hard-pressed to discern the difference. All fish show some variation within a single species, but I've found that with halibut there can be such a dramatic difference between individuals of the same species that they seem a completely different species. The fish are ever interesting, as there is always a subtle nuance to be detected. Taking this even further, the fillets from the topside of these fish can taste quite different from those taken from the bottom.

Another Pacific species, known as the **California Halibut**, is in fact a giant flounder, not a halibut, though for all culinary and market purposes, it is associated as such. These fish differ greatly from the Atlantic and Pacific Halibut and are considered lesser in quality. They are significantly smaller, growing to only 60 pounds, though the market average is 10 to 20 pounds and their flesh is somewhat light green in color. It is a decent fish that gets caught in the middle: larger California Halibut are inferior in texture and flavor to smaller Atlantic and Pacific halibut, and smaller California Halibut are inferior to larger soles and flounders. They are perfectly good fish, but

Fletches of salted halibut on the flakes before going to smoke house, Gloucester, Massachusetts, c. 1885.

they are never the best choice. Their texture is tighter than other halibut, with a more muscular, close flake. These were once known as **Bastard Halibut** or **Monterey Halibut** and are commonly sold indiscriminately as a substitute for the Atlantic and Pacific Halibut.

The remaining species, **Greenland Halibut**, is found in both the Atlantic and Pacific oceans. These are smaller fish, ranging 15 to 30 pounds, and are very dark in color on both the top and bottom sides, with thick skin. These are highly abundant in the northern seas, where there are large-scale commercial fisheries targeting them. Both the Pacific and the Atlantic Halibut are very lean, with two grams of total fat for every three-ounce serving, and the California Halibut is leaner still. This is in stark contrast to the Greenland Halibut, with a fat content so high—about 10 percent—that Harlow related it to the Sablefish or Chilean Sea Bass. Its texture is also the densest of the group, with strong musculature that lends itself to chowder preparations or braising; when exposed to high heat, it can become very dry.

The **Pacific Cherry Halibut** is not a separate species but rather a unique subset of the Pacific Halibut. A migrating fish, the Pacific Cherry Halibut is so named because of its red-tinged bottom, thought to be the effect of rubbing against deepwater red corals. These very muscular, medium-sized fish are considered by fishermen to be the very best eating. You're unlikely to find these at market specifically, but if you ask halibut fishermen, you'll be in his or her good graces as one of the cool kids.

When halibut are at their peak, the flavor will be mild with a somewhat gamey aroma punctuated with a fresh, bright, herbal smell, though its personality fades and becomes stale pretty quickly. Its flavor is not complex, with a very slight brininess, a hint of sweetness, and noticeable sourness. Halibut feed on a wide variety of fish, lobster, and crabs, leading one to think their flavor would be more intense. Though they have an important place in culinary history and remain very popular to this day, they are not a very culinarily charismatic fish. The great writer M.F.K. Fisher scorned, "I always thought halibut a strong and meaningless fish." Female halibut grow larger than the males and are considered to be overall better food fish. The great benefit of finding female halibut is using the roe, which is as good as roe gets, either cured and smoked or sautéed in butter and herbs. The cheeks of all species of halibut are wonderful and very different from the fillets, as these sometimes softball-sized muscles have a sinewy texture that, when braised, becomes quite elegant. The halibut liver is another treasure, milder in flavor than those of most white fish and quite large. It can be cut into steaks and quickly pan-seared as you would foie gras. Halibut do need the addition of both sweet and sour flavor components to bring their personality into full focus. The skin, head, and bones make a very good but basic stock that is bright and honest in flavor. My preferred way to use the often very large bones is to very slowly roast them at 175°F until they are cooked through, about two hours. Then I begin the traditional process of simmering them in water and wine, as this yields a stock of the purest flavor and character.

Halibut are best prepared using low- and medium-heat methods, such as poaching or steaming. High heat can destroy the texture, leaving a coarse and fibrous fillet. The skin is edible, though the heat needed to crisp it sufficiently will sacrifice quality of the flesh. When poaching or steaming, it's best to leave the skin on, as it infuses flavor into the flesh and adds body and gelatin substance to the poaching liquid.

Halibut can be cut in many ways, as they have four long fillets, two each on top and bottom. Very large fish are cut into four sections and then again into long four-inch wide strips known as *fletches*. One unique feature of halibut is that, given the thickness of large fillets, it is possible to cut portions that are perfect cubes. Though this doesn't make it taste any better, it does make for a fun presentation. Smaller fish under 30 pounds can be cut crosswise into steaks or simply into thick blocks.

Chicken Halibut is commonly called for in classic culinary texts, which show a distinct preference for these young fish. Some recipes suggest a two-pound fish be prepared whole, though most recipes call for a four- to six-pound fish, at which size they are cut into steaks. But at that size, I find many of the flounder species to be far superior to very young halibut. They are so young at that point that they haven't had time to develop any flavor, but I guess that's the point—the veal of the sea.

FOLLOWING PAGES, LEFT Dickering on the dock, c. 1950.
FOLLOWING PAGES, RIGHT Fisherman aboard an ice-clad trawler, c. 1930.

New York City mayor Fiorello LaGuardia poses with a 300-pound halibut at the new Fulton Market, 1939.

Given halibut's modest culinary personality, it proves to be quite a versatile fish, providing canvas for a canon of classic French sauces, as is true of its relatives the soles and flounders. In the Pacific Northwest, long strips were dry-cured and cold-smoked into a jerky-like product. And quarter fillets can be cured with great results in a gravlax style. The great James Beard had a unique method to enliven what he plainly considered a somewhat dull fish: first he dipped steaks in lemon or lime juice, then in flour, then dipped once more in the citrus before coating them in fried bread crumbs and gently sautéing the steaks in butter.

Given the high fat content of the Greenland Halibut, it makes for a very good hot-smoked fish, prepared as you would salmon, either in a moderate brine with salt and sugar or a dry-cure before a long, slow hot-smoke over the course of many hours. Orchard woods are best for this, as any wood with significant tannin or bitterness can draw out a strong iodine flavor in the fish. My favorite of all preparations for halibut is cured and marinated halibut fins. Under the skin and between the fins and the fillet lie strips of cartilage embedded in a thick layer of gelatinous and fatty meat. While these can be removed and pan-fried straight from the fish, I tend to lightly salt them and let them sit for two days before rinsing and gently pickling them in a strong broth of Pernod, vinegar, sugar, and spices. They are delightful eaten fresh from the pot but are at their best if allowed to chill in marinade for 24 hours and served at room temperature. They are also great smoked. Halibut fins are not new to the culinary lexicon. Captain John Smith in his *The Generall Historie of Virginia, New-England, and the Summer Isles* wrote of an abundance of halibut so large that two big men would struggle to haul them aboard. He related that, as was common to the wanton waste of the day, they would eat only the heads and the fins, considered the choicest parts, and throw the bodies back to the sea.

Halibut were considered a nuisance in the early days of cod fishing. They do not salt particularly well and there was no opportunity to sell them fresh because of the length of the voyages. In 1835, a well boat (also known as a smack boat) delivered the first shipment of live halibut from Portland, Maine, to the Boston market, and it instantly became a hit—the market for fresh halibut was born.

Halibut, along with other bottom-dwelling flatfish, can have their quality diminished by two factors. One is when a buildup of lactic acid causes the flesh to become "chalky" or opaquely white. Though this chalkiness has no impact on the wholesomeness of the fish, it does reduce the moisture retention of the flesh. Lactic acid is produced by physical exertion and can be exacerbated by high temperatures. This is a very rare occurrence, but halibut caught on longlines, if left to fight against the hook for hours, can cause the onset of this condition. This condition is most prevalent in fish caught in August, when the waters tend to be at their warmest, though the overall occurrence is less than 5 percent. When cooked, a "chalker" has a normal flavor, though it is drier and mealy in texture. Unfortunately there is no way of discerning a chalker in whole fish form, though experts can detect signs of it by the coloration of the flesh.

The second issue affecting quality is a common parasite that infects a wide range of species; it is harmless to the living animal (and to humans), but it destroys the flesh postmortem. These parasites release a proteolytic enzyme, which causes myoliquefaction, a process that softens the flesh to the point that it dissolves when cooked. Similar enzymes are commonly used in culinary applications in the form of meat tenderizers, the most common being papain, an enzyme extracted from papayas.

There are several theories on the origins of the name *halibut*, the most obvious and likely being that it is the combination of ancient English terms *haly* (meaning "holy") and *butte* (meaning "fish"). All evidence aside, I prefer to believe the rather humorous New England legend that halibut is a shortening of "haul-a-boat," which fishermen claimed was the sure and proper name, as it referred to the size and strength of these fish. Halibut fishing in early days was quite dangerous. Though they were once abundant in the nearshore waters of the Gulf of Maine and Massachusetts Bay, they began to be fished farther and farther offshore. Fishermen fishing in small dories would hand-line for these fish, and if a giant fish caught hold of their hook, the men would be taken on what was known as a "Nantucket sleighride," their boat being helplessly towed behind the angered fish. Even after the fish had been subdued and brought next to the boat, hauling aboard the monster, which could weigh hundreds of pounds, was no small feat; one ill-timed flap of its tail could kill a man.

Herring

A.J. McClane wrote: "To eat a herring is to savor history." This appraisal is backed by many authorities. Goode writes: "The herring family contributes more generously than any other group of aquatic animals to the support of man, and the herring is beyond question the most important the food fishes." Given such an introduction, it's hard to believe that herring barely registers on our culinary radar and that its fisheries are now almost exclusively for bait.

Herring is derived from the Germanic term for "host" or "multitude," though some say it's from an Anglo-Saxon word meaning "army." The name bestowed speaks to an unimaginable abundance of these shoaling fish. According to David Starr Jordan, a single shoal of herring was once measured at more than six square miles and estimated to contain at least half as many herring as the whole world caught in 1890.

For most of history herring were one of the most important food fish in Europe and the United States, while also having equally important market as cured products for export, bait, and fertilizer fisheries. In America, herring was mostly used for industry until the mid-1800s. The fish were first steamed in wooden boxes, then pressed to expel their oil. The meal was used as fertilizer; the oil, for everything from industrial lubrication to lamps.

It was not until 1875 that the Franco-Prussian War, having disrupted the importation of highly esteemed French canned sardines, caused investors to look to Maine for opportunities to develop canneries to meet the demand. In that year a single cannery began operating and packed 60,000 cans of small **Atlantic Herring** labeled as "sardines," a standard term that legally applies to 21 different species of small silver fish. By 1880 there were 18 canneries operating, and within the next two decades 23 more would open. Though they were advertised as another fish, the herring had finally earned a prominent place in our economy and our cuisine. By 1950 there were 50 canneries operating in Maine, and during World War II these had produced 80 percent of the canned fish rations that fed our troops.

FOLLOWING PAGES, LEFT Herring spawn on kelp.
FOLLOWING PAGES, RIGHT Promotional comic book, 1967.

But it was not long after peace rang clarion that the effects of changing water temperatures, overfishing, and the introduction of ever-more-efficient technology led to the collapse of the herring industry. The once mighty canning industry that dotted the New England coast limped along as the domestic market for canned sardines decreased. Attrition forced the closure of a majority of these canneries, and by 1975 only 15 were still operating. On April 18, 2010, the Stinson Plant in Prospect Harbor, Maine, the last cannery, closed its doors.

There are many species of herring, each having numerous historic and regional names. The two most notable species, the Atlantic Herring and **Pacific Herring**, are virtually indistinguishable from each other and are the most important commercially targeted species. These are both **Sea-Run Herring**—meaning they spawn in the ocean, in opposition to their many anadronomous relatives that migrate from salt water into estuaries and rivers to spawn. The huge volume of the fishery for Atlantic Herring, also known by the charming name **Silver Darlings** and the more utilitarian **Ocean Herring**, is conducted offshore using trawls, which damage many of the fish, but this is not a concern, as the catch is almost exclusively used for bait. Sea-Run Herring travel in huge shoals in the open ocean, feeding on microscopic organisms and in turn are themselves lunch for myriad predators. They typically reach a maximum length of 18 inches and top out at about 1½ pounds.

The Pacific Herring migrate near shore for their spawning events, which comprise such a magnificent multitude of fish setting their spawn adrift that vast expanses of ocean are recast in milky-white clouds of procreation. Shorelines are concealed, and nearby fronds of giant kelp are laminated with layers of deposit. First Nations tribes long ago discovered how to capture this incredible food source. They harvested the long blades of kelp and hung them onshore; the sticky coating air-dried until it was a caked, powdery dusting. Though the huge majority of this product is now exported to Asian markets, there is a long history of it in indigenous cuisines as well as emerging interest from new generations of chefs rediscovering regional foods. The dried roe adds mild creaminess and a delicate sweetness to the kelp's deeply satisfying umami-heavy flavor and minerality. To prepare it, soak sections of the herring spawned-on kelp, known in Japan as *Komochi konbu*, in water or wine lightly sweetened with sugar or, as I prefer, with a dash of balsamic vinegar.

Once it is rehydrated to an *al dente* texture, I slice it thinly and toss it with shaved fennel and radishes for a unique and captivating appetizer.

Most species of herring ascend powerful tidal rivers in spring and early summer to spawn before returning back to their salty habitat. **River-Run Herring** is a term that generally describes these anadronomous fish that swim on both coasts. The **Blueback Herring**, also known as **Summer Herring** or **Glut Herring**, and its cousin the **Alewife**, which sports the appropriate name **Spring Herring,** are very abundant in the tidal rivers in the Gulf of Maine and were an important food source for early colonists. For many centuries they were eagerly harvested as a harbinger of spring, but a gauntlet of dams erected across their spawning routes diminished populations significantly. Alewife was once so teemingly abundant in Taunton, Massachusetts, that the town was nicknamed "Herring City," and Alewives were called "**Taunton Turkey**."

It is a welcome herald of spring when the first Alewives alight in our harbors before darting convulsively into brooks and tributaries. In a few weeks' time come the Blueback Herring. This slight staggering of their spawning runs is where all disparities stop. Even to trained fishery scientists, distinguishing between the two fish species is difficult and, in my mind, unnecessary. There is no worthy culinary distinction to be made, and they are very often marketed as one or the other. In years past, they were canned together and sold as "sardines." While these river herring are leaner than their ocean relatives, they are interchangeable in the kitchen. But not everyone is so enthused at their arrival. British food writer Alan Davidson remarks that these are "very mean, dry and inspid fish," a point with which I completely disagree.

In the Pacific this dynamic is slightly different, as most species school and spawn nearshore but do not enter freshwater. Between the Atlantic and Pacific there are eight other herring of minor culinary interest or moderate commercial importance as bait. Most often these are not targeted but are bycatch of other fisheries. Another trait common to all in the herring family is what's known as deciduous scales—so named as they slough off as easily as leaves from an October tree. The shimmering scales have long been used in cosmetics and to make jewelry.

OPPOSITE Pickled herring.

The Herring Net, by Winslow Homer, 1885.

Historically, Sea-Run Herring were fished throughout the year and were typically canned. The nearshore and river-run species were often smoked, pickled, or corned. This practice likely owed as much to tradition as it did to the sudden glut of fish during spawning season, which required the bounty to be preserved by every means possible. For centuries, families developed and passed down their own unique curing methods, and now these recipes are still in use as part of the heritage of our coastal communities.

Herring are very high in oil, and their flesh can turn rancid quickly. All members of the herring family are rather bony fish, and preparations such as smoking or corning help make removing the bones an easy task, as they slightly dry the flesh, pulling it away from the bones. But opportunity should not be missed to eat these fish fresh. They are at their very best just prior to spawning, when their fat content can reach as much as 20 percent. When fresh, the flavor is similar to perch, with a distinctly malty, spicy, and acidic character. Like all herring relations, their flesh is quite tender in texture, and special care

needs be taken with whole fish so as not to rip the delicate belly or scrape skin off the fillets. Larger fish tend to be slightly more taut than smaller ones, but across the board I like to firm the texture by conditioning the meat under a thin coating of salt for half an hour before cooking. Or, if the recipe is amenable, I will paint the fillets with lemon juice and a light seasoning of salt. Either way, the salt does not need to be washed off prior to preparation. Taking a cue from the great cuisines of the Mediterranean, where sardines and herring have long been venerated, I will scale and gut the fish and then grill them whole over a fire of green wood and pinecones. The extreme heat renders the fat, which bastes the skin as it crisps and chars, while the meat inside remains moist and rich in flavor. After removing them from the grill, I'll then marinate them with lots of chopped herbs mixed with a scant bit of olive oil and a glug of sherry vinegar.

The roe and milt of herring species are universally esteemed. It's very likely that, in a pailful of fish needed for a proper dinner, one in four will yield a roe that is considered as generous and luxurious as caviar. One of the best preparations I've come across is deviled herring roes. Both the roe and milt are simmered gently in butter with only a suspicion of mustard, a scant twist of the peppermill, and some chopped fresh mint until the butter has been absorbed. The whole is spread on pieces of toast. The roes of Alewife and Blueback Herring were once a very popular canned item, primarily in the South where the industry centered around the Chesapeake and Carolinas.

Every species mentioned above, regardless of their provenance, is perfect candidate for smoking and pickling preparations. As proof, there is a bewildering array of vocabulary describing different cures, cuts, and methods by which these were put up for leaner seasons. Fish that have been scaled, their viscera removed but the gonads left in, are known as *gibbed herring*. Prepared the same way but with the head removed, it is now called a *nobbed herring*. A *bloater* is a whole fish that has been brined and then cold-smoked and meant to be eaten promptly. The name derives from their habit of popping, as enzymes act upon the contents of the stomach causing them to swell. *Hard herring*—or, as they are more commonly known, *Red Herring*—are whole fish that have been lightly pickled and then smoked for three to four weeks until they are dry. The combination of smoke and oxidation of the fish's oils give it a robust rusty red color; hence the name. Due to the drying effect of the process, these were a very shelf-stable product. As you can imagine the lengthy preparation produced an explicit and, well, outgoing aroma. It is said that those wishing to avoid the hounds of justice would brush some Red Herring over their tracks to throw off their pursuers. The fish quickly became a staple food of the merchant marine and gained familiarity in almost every corner of the world; as a result, the term *red herring* has become embedded in our lexicon.

Pickled herring, the fish's most familiar preservation method in these refrigerated times, has been elevated to an art form. To experience the magic that can be conjured from these little fish, take a trip to New York City's to Russ & Daughters, Zabar's, and many other proud outfits that faithfully execute heritage recipes with a precision honed through lifetimes of practice. More on the methods for curing, smoking, and pickling can be found on page 59.

Jack

The jack family is one of the most distinguished and diverse families of fish. It has labyrinthine relations with many important food fish families, including the mackerels and many lesser species that are not common to our food lexicon. Members of this extremely populous family are found in temperate waters all over the world and are generally considered to be among the highest-quality food fish.

Of the different relations, there are those named **Jacks**; the **Selenes**, which include the pensive-looking and cartoonish **Atlantic Moonfish** and **Lookdown**; several **Scad** siblings; and the ever popular **Seriolas**, which include the **Greater** and **Lesser Amberjacks**, the **Almaco Jack**, and the **Banded Rudderfish** in addition to a number of smaller, less important food fish species. The **Pompano** is the most renowned of the family, considered by many and historically the benchmark of quality by which *all* other fish are measured. As the pompanos have a unique history, they warrant a separate entry (see page 332). Identifying the species of the extended jack family can sometimes feel like a shell game, as individual species are often known by many names (often the same name might apply to several species), and many species have nearly identical twins swimming in the opposite ocean that are so similar in culinary characteristics as to be rarely distinguished at market but are in fact different species.

My first experience with jacks was with the farmed **Hawaiian Yellowtail**, known in the wild as **Almaco Jack**, a species from the Atlantic and Pacific Oceans that has gained great popularity as a farmed product known as **Hawaiian Kampachi.** (Yep, all the same species.) When I first cooked it, the prodigious fat content of its fillets gave me pause as I'd not seen a fish that rich, ever. Like foie gras, just the slight heat of fingertips during handling was enough to bring the oils to the surface in a glistening sheen. This has become the most venerated of the family and is a particular favorite of fine-dining chefs, though many of the characteristics of this fish are common throughout the family. The farm-raised jack species can reach fat contents of nearly 30 percent, far beyond that of those caught in the wild. Another jack that is farmed is is the **Hamachi**, which in the wild is a **Japanese Amberjack**, not native to our coasts. The wild species Greater Amberjack (sometimes called the **Yellowtail Amberjack**), is known as **Hiramasa** or **White Salmon** when farmed, an obvious reference to its extreme fattiness.

See how this can get complicated? I'm going to simplify things.

Farmed jacks all share a similar texture that I describe as fleshy or athletic with a concise flake and a greasy richness. The flesh has a distinctive dewey luminescence of the fat: generally creamy white with tan undertones, sometimes ranging to a marked orange tint. These species, both farmed and wild versions, are very popular in sashimi, crudo, and ceviche preparations. Fillets are often seared rare, and they are particularly well suited to broiling and grilling, especially over a live fire, as its generous fat content tames and absorbs the primitive temper of smoke. Like all its close relatives, they have a thin layer of red muscle tissue that should be removed, as its texture is quite dry and its flavor distracting. All members of this family are flattered when salted an hour or so before cooking, giving the dense flesh time to become evenly seasoned.

In wild capture fisheries **Yellowtail Jack** (not the same as Hawaiian Yellowtail) is highly prized, but its history is far more pedestrian, as it was once an important fish in Southern California's canning industry and marketed under the name **Amberfish**. Given the rapid growth of canned tuna and salmon, the canned Amberfish wasn't able to compete on volume or price and the product was soon removed from the market.

Almaco Jack are also targeted throughout their range by commercial fisheries. Almaco range in size from 1 to 20 pounds and the culinary qualities of these fish are constantly evolving as they grow. The smallest fish are the mildest and most buttery in texture and flavor and are perfect for whole-fish preparations. When raw, these smaller fish have a distinguished clean, cucumber aroma that blooms into a fresh herb scent as they cook. At around six pounds, Almaco Jack's flesh gains a pale beige hue, though it cooks up white and very moist. This size range is preferred for any cured preparations, as is traditionally practiced in the South, where the fish are split, salted for a few hours, then rinsed and sun-dried. These cured fish are fabulous when sliced thick and cooked up like bacon in their own rendered fat. As they mature in size, the raw meat becomes tinged a slight pink, and its taste is less focused and the texture gains a sinewy resistance. When cooked, much of the oil renders out and bastes the fish as it cooks. The reduced fat gives the flesh an even mouthfeel and a balanced texture.

Many of these cuts and preparations described below can be made from nearly any member of the extended family. I use this fish as the example, as it is the most versatile of the family. The **"Amberjack"** (as the Greater Amberjack is commonly referred to) is an extremely popular game fish on both coasts. They grow quite large, which lead some island cultures to label the fish **Family Feeder**, a mostly antiquated term that is no longer in use. Most fish landed range from 25 to 75 pounds, though record sizes approach nearly 200 pounds. These fish are extremely prone to parasitic infestation and are usually sold as fillets so as to guarantee market appeal. They have medium-sized scales that are easily removed, though, as with many species of jacks, those running along the lateral line require a bit of extra effort to detach. This is a very hard-boned fish with a thick backbone that provides a rather high ridge over which to train your fillet knife. The rib bones are also quite sturdy, enabling you to cut off the rib section, leaving the flavorful and fatty belly attached. This is a great cut to smoke and serve as one might do with pork ribs. Pin bones run roughly two-thirds the length of the fillet, and the cheeks from larger fish can be quite significant in size and are among the choicest bits. The several inches of flesh that extend from just over the gill plate into the head is another distinctly flavored and prized part of this fish; resembling small "tenders"-like pieces, these are more silken in texture than the somewhat heavy and coarse fillets. Just underneath the gill plate is another delicacy, a band of meat adhering to the collar of the fish. When removed from smaller fish, a few of these strips make a wonderful smoked appetizer, the meat chewed from the bone like chicken wings. In larger fish, the collars can be significant enough to serve as an entrée. The spine also hides a deliciously flavored marrow that has many uses. It can be employed as a finishing ingredient for sauces, mixed with butter to make compound butters, or smashed with butter and breadcrumbs to make a delicious crust.

Smaller Amberjacks are considered far more desirable, as the larger ones have a greater prevalence of parasites and a heavier flavor and texture. Due to the possibility of parasites, Greater Amberjacks of all sizes should not be eaten raw and should be fully cooked, though it does not take well to high heat, as the dense flesh seizes and becomes quite dry. A quick sear for

OPPOSITE Fishing for jacks, Pensacola, Florida, c.1910.

of its body and its high forehead, giving it the appearance of thoughtfulness. Both the Lookdown and Moonfish share a silvery iridescence, with shimmers of mother-of-pearl. These are beautiful fish in a unique and oddly charismatic way. But beauty is not everything—they also deliver on the plate. Many accounts, both historical and recent, regard them as good as pompano. At 12 inches, the Lookdown is slightly smaller than the 15-inch Moonfish, which is also known as the **Dollarfish** and is a bycatch of the shrimp and snapper fisheries. Both Lookdown and Moonfish are caught ranging from only a few ounces to five pounds. The meat of these fish is very similar, and though they do not stand out from the crowd as a particularly memorable pair of fish, there is a lot to recommend them. Smaller fish are perfect for breading and frying whole, medium fish make for great panfish or whole-roast preparation, and the largest fish yield fillets that are uniquely wide and plate-like in their shape. Both fish have a texture that is firm and rather toothsome, much like pompano. Their white flesh is unblemished by the presence of much red muscle tissue, and the flavor can be somewhat muted, though it does have a silky richness that lends itself to many cooking applications. It is good served raw in a ceviche, as the meat tenses up to a very pleasant texture after a soak in lime juice spiked with the heat of chiles.

The Moonfish was once highly esteemed in New York, where it was sold under the name **Blunt-Nosed Shiner**. It found popularity in the Boston area under another alias, **Humpbacked Butterfish**. Neither of these fish is abundant enough to support directed fisheries, but they are of high enough quality that when caught should be sought out and enjoyed.

Jellyfish

I have never met anyone who has a good relationship with **Jellyfish**. Of the hundreds of species found in our global oceans, it seems that none has ever harbored an altruistic thought or contemplated mercy toward them. It's a hard sell to get people to think anything but invective when jellyfish is the topic of conversation. But play along with me here. When I write *jellyfish*, you think "dinner." Let's try it.

The **Cannonball Jellyfish** has long been a nuisance to swimmers and commercial shrimpers in the southeastern Atlantic and Gulf. These bell-shaped beasts swarm in such profusion that they can shut down beaches and clog and damage fishing gear. There are not many predators for this nuisance species, and the population continues to increase. It's like that old *Star Trek* episode "The Trouble with Tribbles."

But there's a newly developing fishery for these **jellies**. Though we have no taste for them in America, there is a significant demand in Asia. As jellyfish are mostly water and spoil very rapidly, the challenge to this emerging fishery is not catching them but rather processing them rapidly enough to prevent deterioration. They must be salted and pressed until dry (a process that can take between 2 and 10 days), at which point they are shelf-stable for a considerable time. Jellyfish are not particularly nutritious, especially in relation to finfish, but are loaded with collagen and calcium, which earns some credit with health food fans.

To prepare dried jellyfish, soak them overnight in a mixture of water and flavored liquids such as wine or vinegar. Once they are rehydrated and pliable (and nearly back to their original size), they can be quickly blanched then used in stir-fries, salads, fish stews, and so forth. I like them best when quickly blanched in acidulated water, then marinated with vinegar, chiles, and garlic. Or taking more of a Mediterranean cue, I slice them very thinly and toss them with fresh mint leaves, shaved fennel, thinly sliced shallots, lemon juice, and olive oil.

Though it's unlikely that Americans will develop a taste for Cannonball Jellyfish anytime soon, there remains great potential to further develop these profitable fisheries in Georgia, Florida, and surrounding states. And we'll never learn to love it unless we give ourselves the opportunity to try it!

Limpet

Among the amazing creatures in the sea, the **Limpet** is notable for its incredible strength and obstinance in clinging to rocks. There's not much of a commercial demand for them, if any, because they are so challenging to harvest. Removing them from rocks in the tidal zone is a task akin to pulling the sword from the stone. Wordsworth mused about the limpet and man's ceaseless vexation over nature's most deceptively simple and humble form.

> *And should the strongest arm*
>
> *Endeavor*
>
> *The limpet from its rock to sever,*
>
> *'Tis seen its loved support to clasp,*
>
> *With such tenacity of grasp,*
>
> *We wonder that such strength*
>
> *should dwell*
>
> *In such a small and simple shell*

These single-shelled mollusks resemble tiny abalone, and various species are found all along the Atlantic and Pacific coasts in shells of various shapes and intricacies. One species is known as **China Hat** for its conical arch shape, while another is simply the **Common Limpet**, a fitting name, as they can be so abundant in some areas that a casual observer might not recognize the individual beings because they can be so common as to completely blanket the shoreline. Limpets on the Pacific coast, particularly the **Owl Limpet**, are larger than those found on the East Coast. On the Atlantic coast, the **Slipper Limpet**, or **Slippershell**, is very common, but unlike other limpets, which are herbivorous, Slippershells prey upon oysters by using a rasp-like tongue to puncture the shell and expose the animal. Given their tasty diet, I find the Slippershells to have the best flavor of all the limpets. The largest limpets attain a shell diameter of about three inches and are the easiest to eat. But I prefer 1½ to 2 inches, as I've found the texture to be at its peak at this size.

Larger limpets, two inches or more, can be treated like abalone, the meat removed from the shell and pounded or rolled into thin steaks, then breaded and fried. Their taste and texture are as fine-grained and smooth as the rare and expensive abalone.

To prepare any species of limpet, start by soaking them in fresh seawater or salted water for 30 to 45 minutes to ensure any grit loosens and falls away. In Hawaii, where limpets are known as **Opihi**, a popular preparation is to marinate them in the shell with spicy chiles, vinegar, and salt before broiling or grilling them.

The first time I had limpets was on the island of Madeira, where they are a prized local delicacy prepared much like the French escargot. A paste made of garlic, chile flakes, olive oil, and a dash of vinegar is slathered over the open side before they are broiled. They are good eaten raw, though I find the texture to be a little too chewy. But if you like raw clams on the half shell these will probably suit your fancy.

The most common way of preparing them is simply to steam or boil them, a two-inch diameter limpet needing only 8 to 10 minutes to become tender and cooked through. A benefit of this preparation is that limpets exude a delicious and fortifying broth that I serve steaming in a mug with a swirl of butter on top. I've had great success steaming limpets and then pickling them in a sweetened vinegar brine heavily scented with rosemary and bay leaf. But my very favorite of all preparations borrows from an old European tradition: place the limpets open side down in a cast-iron pan and then cover them with dried fennel stalks, then set them aflame. The residual smolder is a perfect measure of heat to cook the limpets through while perfuming them with a charred and seductive aroma. A good fruity olive oil or melted butter is all you need to complete the dish, except perhaps a nice cold bottle of rosé wine.

Lizardfish

Lizardfish are commonly caught as bycatch and wasted in a regrettable number of fisheries throughout the mid-Atlantic and the Gulf. Of the several species of lizardfish, most are identical in culinary characteristics, the only variable being size, which typically ranges between 10 and 16 inches. Despite their unmarketable name and bad reputation with fishermen, who intensely despise this aggressive, bait-stealing, often painful to unhook fish, they are surprisingly delicious.

Their torpedo-shaped body is structured like a very thick eel. Their scales are relatively easy to remove, but two sets of pinbones, one running down the spine above the belly cavity and another just above the spine running down half the length of the fish, can make filleting a challenge. Lizardfish's very firm flesh is densely packed with short, small flakes and it holds together nicely during cooking. A diet of mostly shrimp and small fish gives it a clean, straightforward flavor, not unlike that of flounder.

The thick skin crisps nicely, making them a good candidate for broiling or grilling. It takes on very different characteristics when cooked in olive oil or butter—olive oil gives it a very precise flavor, while butter mellows its personality and coaxes its sweetness to the fore. One drawback is that (even when pristinely fresh) it has a faint musty smell that somewhat dissipates but persists even once cooked. In short, it is a fine substitute for many thin-filleted white fish, though it is of no special character.

Lobster

Navigating the coastal waters of Maine tells the story of the working waterfront. The painted buoys, each attached to several traps strung along a line beneath the surface, dot the ocean's surface. I know the color codes of each captain, and they tell me who's active. I can see the Maine work ethic in full glory as captain and sternman slam through the work. Looking upon such a scene, I often think about how the perception of **Lobsters** has changed over the years to become the icon of a region. The first governor of Plymouth Colony, William Bradford in 1623 apologized to arriving settlers as he described the incivility of the situation in America: "the best dish we could present was a lobster or a piece of fish without bread or anything else but a cup of fair Springwater." This was a great embarrassment to the proper Englishman and a poor welcome to the newly arrived settlers. There are many stories and variations regarding agreements between servants and employers that stipulated employees were not to be fed lobster more than twice a week. Though the stories may be slightly exaggerated, the fact remains that the incredible abundance of lobster in colonial times provided just cause for palate fatigue. I live in Maine and regularly work on a lobster boat, giving me access to all the lobster I can possibly eat, and this experience has given me a very small amount of sympathy for anyone who endures monotony in their diet. (It's a tough life here in Maine).

There are many accounts of nor'easters laying siege to the coast, leaving in their wake immense windrows of five-pound lobsters piled several feet high along the beaches. As lobsters were so plentiful, they were widely used as fertilizer, and only those who could not afford anything that Bradford would have described as "better" resorted to eating the lowly shellfish.

It is not until several decades later that we find record of lobsters sold in markets. According to author and chef Howard Mitcham, the first such account places Provincetown lobsters in the Boston market in 1740. Thomas F. DeVoe, a chronicler

of New York life in nineteenth century, relates the presence of lobsters in New York shops as early as 1815. Likely the lobsters were local product from Long Island Sound. But even with local lobster availability, live product was the exception, as pickled was the preferred market form.

One of the difficulties in developing the lobster trade is that lobsters must be sold alive, and in the days before refrigeration and rapid transit, getting freshly caught lobsters, still vigorous with life, onto city market stalls from the small rural fishing communities where they were caught proved a considerable obstacle. One breakthrough that allowed lobster to expand its footprint was the introduction of a small fleet of well boats, or smacks, cumbersome constructions fitted with cargoholds that allowed for sea water to pass through, creating a live holding tank to ease the attrition of transport.

Historically the American lobster occupied a broad geography that stretched as far south as North Carolina all the way through the Maritime provinces of Canada, with the vast majority of the population centered in the Gulf of Maine. It was there in the 1830s that industry began to capitalize and operate at an increasing scale. Until this time the lobster industry was still handicapped by the public perception of lobster as food for servants and the poor, or fertilizer and fodder feed for livestock. This cultural barrier lingered even as the sweet salt-fragrant steam of lobster pots slowly percolated among metropolitan epicures. One lobsterboat captain, Thomas Fairfax, supposedly remarked, "Lobsters are very good as an article of commerce, and pretty enough to look at, after they're boiled; but as to eating them, I prefer cast-off rubber shoes."

And as history judges Captain Fairfax, it is clear that he was on the wrong side of the argument. However he was correct in his assessment of their value in commerce. It was in the early 1840s that Maine lobster became one of the first foods to be canned commercially in United States. The industry started in Eastport, Maine, and was rapidly replicated in small towns along the coast as canneries sprung up to cash in on this new technology and suddenly *en vogue* product. By 1844 there were 23 canneries operating in Maine, marking the advent of the canned seafood industry, which was one of that state's most important economic sectors for more than the next

century and a half. As the quality of Maine products gained reknown, a lucrative market for canned lobster developed in Europe and beyond. British customers were accustomed to using lobsters whole, as was the style of classic French cuisine that was dominant in that era. Lobsters and crawfish were primarily used as garnish on opulent hotel platters, and this led to a quirky bit of customized food processing. Enterprising operators developed a can specifically sized to accommodate an entire lobster, shell and all. The success of the canneries negatively impacted lobster populations as canners preferred either smaller, garnish-size immature lobsters or those over five pounds, as labor in processing them was more efficient— the combination of this dual demand removed the breeding stock as well as targeted the yet-to-mature juveniles. By 1880, 13 canneries were operating in the tiny town of Eastport alone. Such pressure on the resource could not be sustained. By 1895, the Maine lobster industry failed and the last cannery closed. Strict regulations were put in place on the lobster fishery in one of the first examples of the federal government asserting authority over the extraction of a natural resource in state waters. Lobster populations soon rebounded, but by then the cannery infrastructure had been retrofitted for processing canned sardines and the market for canned lobster had shifted its attentions to other products.

OPPOSITE Lobster traps in a foggy Maine harbor, 1891.
ABOVE Canned lobster label, c. 1915.

LOBSTER FISHERMAN · STATE OF MAINE

TRAVEL A NEW WORLD
SEE THE U.S.A.

A Maine lobster bake.

In 1846 the first known recipe for lobsters "in the rough"— or, as we most commonly enjoy them today, in their shells—was published in *Miss Beecher's Domestic Receipt Book*. The first train-load of live Maine lobsters arrived in Chicago in 1842 to great fanfare. In New York City, Charles Ranhoffer and Louis Diat, the greatest American chefs of their time, began featuring them prominently on menus. Over the coming decades, rapid expansion of rail networks, combined with the growing population and the widespread adoption of the newly invented icebox, allowed live lobsters to be successfully shipped beyond regional markets. The stage was set for continuous pioneering of new markets. And in 1896, Fannie Merritt Farmer solidified lobster's place in the domestic kitchens of America when she published recipes for lobster bisque and lobster Newburgh in her hugely influential *Boston Cooking School Cookbook*. Gone were the days of reluctant lobster consumption. America's population had nearly doubled in the second half of the nineteeth century and its complexion had changed too. Whole generations of aspiring Americans had never known the cultural biases of yesterday. Lobster was big business and it was acknowledged as one of America's most iconic seafoods and one of its most treasured.

In the decades to follow, social and economic shifts served to increase the stature of lobster and access to it. After World War II, Americans were flush with newfound economic freedom— freshly paved interstate highways gave vacationing families access to "authentic" coastal experiences, where the lobster bake, a method appropriated from Native Americans, became part of the individual's American experience. In the 1960s, with the expansion of commercial airlines, the cost of air freight dropped, allowing perishable seafood such as salmon and lobster to rapidly access markets across the nation.

In short order lobster became a vital pillar of the Maine economy. According to chef Jasper White, lobster was the subject of America's first appellation control laws requiring any product marketed as lobster to be the American lobster, *Homarus americanus*. Abundant lobster fisheries were thriving in Long Island Sound and along the Connecticut coast to around the tip of Cape Cod. But fishing pressure, environmental changes brought on by cyclical trends in water temperatures, and the onset of devastating disease began to take a toll on lobster populations outside the Gulf of Maine,

A great example of the prevailing optimism of the era: if a lobster fishery was profitable in Maine, the thinking was to create new lobster fisheries elsewhere. In 1907, the federal government attempted to transplant more than 1,000 mature and egg-bearing lobsters into Puget Sound near Seattle in hopes of establishing a new industry there. The ill-conceived experiment came to a quick end as the lobsters failed to achieve a biological foothold.

which is segregated by Cape Cod and prevailing water currents that effectively create a biological barrier. The Long Island Sound lobster population had decreased by 95 percent by 1995.

The lobster harvest in the Gulf of Maine has been steadily increasing. Since 1970 landings have jumped by 600 percent, from 20 million pounds or more to now consistent landings of 120 million pounds or more, and this boom is one of the great success stories of fisheries management. Today, the very same number of lobstermen are fishing the very same number of pots as they were in 1970. Without an increase in effort or efficiency, the industry has realized such exceptional gains simply by great management. To start, in Maine, where the vast majority of U.S. landings occur, it is illegal to land a female lobster that is laden with eggs on the underside of her tail. Further, the lobsterman, is required to cut a notch in the tail of that lobster marking it as a known breeder. If a lobster is caught that has this notch, even if it is not bearing eggs, it is required to be released. By protecting the breeding stock, the lobstermen ensure that a robust population will follow. As lobsters get older they breed exponentially more, and so another protection is in place regarding size. A legal lobster must measure at least 3¼ inches from its eyesocket to the edge of its carapace, but any lobster larger than five inches by that same measure must be thrown back. What's most amazing about this management scheme, which includes many other conservation-oriented practices, is that they were designed and implemented by the fishermen themselves. The lobster community—more than 5,000 individually licensed small business owners—takes incredible pride in the prudence and permanence of their industry. Despite there being very little law enforcement oversight on the water, lobstermen abide by the rules, their rules, as they know they ensure their own future as well as that of their kids and community

A lobster has two claws, the larger one is known as the *crusher*, which, well, crushes, and the smaller, more elongated one is the *pincer*, which reaches out and grabs. The sex of lobster can be determined by the last set of swimmerets found on the underside, where the tail meets the carapace. Female lobsters have swimmerets that are hairy and unjointed, while male lobsters' swimmerets are smooth and jointed.

ABOVE Stevedore holding a giant lobster claw, New York City, 1943.
FOLLOWING PAGES The iconic New England lobsterman.

Female lobsters are often full of roe, a dark green mass found mostly between the tail and the body. As it cooks, it turns from dark green to a brilliant coral red and, as such, is commonly known as *lobster coral*. The cooked roe can become quite grainy, though it lends wonderful flavor when crumbled and added to butter or mayonnaise. The heptatopancreas, more commonly known as the liver or its culinary name *tomalley*, is another underappreciated part of the lobster; it's light green and incredibly robust and sweet in flavor. I prefer to make a smooth compound butter with it that I use as a sauce for broiled fish or melted over pasta or tossed into steamed rice. One note of caution: lobsters can aggregate toxicity in the liver, so it's wise not to eat too much of the tomalley. If you're just in Maine on vacation or, like most people, you don't eat lobster every single day, you'll be just fine. Go ahead and enjoy it for all that it is—the sweet taste of Maine.

A pervasive myth about lobsters is that larger ones are inherently tougher, which is simply not true. They often end up that way because we cook them in the same manner as we would a smaller lobster, subjecting the meat to withering boiling heat for a longer period of time, which does indeed tense the meat and render it slightly rubbery. The key is to cook larger lobsters at lower temperatures for longer time, which will result in a flavor and texture equal to that of smaller lobsters.

Lobsters grow very slowly. A one-pound lobster is between six and seven years old. In order to grow, lobsters must molt, or shed their shells, and in the process grow a new shell that is 14 percent larger than that which they just vacated. On average, a lobster will shed its shell three times a year and mostly in the warmer summer months. This coincides with the peak of the lobster fishery, as the lobsters have moved from their deepwater, offshore winter habitats into the warmer nearshore waters.

When a lobster sheds its shell, its flavor and texture profile changes as its system is busy building and hardening its new protective armor. As it builds this larger shell, its body is not quite big enough to fill it out, and so it takes in seawater to fill the gap, and this has led to a great deal of heated debate and consternation among those who consider themselves authorities. Commonly lobsters are broken into two categories, new shells (those recently shed), also known regionally as soft shells or shedders, and hard shells (those that have occupied their current shell for a time). Hard shells are quite packed with meat, as the animal has grown and is pressing against its current confines before it sheds to continue its growth. The new-shell lobsters do not yield as much meat and, when cracked open, release seawater from inside. Many chefs and consumers are turned off by this, but I believe a new-shell lobster is at its peak. Taking on that sea brine helps to season the meat, and during cooking the more porous new shell releases some of its spirit into this liquid, thus infusing the meat further with rich lobster flavor. And as for the liquid itself, there can be made no better lobster broth or stock than the pure essence that comes from within. I think of it like an oyster—no one would think to open an oyster and pour off the unctuous salty brine surrounding the plump morsel. Indeed, the oyster's liquor is one of its best assets. New shells are also quite a bit easier to clean, as often nothing more than a strong set of hands is needed to crack the shells. But for all my championing of new shells, there are legendary chefs whom I look up to and greatly admire who wouldn't waste a second telling me how ignorant and wrong I am in this matter.

Regardless of this professional, and perhaps personal, disagreement, the bottom line is you simply cannot go wrong with lobster any which way it comes. What I think is the most compelling aspect of the new-shell versus hard-shell argument is that it asks us to look at a familiar ingredient and to see it anew through the lens of seasonal ingredients, always available but having subtle differences worth celebrating. Recipes for new shells call for different methods and lighter flavors, whereas the robust flavors of hard shells want to be pan-seared with heavy booze and herbs or grilled over a wood fire. Regardless of what you choose, you absolutely must buy a lobster that is vigorously alive. When you hold the lobster by its shell with its head upright, it should snap its tail rapidly, a sign that it is fresh from the water and still energetic. Any lethargy shown by the lobster at the time of purchase will likely be reflected in its flavor.

The shells of the lobster should never be wasted. Their rich flavor can be used in so many ways, adding great elan to risottos, pastas, seafood stews, and many other dishes. I suggest baking the shells until they are dry and brittle before simmering them gently in wine and water to make stock. And as a last piece of advice, don't let your overly creative inner chef get the best of your lobster. Lobster steamed over a few inches of heavily salted water and served with salted drawn butter and a wedge of lemon is truly an iconic American experience.

Though the American lobster, most often referred to as **Maine Lobster**, is this country's cold-water treasure, we are also blessed with **Spiny Lobster** fisheries both in the Gulf and in California. Though both are fairly significant fisheries, they are but a fraction of Maine lobster in terms of volume. The **Caribbean Spiny Lobster** lives in the Gulf and the **California Spiny Lobster** in the Pacific, and both are very similar in culinary qualities and appearance. They are both elongated, with a recognizable lobster shape, but are noticeably lacking claws. The tails are the only edible part of the animal worth the effort of eating. These make for wonderful presentations, as the shell can be split along the back by scissors and the meat removed and splayed within the shell, brushed with seasoned butter, and broiled. They have a much firmer muscular texture, and due to how they break down after death, they must be cooked from frozen to prevent the meat from becoming quite rubbery.

There is a very small fishery in Florida for the **Slipper Lobster**, which is usually enjoyed as a regional specialty given the small quantity caught. Beware: these do not look like a typical lobster but more like a moccasin or a mitten worn by Spock while giving his "Live long and prosper" salute. The meat is noticeably less sweet than other lobsters but has a wonderful and pleasant chewy texture that is quite well balanced by a tropical fruit salsa, which traditionally accompanies the broiled tails.

OPPOSITE California Spiny Lobster, c.1950.

Lobster Newburg

There are many tales surrounding the "invention" of what was one of the most famous and important dishes in fine dining in the late nineteenth and early twentieth centuries, but like so many stories widely reported upon by gossips and amateur historians, any truth has been obscured by time. In summary of the various legends, a Mr. Ben Wenberg, a successful businessman involved in shipping (or brokerage) (or philanthropy) was a regular customer at the famed Delmonico's restaurant, the top table in New York for many decades. After returning from a trip during which he had enjoyed a lobster dish, Mr. Wenberg asked if he could prepare it tableside in the restaurant for the owner. As the two gentlemen were friends, Mr. Wenberg was obliged, and the resulting dish was proclaimed delicious and subsequently appeared on Delmonico's menu. It quickly became a favorite of the discerning clientele, and the dish was named in honor of its "creator" (or, rather its introducer). As the story goes, at some point Mr. Wenberg fell from the good graces of Mr. Delmonico, and his namesake dish was dropped from the menu. His patrons' resounding and vociferous outcry convinced Mr. Delmonico to reinstate the dish on his menu. So as to not concede anything to his antagonist, he used a clever twist of typography and changed the name Lobster Wenberg to Lobster Newburg. The famed chef at Delmonico's, Charles Ranhofer, later standardized the recipe in his cookery tome *The Epicurean* (1894):

Cook six lobsters each weighing about two pounds in boiling salted water for twenty-five minutes.

Twelve pounds of live lobster when cooked yields from two to two and a half pounds of meat and three or four ounces of lobster coral.

When cold detach the bodies from the tails and cut the latter into slices, put them into a sautoir, each piece lying flat and add hot clarified butter, season with salt and fry lightly on both sides without coloring, moisten to their height with good raw cream; reduce quickly to half and then add two or three spoonfuls of Madeira wine; boil the liquid once more only, then remove and thicken with egg yolks and raw cream.

Cook without boiling, incorporating a little cayenne and butter; warm it up again without boiling, tossing the lobster lightly, then arrange the pieces in a vegetable dish and pour the sauce over.

Mackerel

"Active and beautiful, strong, hungry and courageous, the mackerel possess many noble attributes."

—GEORGE BROWN GOODE

The *Scombridae* family, which includes both mackerels and tunas, has been a mainstay of the human experience and catalyst for cultural and economic development. As both **Mackerel** and Tuna both deserve an entire book's study I will address each as separate entries. Mackerel swim in nearly every ocean and have a unique history as represented amongst their kin is the entire economic spectrum having many of the most abundant and accessible species as well as more rarified and esteemed species.

Mackerel, like cod, is more than just a fish; it also is a mainstay in our culture and economy. As such, it makes perfect sense that mackerel has become part of our colloquial language through which we can examine how we describe our world and our relationships in it. Mackerel is a fish of many moods. It is confident, charming, tempting, elegant, and pugilistic all the same. The word *mackerel* is just as colorful as the fish itself. It is used to describe an awkward social setting (someone being a "cold mackerel"), weather (a "mackerel sky"— wispy clouds undulating in a ripple pattern, which presage unsettled spirits or the approach of unsettled weather), and more. Some entomologists believe the name *mackerel* derives from the Latin word *macula,* meaning "with spot," with reference to the constellation-like golden markings of the **Spanish Mackerel**. I prefer the theory that it derives from the Middle French word *maquereau,* meaning "elegantly or alluringly dressed." In modern slang, *maquereau,* and its derivitive *mack* mean "pimp," a validation no less flamboyant.

The history of mackerel has been one of boom and bust, periods of immense popularity followed by disdain. Many accounts in our nation's early history tell of long periods marked by a total absence of mackerel and then the subsequent return of impossibly vast schools, more than 20 miles long and a half mile wide. When stock was plenty, catches were immense. In 1830, the U.S. catch was 99 million pounds. In 1885, the most prolific year on record, more than 100 million pounds were harvested in Massachusetts alone. Until 1870, nearly all mackerel consumed was salt-preserved product. In the 1800s salt mackerel was so popular as to be one of the most widely eaten seafoods in America. Goode remarked that it rivaled cod for the claim of highest rank among food fishes.

While our current tastes and modern cuisine do not revere mackerel's confident flavor, it's hard to overestimate the defining role this fish played in our economy, in our cuisine, and in our history. Goode states, "The mackerel fishery is peculiarly American, and its history is full of romance. No finer vessels float than the American mackerel schooners— yachts of great speed and unsurpassed for seaworthiness. The modern instruments of capture are marvels of inventive skill, and require the highest degree of energy and intelligence on the part of the fisherman."

The center of the Atlantic mackerel fishery was in Boston, and both the fish itself and the salt-cured product made from it became synonymous with its home port, known simply as **Boston Mackerel**. In 1880, a sardine cannery in Maine began experimenting with canning broiled mackerel. Small fish were dressed, then singed over coals for a few minutes to char the skin, render some of the fat, and give the fish a light smoky flavor. The resulting product was a huge success, and as sales rose, the process was soon replicated and produced by several canneries throughout the state.

I have the incredible good fortune to fish mackerel just a few steps from my house. Even though I can have them in the pan less than five minutes after they strike my line, I prefer their flavor when aged in the refrigerator for two to three days, which allows their oils to oxidize and mature in flavor, becoming rounder, less pungent, and more ebullient in character. Regardless of the preparation, mackerel's meat is equally good served hot or cold. One of my favorite methods is marinating pan-fried fillets in a potent mix of aromatic vegetables and vinegar in the style of *escabeche*.

To ensure quality, mackerel must be bled and iced immediately after capture, as their flavor diminishes rapidly. This is due not to spoilage but to enzymes that are activated during capture that quickly begin to squander the vibrant flavor of the fish. Despite their oiliness, mackerel when properly maintained retain their quality for a long time—up to 19 days, according to a Canadian fisheries research study.

A fresh mackerel should be bled around the gills, carefully eviscerated so as to not puncture the gallbladder, and washed in salt water. Such a process results in a fish with a highly aromatic, buttery, and nutty-sweet briny flavor, a sharp somewhat sour aftertaste, and a rigid texture. At this level of quality it is one of the most versatile and interesting of all the fish. Mackerel's culinary uses are unlimited—they are among the best fish for pickling, canning, salting, smoking, air-drying, and using fresh or frozen. Depending on the season, the flesh can sometimes seem a touch mealy. One way to prevent this, though it can only happen at the time of capture, is to make slight slashes in the skin just after death but prior to rigor mortis. This will preclude some of the physical processes that degrade the meat. This method, called *crimping*, can be used to preserve the quality of most highly active fish species. Another remedy that will both firm and frame the flavor and texture of the fillets is to simply sprinkle some salt and leave the fish to sit for 20 minutes prior to any preparation.

All mackerels are exceptionally fast, torpedo-shaped fish. They have considerable amounts of red muscle tissue—12 to 28 percent of their weight—to support their constant motion and steely gray muscle capable of quick bursts of speed, up to 30 miles an hour in some species. Most mackerel spend winters in deep water offshore, coming near shore in spring to spawn. After spawning, the fish can be slack in richness and stale in flavor, but these voracious fish immediately begin their summer-long predatory indulgence, fattening up through the fall when they are at their peak.

Mackerel milt and, even more so, their beautiful cashew-shaped orange roes make for fabulous eating. The roes are traditionally cooked just as you would shad roe. They are also excellent when salted and air-dried in the manner of bottarga. When smaller, they are delightfully sweet and aromatic, and I gently poach them, then pound them to mix into vinaigrettes or with egg yolks to make a highly flavored aioli. All mackerel, with their rich flesh, are best flattered with acidic ingredients such as lime juice, vinegar, or wine. In classic French cuisine, mackerel is paired with the gooseberry to such an extent that the berry is commonly known as the "mackerelberry." In our Southern cuisine, fennel has long been considered a top pairing with mackerel, with fillets poached in a fennel-scented broth, whole fish laid on a bed of fennel stalks and grilled over charcoal, or marinated in a brine with an anise-flavored liquor such as Herbsaint. According to author Jane Grigson, fennel is to mackerel as mint is to lamb. That said, one of my very favorite preparations is to coat mackerel fillets with fresh mint leaves, a sprinkling of lime or lemon juice, and salt, and let them sit for an hour; I remove the leaves prior to almost any method of cooking. Rosemary, with its brawny, woodsy perfume, charms the fish into a state of rare grace, and the candid and brave flavor of mackerel is generous enough to stand up to even heavy red wines and Ports as partners.

The classic preparation for salt mackerel was to soak it in milk prior to poaching it in the same liquid, then to thicken the milk with flour and butter. Soaking mackerel in buttermilk is another classic and uniquely New England tradition. When mackerel is smoked, the strength of its flavor allows it to pair with nearly any wood, although the softer and less angular, sweet-scented orchard woods offer the best accord.

According to Paul Johnson, mackerel are best split into two categories: small, oily, and full flavored, and larger, more mild varieties. The fat content of mackerel ranges from just over 2 percent to upwards of 30 percent depending on the season and species. **Atlantic** and **Chub Mackerel** tend to be at the higher end of the spectrum in late autumn. These oils give mackerel an omega-3 content greater than just about any other fish. When at their most unctuous, they can self-baste in cooking processes almost to the level of a confit. The edible yield on a mackerel is very high, with only 35 percent of its body weight being bone or refuse. Further, many classic culinary texts recommend mackerel bones for use in making stock, and the skin, unlike most fish, is flavorful and well textured and should be used. Their bone structure is uncomplicated. Filleting them takes no more than a flick of the wrist, and only two simple cuts are required to free the entire row of remaining rib and pin bones. Smaller fish make a wonderful presentation when butterflied from the dorsal side, leaving the belly cavity connected.

The Atlantic Mackerel, also known as the Boston Mackerel, and both the **Atlantic Chub Mackerel** and **Pacific Chub Mackerel** are so near each other in quality and appearance that I will herein treat them as one. The only difference is one of taxonomy: the chub mackerel can be distinguished by the presence of distinct spots below its lateral line and the presence of an air bladder. Historically, these northern species were the most commercially important of the mackerel species and were once the dominant fish used for canning. They have long been considered an indispensible part of a traditional New England breakfast fillets or whole small fish seasoned and pan-fried in butter or bacon grease and served with biscuits. These fish are as beautiful as fish can be, their virtue painted on their verdurous and iridescent bodies in eventide and cerulean blues. These mackerels were widely considered to be the superlative member of this already exalted family of fish and mentioned as such in many historical cookery texts as the finest tasting of all foods of the sea. The flesh is darker than that of other mackerels, and its meat is prone to bruising and gaping. Careful handling negates any of these issues. The fat content can be ascertained both by season and by examining the belly flaps—when very fat, they will crack halfway between the backbone in the center of the belly cavity. At this stage they are best suited for smoking or salting preparations. One-year-old fish are known as **Tinkers**, historically as **Spikes** or **Blinkers**,

and are considered to be the sweetest and best quality. When such a small size, between five and eight inches, their bones are still tender and can be soaked in a heavy brine for a few hours, then deep-fried for a crunchy and delightful snack or garnish. When slowly cooked, skin-side down to render their rich oils, they can be pan-fried until crisp in the same manner as duck breast. When cooked over high heat the oils can develop a very flattering singed or burnt aroma that balances perfectly with their sweet flesh. The meat is salty and juicy in flavor and retains its moisture during cooking; when done, it will still present a sheen of fat covering its velvety texture.

The Spanish Mackerel, described by James Beard as "a handsome wanderer," is slightly larger than the Atlantic Mackerel and chubs, and its territory is farther south and throughout the Gulf. Two Pacific species, the **Gulf Sierra** and the **Pacific Sierra**, are for all purposes identical to the Atlantic-swimming Spanish Mackerel. These are just as beautiful as their kin, as Goode describes "the Spanish mackerel, darting like an arrow just shot from the bow, its burnished sides, silver flecked with gold, thrown into bold relief by the cool green background of the rippled sea; the transparent grays, opalescent whites and glossy blacks of its trembling fins, enhance the metallic splendor of its body, until it seems to rival the most brilliant of tropical birds." However, post-spawning, they can be described as no more than wretched skeletons. Spanish Mackerel have long been popular in Southern cooking, but when the fish was first recorded caught off Long Island in 1838 people were afraid to eat them, as they had never before been seen so far north. They are considered of best quality and most delicate flavor when caught in the Chesapeake Bay and from areas north. Those that swim south are still notably delicious, just not as delicate and nuanced in flavor and rich in oil. These have less red muscle tissue than other mackerels and are generally leaner in comparison, with the lightest-color flesh. This is the most mild-flavored of all of the mackerels (smaller fish being milder than larger ones). Well suited to any preparation method, they are particularly good pickled.

The Spanish Mackerel is sometimes confused with the **King Mackerel**, a wicked and dangerous-looking fish with vicious teeth, suspicious eyes, and a body that cannot hide its strength. These grow much larger than the Spanish and Atlantic mackerels; 30 pounds is a fairly common size, though they have

been taken up to a hundred pounds. But don't let looks fool you. King Mackerels have a well-developed flavor and a rather dense but flaky texture that takes very well to marinades, especially ones using citrus juice. Its dull gray flesh is lightened by acid, and it bleaches further when cooked. This fish, sometimes regionally called **Kingfish**, spoils quickly, but when fresh, it makes for delightful eating. It does not benefit from brief aging as do the Atlantic and Spanish mackerels. They can be cut into steaks and are especially good over a smoky grill. Given their size, their roes are large enough to accommodate many cooking methods, from smoking and poaching to salt-curing and sautéing.

The **Cero Mackerel**, also known as **Painted Mackerel**, is abundant in our southern waters. It grows as large as 35 pounds, though it averages only 5 to 10 pounds. They resemble Spanish Mackerel and share a similar delicacy in their flavor with flesh that is more beige than dark. Smaller fish are the perfect substitute for and nearly identical to Spanish Mackerel, while larger fish are similar to and substitute for King Mackerel. The Cero Mackerel does not support a major fishery, with only a fractional amount landed in comparison to the other species. Admired for its eating qualities, this important game fish is worth seeking out.

Two other mackerel species that swim in waters across the globe are the **Bullet Mackerel** and **Frigate Mackerel**, more commonly referred to as **Bullet Tuna** and **Frigate Tuna**. Their qualities are equally likened to those of tunas, and so I include them in that section (page 473).

ABOVE Spanish Mackerel.
OPPOSITE Bull Mahi.

Mahi Mahi

Early in my career, my fish purveyor once tried to sell me **Dolphinfish**, also known as **Dolphin**, and I was having none of it. He then explained that the fish (not Flipper) also was known by several names, including **Dorado** or, as it is best known, **Mahi Mahi**, and that these beautiful fish are completely unrelated to the marine mammal. Most often referred to by the abbreviated **Mahi**, Mahi Mahi comes from the Hawaiian language, and means "strong," while the scientific name is derived from the Greek word *koryphe*, which appropriately means "top" or "apex." The alternative, Dorado, derives from

Mahi, are instantly recognizable by their angular, squared-off head and muscular collar. This peculiar shape, a cross between a battering ram and a raindrop, gives them a potent and unrestrained look. The females are more traditional in profile, though they present as powerful with an energetic and wild agility. When a Mahi is just from the water, its skin is more vivid than the most riotous firmament—a truly magical sight. This fleeting brilliance has often been eulogized in literature, my favorite being James Montgomery's poem "The Pelican Island," in which he describes them "[glowing] with such orient tints, they might have been / The rainbow's offspring, when it met the ocean."

Mahi was long a welcome bycatch of tuna and Swordfish fisheries. As the fish gained a following (and people realized that Mahi and Flipper are not related), dedicated fisheries emerged in many regions. The fish can grow up to six feet and 85 pounds, though 20 to 30 pounds is the average. Smaller fish ranging from two to five pounds are called **School Fish**. Unlike many fish, Mahi is excellent eating at any size. According to Paul Johnson, young Mahi grow prodigiously, up to five pounds a month. Though they reach considerable size, they are short-lived, with just a three- to four-year life expectancy. This hastened mortality is balanced by prolific reproduction rates as males reach sexual maturity within six months and spawn two to three times a year. They're the James Dean of the seas: Live fast, breed often, die young.

Mahi has a guiltlessly rich flesh, mild and savory flavor, and a moderately firm texture with large, angular flakes. The flesh color ranges significantly, from nearly translucent to pink-beige to an overcast-sky gray. A band of bright red muscle tissue divides the handsomely shaped fillets. When the fish is fresh, the red tissue, or bloodline, is tight, compact, and vividly colored. As it ages, the dark muscle fades to ruddy brown and the flesh develops a distinctive cardboard aroma and its taste becomes stale.

Mahi needs attention immediately after capture in order to preserve quality. Fishermen have to be vigilant, handling each fish as it's caught, cutting the tail to bleed the fish before chilling in a slurry of salt and ice. The result is a fish with clear, bright flesh, enviable texture, and an elegant flavor. The skin is covered with micro-scales and is too thick to be edible.

a Latin American colloquialism meaning "gilded." How we choose to name something tells us a lot, and this fish has some pretty flattering names.

Mahi swim all over the world, in open ocean and make seasonal appearances along the mid-Atlantic and North Carolina coast to points south, and in the Pacific from Washington to San Diego. They are also common in the waters around Hawaii and are a revered and important fish in native cuisine. These empyreal-colored torpedos are as stunning as a fish can be, and they are made for swimming fast. Males, known as **Bull**

FRANK E. DAVIS FISH COMPANY

PACKERS, IMPORTERS AND DISTRIBUTORS

Salt Mackerel
Codfish, Fresh Lobster, Etc.

MAIL ORDER DEALERS

FOUNDED IN 1885   INCORPORATED IN 1905

REG. U.S. PAT. OFF.

FRANK E. DAVIS, PRESIDENT
ARTHUR C. DAVIS, TREASURER

Gloucester, Mass.
October
Nineteen
Twenty-Eight

Dear Customer:-

"What shall we have for dinner tonight?" Isn't that
a daily question in your home?

But you needn't worry anymore. For when you can go to
your storeroom or pantry shelf and say, "WHICH shall I have — Lobster
Stew, Baked Mackerel or Halibut Pie" — that's the answer, isn't it?
And you can say just that when you have a supply of Davis Seafoods
handy. No worry as to what to have. No long hours spent preparing.
Just — "That's what I want" — and it might be a chowder, creamed haddie,
mackerel or codfish, or perhaps stuffed baked sardines, fancy herrings,
halibut or fried oysters. Whatever you want — you'll have it — and
quickly, too.

However, there's one sad thing about my "harvest" this
year. My Mackerel supply is almost exhausted. Gloucester fishermen
have been searching the waters off our Cape for days — hoping that a
"school" will show. But the Mackerel have disappeared. Severe storms
have driven them somewhere. Some fishermen say they've hibernated early,
in the Gulf Stream. Others say they're in deep water and will return.
So we're not discouraged — nature has located us close to the richest
waters there are.

But I don't want you to be disappointed. So, if you
haven't sent for your winter's supply of Mackerel, do so now. The few
Mackerel I have on hand are wonderful fish. Fat, tender, juicy — just
the kind you'll enjoy for your next Sunday morning's breakfast.

And when you check your Mackerel on your order sheet — don't
forget my new pack of Lobster, Clams, Finnan Haddie and the like. You'll
find them all included in my "Ever-Ready Supply". So just read my circular carefully now — check your favorites on your order sheet and hurry
it right along to me. As usual, I'll guarantee your complete satisfaction
from the time your seafoods leave my shop — until you say, "they're fine".
May I hear from you now?

Faithfully yours,

Frank E. Davis,

The Gloucester Fisherman

FRANK E. DAVIS FISH CO.

FED/RBL

Right from the
Fishing Boats to you

The original mail-order fish house—the only concern in
GLOUCESTER selling fish exclusively direct to the consumer.

Because of its unique bone structure, the Mahi is the most fun fish to fillet. The vertebrae are a series of small round knobs; using a knife requires following their contours for the length of the fish as you would follow a difficult slalom course. But here's an amazing trick: cut the fillet free from a few vertebrae at the tail end and cut the skin running along both dorsal ridge and the bottom of the fish. Then put the knife aside. Lift up the disjoined section of meat and slide your hand between the fillet and bone with the pinky side facing toward the head. Holding the tail with a very firm grip and with your other hand directly on the spine, slide your hand along the spine in one strong, rapid motion, like an exgaggerated karate chop, until you hit the collar. The fillet will part cleanly from the bone with surprising ease. The best part about this method is it often yields a cleaner cut than most people can accomplish with a knife. And, you get to channel your inner Ralph Macchio and karate chop a fish. Pull this off, and you are officially cool. Just make sure to get video evidence.

Mahi is well suited to many preparations, but in restaurants you'll find it most often grilled. At some point in the early 1990s, it seemed every menu paired grilled Mahi with with tropical fruit salsa. A combination of fruit, citrus, and chile really does do wonders for Mahi's character and helps tame and integrate the red tissue flavor. I prefer the meat of the females, which I find to be more nuanced and slightly less assertive than the males', with an approachable sweet-savory flavor. Another reason I prefer the females is that the roe of Mahi is as good as that of any other fish. Because females spawn multiple times a year, finding heavily roe-laden fish is common. The Velveeta®-colored roes weigh from one to five pounds. These can be prepared as you would shad roe, simply sautéed in bacon grease or butter until medium rare. Or, put to their best use, they can be cured and dried to make bottarga (see page 76). Once the roe has cured, it can be grated on top of any dish to add a rich, umami-like accent. Or, while still curing, it can be sliced very thinly for a meltingly tender and explosively flavored taste experience.

I find that Mahi fillet is well flattered by gentle smoking. For any smoke process, the skin should be scaled and left on. Either dry-cure or brine is equally appropriate, though the brine method is recommended for a hot-smoked product that is as smooth and pliable as the best smoked sturgeon. If dry-cured and cold-smoked for several hours, the Mahi is deeply penetrated by the seductive smoke, which matches its bullish personality perfectly. Assertive woods such as spicy oak or hickory are best, as softer flavored orchard woods seem to humor the fish's flavor rather than augment it.

Another related species is the **Pompano Dolphinfish**, also known as **Pompano Mahi** or **Chicken Mahi**. Most often it is simply called Mahi and not distinguished in the market. These smaller fish range from one to four pounds, rarely growing as large as 10 pounds. The meat of the Pompano Dolphinfish is nearly identical to that of Mahi, though it is distinguished by a smaller flake and softer texture. Like its larger relative, it is a very fine food fish, and its smaller size enables a range of unique preparations. Pompano Dolphinfish are perfect for whole fish preparations such as stuffed and baked, marinated and roasted, deep-fried, grilled, or baked in salt.

Mail-Cheeked Fishes

The Mail-Cheeked Fishes of the Pacific make up one of the largest and most complex of the seafood orders. There are several families belonging to this grouping, including the **Sablefish** (page 345) and **Greenlings** (page 224), which are treated separately as their culinary qualities are distinct from the broadly similar qualities of the other families. **Rockfish, Searobin, Sea Raven, Sculpin**, and **Scorpionfish** families represent some of the most important food fish species—and some of the most underloved.

The scorpionfish family includes three species in the Pacific known as **Scorpionfish**: the **California Scorpionfish, Stone Scorpionfish**, and **Rainbow Scorpionfish**. Confusingly, these are most often known as **Sculpins**, and their culinary qualities are similar to the true sculpins. Among the most important mail-cheeked species are the **Pacific Rockfish**, members of the Sebastes family (from the Greek, meaning "venerable"). The 70-plus members of this family range from Southern California to the Aleutian islands of Alaska and represent a diversity matched only by the jack family in its complexity and versatility.

While it is tempting to make broad statements to describe the culinary character of this group, their sheer diversity makes that an impossible task. But I'll try anyway. Generally, their white flesh is tame and classy in flavor, and their aroma is sweet, with the punctuation of a briny sea scent. For the most part, these species are interchangeable in recipes, though some are better suited to moist cooking as in chowders or stews while others perform better in sauté or broil preparations. While there are certainly species that stand out for their culinary qualities, given the vast range of species your best bet is to buy the fish that is freshest rather than seeking out any specific type. More wild and confusing than this culinary pageant of fish are the wonderfully ridiculous names given to them, each representing a blend of physical characteristics and personality. Reading a list of these names, one would be forgiven for thinking it the lineup of the next Wrestlemania® matchup—the **Pop**, **Dragoneye**, **Rougheye**, **Halfband**, **Dark Dusky**, **Thornyhead**, **Rosethorn Idiot**, **Chucklehead**, **Sharpchin**, **Aurora** . . . the list goes on.

Thornyhead.

Historically known as **Pacific Rock Cod** or **Rock Cod** (though they bear no relation to true cod), these fish have long been important as both sport and commercial fisheries, and given the diversity of immigrant populations along the West Coast over the years, the many regional and colloquial names represent a fascinating window into the history of the region. Greek, Italian, and Portuguese fishing communities among others all appreciated and sought out these prized delicacies. In particular, they have has long been popular with the large Chinese population that settled in the San Francisco Bay Area in the nineteenth century, and the fish has come to be is identified with the Chinese cuisine so prevalent along the coast.

Pacific Rockfish are generally very long-lived. Given this slow growth and long life, coupled with the fact that many species of varying abundance inhabit the same waters, this family is particularly susceptible to fishing pressure. It is hard to protect one species while exploiting another. Throughout the 1960s and 1970s, heavy fishing led to a significant decline in populations, and some of the more vulnerable species were extensively depleted. In the decades since, good management, led by the fishing community itself, has restored this fishery to sustainable levels. For instance, developments include techniques like a weighted release mechanism that can quickly return protected or vulnerable species to their deepwater habitats before they succumb to barotrauma when hauled from great pressure to the surface, a trip that can cause their internal organs to get crushed by the inflation of their air bladder. This ability to dramatically increase the survival rates has allowed the fishery to target healthy populations while protecting and rebuilding those that are more sensitive.

By far the most important commercial species in this family is the **Pacific Ocean Perch**, most commonly fished in Alaska, where more than 100 million pounds are caught annually. These are the Pacific equivalent of the historically important **Atlantic Acadian Redfish** and **Golden Redfish**. These make up such a large and important category of food fishes that I treat them separately (see page 89). These modest-sized fish are nearly always processed into thin fillets destined for the frozen market and processed into value-added products such as fish sticks or breaded fillets. Each state's rockfish fishery has a different principal species, as the diversity ranges as you travel along the coast. In Alaska, it's the Pacific Ocean Perch, while in

Washington the Yellowtail Rockfish is the predominant species. In Oregon, it's the **Widow Rockfish** and Yellowtail Rockfish. And in California the **Chilipepper** is the most important by a longshot.

The market term *rockfish* applies broadly to scorpionfishes, but a dizzying array of names are applied on a state-by-state basis and in regional vernacular, including **Red Snapper** and **Pacific Red Snapper** which causes some confusion (neither being snapper). While most are legally named _____ **Rockfish** (fill in the blank), each starting with an appropriate descriptor, some species are known by a single name such as the **Cowcod** and **Treefish**.

In this family there are species of every color, pattern, and personality. Those with red coloration are typically sold with the skin on, as they visually relate to the ever popular Red Snapper. Those with brown or greenish colors are typically sold skin-off. And recently there's been a trend to keep some species alive in aerated tanks, which allows them to be sold at a premium in the live market.

In his wonderful book *Fish Forever*, the West Coast's preeminent seafood expert Paul Johnson very helpfully organizes the 70-plus species of rockfish into three categories. The first category includes small fish with very thick skin, firm, coarse-textured flesh, and the heavy armor and scales often associated with the scorpionfishes order. These are solitary fish dwelling in deep water and are inaccessible to trawling. Johnson lists species in this category as yellowtail, **Gopher**, **China**, **Black**, **Yellow**, **Copper**, and **Quillback Rockfishes**, as well as the **Kelp Bass**.

He defines his second category as deep-bodied fish having similarly heavy armor as those in the first category. These are also solitary fish caught by hook and line and, in his opinion, are the best eating, as their fillets are meaty and thick with their coarse texture and flavor resembling that of grouper. This category includes the **Goldeneye**, **Vermilion**, **Redbanded**, **Canary**, and **Turkey Rockfishes**, as well as the Cowcod (unrelated to cod).

The third category includes the multitudes of schooling fish, which are found in such number that they require a less-hardened façade as armor against predators. These tend to be more slender shaped and softer in flesh but with the same mild flavor common among the family. The **Yellowtail**, **Widow**, **Black**, **Blue**, **Blackgill**, **Shortraker Rockfish**, **Boccacio**, and Chilipepper round out Johnson's third category.

I find that fish from Johnson's first two categories are better suited to braises and stews, though they also are well represented in slow-roast preparations and when deep-fried whole until shatteringly crisp. Those in the third category take better to quick cooking preparations, such as sautéing, whole roasting, salt baking, or grilling. I've not found a great affinity between rockfish and smoke—the flavors clash and accentuate a tinniness in the fish. All species make good stock, though attention must be paid to the temperature—only a very low simmer will retain the bright, clear flavors for which these fish are well regarded. And though each species is good eating, the greatest enjoyment comes in discovering all their nuances in texture and flavor, which are as diverse as the communities who fish them.

Of the remaining families of mail-cheeked fishes, each with dozens of species, most are not fit for food use though there are several very notable exceptions. Their culinary merit depends primarily on their size, as these highly armored fish have low edible yields. Generally, only those larger than 10 inches are worth the effort.

The species most noted in these families are the **Sea Raven**, the **Horned Sculpin**, and the **Bighead Searobin** and **Striped Searobin**. A nonrelated but identical species, in culinary terms, is the **Oyster Toadfish** of the Gulf. Another relation, the **Flying Gurnard**, is similar in features, though its culinary qualities are among the finest of all. In France this fish is known as Grondin and, to the Marseillais, no stew can be considered a bouillabaisse without it. That is a pretty good recommendation for seeking out these fish!

While nearly all members of each family have equal-quality meat, the aforementioned species, mostly the larger and more common species are most often considered to be food fish. The roes of these fish have long been a source of caviar and of moderate importance to industry. Historically, the **Striped Searobin** alone has any record of consumption on the East Coast, specifically in

Lionfish.

Hartford, Connecticut, where they were known as **Wing Fish**. Despite this, there is also record of tens of thousands of pounds of **Sea Robin** being sold at the Fulton Fish Market in New York City each year, though there is no single constituency or cuisine to account for this consistent demand—I can find no recipes, articles, or menus featuring them.

Commercially, all of these fish are taken only as bycatch, but their prevalence and abundance can ruin the day's fortune for fishermen seeking out other catches. These bizarre-looking fish have huge fan-shaped pectoral fins used to "walk" along the sea bottom and stir up mud and sand while looking for food. In some of these species, the spines can be venomous, but I've never found this to be an issue with the flesh.

These families have a texture similar to monkfish—snappy and somewhat elastic though flakier. The flesh ranges from pearly to milky white. Somewhat opaque when raw, it firms up to a pale, dense white when cooked. Their flavor is like that of many other bottom-dwelling species—mostly mild, taking on notes of the crabs and shrimp in their diet with a general level of sweetness like hake. They are a near perfect substitute for cod or flounder and even more robust fish such as tilefish or Striped Bass. These fish braise well, and are excellent fried as finger-size portions of fish and chips. Their fillets are best when they are brined in a weak solution before cooking; this step helps to maintain the integrity of their flesh, as well as capture and accentuate the sweetness for which they are increasingly being recognized by chefs. Adding a little vinegar to the brine really enlivens the fish's flavor, especially for preparations in which it is to be deep-fried or breaded and baked.

Lionfish, a related species, is not native to our waters but have gained a startlingly strong foothold that has proved to have quite a negative impact on ecosystems. In particular, the Lionfish are decimating juvenile populations of reef-dwelling

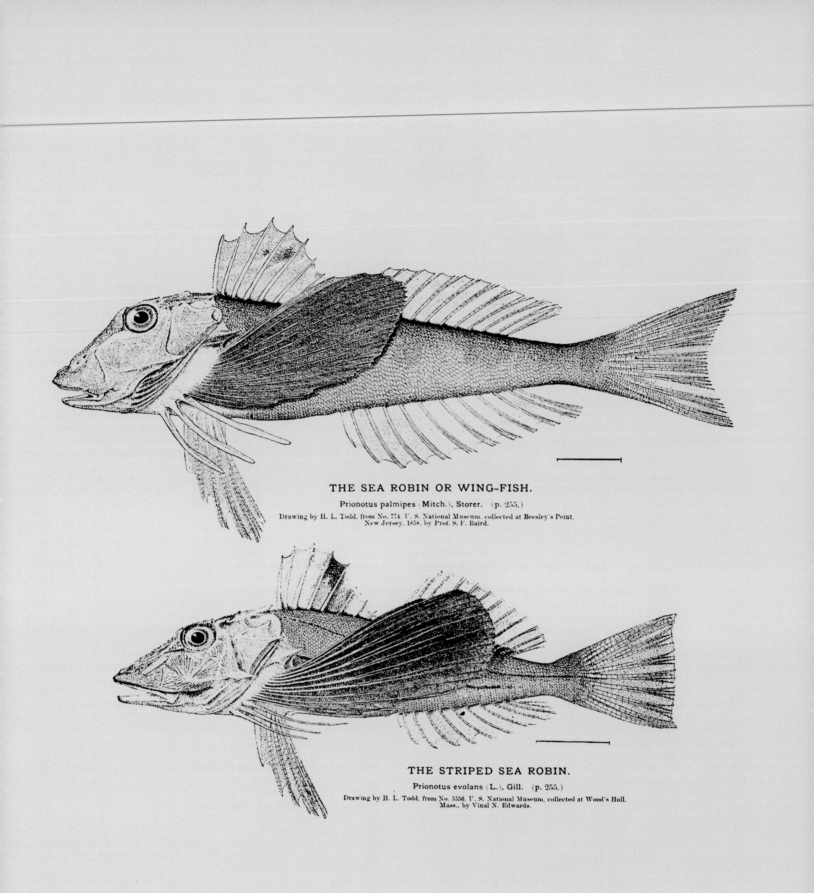

THE SEA ROBIN OR WING-FISH.

Prionotus palmipes (Mitch.), Storer.   (p. 255.)

Drawing by H. L. Todd, from No. 774, U. S. National Museum, collected at Beesley's Point,
New Jersey, 1858, by Prof. S. F. Baird.

THE STRIPED SEA ROBIN.

Prionotus evolans (L.), Gill.   (p. 255.)

Drawing by H. L. Todd, from No. 5556, U. S. National Museum, collected at Wood's Holl,
Mass., by Vinal N. Edwards.

fish such as snapper, grouper, and parrotfish, thus diminishing catches of important market species but also threatening the underlying health of the ecosystem. Urban legend has it that during Hurricane Andrew in 1992, just a few specimens of this species were set free from the home aquariums of Columbian drug lords living in Miami. Though evidence points to the invasion beginning before this time, the story makes for colorful conversation. One of the most ornate fish in any waters, the Lionfish has long-spined fins that drape from its body like willow branches, creating a constellation of crystalline threads and camouflaged webbing. As with many invasive species, initiatives have been undertaken to eradicate Lionfish from their new habitats by creating a market for them. Unfortunately for the Lionfish, this initiative has been successful, as their texture is a perfect cross between the meaty monkfish and the taut, firm grouper with all with the sweetness of snapper.

Another member of this family is the **Lumpfish**. Having no discernible hard skeleton, these odd creatures seem to be made of Play-Doh®. I've taken them as bycatch in lobster traps, and while I've never cooked Lumpfish myself, it is commonly hot-smoked in Nordic cuisines. The roe is also popular, salted and used much the same way as sturgeon roe.

Thornyhead.

Cioppino

San Francisco proudly claims cioppino as its own. The heritage of this dish links back to the Portuguese communities who immigrated to the area around the time of the Gold Rush. Cioppino, like most fish stews, is a concoction of the day's catch, and so there are numerous variations, but a few constants. Dungeness Crab, shellfish, and a mixture of fish, such as rockfish, are all simmered together in a broth of tomato, celery, onion, dried mushrooms, and lots of garlic, the whole of it fortified with red wine, a somewhat unique addition but one that is in keeping with the preferences of the Portuguese. Some versions call for sherry or white wine, though arguments over preference are not nearly as divisive as those over red versus white chowder. James Beard praised this truly Californian dish as "having a noble history" though he lamented how it had become tarnished by commercialism and ubiquity on tourist-oriented menus. The following version is adapted from *The Gourmet Cookbook* (1950).

Scale and remove the gills of 1 whole rockfish (2 to 3 pounds) then cut into slices. Remove the shells of 2 large raw Dungeness crabs and scrape out the lungs and greenish fat, discard, and cut the remaining crab into pieces. Thoroughly wash and de-beard 1 pound of mussels and 24 each littleneck clams. Steam them open in white wine, reserving both the shellfish and the strained liquid. Cut ½ cup dried mushrooms, preferably porcini, into small pieces and soak in the clam/mussel broth for 10 minutes then drain and reserve both liquid and mushrooms.

Heat ½ cup olive oil in a large pot. Add 1 large onion, chopped, 2 cloves garlic, finely chopped, 1 large green pepper, chopped, and the soaked mushrooms. Cook the mixture over a low flame for about five minutes, stirring frequently. Add 1 generous cup cooked or canned tomatoes, 4 bay leaves, 4 whole cloves, 1 cup red wine, and the liquid from the clams and mussels. Cover the pan and simmer for one hour. Season with salt and cayenne.

Add the sliced fish, crab, and 1 pound raw head-on shrimp, and cook for 15 to 20 minutes without stirring. Last of all, add the mussels and clams and heat them through. Serve the cioppino in heated soup plates or bowls, with crisp Italian bread and butter and a bottle of red wine.

Menhaden

One of the most confusing fish to follow through the canons of culinary and marine science literature is the **Menhaden**, both because of its ubiquitous presence and, even more so, multiple regional monikers. The **Pogy** and **Moss Bunker** and **Bony Fish** and **Green Tail** and **Bug Fish** and **Bug Shad** and . . . over *30* in total. These relatives of the herring often grow just over a foot in length and weigh up to two pounds. They are rounder than the sleek herring, with a deep body that has heft and attractive color. The bluish-green back fades into burnished sides with silver accents and a brassy luster. A large head and conspicuous blotches on the side are the telltale signs that this is indeed the menhaden, or whatever you choose to call it.

Menhaden range throughout the East Coast from the Gulf of Maine through the Gulf of Mexico. There are several species of menhaden, though they are never distinguished in their use. The only significance of each species is in which waters it swims. They travel in such immense schools, darkening the waters, that they can be spotted from the shore. This incredibly abundant fish has long been the target of one of America's largest fisheries, with over a billion pounds landed annually. Goode described the menhaden as "swarming in our waters in countless myriads, swimming in closely packed, unwieldy masses, helpless as flocks of sheep, near to the surface and at the mercy of every enemy, destitute of defense and offense, their mission is unmistakably to be eaten." I disagree with the notion that they are defenseless. They breed so prolifically that exponential reproduction is their survival mechanism, which allows predators to satiate themselves and still leave enough fish to carry on.

These are filter feeders. They swim with their mouths open, filtering four to eight gallons of water a minute and sieving from it plankton. It is estimated that a single fish filters 5,760 gallons of water a day! In doing so, these fish perform an exceptionally important ecosystem function in that they remove excess nutrients that wash into our waters from our upstream lives. These nutrients, including nitrogen and phosphorus, feed the phytoplankton and, in excess, can cause algal blooms that die and deplete oxygen from the water as they decompose. This effect is called *eutrophication* and creates dead zones, where nothing can live. Oysters perform the same function, though they are stationary at the bottom of the water column, whereas menhaden swim at the surface. Menhaden is a keystone species—essential in preserving the health of an entire ecosystem by maintaining water quality. As these nutrients are common fertilizers for plant life, it is quite appropriate that menhaden's regional name Pogy is derived from the Abnaki Indian name *Pookagan* or *Poghaden*, meaning "fertilizer." The name *menhaden* is a modification of the Narragansett word that means "that which enriches the earth." The legend goes that, when planting corn, members of various tribes of the Wampanoag people taught the Pilgrims to bury a menhaden in the hole along with the seed to help the plant grow heavy and strong.

Menhaden were once considered the farmer's fish, as their use as fertilizer enabled the development of large-scale agriculture in New England and Long Island Sound in the eighteenth and early nineteenth centuries. But as the Industrial Revolution transformed the nation, menhaden became the fish of the factories—oil rendered from the fish was the principal industrial lubricant. The menhaden oil industry was so productive that by the 1870s it exceeded the aggregate sum of whale, seal, and cod oil.

The brilliant writer H. Bruce Franklin declared them to be "the most important fish in the sea" in a book by the same title. Not only do menhaden maintain ecosystem health, it is the most important prey species for so many of the fish that we eat. Goode wrote: "People who dine on saltwater fish are eating nothing but menhaden." He further described their importance: "[I]n estimating the importance of menhaden to the United States it should be borne in mind that its absence from our waters would probably reduce all our other sea fisheries to at least one-fourth their present extent."

In addition to the fish's long history of industrial use, there is also an important history of salting them for domestic use. Salted menhaden was first produced as a source of cheap food for slaves, but this tradition persisted well past the institution of slavery, and the fish continued to be eaten along the coast, mostly by poor families. There is minor mention made of menhaden being sold as a fresh product in the New York market, but its largest use as a food product was canned menhaden packed in oil, similar to sardines. At its peak, canned menhaden production was over 500,000 cases a year. Marketing efforts sought to rename this fish as "**American Lunch Fish**," "**American Club-Fish**," and

my favorite, the "**Shadine**." None of these proved successful in shedding the taboo associated with this industrial fish, and in 1874 the canning effort was abandoned. In recent years, there have been a few failed pilot efforts to recreate this industry under various marketing names, such as **Mahimi**.

Menhaden are too bony and oily for most people, I'll give you that, but this oiliness can be diminished through proper preparation, either through curing or brining and allowing to air-dry. I then stew them with potatoes and other fish in bouillabaisse-type preparations, where I am layering flavors rather than making the menhaden the sole component. I also "red-cure" Menhaden exactly the same way I do anchovies (see page 59), and use the unctuous fillets to add depth and savor to many dishes.

There is a long tradition in North Carolina of using menhaden roe in the same manner as shad roe. While the roes of menhaden are a little bit smaller than those of shad and have a somewhat nuttier flavor, the two types of roe can be prepared in exactly the same ways. In the South, the roes were commonly cured, pressed, and sun-dried like mullet roes. This is the product many of us are familiar with as bottarga.

But the most common use of menhaden remains industrial products. In his book *The Bottom of the Harbor*, Joseph Mitchell wrote: "It is a factory fish, it is turned into an oil that is used in making soaps, paints and printing inks (which is why some newspapers have a fishy smell on damp days) and into a meal to feed pigs and poultry." Often used in livestock feed, it has also been a common component of aquaculture feeds and cosmetics products. The fishery is virtually controlled by a single company, Omega Proteins, operating out of Virginia and the Gulf. And though I can't say menhaden will ever be a popular culinary ingredient, I hope that ambitious cooks will begin to explore the history of its culinary potential.

Milkfish

Milkfish, known as **Awa** in Hawaii, is a little-used fish caught only in Hawaiian waters. They are historically important as they were once the most revered fish by island natives. The herbivorous fish, with their snow-white flesh, were so esteemed that they were often reserved for the chiefs. When Captain Cook first encountered the indigenous populations on the Hawaiian Islands, he discovered and documented one of the earliest examples of aquaculture. Using an intricate series of tide pools and spillways, small fish swam into and were trapped in the pools by receding tides. They were then held and fattened in tidal-fed ponds until, at their peak of richness and flavor, they were served with ceremony at the chief's table. Milkfish is one of a group of unrelated species known as the **Hawaiian Pond Fish** that were commonly produced this way. Other species included the **Threadfin (Moi)**, **Striped Mullet ('Ama'ama)**, and **Sharpnose Mullet (Uouoa)**. These fish are all excellent eating fish, with more or less similar culinary qualities. The binding trait of this diverse group is that they are all well suited to pond culture as they can easily adapt to the constructed brackish water environment.

Given the seasonality of fishing and dynamic conditions surrounding oceans, fishing was sometimes impractical, and these ponds ensured consistent access to this important source of food. The practice of tidal pond rearing is no longer widely used. Though Milkfish has mostly faded from popularity in Hawaiian cuisine, it remains very popular in Chinese and Indonesian preparations, where it is the preferred fish for making fish cakes. The flesh is also well suited to serving as sashimi, as its rich oils and courteous flavor make for interesting eating.

Mojarra

The **Mojarras** are a family of small silver fish known by colorful monikers such as **Silver Jenny** and **Irish Pompano** (no relation to the true pompano). These fish are landed almost exclusively in Florida although they are found throughout our oceans (two Pacific species are abundant but not targeted). It's a relatively significant regional fishery that lands about 375,000 pounds, nearly all of which goes to bait. A small portion of the catch goes to ethnic markets, where it is considered to be a food fish of average quality. These fish are often 6 to 12 inches, and their white flaky flesh makes them fairly versatile. In Latin American countries *mojarra* is a common name for tilapia, to which these fish have no relation, though their qualities are quite similar.

OPPOSITE Shoveling menhaden.

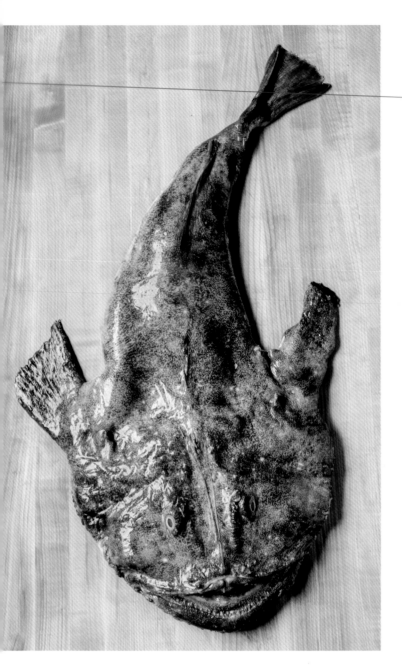

Monkfish

I first saw the terrifying mug of a monkfish on a Saturday morning. PBS was airing a famous episode of Julia Child's cooking show in which she first introduced America to what would soon be a beloved food. She stands alone as an outsized personality, and to see her tackling this truly hideous sea monster left quite an impression on my budding culinary mind. This fish's form is so unique and its appearance so odd, but a host of vernacular names do some justice in describing it: **Anglerfish**, **Allmouth**, **Fishing Frog**, **Sea-Devil**, **Belly-Fish**,

Goosefish (which is actually the official name) . . . well, you get the idea. Alan Davidson nailed it when he described it simply as an "uncouth fish."

Monkfish is a voracious predator and quite a cunning one at that. The fish are somewhat flat and rest like a rug, hidden against the ocean floor. A thread hangs off the tip of its dorsal fin and floats just above its mouth, and this "fishing lure" proves quite successful. The sedentary creature attracts small and large fish and even birds to come and take what they see as an easy meal before becoming one themselves. It's known as the Allmouth for good reason; its head is more than 50 percent of its weight and its width is two-thirds the length of its entire body. Its long, jagged-toothed jaw juts out in a significant underbite.

Monkfish had long been considered a nuisance fish—a bycatch of bottom trawls that target groundfish and scallops. It wasn't until Julia Child and French chefs began their haute cuisine cultural invasion of the American restaurant scene in the 1970s and 1980s that this fish began to enjoy the limelight it deserves. Monkfish has long been an important part of seafood cuisine in France, where it is known as *lotte*. These chefs, newly arrived in America, took full advantage when they found this familiar species available for pennies on the dollar. Recipes for monkfish started showing up in national newspapers. In 1979 it was featured in five different articles in the *New York Times,* and Pierre Franey wrote of it that this "culinary oversight is finally being corrected." By the early 1990s, this ugly fish became the darling of chefs all over the country, and a directed fishery was in full swing. It also became the darling of the conservation community as it quickly fell victim to overharvesting. Landings in 1986 were at a modest 5.5 million pounds. By 1993, that figure had multiplied tenfold. The populations declined significantly and fishing was limited in order to protect the fish whose existence we were largely unaware of just a decade earlier.

Monkfish are available year-round but are at their best from late fall through early spring. Unlike many other species, monkfish have a flavor and texture that get better the larger the fish gets. They feed on anything, including flounder, skate, lobsters, crabs, and eels, and consequently their flavor is duly sweet and complex, with a buttery lobster aroma. Its flavor is appealing without being assertive, and its finish is sharp, having notes of brine and seaweed.

The monkfish amasses a large fatty liver (plumpest in the dead of winter), which is popular in Japanese cuisine and known as *Ankimo*, which is considered the *foie gras* of the sea. The liver can weigh several pounds and is delicious made into cured or cooked pâtés or into compound butters, or puréed and added to finish soups or sauces. It can also be sliced thickly and sautéed with sweet apples and finished with vinegar.

Given the monkfish's very low yield, about 39 percent meat, its body is almost always separated from its head, which is tossed overboard, and just the tail, or loin, lands at the dock. If you are lucky to find a monkfish head, grab it. As this fish is almost all mouth, it has some pretty impressive chompers powered by wonderfully meaty cheeks. These disc-shaped muscles have a slightly smaller flake than the loin meat, though they cook in the same fashion. The tail meat consists of two loins running alongside a single cartilaginous spine. From larger fish the two loins are cut off the bone, whereas smaller fish are often sold as whole tails. Monkfish is robed in a slippery and elastic purple-mottled skin that should be removed. Underneath lies a purplish membrane that covers much of the loins; this must also be removed, as it will curl when cooked and ruin the texture and presentation.

Monkfish can be grilled, broiled, butterflied and sautéed, or simply roasted, but I think it is best braised. Its rich flavor and springy texture make it a good pairing for the heartier ingredients typical of winter cuisines. Monkfish is equally comfortable bathed in red or white wine and takes well to deeply scented herbs like rosemary and bay leaf and seductive spices like mace and allspice. One go-to preparation is to sear loin medallions with whole garlic cloves in butter, then layer the fish, adding juniper berries and thyme over wedges of winter squash and dousing the whole in fresh-tasting Beaujolais for hours of gentle cooking.

The bones and head yield what I consider the best of any fish stocks. This resulting broth is clear, sweet-sour, and redolent of clams and lobster. It has a uniquely voluptuous body, layered with gelatinous texture that is near equal to veal stock in its palate-coating richness. There is no better stock to use as a base for paellas and rich seafood stews.

The monkfish is really delightful when smoked. The loin is tensed by a heavy brine, well seasoned with onion powder, bay leaf, cinnamon, and thyme, then hot-smoked over a slow, flavorful fire for several hours. As it cools, the smoke permeates the flesh, giving it a very integrated flavor. I particularly like it sliced very thin and served cold as a carpaccio, topped with a shaved fennel and herb salad, or sliced slightly thicker when it becomes a perfect replacement for bacon in a BLT or flaked over a Cobb salad.

Given its resilient, firm texture that snaps back to the bite and its smooth, buttery shellfish flavor, the monkfish truly deserves the moniker bestowed upon it by fishermen long before it was popular—**Poor Man's Lobster**. But these days the two seafoods are not so far apart in price, and in many dishes, it could be well argued that monkfish might just upstage its famous neighbor.

Mullet

Mullet is one of the most wide-ranging seafood species in the world, and the vernacular surrounding it often muddies the line between species, region, and even families of fish. Many high-end chefs know the term *mullet* primarily through the unrelated Red Mullet, or *rouget*, celebrated in European cuisine.

Historically in the United States, according to Goode, "it is hard to overstate the importance of mullets in fisheries from Delaware south throughout the Gulf states." According to fish expert David Starr Jordan, the mullet was the most popular and abundant food fish of the Southern Seaboard, and its abundance made it accessible to everyone. So entrenched was its long-standing role as first among all edible fishes of the South that its importance and value exceeded snapper. Calusa Indians cooked whole mullet impaled on sticks of green wood and roasted over live fires. After the Civil War, fresh fish consumption in both the North and South increased, and as one of the fish most abundant in the fall months when the temperatures were cool enough to transport this oily fish, mullet became an important market item and was shipped throughout the Southeast. Until the 1950s, mullet accounted for up to one-third of all fresh fish consumed between Louisiana and North Carolina.

On the Florida coast, where the majority of mullet fishing is based, smoked mullet has historically been the working person's lunch, and in lean times, the fishery provided a source of supplemental income for a large range of the population. In the 1840s, due to a scarcity of fish in New England in the autumn, Gloucester schooners made their way south to Florida to fish mullets. After the Civil War, it became not only an accessible foodstuff and but also an important source of employment for freed slaves unshackled from plantations throughout the South.

The **Striped Mullet**, the most common in our waters and the only species in the Pacific, was significantly fished in the San Diego area and in Hawaii, where it's known as **'Ama'Ama**. It has long been a very important food fish, where it had for centuries been cultured in human-made ponds—stone walls erected in tidal areas that captured in-flowing waters and the fish that came with them. These ponds, numerous across many islands, held great importance in Hawaiian culture: the building of them was such a significant achievement that the structures are still known today by the name of the chief who erected them. Captain Cook described these ponds in his journals, and they are one of the first examples of wide-scale aquaculture in the Western Hemisphere.

The Striped Mullet, the largest of the five commercial species (growing up to four feet), is also known as the **Sea-Going Mullet** and **Black Mullet**. The **White Mullet** grows up to three feet and is also known as **Silver Mullet**; it is similar to the Striped Mullet, but leaner. The **Liza** (or **Lisa**), growing up to three feet, was given its romantic name by fish and game officials in state of Florida in hopes of increasing its popularity. (It didn't work.) Averaging less than a foot in length, the **Mountain Mullet** and the **Fantail Mullet** are the smallest and least important commercial species.

Mullet has not always been held in high esteem, as evidenced by its significant use as bait, especially in the western Gulf. These fish are catadromomous—spending their springs and summers in freshwater rivers and migrating in immense schools to colder brackish waters come fall. When these schools converge in large numbers, the mullets' habit of jumping from the water and splashing down is an ever-present sound, resembling the roll of distant thunder. As the fish enter colder waters, their gray, muddy-tasting flesh becomes white, firm, and admirably fatty. Mullet are at their very fattest and most delicious just before spawning, their skin bright blue and silver in color. After spawning, they are thin and emaciated with little value as food, their color darkened to deep brown and the vibrancy of their personality sapped. The fat, pre-spawn fish are most plentiful beginning in September into early winter. During this season, the mullet is almost always sold whole, as the roe and milt are often more valuable than the fillets.

Because of its high fat content, mullet is one of the very best smoking fish, treated in varying methods of cure (for more information, see page 59). It is traditionally smoked over sweet bay, hickory, oak, pecan, or eucalyptus woods, though it is at its zenith when smoked over dried palmetto roots. The smoked fish were historically referred to as "Biloxi Bacon," as they were so prevalent at the breakfast table. Mullet was in such demand in the region that it never had to travel far to find market. The fish itself is enjoying a period of increased appreciation, and innovative chefs are becoming aware of its culinary qualities and are using new supply chains to overnight ship these fish to top kitchens all over the country.

In the kitchen, mullet has an incredible range of uses. Their flavor is mild and nutty, and their texture is firm and flaky with a silken fattiness. The bloodline is roughly one-third of the fillet, and it can add a bold iodine flavor. They are known to have a somewhat muddy flavor, but that depends on where they are caught. Those hauled from the sandy bottoms on the west coast of Florida have a cleaner, brighter flavor than those caught to the west, where the Mississippi is a greater influence and the bottoms are muddier. This dull flavor can be eliminated through several soakings in salted and acidulated water.

According to chef Greg Baker: "It's an oily fish, but mild tasting. Its not as prevalent as it used to be, but it's kind of our de facto barbeque fish." I find the fillets best when pan-fried or grilled, as they self-baste in their own fat. I think mullet is at its best when the flesh is dry-salted for about an hour, then washed clean of the salt, brushed with lemon juice, and rubbed with olive oil before grilling over wood or charcoal. This "green salting," or soft-cure method, augments the quality of the meat, regardless of the intended preparation. Its fillets are about 50 percent yield, thus making an already economical fish even more attractive, but the real culinary creativity and value comes in the use of its roe, milt, and liver.

OPPOSITE Fresh mullet catch.
ABOVE Mullet roe.

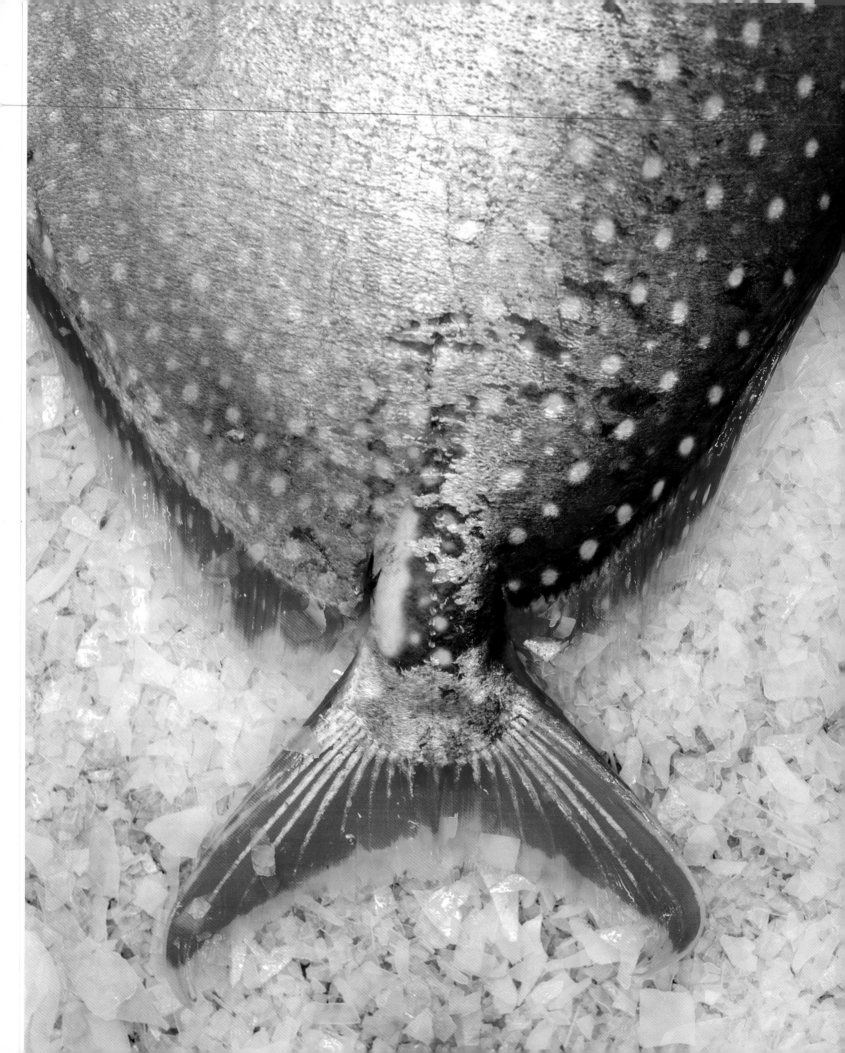

There is meat on the underside of the jaw, also liver-red, that is alternately referred to as "chin meat" or "jowl meat"; further, there are small bits of muscle in the cheeks just under the eyes. Given the range of cuts and colors, and that each of these have different textures, Opah offers a versatile palette to the chef. The top loin is great sliced thin and served raw or cut into large sections as you would a pork roast and cooked in a similar fashion. The top loin and belly are flattered by smoking, as the fat absorbs the rustic flavor. They sear very well, forming a crunchy exterior as they self-baste. The belly and the loin are to be cooked no more than medium for the best texture and flavor. The breast, cheeks, and chin are much tougher and are ideal for braising. I think they take particularly well to warm spices such as cinnamon and allspice, balanced with the bite of chiles, ginger, and garlic.

Regardless of the cut, Opah's meat is very dense, noticeably oily, and flaky. During cooking, it releases a lot of fat; its fat content is on par with, if not greater than, that of salmon. When cooked in butter, the flesh absorbs its sweet buttermilk and cracker-like scent, and the flesh gives off a very floral aroma, matched well to the buttery richness. The belly and the loin are wonderful treated to a gravlax or pickling preparation. The skin is quite thick, but if scored and cooked slowly, it can be made crispy, as when rendering the skin of a duck breast. Given its culinary versatility, Opah is among the most interesting and fun-to-cook species.

Another fish similar to Opah is the **Ocean Sunfish**, also known as **Mola Mola** in Hawaii. Though Opah and Ocean Sunfish are not related, they share the same general body type and in cookbooks are often misrepresented as the same species. (Another potential confusion is with the very common freshwater sunfish, a small panfish about as different as can be from the Ocean Sunfish.) Ocean Sunfish are longer from top to bottom than they are lengthwise. Growing slowly in excess of thousands of pounds and living up to 100 years, these fish are quite rare and are found alone, never schooling. They feed mostly on jellyfish and augment their diet with sponges, small fish, and squid. Most often seen resting on their sides on the water's surface, as though they were sunbathing, these large fish are rarely taken either recreationally or commercially, though they are sometimes hauled in as bycatch, though rarely taken to port. There is some history of their being used for food, but reviews of quality vary greatly. Like the Opah, given the vast area of their fillets, they are naturally segmented in multiple sections. When mentioned in culinary references, nearly all point to the loin running just above the spine, claiming it as the only section worth the effort of eating. This strip of flesh when raw is gelatinous and jellylike in texture and nearly translucent. Prior to cooking, the meat must first be gently poached for about 20 minutes to firm the texture, which also shrinks it in size by nearly half. At this point it's ready for nearly any preparation. Some swear off this fish as food, calling the flesh insipid and simply not worth eating. Others rave about its succulence, comparing its texture to that of Sablefish, with the meaty and rich flavor of bass. Given the enormous waste involved in preparing this fish and the majesty of its size and longevity, I cannot in good faith recommend seeking this fish out.

OPPOSITE The unique contours and colors of Opah.

FOLLOWING PAGES Hand harvesting oysters, Beaufort, South Carolina, 1938.

Oysters

In *The Oysters of Locmariaquer*, Eleanor Clark writes: "Intimations of the ages of man, some piercing intuition of the sea and all its weeds and breezes shiver you a split second from that little stimulus on the palate. You are eating the sea, that's it, only the sensation of a gulp of sea water has been wafted out of it by some sorcery, and are on the verge of remembering you don't know what, mermaids or the sudden smell of kelp on the ebb tide or a poem you read once, something connected with the flavor of life itself."

This rather blunt creature, capable only of opening and closing its shell, does not share any of its charm until a knife reveals its inner life. The pearlescent lining of the shell, the dark-lipped mantle, the plump meat swimming in lusciously salty brine . . . all are the result of experience. Every tide, storm, and season seen in the oyster's lifetime is reflected in its taste, aroma, and texture. It is through the oyster that we are able to engage with the unseen, overcrowded circus of microscopic ocean life. When we eat oysters, we taste the very essence of a life aquatic.

In America, five different species of oyster are commercially cultivated. Though these each reflect their home waters, there are general characteristics that are common to each variety. The **Eastern Oyster** (*Crassostrea virginica*), native to our Atlantic shores, tend to be briny and somewhat buttery. Of all the oysters, this most represents its origin, as its geographical range runs from Texas through Maine. The **Pacific Oyster** (*Crassostrea gigas*) grows very large and is soft-textured, with a cucumber aroma and mild, sweet flavor. **Kumamotos** (*Crassostrea sikamea*) are small, with a very deep cup, and have hints of cucumber and a noticeably creamy finish. The **Olympia Oyster** (*Ostrea conchaphila*), native to our Pacific shores, is tiny, about the size of a nickel, and has a flavor that the great oyster authority Rowan Jacobson describes as coppery and smoky. The **European Flat Oyster** (*Ostrea edulis*) has a distinct copper-iron flavor with a tangy and briny personality. These are grown on both coasts and are native to the waters of France, where they are known as *Belon*, though they cannot be called such when harvested outside of France.

It is no surprise that oysters have long been one of the most celebrated seafoods in America. Oysters are a product of their environment, and as such they have always been identified and sold by their provenance. Wherever they grow, they are a keystone species, meaning the health of the entire ecosystem is based on their presence. Oysters freely spawn, and the larvae, once hatched, remain in the water column until they are just barely visible, no bigger than an apple seed. Known as *spat*, they are large enough to settle to the bottom. At this stage it is all luck that they will find suitable substrate, or bottom conditions, that will allow them to attach and make their home for the rest of their lives. If they land in sand or mud, they are very likely to be buried and suffocated. If they land on more solid bottom or hard substrate, such as older oysters, there they will grow generation over generation to form huge reefs that provide habitat for juvenile fish and crustaceans.

In their process of feeding, oysters filter up to 50 gallons of water a day, taking nourishment from microscopic plankton sieved from the passing waters. The oysters "clean" the water of the microscopic organisms that give the seas their murky attitude, allowing for light penetration to reach the bottom. This is especially important in shallow estuarine ecosystems like the Chesapeake Bay, as this expanded photic zone allows for eelgrass and other bottom-dwelling plants to thrive, which also provide essential spawning and growth habitat. When Captain John Smith first documented the Chesapeake Bay, the waters were as crystal clear as those of the Caribbean, with visibility all the way to the bottom. In these ways, oysters influence not only the quality of life but the ability of every creature with which they cohabitate to live. The oyster is more than just a singular species; it is one upon which everything else thrives. The downfall of the oyster has led to widespread loss of resiliency in many major fisheries and in the health of our terrestrial ecosystems.

All along the coast, oyster reefs provided a large measure of protection against the ever-eroding tides of an angry ocean. Without these barriers to stop storm surge, we have witnessed incredible devastation to some of our most cherished cultural centers. The destruction wrought by Hurricane Katrina in New Orleans and Hurricane Sandy in New York are but recent examples of how we have eaten our way directly into the storm's grip.

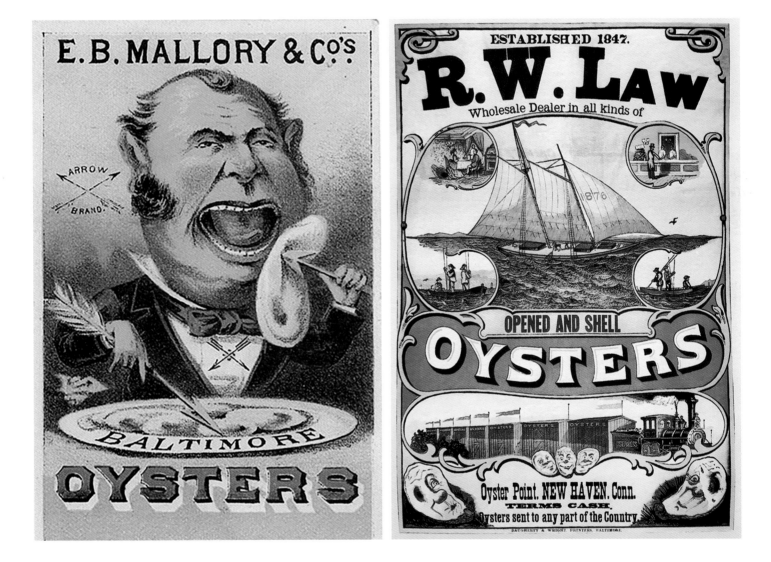

For many decades, the oyster population has been less than one-tenth of its historical abundance. But it wasn't always this way. America was once home to the most abundant oyster beds anywhere in the world, but as the oyster was both the food of the rich and the poor, unregulated harvests soared into the late 1800s. By the early 1900s, when landings peaked at 27 million bushels per year to supply eastern and midwestern markets, the oyster beds around New York had already been decimated by fishing and increasingly by pollution. How did we get here? It was around the time of the War of 1812 that New England and New York schooner fleets began sailing to the Chesapeake to dredge for oysters. This marked the beginning of dredging under sail power. The skipjack, a unique sailboat with vertical sides, was developed specifically for the shallow waters of the Chesapeake, and to this day it remains among the most beautiful examples of craftsmanship and craft in America. In the winter, the oyster industry in the Chesapeake was to catch the oysters and bring them to the markets of New York to be consumed on the half shell. In the warmer months, oysters were shipped and released into the waters surrounding New York, where they would continue growing and take on local flavors in a process known as *bedding*.

The oyster industry has been centered on several estuary ecosystems that have provided the bulk of the product. The first major area to be exploited on the East Coast was in Long Island Sound, just off New Haven. Later, both the northern part of the Chesapeake as well as the southern reaches around the James River were the most productive. As these beds were gradually depleted, the industry continued to move south into Apalachicola, Florida, and into the bayous and lakes of Louisiana. In the Pacific, Puget Sound and Willapa Bay were the major regions.

By the 1840s, oysters were a principal product in the emerging canned foods industry. The hotbed was in Baltimore, where more than a hundred canning houses were operating by the mid-nineteenth century. Thanks to its easy access to the bounty of the Chesapeake by water and ready access by rail to the rest of the country, Baltimore was the perfect home for canned oysters. In the packing houses, the job of shucking was mostly performed by women and boys. A good shucker could open 4,000 to 5,000 oysters a day, equaling about a hundred quarts, depending on the size of the oyster.

As southern oyster fisheries began to grow, the packing industry moved south and to the west, first developing in Apalachicola, Florida, then Brunswick, Georgia, and then on to Biloxi, Mississippi, which eclipsed Baltimore's production by the early 1900s. For a time, Biloxi was known as the Seafood Capital of America, as oysters from throughout the Gulf were brought there for packing and shipping. Oysters from Puget Sound were the first canned on the Pacific coast when that industry began in 1931.

The **Olympia Oyster** once carpeted the Pacific coast, until the year 1849 brought with it an avalanche of prospectors. In the boomtown culture, the oyster was central to some of the cuisine that developed to please the newly wealthy, such as the Hangtown Fry. But as they were on the East Coast, the oysters also were a plentiful and accessible protein source for the masses, and small localized fisheries rapidly took their toll. The Olympia Oyster was first commercially harvested on a major scale in Shoalwater Bay, Oregon, and it was first shipped to San Francisco in 1851. By the early 1900s, the population was in steep decline.

In 1919, an effort was undertaken to introduce the **Pacific Oyster** into the depleted waters of the Pacific Northwest. The species, native to Japan, took several years to gain a foothold in the new environment but ultimately it found a good home and now represents the vast majority of the Pacific production.

Oysters were once so plentiful in New England and throughout the Southeast that there was an industry called *shelling*, in which small oysters were sold as fertilizer. Oysters were also harvested to make lime, substrate for roads, and chicken feed. Shell middens provide us proof that long before our taste for oysters sailed with us on the Mayflower and successive voyages, oysters sustained Native Americans for eons. Archeological sites along all our coasts attest to this ancient history and the ecological resilience that we have lost. And our taste for oysters has not abated. Now oyster farming, or mariculture, is the principal source of this once-prolific food. This is why I encourage people to eat as many oysters as they can. I believe that it is our patriotic duty to do so (along with clams and mussels, which provide similar ecosystem services). A planted oyster offers all the benefits of a wild oyster, and our support of mariculture industry ensures that more oysters will be planted.

Please Post Conspicuously

DEPARTMENT OF COMMERCE
U. S. BUREAU OF FISHERIES
WASHINGTON

WHY YOU SHOULD EAT OYSTERS

The *Oyster Production* of the United States is the *Greatest in the World.*

It can be *Made Much Greater* because vast areas of unproductive bottom can be made productive *by Oyster Culture.*

The *Purity* of oysters placed on the market is now *More Assured by United States and State Inspection* and the cooperation of the large producers.

Don't be afraid of *Green Gilled Oysters.* The gray-green color, which is of vegetable origin and derived from their food, forms a deep fringe within the open edge of the oyster. Such oysters are *Often the Best* and in France are prized above all others.

Therefore Eat Oysters

It is *A Duty* to utilize this vast food resource as far as possible and save other foods of which there is a dearth.

It is also *A Pleasure* to use the oyster which in other countries than ours is a luxury rather than a common food.

It is not one of the cheap foods when measured by the cost of its useful constituents, but it is valuable as *an Appetizing Variant of the Diet.* A reasonable variety of food is necessary to the health of a civilized people.

The oyster is *Without Waste, Digestible, Wholesome, and Delicious,* and it may be *Prepared in Many Ways.* If you wish to know how, *Write for a Cook Book,* to—

U. S. BUREAU OF FISHERIES, DIVISION F, WASHINGTON, D. C.

OPPOSITE Island Creek Oysters at the farm in Duxbury, Massachusetts.
FOLLOWING PAGE Shucker at Bevans Oyster Co.

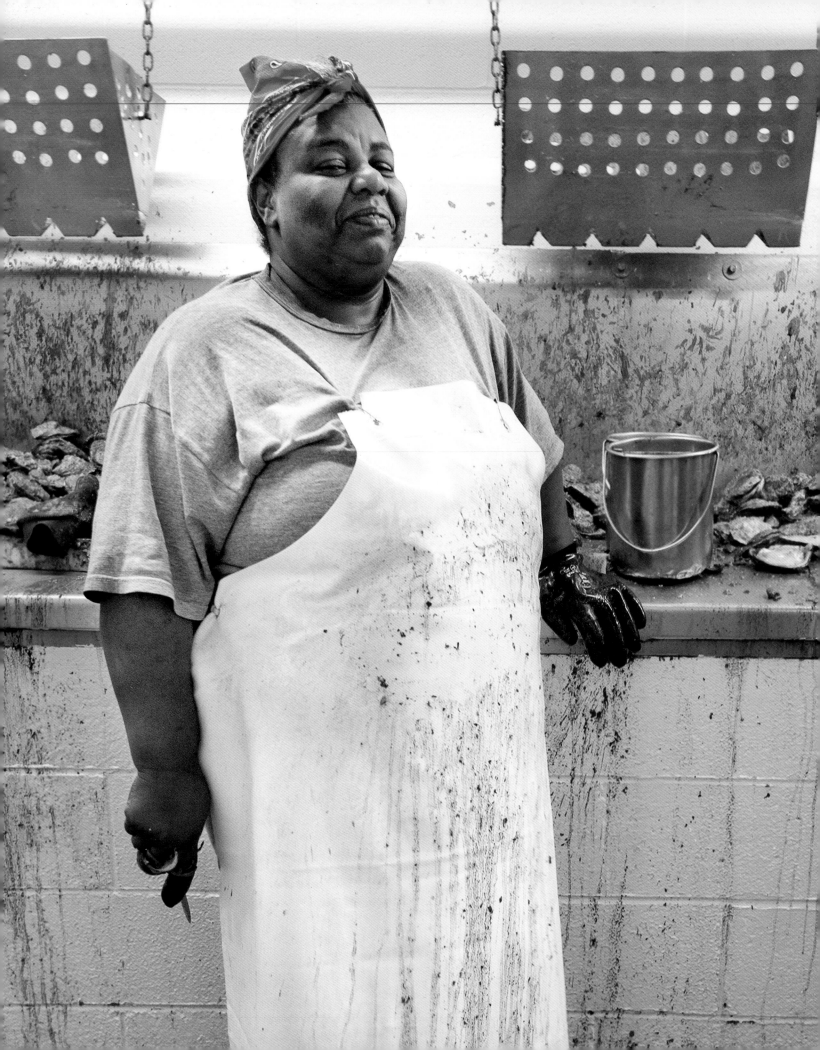

It's quite common to find several dozen recipes for oysters in classic cookbooks, a far greater number than for most other seafoods. Their versatility and their multicultural popularity led to the creation of so many fabulous dishes. In New England there is the oyster stew, pickled oysters, curried oysters, oyster pie, scalloped oysters, and so many others.

It's down New Orleans way that I think oysters find their best culinary partner in the creative and rustic French-influenced Creole and Acadian cuisines. One of the first oyster dishes to be exported from that great region was canned fried oysters, made by the Gulf of Mexico Oyster Company. Large oysters were rolled in cracker meal and fried in a mixture of lard and beef tallow until crispy and deeply browned. While still hot, they were packed in square tins which were then filled with the hot fat. Eaten straight from the can, these were a very popular item nationwide, but the preparation just doesn't suit the modern diet.

For oysters that are to be fried, I suggest first poaching them for no more than 15 seconds in an acid-spiked court bouillon. This removes some of their slippery, viscous liquor and sets the meat, allowing an easier and more even coating of bread or cracker crumbs. Fried oysters are, of course, the star of the Po' Boy sandwich. Made with fried oysters laid over shredded lettuce and spiced mayonnaise on a not-too-crusty loaf, this is a classic street food of the great polyglot city of New Orleans. It's sometimes called an oyster loaf, but it's true character is revealed in another name, *la mediatrice*, or "the peacemaker." This colloquialism, according to Howard Mitcham, was earned "when a New Orleans husband came home in the small hours of the morning without an excuse, he brought a hot fried oyster sandwich to share with his wife, because how could anyone be angry with such a thoughtful spouse."

Then, of course, there's Oysters Rockefeller, possibly the best known of all oyster dishes. This is truly a heritage recipe that originates from around 1900 when it was created by Mr. Jules Alciatore, owner of the legendary New Orleans restaurant Antoine's. The restaurant is still alive and well today, the original recipe is still on the menu, and it is still a family secret. Beyond Antoine's kitchen, it has been adapted by nearly every cook that's ever made it, but the general concept is the oysters are topped with a rich béchamel sauce flavored with spinach and herbs and sprinkled with breadcrumbs, possibly cheese, then broiled to a bubbling and crisp texture.

The oyster industry in the Gulf became an economic beacon for a Croatian immigrant community, whose presence is still very strong in both the industry and in coastal parishes of Louisiana. Many of these family businesses have spread throughout the Gulf, and the culture has influenced Gulf Shore's cuisine, notably Drago's restaurant, home of the world-famous New Orleans char-broiled oyster.

Another classic is the ubiquitous oyster cocktail, a simple preparation of raw oysters often served with a wedge of lemon and a ramekin of cocktail sauce. I don't much care for this pairing, as it does nothing to flatter or elevate the oyster. I'll turn again to the inimitable James Beard in his summary of cocktail sauce: "This is my pet abomination. A sauce of this kind entirely destroys the delicate flavor of the oyster." Other than being served with a squirt of lemon juice and perhaps some fresh cracked pepper, "the only tolerable variation is the addition of a dab of caviar" says Beard.

On the West Coast, two dishes come to mind: Oysters Kirkpatrick, which involves variations on the theme of Worcestershire, cheese, and bacon, and the Hangtown Fry, a dish claimed to have been invented in a California boomtown when a lucky forty-niner ordered up the most expensive dish the kitchen could make. Out of the kitchen came fried oysters cooked into an omelet. It's a great way to start or end the day.

Regardless of how it is prepared, eating an oyster is always a pleasure; it reminds me of a favorite book, *The Bottom of the Harbor* by Joseph Mitchell. Meditating upon the pulsing life of New York and the hidden wonders of its surrounding environment, Mitchell writes, "Every time I eat harbor oysters my childhood comes floating up from the bottom of my mind." For me it's a Chesapeake oyster that recalls the same quiet remembrance.

Char-Broiled Oysters

In the 1970s, Croatian immigrant Drago Cvitanovich opened what is now one of the legendary haunts of New Orleans cuisine. (To stand out among that crowd is saying something!) For over 100 years, Croatians have been deeply embedded in the oyster industry of Louisiana, and Drago's has long had a reputation for serving the finest seafood. In 1993, they became even better known for their char-broiled oysters, an impossibly rich preparation that, by all accounts, was created by Drago's son Tommy and involves quantities of butter that are borderline excessive even by New Orleans standards,

Freshly shucked oysters are placed on a sizzling-hot grill and drizzled with melted butter seasoned with garlic and spices. The grill erupts as the butter flames around the oysters, leaving a delightfully bitter, charred flavor. The now-bubbling oysters are topped with a mixture of cheeses and, for good measure, another splash of butter and served still sizzling in their shells.

For three dozen oysters on the half shell, count on one pound of melted butter mixed with ¼ cup finely chopped fresh garlic, ½ teaspoon black pepper, and a pinch of dried Italian seasoning, plus ½ cup mixed grated Parmesan and Romano cheeses for sprinkling and chopped parsley for garnish. An ice-cold Abita beer perfects the picture.

Hangtown Fry

This dish with the intriguing name has an equally intriguing backstory. According to Erica J. Peters in her book *San Francisco: A Food Biography*, a miner in the wild days of the California Gold Rush claimed to have been robbed by two men who were later hung for the crime from an oak tree in the center of the encampment. The place became known as Hangtown, despite efforts to the contrary. A year later, a hotel opened there and became famous for its food. One day a fortunate prospector, flush with newfound riches, came in and requested the most expensive dish in the house. He was presented with a plate of oysters cooked in eggs, both luxury items in that time and place.

There are plenty of other legends surrounding the origins of this dish. All are colorful, most ridiculous, but they all lead back to a dish that itself has many variations. At its core, it is a combination of shucked oysters and eggs. In some forms, this is in an omelet. In others, the oysters are mixed with beaten eggs and then scrambled. My favorite comes from Helen Evans Brown's excellent *West Coast Cook Book* from 1952. In her recipe, she calls for several shucked oysters to be dusted with flour, dipped in beaten egg, and rolled in cracker crumbs before being browned in butter. Once the oysters are crisp, beaten eggs are poured over them and cooked gently until set—basically a fried oyster frittata.

Regardless of how it is prepared or the story that is told, Hangtown Fry is a uniquely Californian dish that offers a glimpse into the wild days in an untamed land.

Fishermen at the Wharf, Potomac River, Washington, DC, 1938.

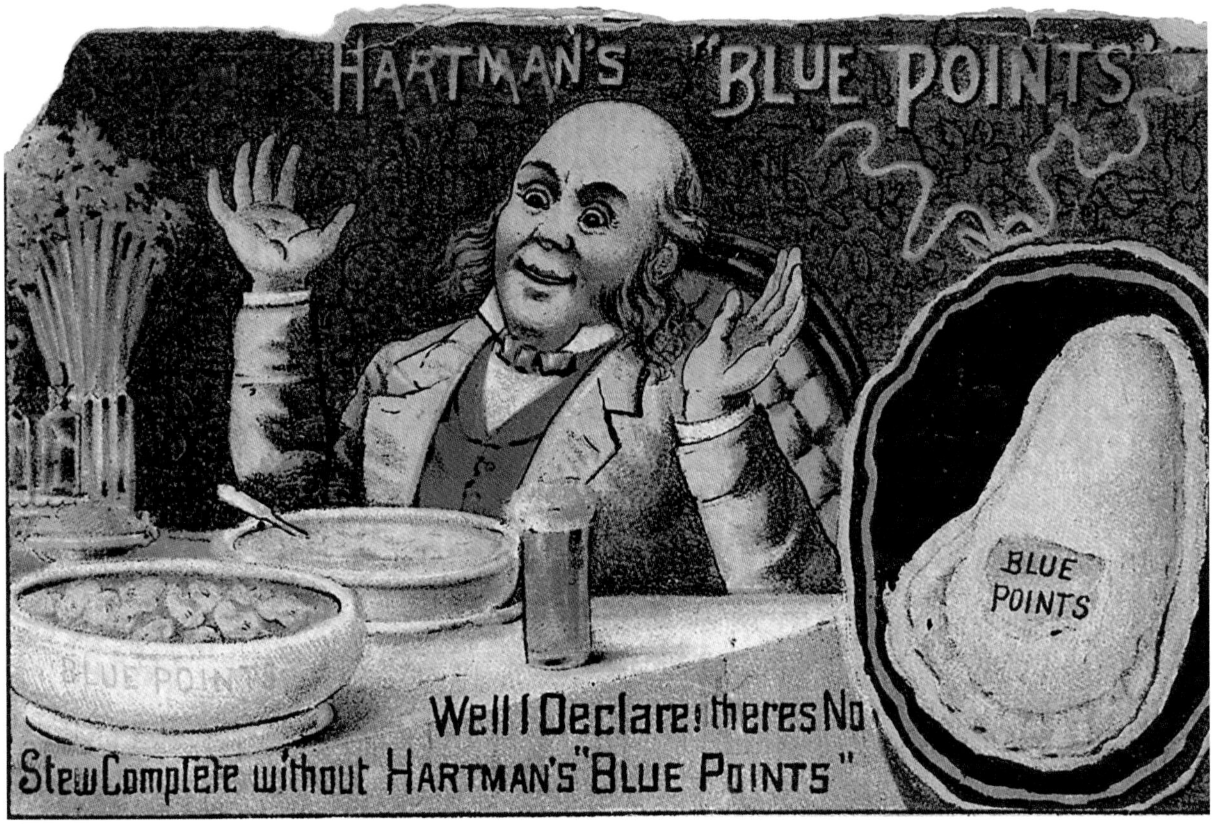
HARTMAN'S "BLUE POINTS"
BLUE POINTS
BLUE POINTS
Well I Declare! theres No
Stew Complete without HARTMAN'S "BLUE POINTS"

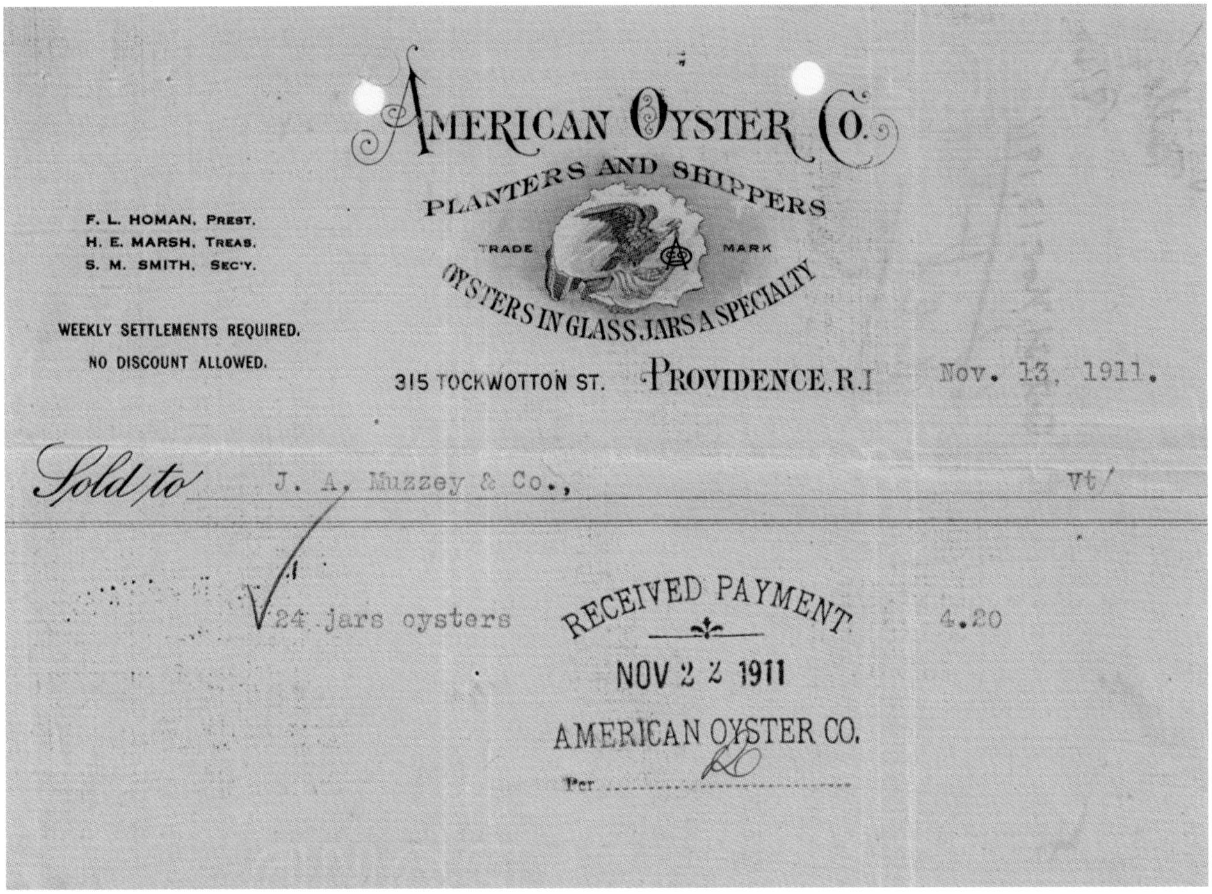

AMERICAN OYSTER CO.
PLANTERS AND SHIPPERS
TRADE MARK
OYSTERS IN GLASS JARS A SPECIALTY

F. L. HOMAN, PREST.
H. E. MARSH, TREAS.
S. M. SMITH, SEC'Y.

WEEKLY SETTLEMENTS REQUIRED.
NO DISCOUNT ALLOWED.

315 TOCKWOTTON ST. PROVIDENCE, R.I Nov. 13, 1911.

Sold to J. A. Muzzey & Co., Vt.

24 jars oysters 4.20

RECEIVED PAYMENT
NOV 22 1911
AMERICAN OYSTER CO.
Per

Pacific Surfperch

Pacific Surfperches are an important fish in the outdoor culture of the Pacific Northwest. They are very popular with many recreational fishermen, and though catching them is never guaranteed, the process is easy to grasp: stand on a beautiful beach and cast your line into the surf. There are 18 species of surfperch in this family, and they can be seen easily gliding through the breaking waves, almost onto the shore itself, to snap up little crabs and shrimp from the sand. On average these are no bigger than a hand, though the largest species grows up to 19 inches. There's a small commercial fishery for surfperches, most active near San Francisco and north into Oregon.

There is a centuries-old disagreement regarding the quality of these fish. In the early days of California, surfperch was shunned by many for its mushy texture and watery flavor, yet the fish was very popular with the Chinese immigrant communities, who often salted the fish, then dried it on open-air racks for several days. This technique firms the flesh and intensifies its flavor as it dries. The Chinese also salted and dried another fish that was widely shunned by the new Californians for similar reasons: flounder. Sometimes I think that we just don't give things a fair shot. We seem to have changed our minds about flounder, but since I've not seen surfperch on any restaurant menus or offered by any wholesalers, I'm left to guess that its day in the sun, other than on an open-air rack, has yet to come.

Parrotfish

The dozens of species of **Parrotfish** swimming worldwide all seem to be competing for the title of "Most Flamboyant." Their beautiful appearance looks like a mash-up of puffy paint, tie-dye, and a coloring book, and they can make an impressive splash at the table, too.

Parrotfish are caught around the reefs upon which they graze for algae. Their parrot-like mouths (hence their name) and strong teeth chomp off bits of coral in order to eat the algae. The ground coral passes through, and the parrotfish are proved essential to the health of reef ecosystems as they prevent the algae from suffocating the living coral. The healthy, manicured reef in turn provides critical habitat for every other species of fish that swims in or passes through the area.

The several species in our waters range in size from less than a foot in length to more than four feet and are targeted by divers using spear guns and also taken as bycatch in snapper fisheries. Small specimens and smaller species are captured for the aquarium trade. The larger species that command some market value as food fish, sold under the common parrotfish moniker, include the **Midnight**, **Blue**, **Rainbow**, **Queen**, **Redtail**, and **Stoplight Parrotfishes**. Though they are found in reef ecosystems along all of our coasts, they are not much appreciated in the kitchen outside of Hawaii, where they are known as **Uhu**.

The scales are very thick and large, about as tough as a thumbnail, and removing them is a messy task as they fly about like the contents of a busted piñata. What lies beneath are thick fillets of tender white flesh covered in a thin colorful skin that crisps nicely and adds a pleasant taste. The flavor is predictably mild and moderately sweet. While parrotfish doesn't possess much overt charm, its elegance is revealed when paired with aromatic ingredients like lemongrass, ginger, herbs, and citrus. When the fillets are sautéed, olive oil does the fish no favors, as it amplifies an inherent algal taste and aroma. The nuttiness of butter accentuates the fish's sweetness and highlights its briny and floral flavors. Parrotfish fillets are well suited to grilling or broiling, and are best served with a simple nut-oil vinaigrette or compound butter. Some Hawaiian culinary references proclaim that steaming them whole over aromatics is the only way to do justice to these gorgeous fish. While I disagree that this is the only way, I do very much enjoy the results!

Periwinkle

As seafood goes, **Periwinkles** offer much more of a seaside experience than a market one. The untold number of these small snails that cling to the rocks all along the coasts are the ultimate expression of tidepool cuisine. I can take a short walk from my house and, armed with little more than patience and a bucket, pluck hundreds of periwinkles from the rocks. These are a perfect summer treat when served up before a lobster dinner or after a long hike while relaxing in one of the little seaside seafood shacks lining the New England coast.

The **Common Periwinkle** in New England, the **Marsh Periwinkle** (or **Marsh Snail**) in the mid-and southeastern Atlantic, and the **Checkered Periwinkle** in the Pacific are members of the *Littorina* family; the name references the Greek for inhabiting intertidal zones. They have long been a popular pub food in the United Kingdom, where they are commonly referred to simply as "'Winkles." In the Sicilian and Italian-American tradition they are called **Lumache**, while similar species along the Gulf coast are known as **Bigoneaux**, French for "snail." Sometimes the term *periwinkle* is used as a name for whelks, a larger snail.

These small, conical shellfish, usually about a half inch or so, blanket the rocks of tidal pools and are accessible in profusion at low tide. They have modified gills that allow them to breathe air and thus survive out of water for a significant amount of time, long enough to be shipped to market. A seemingly unlikely food source, they are not sufficient to provide any substantial sustenance. And the effort involved in gathering them sometimes feels like a Sisyphean task, with the reward being stone soup, as the edible yield is very low.

Varying accounts exist regarding the origin of the periwinkle on the East Coast. Some claim that they are an indigenous species that were wiped out by an unidentified circumstance, only to be reintroduced to the eastern shoreline in the 1840s, either by accident through the ballasts of ships or by immigrants planting them in hopes of replicating a taste of home on their new shoreline. There is reference in Jeffrey Bolster's *The Mortal Sea* that they were first introduced to this continent via a Viking expedition, though they did not gain a foothold at that time. Whatever their genus is here, periwinkles now populate coastlines as far south as North Carolina.

The current market for periwinkles, the commercial term common to all like species, is very small, consisting of live specimens sold by the bag, mostly to communities of Chinese, Italian, and other Mediterranean origins. The demand for periwinkles is unlikely to expand beyond small ethnic markets due to the effort and expense of harvest and the low value they bring. But they should be sought out and enjoyed as a coastal treat whenever you find yourself wandering down a rocky beach. Marsh Periwinkles, particularly abundant in the Chesapeake Bay, are plucked from the blades of marsh grass, hence their name.

Periwinkles eat algae, giving them a distinct mossy or vegetal flavor I describe as herbal or peppery with a tarragon-like note. While they are available year-round, they are at their best in July and August, as they have grown full after a summer of feeding.

These should only be cooked from the live state, which can be tested by their reaction when the opening of the shell is gently touched. If it doesn't flinch or close tightly, don't bother cooking it. Prior to cooking, soak live periwinkles in seawater or heavily salted water for about half an hour, then give them a vigorous rinse in cold water before draining and cooking. Their texture once cooked is springy, chewy, almost scallop-like. Plucked from its shell, the animal's shape is helical in form, mimicking the curve of the shell.

Periwinkles can be cooked via a variety of methods, the most common of which is simmering in seawater or a flavored broth. The liquid can be augmented with heavy seasoning, such as bay leaves, rosemary, or black peppercorns. Adding wine or beer only dilutes their natural briny flavor and is not really necessary (better just to drink it!). They can also be roasted, which I like to do over a bed of hardy herbs, such as thyme. They are also great grilled (in a fine-mesh grill basket)—the gentle smoke flatters the herbal flavor and salty tang of the meat. Cooking time by any method is always just about five to seven minutes, and doneness is tested when the thin disc at the bottom of the shell, the operculum, is easily flicked off using just a toothpick. No further utensils are needed. It's not practical to keep periwinkles hot once cooked, but they are perfectly delicious served at room temperature or alongside a bowl of the warm cooking broth. I think they should always be accompanied by melted butter or, my favorite, aioli. They are perfectly paired with a bitter beer such as an IPA that draws out the "sea-ness" of their flavor. Periwinkles make a delightful way to start to a casual meal or spend a seaside afternoon, but as Jasper White writes, "They are not for people with a short attention span."

Periwinkles have many relations that are similar and, though they range significantly in size, their culinary applications are close enough as to not warrant separate entries. These include the larger **Moon Snails** of both the Atlantic and Pacific coasts (see also Conch, page 159), and the **Oyster Drill**, carnivorous snails that use their rasp-like tongue to drill through the shells of its favorite food and eat the vulnerable bivalve. Oyster Drills are native to the East Coast, and found throughout New England to the Gulf but were introduced to the West Coast during efforts to build populations of eastern oyster varieties. These are cooked in the same ways as are periwinkles, but their flavor is sweeter, reminiscent of the shellfish they feed upon.

Pomfret

Pomfrets are highly migratory oceanic fish that are found near the surface to depths of 3,500 feet. They are excellent food fish, and while there is a major fishery in Hawaii, they are not extensively targeted in fisheries along continental coastlines. A small amount of **Atlantic Pomfret** and **Bigscale Pomfret** are bycatch of various fisheries in Florida and find easy sale.

In Hawaii the fishery targets three species, but it is the **Sicklefin Pomfret** that accounts for the majority of the landings. The **Pacific Pomfret** and **Rough Pomfret** are more often taken as bycatch in the tuna industry but are of similar quality and equally appreciated at the table. All three species are known locally as **Monchong** and sold under that name. They are all of a similar size and can weigh up to 25 pounds, though market size averages between 5 and 10 pounds. Fillets are nearly always sold skinless due to the fish's very large, tough scales. They share a translucent pink-toned flesh that is moderately dense with a buttery richness. Its texture is akin to skate's as it flakes into long strands. It is great on the grill, as its high fat contest self-bastes the fillets and retains moisture. It has a moderate flavor characterized by a salty hint that is followed by a lush and savory personality. It is best prepared poached, especially in a broth heady with fresh herbs to complement its clean flavor. It has recently become a popular fish for use in sashimi and sushi preparations. When raw it is likened to Hamachi, as it has a meltingly rich texture and crisp melon-cucumber aroma.

Pompano

The **Pompano** and its close relations are the most celebrated member of the jack family and so legendary as to warrant their own entry in this catalog. From the earliest records to the present, the pompano has been the standard bearer of quality against which all other Atlantic and Gulf fish are measured. For many years around the turn of the twentieth century, pompano was the most expensive fish in New York markets. In one of my favorite commentaries upon a fish, the great Mark Twain said, "The renowned fish called the Pompano is as delicious as the less criminal forms of sin." That said, there are those who disagree, namely the eminent James Beard: "Many people—I am not among them—think that Pompano is the finest fish caught in American waters." (As an aside, I would so love to witness a conversation between Twain and Beard.)

Pompano, also known as **Florida Pompano**, is rumored to have been named by early Spanish colonists in America for an old Spanish word for "grapevines," a description of the fish's grape leaf–like shape. They are a unique fish in that they swim upright like a round fish though their skeletal structure is more similar to that of a flat fish, with a small, shallow belly cavity and very few bones. The edible yield is just about 50 percent.

The famed **Florida Pompano** has an equal match in the Pacific, its close relation the **Paloma Pompano**, though the commercial catches of this fish are relatively low. Very confusingly there is an unrelated species of pacific butterfish that is called the Pacific Pompano. Pompano range from the South Shore of Cape Cod down to Florida and into the Gulf of Mexico, the vast majority of the catch coming from North Carolina and south into the Gulf. Catches peaked at over 1.5 million pounds in the 1970s but have been declining ever since. Recent catches have been less than 500,000 pounds. These beautiful sleek fish are built to swim fast. They have a charming habit of jumping from the water, sometimes rocketing over the surface. At other times they are known to skim across the surface of the water like a flat stone skipped by a child. The dorsal ridge is a mirror-like cast mixed with blue-green shades fading into various intensities of silver near the belly. The underside of the fish is a bright yellow, which is repeated in the tail and anal fin. They are easily identified by these yellowish streaks running along its lower edges. This coloration is shared by the pompano's close relation the **Permit**, which is comparable in taste and has similar yellow markings but distinguished by black on the tips of its fins and tails. The Permit grows slightly larger than the pompano, up to 2½ feet with an average market size of two to four pounds; the pompano grows up to two feet in length with a market average of 1½ to 2 pounds in weight. Though it is still highly regarded as among the better food fish, the Permit is thought to be a lesser-quality fish than the pompano.

Another species of jack, not a true pompano, but so similar in qualities as to warrant inclusion here, is the **African Pompano**. This fish grows up to four feet and has a slightly more squareish head, with a gray-blue chevron pattern running along its sides. These treasures, delightful eating at any size, arrive at market as bycatch from the snapper industry, lacking sufficient abundance to merit a targeted fishery. Smaller fish run four pounds, and larger specimens are regularly caught weighing 12 to 25 pounds. These fish have rich, oily flesh common to the jack family and make for excellent raw preparations, as their buttery flesh needs little improvement by cooking or other ingredients. When it is to be cooked, the flesh excels under marinade, absorbing flavors

TOP Pompano at GW Fins in New Orleans, Louisiana.
BOTTOM Legendary seafood chef Tenney Flynn.

deep into the flesh—perfect for the grill or broiler. The head of the African Pompano is sufficient for making a flavorful but somewhat oily stock (the fat can be skimmed off) or as the centerpiece of fish head soup. While the fish is certainly great eating, the flesh has a noticeably squid-like flavor balanced by an acidic tang and lacks the nuance and delicacy in flavor so celebrated in the pompano.

Another delicious member of the pompano family is the **Palometa,** which is almost entirely a recreational catch with no market presence, so I will not mention it further. A Pacific species of pompano known as the **Gafftopsail** or **Pompanito** is closely related to and a culinary equal of the pompano.

Juvenile pompano form large schools and swim near shore. They can sometimes be seen in the breaking surf, driving their prey straight onto the beaches. As they grow older they become more solitary and settle down to occupy deeper waters. Originally pompano were found mostly around oyster reefs and barrier islands in the Gulf and Southeast Atlantic. In the past few decades they have expanded their territory as populations are now found to aggregate around offshore drilling platforms. The platforms act as artificial reefs, providing a micro-ecosystem attracting fish and marine life of all sizes and creating productive fishing spots for both commercial and recreational fishing.

Pompano spawn throughout spring into late summer, with most catches made in the fall and winter. They are at their peak quality in the fall, when they are fat and are in every way superior to those caught during spawning season. The pompano feeds upon small shellfish, from which it gains its distinctive flavor, and the flesh is fatty with a texture between Sablefish and Hamachi. The skin crisps beautifully, and its corselet of scales does not need to be removed prior to cooking.

The fish is wonderfully balanced, as its fatty and rich mouthfeel flatter the small but silky flake of the fillet. Its flavor is reminiscent of sweet crab, and its distinct ocean brine needs very little embellishment to accentuate the beauty of this fish—just a few herbs, aromatic vegetables, and a splash of wine or flavored spirits such as Pernod are enough to enliven any dish. There is a tradition in Florida of serving pompano cooked in and drizzled with olive oil, a combination popularized by the large Greek fishing community in the area. Though butter is certainly a fine medium, the olive oil enhances the fish's flavor, making it more robust. I am particularly fond of pairing these fish with mint and ginger, which elevate the fish's remarkable flavors by adding a slight spice and comforting aroma. Given pompano's high oil content, all members of the fish's family are well suited to smoking, either for preservation or as a mild treatment for flavoring prior to cooking.

Not only is the pompano regal in and of itself, but it is the basis for a legendary dish—*Pompano en papillote*, an American classic and a staple of fine dining for over a century. The great New Orleans restaurateur and chef Jules Alciatore first unveiled this dish in 1901 at Antoine's restaurant to honor a visit by the famous Brazilian balloonist, Santos Dumont. The delicate fish is laid on a sheet of parchment paper and layered with aromatic vegetables, a splash of liquid, such as Pernod or wine, and butter, then wrapped in the paper to form a half-moon shape with an airtight seal. When baked, this packet puffs like a balloon (hence, the relation to the balloonist) and is served tableside. A service captain completes the pageantry making quite a show of cutting open the parchment, releasing a cloud of sensuously aromatic steam.

Although pompano were very popular as fresh product, significant quantities were salted, prepared in the same manner as mullet (as were other popular fish such as the Bluefish, Sheepshead, and Redfish). This practice was undertaken in January through early spring, the trade ending around May when hot weather decreased quality and turned oils rancid. Before it was served, the salted pompano would be washed of its salt crust and soaked in water and vinegar, then broiled with butter, poached with herbs, or added as part of a New Orleans–style court bouillon.

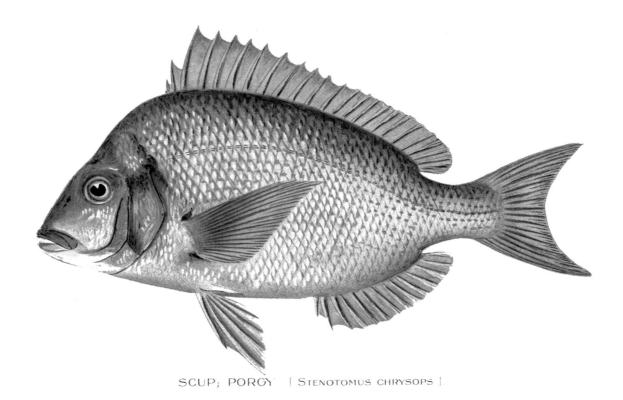

SCUP; PORGY [STENOTOMUS CHRYSOPS]

Porgy

I find the porgies (the *Sparidae* family) to be one of the most appealing of all the families of fish. The many species have a lot going for them: a pleasing shape, beautiful colorations, and an exciting and charismatic array of flavors and personalities. The profusion of bones in these fish's relatively small bodies is the only thing that keeps them from being among the most highly regarded seafood species. But that's never stopped me—the bones are easy to remove, and the fish are so plentiful in our waters that they can be found at a great price point. The porgy family is one that has important history in our cuisine and fisheries. According to Goode, one species, the **Scup**, also known simply as **Porgy**, was "by far the most important food fish" in early America, from Rhode Island into the southern reaches of the mid-Atlantic. The names Porgy and Scup are both derived from Narragansett word **Mishcuppaug**, meaning "thick scaled." In the North, the name **Scuppaug**, shortened to Scup, came into fashion, while to the south the **Paugy** and its subsequent derivation, Porgy, came to be the common moniker. Grigson describes this fish as having such a "cheerful name" as to be endearing to the cook. Though Scup/Porgy is a single species, there are more than a dozen other species that fall under the name porgy, and this creates some confusion.

In early fisheries, before the use of refrigeration, smack boats were used to transport fish in live wells. The Scup was the first fish to be transported by such method. A boatload arriving in Boston Harbor was released into the water in hopes of proliferating a new fishery. A small number of these fish were caught in the ensuing decades, but they did not ever become permanent citizens. These fish are particularly abundant throughout Rhode Island and along the southern coast of Cape Cod.

Their abundance led them to be incredibly popular and important, though that abundance also became their downfall as in subsequent years they became undervalued and thus underappreciated. "The Porgy soon became too common for profit or pleasure and the fishing was abandoned," says ichthyologist David Starr Jordan. The profusion of bones in this fish's relatively small bodies is the only thing that keeps this fish from regaining its popularity. "The effort required to capture more than was needed was not even a matter of sport." According to sportfishing expert A.J. McLane, smaller fish were marketed as "porgies for poor young men," and this bias continues, as they are not considered worth the time and effort if more esteemed fish are available.

PREVIOUS PAGES Scup.
ABOVE Jolthead Porgy.
OPPOSITE Sheepshead.

Larger fish are certainly easier to work with, as the bones are more easily removed than those of smaller fish, and they have a more developed and nuanced flavor. All members of the family have thick skin that holds fast to their scales, which must be removed quickly after capture. If the scales are allowed to dry even slightly, they become very hard to remove.

Some species are considered far better for their culinary qualities, though across the board these are all fine food fish and share similar culinary characteristics—mild and aromatic with a sweet cucumber brininess to them. Their flesh is flaky and firm. Most species are quite small, weighing just about a pound, and lend themselves to whole-roasted preparations or use as panfish. If baking or salt baking, leave the scales attached, as that will help to preserve moisture and flavor. The skin of most porgies is quite thick and is prone to significant curling when cooked; therefore, I recommend scoring it in several places.

Scup are dull silvery fish that are marked with iridescent patches of blue above each eye. Scup has is always been an important fish in the markets of Boston south to New York, especially in the summer when it is particularly abundant. Though these fish grow to five pounds, more commonly they are caught weighing between one and two pounds. These fish range farther south,

with their boundary being in the Carolinas, where they are also common food fish. In Virginia this fish has gone by the very elegant historic name **Fair Maid**, though the reference does not carry into any other region.

Jolthead Porgy is one of the larger members of the family, growing up to two feet in length. These are gorgeous fish—silvery and pale brown in color and coated with silvery scales flecked with brassy edges. Thin bands of bluish mascara-like markings accentuate the eyes. While these handsome fish range from Rhode Island throughout the Gulf, they are most abundant and popular in the Carolinas, where they are often caught weighing two to four pounds, making them best suited to use as fillet fish. Their body is quite round, with a full and meaty fillet. The flesh is perfectly textured with snap and a tight flake. I find it to be one of the most compelling and beautiful fish I've ever cooked, a cross between the richness of Sablefish and the coarse grain and meatiness of snapper. Raw, the delicate flesh is quite soft and can gape easily, though it firms perfectly when cooked. Jolthead Porgy's bones are very thick and somewhat bulbous in shape, making filleting a little tricky. Often there will be some intercostal tissue left between the thick bones; it can be scraped out and used in chowders or stews. If left between the bones, the small amount of flesh lends a truly nuanced and delicate flavor to stock. The flesh is milky white with a very light red bloodline. The cheeks are a special treat on larger fish and are worth the effort to remove; this meat is colored deep beige with a reddish tone, similar to that of raw chicken leg meat. As is typical with most porgy, there is quite a lot of meat in the nape and around the collars. On larger fish a collar can be a wonderful cut to serve on its own—the meat is more firm, and the bone itself adds dramatic appeal, especially when simmered into soups or stews. Or, gather several collars from smaller fish, marinate them in vinegar, chiles, and salt then deep-fry them, and serve like chicken wings. Another unique quality of this fish is that the flanks of meat covering the belly are quite thick—fatty and wonderfully flavored—and every effort should be taken to make use of them.

Sheepshead has a couple of pretenders swimming under the same moniker, though the true Sheepshead is supreme in culinary qualities to the California Sheephead (no *s*), which is indeed a species of wrasse, and the freshwater Sheepshead, which is a regional term for the freshwater drum. Though the

Scup is the most common member of this family, the Sheepshead has often upstaged it in garnering culinary attention. They were quite prevalent along the entire East Coast, particularly in New York and New Jersey—indeed, Sheepshead Bay in Brooklyn is said to be named for the fish. Thomas F. DeVoe quotes of the Sheepshead: "There are many who think it's the very best fish for a boil that swims." In many historical texts, Sheepshead were used as a benchmark against which to compare other fish as a qualifier of status and quality with some preferring it over salmon while others compared it to the English turbot. Neither of these comparisons is very accurate, though it does demonstrate how a nation of immigrants often made sense of their new environment by relating it to their old one. Sheepshead, with its distinct look of sadness or confusion, is so named for the shape of its head as well as its incisors, which resemble those of the sheep. They feed on a diet of oysters, mussels, and barnacles, for which their protruding teeth are perfectly adapted to grinding shells grabbed from pilings and rocks in nearshore areas. As their diet is heavily laden with crustaceans and shellfish, their flesh is similarly succulent and sweet—so much so that, according to author and chef Howard Mitcham, unscrupulous fishmongers have diluted crabmeat with that of cooked and flaked Sheepshead meat. Though once very common in the New York area, these are now most abundant from the Chesapeake Bay throughout the South. When young, they are particularly well marked by several black bands running vertically along their sides, a pattern that earned the name **Convict Fish**. As their head makes up such a large portion of their body, they have a relatively low yield, though there is quite a lot of meat in their heads and so lend themselves perfectly to whole preparations. They make a wonderful whole braised fish or excellent stock, as the bones are rich with gelatin and the meat lends delicate flavor to the broth. While Sheepshead grow up to three feet and can weigh 20 pounds, they are most often caught at around three pounds. Both the roe and milt have long been considered delicacies.

The **Red Porgy** are somewhat unique among the family, as they are caught in deeper waters, often as bycatch of the snapper and grouper industry. These fish are iridescent pink, glowing deeper red along the dorsal ridge, and fading to silver along the belly. They can grow up to three feet long, and their average size, the largest among the family, ranges from five to seven pounds. These are one of the highest-volume catches of the porgy family and are considered equal in quality to that of the Jolthead Porgy. Due to their appearance and origin, Red Porgy are often confused with and sold as **Silver Snapper**. The flesh is grayish white, changing to pinkish white just under the skin, and the bloodline is very thin and compact with a rather muted flavor. The fillet itself has a very mild aroma that betrays its particularly sweet and unabashedly briny flavor. When cooked, it can tend to dry out on the surface, though its interior retains moisture well, and its somewhat coarse-grained flesh is similar to that of grouper.

There are several other species of porgy that are not as important from a commercial standpoint, but small regional fisheries or quantities taken as bycatch provide a source of these truly excellent fish. They are generally grouped by their size. The smaller **Grass Porgy**, **Silver Porgy**, and **Longspine Porgy** rarely exceed a foot in length and are best suited to use as a panfish or for whole preparations. More generously sized species ranging from a foot and a half to just under two feet include the **Sheepshead Porgy** (yes, a different species than the Sheepshead mentioned above), **Littlehead Porgy**, **Knobbed Porgy**, **Saucereye Porgy**, and **Whitebone Porgy**.

The family also includes the **Sea Bream** and its comparable relations the **Pinfish** and the **Spottail Pinfish**. These have similar qualities to butterfish, as their flesh is finely grained and smooth, and they are plumper in shape than most other porgy. Their flesh is dull gray with threads of pink tissue coursing through it, but it becomes bright white when cooked and has the typically fatty, sweet, and mild brine flavors of the family. The pinfish are particularly common throughout the Carolinas, and smaller ones are often used as bait, though they make great panfish. Their attractive coloration and great flavor caused them to be considered as a potential fish for aquaculture production, though there is no effort that I'm aware of.

Only one member of the family is found on the Pacific coast, the aptly named **Pacific Porgy**, which is found in the southern regions of California and below. Though it is a popular game fish, it is not subject to major commercial fishing. In Hawaii there is a fish called **Mū**, or the **Humpnose Big-Eye Bream**, which is often considered and sometimes sold as porgy. Though it has very similar culinary qualities, diet, and physical characteristics, it is indeed a member of the Emperor family (page 205) and unrelated to the Porgy.

Puffer

These delightfully amusing creatures are abundant along our shores and are stamped with a wide variety of regional names. There's the **Blowfish**, **SugarToad**, **Globefish**, **Swellfish**, and my favorite, the rather elegant **Sea Squab**, so named as the cleaned meats look a bit like the drumstick of a gamebird. These fish are distinguished by their effective defense mechanisms. They not only are covered in sharp spines but can inflate their bodies into a balloon shape. And sometimes they are poisonous. This combination makes predators wary, but humans are strange animals and not so easily deterred. According to McClane, some species were quite popular in the United States between 1950 and 1970 before catches began to decline. The meat of these strange and unique creatures is some of the most delicate seafood in the world's oceans. It is at once creamy and custard-like in richness while having an engaging elasticity to the bite. The texture is often related to that of frog legs or—how about a more relatable example?—they are like the best chicken wings you could possibly imagine. Only the small tails are eaten, and if you can find them, they will usually be pre-cleaned at market, where they look like large skinless chicken drumsticks.

This many-membered family of fish includes among its relations the famed and deadly *fugu* of Japanese cuisine. And make no mistake: many of the puffers that swim in our waters are quite toxic. The **Northern Puffer**, found from New England to Georgia, is claimed by some sources as the least toxic in the family (note: "least toxic" is still toxic, but it's the dose that makes the poison). Another prominent puffer is the **Smooth Puffer**, commonly called **Rabbitfish**, which is abundant throughout eastern waters and into the Gulf. It is the largest of the family, growing to over three feet in length. Despite the potential risk of consumption, it's long been fancied at the Southern table. And I must admit that I do very much like this fish.

Great care must be taken when handling these fish to avoid the toxins usually contained in the organs and sometimes present in the flesh. Some species are less dangerous than others, which can lead you to think you should prepare these yourself using a YouTube video guide. *Please don't. Leave it to a professional.* Proper preparation is, of course, essential, but much of the risk first comes from identification of the fish, as more than a dozen species swim in our coastal waters. Though I know that these are truly delicious fish, I cannot in good faith state that any puffer is safe to eat, and personally I've more often than not declined to eat it. Good rules of thumb: Don't carry someone else's bag through airport security. Don't eat wild mushrooms from strangers. Don't eat puffers unless they come from a known, trusted, and experienced provider.

Remora

There is very little regarding the **Remoras**, or any of their relatives, in the history or culture of fishing. Indeed, the only references that I've found have been to the "remora class of lawyers," a derogatory term meaning the leeches in the otherwise noble field of law. Remoras go by the common name of **Suckers**, as they have a hard, scratchy plate on top their heads, which they use to grasp on to the sides and underbellies of large species such as sharks and whales. Members of this family tend to be named after what they adhere themselves to, thus the **Sharksucker**, **Whalesucker**, **Marlinsucker**, and so forth. Of the eight or so species, only the Remora and the Whalesuckers reach a size worthy of any culinary effort, growing over two feet in length. They have no scales and range in color from a sooty, mottled black to a sporty striped look.

The yield from these fish is quite low. This is somewhat helped by its small ribcage, though its pin bones run back in the fillet nearly half its length. And though it is of generally admirable culinary quality, both the shape and size of the fillets make for somewhat awkward presentation. Their smoky pink flesh has very dense muscle ribboned throughout with fat. Its texture is a cross between Sablefish and Mahi, missing the tiny flake of the former and the meatiness of the latter. Its taste is savory and salty, with hints of a green seaweed–type aroma and a flavor and aftertaste very rich in umami, though somewhat sulfurous. Its oily mouthfeel is ameliorated if it is cooked slowly so that its inter-muscular fat renders out.

Blanching the fish prior to cooking in a very slow, gentle poach both adds flavor through the broth and helps to render out some of the fat, making it suitable for just about any preparation. It's rather unique among fish in that it can be at its best when cooked twice, as its texture becomes wonderfully soft and yielding, though it maintains its resilience to handling. Because of the streaky fat in its fillets, it takes flavors of smoke very well. Though its presentation is nothing to be admired, it is a wonderful fish for mixing into chowder or smoked seafood dip, if you can find it, as it provides all the desired flavor and texture and at an extremely low price.

Remora.

Sablefish

I first began cooking with **Sablefish** when I became aware of the sustainability issues surrounding Chilean Sea Bass. I was a young chef when the sea bass craze hit, and though my customers demanded it, I chose to take it off my menu in favor of Sablefish, also known colloquially as **Butterfish** or **Black Cod** (unrelated to either). Sablefish has many of the same characteristics as Chilean Sea Bass—its glowing, deliciously silken flesh is very forgiving, maintaining its richness and moisture in almost any preparation. Sablefish came to the culinary fore when chefs such as Hiro Sone introduced his sake-marinated Black Cod, and Nobu Matsuhisa his miso-lacquered preparation, dishes that came to be replicated on menus all over the country.

Sablefish was an important fish for coastal dwelling First Nations peoples and has a long history in their cuisine. Prior to World War II, there was a large Japanese fishery for Sablefish in American waters, though that effort has turned domestic since then. They are taken by various methods, mostly longline, and are also bycatch of the halibut fishery. Given the size of their heads, the fish are often landed with the head off, cut just before the collar. On fillets, the bones are not easily pulled but can be removed by making shallow incisions on either side of the bones, known as a V-cut, to remove the entire strip. The bones can also be removed after cooking as the flesh pulls away and exposes them. The spine and ribs are relatively soft, and those from smaller fish can be soaked in a heavy brine then deep-fried until crisp or barbecued over a wood fire for a crunchy snack. Sablefish collars also make a delightful nibble, as the bone holds a very tasty chunk of meat. These are great when smoked or glazed in teriyaki-type sauce.

Sablefish's small, buttery flake melts in the mouth, though I recommend a quick, dry-cure in salt and sugar for about an hour to firm up its texture and accentuate its flavor. The flavor is complex and savory, with a shellfish-like sweetness, and takes on a caramelized pecan nutty finish when cooked, especially over high heat. The skin is dark black with very small, firmly attached scales. These should be removed before serving as the skin crisps well and adds a nice counterpoint to the texture, though the flesh is equally good with the skin off.

James Beard remarks on Sablefish's "peculiar, gelatinous fat," which is very high in omega-3s, and states: "Especially when it is kippered or smoked, the sablefish has few rivals." Indeed, it's a very versatile fish for both hot- and cold-smoking. After curing, it is generally smoked over alderwood—a very popular product in New York delis. Though fresh product has long been exported to Japan, Americans have developed a taste for this species, and a domestic fresh market has boomed since the 1980s. In addition, Sablefish freezes exceptionally well, thus enabling its largely remote Alaskan fisheries to deliver high-quality product year-round to the lower 48 states. More than two-thirds of the fish is taken in Alaska, where they reach a larger size—roughly five pounds or greater—and have a higher oil content and a richer, more developed and mature flavor. They are also caught along the entire Pacific coast, including Puget Sound, where it was historically known as **Horse Mackerel**. In San Francisco, it was known as **Candle Fish** due to its extreme fattiness. In its southern reaches, they tend to run smaller in size.

Fish that are three pounds or less have become commonly known as Butterfish and are preferred for pan preparations, as they have a slightly lighter and cleaner flavor with less oil. In this way, they resemble the Bluefish, as they have gradations of texture, flavor, and fat that are determined by age. Sablefish are widely considered best quality when caught in the late summer and fall, after they have been heavily feeding on crab, squid, and Eulachon, building up fat reserves for the winter.

Given the abundance of regional and historical names, the fish is officially known only as Sablefish, a name given to it as a reflection of its silken flesh that, some say, is as luxurious as the fur of a sable.

The Sablefish has a rarely caught cousin, the **Skilfish**, which is nearly equal in culinary quality though its flesh is said to be firmer. They grow nearly double the size of Sablefish. Given the rarity of Skilfish, it is cause for celebration when one is taken, and local newspapers herald the event. It will never be a market fish but it's fun to mention here.

OPPOSITE Sablefish.

Salmon

"In all the realm of food is no story more tinctured with romance and adventure than that of the salmon," reads a World War II–era pamphlet titled "Cattle of the Sea." They are a fish that we can relate to as they swim into our world and into our lives. And they have been an essential part of the history of so many human communities for so many centuries. Celebrated by the Greeks and Romans, salmon has found a welcome home on tables of both the richest and the poorest. It is the king of all of the angling fish and so inspired Isaac Walton's timeless classic *The Compleat Angler*.

The Atlantic Salmon, known to science as *Salmo salar*, meaning "the leaper," was well regarded by Europeans in the Mediterranean and throughout northern Europe. When America was first settled by European colonists they found our rivers as teeming with salmon as our seas were with cod, and for a long time those two were among the new country's most important fisheries species. In Maine, where some of the largest salmon rivers run, salmon was a staple food of frontier communities, from loggers to the settlers pushing the boundaries of the new America. The very highest-quality fish were considered to be from the Kennebec River in Maine, and by 1832, according to Thomas F. DeVoe, New York City was supplied with fresh salmon from there. The fish he describes were very large, abundant, and cheap. According to

Goode, there are accounts of people reminiscing about their grandfathers going to the rivers to buy shad and the fishermen stipulating that a certain number of salmon must be purchased along with the shad. In New Hampshire there is legend of an old folk tradition that farmers' wives would spear salmon with a pitchfork to feed the field hands.

At the dawn of the salmon fishery, what wasn't eaten fresh within the immediate region was salted, packed into barrels topped off with brine, and transported all over the colonies. As technologies advanced, the abundance of salmon provided one of the first opportunities for a new industry to gain a foothold. Salmon, along with lobster, were among the very first foods to be canned in America.

Salmon have a very complicated life cycle, which culminates in their return to the river of their birth in the spring and throughout the summer. Salmon runs on the East Coast began in March and ran through September, with the peak runs in the northern range being just around July 4. A traditional culinary pairing in Maine is the that of grilled salmon with the first peas plucked from the vine and freshly tilled new potatoes. It was a feast to celebrate not only the founding of our country but also the waking of nature's sleeping bounty.

PREVIOUS PAGES Pike Place Market, Seattle, Washington.
OPPOSITE AND ABOVE Canned salmon labels, 1881–1897.

The adult fish returning to the river make their way upstream, leaping over obstacles and swimming into shallow tributaries and creeks, where the females, laden with as many as 1,000 eggs for every pound the fish weighs, will use their tails to dig a deep nest called a *redd* into the gravel streambed and deposit their eggs. Male salmon compete for the chance to fertilize the eggs, which the following spring will hatch into *alevin*. This first stage of salmon is still larval, with the fish attached to and feeding from the remaining egg yolk sac, but it will grow quickly over the next six weeks. Once this built-in nutrition is gone, the alevins become what are known as *fry*, and over the course of the next year they will feed on insects and plants and nearly quadruple in size. At this age, they become known as

parr. These fish, about 3½ inches in length, will spend the next one to five years feeding, growing, and readying themselves for the first great journey of their lives. The disparity in growth rates depends on the water temperature of the creeks and the availability of food. Once they measure between six and nine inches, the baby salmon are now juveniles known as *smolt*. In springtime the newest class of smolt will begin to undergo an incredible transformation as they lose their effective river bottom camouflage coloring and take on the silvery sheen and striking black spots of the adult salmon. For all of their lives, these young salmon have been swimming against the stream, maintaining their place, but now they turn and swim with the current toward the river's mouth and the great ocean's embrace. As they swim between fresh and salt water, a special adaptation in the gills allow the fish to modify their physiology (osmoregulation) to adapt to the new environment. As these young salmon journey downstream, their minds are imprinted with a map of the earth's magnetic field as it pertains to their specific location. They will use this to navigate back to the very spot from which they departed.

Once in the ocean, the now-adult salmon migrate in schools across great distances, feeding on small fish, especially herring, shellfish, and crustaceans. After one to four years at sea, depending on how fast the individual fish grow and mature, hormones will direct them to return to their home river. Salmon that return from the sea after just one year are named *grilse*; those that remain longer become known as *multi-sea winter salmon*. Once the fish head toward freshwater—in what's known as the *salmon run*—they will stop feeding and live off their accumulated fat reserves. This is when the fish are at their peak, their flesh streaked with luxurious fat that will sustain them all the way through the spawning process. After the salmon have spawned, they become known as *kelts*. In this stage they are very weak, as they haven't fed in weeks and are worn down from mating. Their natural instincts turn them once again to the sea, though the vast majority will not complete the journey. Those kelts that do succeed begin to feed and grow strong until nature calls them home again. It's estimated that only 5 percent of Atlantic Salmon survive the arduous trials and return to successfully spawn again. These strongest fish are known as *mended kelts*. That Atlantic Salmon can survive after spawning is unique; all Pacific species die in the waters where they have just mated.

Salmon rivers vary in length from just a few dozen miles to almost 2,000 miles. Within each river there are multiple genetically distinct runs, with each finely calibrated to the unique strengths demanded of them by their particular tributary. Salmon that must swim only a short distance to their spawning grounds will carry less fat than those continuing farther upstream to more distant home waters. Within each river system, the salmon population will be more or less uniform in their culinary qualities, but populations from different rivers can show incredible diversity in size, strength, fat, age, and flavor. Unlike the Atlantic Salmon, Pacific salmon is not one species but five. From the Pacific Northwest to Alaska, rivers are likely home to multiple salmon species, each returning at slightly different times in the calendar year and each having its own genetic diversity.

Salmon fisheries are for the most part conducted to capture returning fish just as they near or enter freshwater. As the quarry swims toward land and funnels into the confines of the river, it makes good sense that fishing effort would be well rewarded. Traditional methods have used weirs, gill nets, fish wheels,. and simple dip nets to easily land all that was wanted. Despite the efficiency of these methods, far more salmon succeed upstream than are taken. Those that swim unmolested past human's guard are counted as escapement, an important part of fisheries management. In Pacific salmon fisheries, a certain number of fish must pass beyond the gauntlet before fishing may even begin. This escapement ensures that an adequate breeding population finds its way home.

The awe-inspiring predisposition toward home, and the backbone and brawn that brings them there, animates the very identity of the species. But such singular motivation acted out in an equally singular geography makes them quite vulnerable to fishing and environmental stressors. As each geographical area has its own genetic variations, it has proven far too easy to eradicate entire populations. Many of the salmon fisheries in the Pacific are enhanced by hatchery-released fish. While these human-raised salmon released into the wild certainly increase the returning biomass, there is some controversy about the practice, as it is a manner of selective breeding (as we choose only certain genetic strains of salmon it is considered artificial selection).

For most of human history, rivers have been the most powerful mechanism of commerce, providing avenue for people and goods. Very often, communities founded agricultural sites in the alluvial floodplains that extend from rivers, the soils richly fertilized by centuries of deposits. Just as oceans bore life on earth, rivers birthed thriving human communities. As populations grew and our society advanced, rivers not only transported goods but also powered industry itself. Hydropower captured by dams milled our grains, cut timber, and wove textiles. To power early New England, the once free-flowing aqueous arteries were severed by more than 14,000 dams, which disassociated rivers from the sea and interrupted the migration of fish that swam between.

Atlantic Salmon's range extends from northern Québec and the Labrador Sea south into Long Island Sound. There are some accounts of the fish swimming as far south as North Carolina and through the Chesapeake into the Potomac River, but if they swam into these waters there were never significant populations. Most of the 875 Pacific and Atlantic salmon rivers in North America have suffered significant declines in salmon populations, with many river runs classified as endangered. By 1815 the proliferation of dams along the Connecticut River, and the pollution and sewage discharged from the industries they fueled, had wiped out what was once the most abundant Atlantic Salmon population. Over the next few decades populations collapsed in all of the most important rivers,

including the Merrimack by 1860. By the 1870s, populations in the Androscoggin, Kennebec, Penobscot, and Damariscotta rivers had been suffocated under a cloud of sawdust from the timber industry. In 1872 it was recorded that in the 28 most important Atlantic Salmon rivers, the fish appeared in only eight of them with any regularity. The loss of these fisheries was greatly lamented, though the powerful drug of progress prevailed over our judgment. Goode gave voice to this sentiment, writing: "In 1798 a corporation known as the Upper Locks and Canals Company built a dam 16 feet high, at Miller's River, 100 miles from the mouth of the Connecticut. For two or three years fish were observed in great abundance below the dam, and for perhaps 10 years they continued to appear, vainly striving to reach their spawning grounds; but soon the work of extermination was complete. When, in 1872 a solitary salmon made its appearance, the Saybrook fishermen could not give it a name." All commercial Atlantic Salmon fisheries in the United States were closed by 1948.

Atlantic Salmon is now farmed all over the world in oceans far from the Atlantic. It has rapidly become one of the most important globally traded seafoods and has had an impressive impact in increasing the seafood intake of Americans. While much of the volume is produced as a low-priced commodity, there are also luxury-level brands that have raised the culinary profile of this newly innovated favorite. While it has become a staple on menus it has not been without controversy. There have been a host of abuses associated with farming salmon that have turned many chefs and consumers away from it. The market for wild salmon was threatened by the emergence of the often lower-priced farmed product, and fisheries fought back with marketing campaigns and lawsuits. These focused on salmon producers artificially coloring their products with chemically derived pigments. This led to the mandate that farmed salmon be labeled "color added." By nature, salmon is a white-fleshed fish; its signature "salmon" color is derived from naturally occurring pigments in the shrimp and krill they feed upon. Though the relationship was (and to some extent still is) contentious, the market for salmon is growing and there has been plenty of room for both wild and farmed fish to gain share, plus the industry has been consistently advancing its sustainability practices.

OPPOSITE, TOP Wilson Dam. Alabama, 1927. MIDDLE Grand Coulee Dam. Washington, 1942. BOTTOM Bonneville Dam. Washington, 1934.

FIG. 2.—CHINOOK SALMON. BREEDING MALE.

FIG. 3.—SOCKEYE SALMON. ADULT MALE.

FIG. 4.—COHO SALMON. BREEDING MALE.

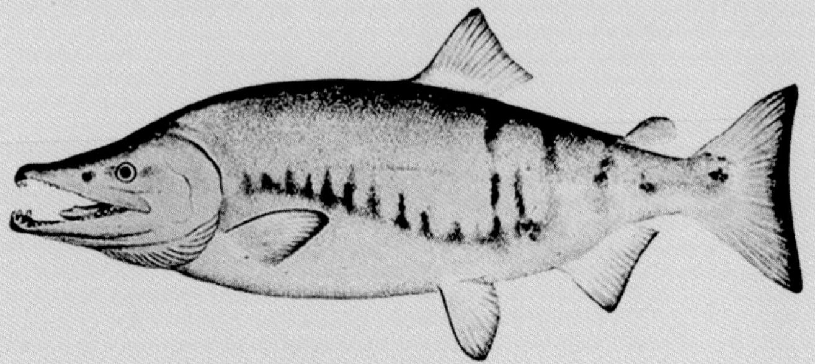

FIG. 5.—CHUM SALMON. BREEDING MALE.

FIG. 6.—HUMPBACK SALMON. ADULT MALE.

FIG. 7.—STEELHEAD TROUT.

Kodiak, Alaska.

A detriment of having ready access to farmed Atlantic Salmon is that consumer interest in the fate of wild Atlantic Salmon has dulled. There are still glimmers of hope in some New England rivers where dams have been removed or fish ladder installed, and salmon populations protected and enhanced, all resulting in a slow increase in spawning runs of the once-mighty salmon. These charismatic creatures provide an economic and cultural incentive for us to end the legacy of environmental abuses. While we should have (and need, from a health perspective) farmed Atlantic Salmon, we must never forget to protect and restore the wild Atlantic Salmon that once fed so many millions.

In 1792 a trader named Robert Gray sailed into the Columbia River and discovered what Native Americans in the area had known for centuries—that it was the greatest salmon watershed in the country. Lewis and Clark noted in their journals that salmon from the Columbia was the principal food of the local Indians. Carbon dating indicates that indigenous salmon-eating peoples were living in the Columbia watershed around 11,000 BC and that this fish had sustained civilization for almost 13,000 years prior to the Lewis and Clark expedition, Corps of Discovery. Salmon's role in native lore, culture, mythology, and animism is foundational, and to many tribes throughout the Pacific Northwest and Alaska, salmon is central to their identity.

As early as 1830, a small but growing fishery was under way in the Columbia and in many rivers in Northern California. Nearly all of this fish was salted in barrels and shipped to remote markets as far east as the Mississippi River and west to Hawaii. A few producers would pack only the bellies of the salmon, discarding the rest. This fattiest and choicest piece of the fish was in high demand, and salmon were so plentiful that such wanton waste was economical. This practice ended in 1906 when regulations began requiring that no belly could be packed unless economic use was made of the remainder of the fish. This was among the first of so many contentious regulatory issues to come.

The population boom and cultural avalanche that followed in the wake of forty-niners seeking riches provided a workforce and market for the rapidly growing industry. In a letter dated 1851, Dame Shirley wrote in adulation of the bounty of the West Coast, where she found "salmon in colors like the red, red gold." The moniker proved to be quite accurate, as the Columbia River salmon industry proved over time to be far more lucrative than gold mining. As salmon had been an important resource for the canning industry in the East, it was only a matter of time before the technology arrived on the West Coast. It started in 1864, when a bunch of Yankee entrepreneurs from Maine packed 4,000 cases of canned Sacramento River salmon. Canneries quickly popped up along the shores of every major river all the way up to Alaska, where the first cannery in that state was opened in 1878.

The industry exponentially increased their market when on May 10, 1869, the golden spike was driven into the ground in Promontory, Utah, completing the transcontinental railroad. But such market access didn't come without incredible loss.

While European settlers were vigorously expanding the geography of their America, Indian populations were rapidly losing their country. Between 1850 and 1900 the Native American populations in the Columbia River watershed declined by 95 percent due to disease, displacement, and death. At the same time, the non-native population in the area increased 1,000 percent. Gone were the sustainable fisheries thousands of years old, the mythology and lore imbued in traditional fishing sites, and the indigenous skills that had sustained people from time immemorial. By the 1890s, the Columbia River salmon fishery was so extensive that it accounted for more than one-third of the entire value of West Coast fisheries. Of the Columbia, David Jordan commented that "the river has become a perfect web of nets." Fishing pressure was so intense that a declining abundance was noted early on, and the industry vigorously lobbied for the government to open a salmon hatchery to augment natural populations. The very first such hatchery on the West Coast was established in 1872 on the McCloud River in California. Shortly thereafter, hatcheries were operating in every commercially important river. In 1898 U.S. Congress passed the first law protecting salmon after Alaska's Karluck River had been completely obstructed by commercial fishing interests. And still the industry grew, principally by expanding into salmon-rich Alaska. In 1917 the production in Alaska alone was so immense that if the product had been shipped in fresh condition it was calculated that it would have required a train of 12,000 cars, each holding 30,000 pounds of fish.

OPPOSITE, TOP Postcard depicting Native American salmon fishery, 1874.
MIDDLE Sliced salmon ready for canning, Oregon, 1941.
BOTTOM Unloading salmon at the docks Astoria, Oregon 1941.

If those fish had been placed end to end, they would have formed an unbroken line five times the distance between New York and San Francisco. Canned salmon was a vital food source in early America and provided affordable and accessible healthy food to millions living in urban centers. This passage from a World War I–era government pamphlet sums up its contribution: "Of them it may be said that they did almost as much to win the war as their larger brothers, the submarine chasers, for canned salmon was one of the chief articles of food sent abroad to sustain our own soldiers and those of the Allied forces."

Fresh salmon sold as fillets has steadily gained popularity since the 1940s. Cookbooks from this period began espousing the virtues of fresh salmon and featuring recipes calling for fillets. And as the salmon industry slowly shifted into remote Alaskan waters, transportation of product became a paramount issue. (The difficulty in getting anything in and out of Alaska is still exemplified by the shape of salmon cans. The slightly tapered bottom allows empty cans to nest in compact stacks, maximizing shipping efficiency.) A reduction in the cost of air freight during the 1960s allowed these fisheries to access markets for fresh fish all over the country.

The exemplary success of Alaska's salmon fisheries continues, but salmon have fought a losing battle against many foes in the lower 48 states. The booming agricultural industries in California and the Pacific Northwest are heavily dependent upon irrigation drained from rivers. Decreased flow has cut off some rivers from migrating salmon, and shallower waters are warmed by the sun reaching temperatures that prevent spawning. In 1942 construction of the Friant Dam, one of the first major irrigation projects in the California Central Valley, cut off the King Salmon run in the San Joaquin River, which made the King Salmon extinct within the decade in that river system. Intensive logging, animal grazing, and the paving of land for expanding urban developments have resulted in siltation that smothers spawning habitats. And dams, 13 on the Columbia alone, have dismembered the skeletal structure of the salmon's ecosystems.

The five species of salmon native to the West Coast have many historical names and traditions associated with them. They are all easily distinguishable from each other and from the Atlantic Salmon, which differentiates itself by having a white tongue while all Pacific species have black tongues. All of them freeze very well, allowing great quality product to be accessible to nearly everyone.

King Salmon is known by its native name **Chinook** and a host of others, including **Tyee Salmon**, **Spring Salmon**, and **Quinnat Salmon**, and these range in size from an average of 10 to 15 pounds to more than a hundred pounds. These monster fish are called **June Hogs** and are quite rare. The King Salmon are caught throughout Alaska, the Pacific Northwest, and California, mostly near shore when they are making their spawning return. It's the most luxurious, richest, fattiest of the salmon and represents about 1 percent of the entire catch. It is the highest value per pound of all of the species and also very important in subsistence fisheries for indigenous peoples, making up a considerable portion of rural Alaskans' diets.

A significant number of "**Kings**" are taken as bycatch in the Alaska pollock fishery. There is also an extensive troll fishery that catches the fish while at sea. These hook and line fish are considered the best-quality product, as they are urgently handled, promptly bled, and iced to preserve quality. They are not as rich as the river-run fish since they have not yet packed on all the additional fat needed to sustain their journey home. Yukon River Kings swim the longest distance of any of their kin (up to 2,000 miles) and can have a body fat percentage of up to 35 percent. Kings spend the longest time at sea, up to eight years before returning to spawn. King and Coho salmon are what most consider traditional salmon color, with streaks of white fat running between the muscle tissue. A very small percentage of Kings landed are **White** or **Ivory Kings**. These are fish that, by result of genetic variation, cannot absorb the red pigments found in the copepods and krill on which they feed. Historically, these were seen as undesirable fish and sold for much less than the traditional colored Kings, but now they are considered a novelty and have recently gained in popularity, as they have all the rich flavor associated with the species but an unexpected color, adding a bit of surprise to its presentation. About 1 in 20 King Salmon are white, though it is impossible to tell the color until the fish has been cut. Of the five species of wild salmon, King Salmon is the only one to manifest this trait.

Coho Salmon, aka **Silver Salmon** or "**Silvers**," is the fourth-largest of the Pacific salmon fisheries. The fish average about eight pounds and spend two to three years at sea. Coho Salmon has a robust flavor that I think is most comparable to Atlantic Salmon, and the flesh's appearance is similar to that of the King Salmon. The fish run occurs during late summer and early fall;

although they were once a very important commercial species, their abundance has declined. Because their spawning tends to be centered in shorter rivers more susceptible to the impacts of coastal development, they have suffered more critical habitat loss than other species. The shorter rivers allow Coho Salmon to have a more moderate fat content.

Considered the least of the Pacific species and the third-largest salmon fishery is the **Chum Salmon**, aka **Keta Salmon**, **Silverbright Salmon**, and provocatively as **Dog Salmon** (because it was once used to feed sled dogs). These range from 10 to 20 pounds, and their run is the latest of all the species, starting in September going into November. Like the Coho Salmon it also spawns near to the ocean and does not put on much fat, but in my opinion, its pale pink flesh has a very charming flavor, more subtle and intriguing than the sometimes overly rich King. Chum Salmon begins to degrade quickly once it returns to freshwater, so the fishery focuses on catching them while they are still feeding and in their prime ocean form. The name Silverbright, which sounds like something my dentist would try to sell me, refers to them at this stage. They are also the largest source of salmon roe, which is typically salt-cured with much of the product being sold in Asian markets where it is known as *Keta roe* or *Ikura*. Chum Salmon was at one point the salmon most likely to be found in fresh markets until its market prominence was obscured by the introduction of farmed Atlantic Salmon. Both Chum Salmon and the diminutive Pink Salmon store much of their fat in a subcutaneous layer under the skin and between the flesh (the other species store fat throughout their bodies). Cooking these species with the skin on helps preserve that fat and baste the meat, adding flavor and preserving moisture.

The **Sockeye Salmon**, also known as **Red Salmon** or **Blueback Salmon**, is the most wild looking and flavored of the Pacific salmon. These five- to six-pound fish spend two to three years at sea feeding mostly on krill, shrimp-like copepods, and plant matter. A flavorful diet leads to a flavorful fish, and their deep scarlet-orange flesh, colored from the caratenoid pigment in their diet, has a gamey flavor that is unique among salmon.

OPPOSITE Brining salmon in preparation for hot smoking.

ABOVE Salmon fisherman in Alaska, 1992.

OPPOSITE, TOP Lucy Ben stands beside a line of drying fish, Nome, Alaska, 1949.

OPPOSITE, BOTTOM Eskimo women cutting fish on beach, Aleutian Islands, Alaska, c. 1940.

This is an incredibly high-volume fishery, and though Sockeye swim in the waters of California and range north, this fish is really at home in Alaska. North of the Aleutian Island chain lies a massive body of water called Bristol Bay. Eighty percent of the planet's Sockeye Salmon comes from this region, which is fed by countless rivers flowing from lakes and glaciers perched upon the tundra, their tributes running down through the Tyga forest and into the deltas. The enormous volume of this fishery, second only to the Pink Salmon, counts runs of 40 to 45 million fish caught in a year. Historically, it is the only salmon fishery that is not enhanced by hatchery spawn. This is truly nature operating at her peak capacity. The incredible wealth of this resource is a national treasure and something to celebrate at the table. A very small amount of Sockeye Salmon became landlocked due to glacial influences on topography, and these fish, known as **Kokanee**, are prized by anglers and cooks alike. Likewise, a small population of landlocked Atlantic Salmon exists for the same reason in the lakes of northern New England, and is there called **Ouananiche**.

Pink Salmon, aka **Humpback Salmon** (or **Humpy**), is the most abundant of all the salmon, representing in some years 40 percent of the entire salmon population with runs in some years topping 100 million fish streaming back into rivers. They are the smallest, shortest-lived, and often the leanest of the Pacific species. The fish average between two and five pounds and have the highest yield, 75 percent of their weight being fillet. They have the most delicate flavor, and their finely textured flesh is colored a muted orange to pale pink, almost like an Easter pastel. The largest runs of "**Pinks**" happens in the far northern regions of Alaska, limiting its ability to be marketed fresh, and the vast majority is canned. As volume has traditionally been the profit drive, fishermen never had much reason to carefully handle the product. Now a new generation of fishermen are looking at these as an opportunity species and are producing an increasing amount of high-quality frozen fillet product that is very economical and makes great eating. As the fish are small and their bones somewhat soft, I will pickle the back and rib bones of the Pink Salmon or marinate them for two days in wine, salt, sugar, and water. Salt penetrates the porous bones, helping to make them even more brittle. I then cook them either in an oven under low heat until they are shatteringly crisp or grill them over a white-hot fire.

James Beard wrote: "Salmon has an international reputation, richly deserved, as a gourmet food. Like beef, it is also popular among people of plain taste, and it is eaten even by some members of that minority of Americans who dislike fish in general." Salmon has long been an American favorite and continues to be so, seemingly as an obligatory offering on any menu from the temples of haute cuisine to the neighborhood diner. When cooked, all salmon share a similar quality in that they have a somewhat nutty or buttery taste and the faint aroma of baked potato. The flavor of salmon intensifies as it cooks, much the way lamb does, not reaching its potential until cooked at least to medium temperature. When raw, fresh salmon has a cucumber scent and a very mild and nuanced flavor. Salmon are about 99 percent edible, with everything except the gallbladder and the contents of the stomach having culinary merit. The skin of all salmon crisps well and adds a good texture to the dish if sautéing, grilling, or broiling. Salmon skin is also rather unique in that it doesn't curl or buckle when placed in a hot pan, allowing for even cooking. When cooking Pink or Chum Salmon, which have less robust musculature, the skin provides necessary structural integrity. Beard, along with other writers from his time, mentions salmon cheeks as the very best part of the fish and recommends they be kippered (steamed, then hot-smoked) and served as "cocktail tidbits." These bite-size muscles are worth removing only from very large fish; otherwise they are too small to bother with. Beard notes that his experience comes from his childhood in the Pacific Northwest, where he lived near a cannery and could easily get all that he wanted, and admits that salmon cheeks are likely hard to come by for the rest of us.

Salmon are perfectly suited for cutting into steaks, which I think is one of the best ways to enjoy all the nuances of flavor and texture in one dish, from its crispy skin, the firm fillet, and the buttery soft belly meat. When preparing salmon for steaks, cut off the tail from the dressed fish and locate the small blood vessel directly below the backbone. Using a turkey baster, force water directly into this vein to flush blood out of the body. This not only produces a cleaner presentation but also gives the fish a cleaner flavor. This process, called "pressure bleeding," is sometimes used on just-caught fish with a high-pressure hose to give them added quality and shelf life.

King Salmon.

smooth, I'll pass the mixture through a fine-mesh sieve, portion it into jars, and top each with a shot of Amontillado Sherry or a rich Madeira before capping it off with a thin layer of clarified butter, the whole to be served on toast. My other favorite is a French preparation in which the flesh is cut thinly on a sharp bias and poached in red wine. The fish is served over stewed lentils and the poaching liquid is reduced to a thick syrup and mounted with butter to be drizzled on as a sauce.

Salmon roe is most often cured in a mixture of salt and sugar. Mature skeins of eggs should be first rubbed in a colander to separate them from the outer membrane. Each individual egg, or berry, is now separate and in this state can take the cure easily. With unripe or immature skeins, I like to sauté them in butter with hard herbs such as rosemary or thyme. In this manner, they are very much like shad roe. The milt, or the male's sperm, aka *soft roe*, can be treated in the same way, though I prefer to lightly coat them in flour before sautéing.

There's a lot of meat with a range of textures and tastes in the head of a salmon, leading to many uses. In Southeast Asian cuisine, salmon head soup is very popular. The heads make a full-flavored and hearty stock that must be simmered over the lowest heat to avoid becoming murky and overly flavored. I like to split salmon heads and coat them in salt for about a day before rinsing and hot-smoking them. I'll use a half of a smoked salmon head in place of ham hock when cooking beans for a cassoulet or soup. The smoked salmon heads themselves make a wonderfully rich, smoky stock that only needs to be used in small quantities.

Of all fish in the sea, salmon ranks as the very best for various methods of preserving and smoking. The salt-cured salmon upon which the West Coast industry was founded made its way to Hawaii and became part of a traditional dish called *lomi lomi*, meaning "to massage" in the native language. This dish calls for salt salmon that has been soaked in freshwater overnight and minced or diced, plus fresh tomatoes, sweet Maui onion and spicy chile, which is all then hand mixed together (i.e., massaged), resulting in a dish much like ceviche or tartare in its presentation.

Salt salmon was regularly featured in West Coast cookbooks prior to 1950. Uses varied from chowder to fish cakes, or the soaked fillets were poached in cream to make a wonderfully flavorful

Salmon liver makes for a great campsite breakfast when sautéed with bacon and served with a good squeeze of lemon juice. But if there's no campfire in sight, the dish is equally compelling cooked in the home kitchen.

Two of my favorite classic salmon dishes involve pairing it with pretty strong wine. To make traditional potted salmon, I poach fillets in a court bouillon flavored with peppercorns, mace, and allspice. Once cooked and chilled in the liquid, I pound the meat with a mortar and pestle with half as much butter. Once it's very

PREVIOUS PAGES Canned salmon at the Koenig and Sons Cannery, Pacific Coast, n.d.

ABOVE Salmon strips, brined for smoking.

and rich casserole-style dish. As a staple in early Continental cuisine, salt salmon was simmered for 10 minutes, then soaked in cold water for another 10 before being broiled with butter and cayenne. This was commonly served with lemon wedges over toast as a breakfast dish. I also make a dish of pickled salt salmon: after soaking the fish overnight in water, I slice it into half-inch portions and pickle it in a hot sweetened vinegar brine flavored with onions and peppercorns. A preparation like this will last in the refrigerator for at least a week, if not two, and its flavor will only improve over time. Brine-pickled salmon is often made with hot brine and then allowed to cool in the brine so that the fish's oil separates and can be removed to prolong the shelf life of the flesh. The oil can be used as a garnish, drizzled over vegetables, or as a sauce for the fish.

Smoking salmon is an art form all its own, which I explore in greater depth on page 69. One of the very best methods for cooking salmon is a hybrid form of smoke and roast. From the Native Americans of the Pacific Northwest, we were gifted with the method of plank cooking salmon—roasting fillets on a plank of cedar or alderwood that is set into the embers of the fire or into an oven. As the wood heats, it begins to release its essential oils and aromas, which perfume the fish, and the edges of the wood begin to singe, adding a whisper of seductive smoke, a flavor that pairs

so well with salmon. Another method learned from the Native Americans involves splaying a whole fish (head and tail removed) and skewering the body on sticks of green wood. The skewers are secured into the ground to lean over a fire made of driftwood, and the fish cooks slowly in the swirling smoke and rising heat. This traditional barbecue salmon method is also known as *salmon sluitum*; the dish is best served with melted butter and lemon.

Native Americans throughout the Pacific Northwest and Alaska continue their tradition of smoking salmon in large quantities to suffice them through the year. When the salmon bounty is running, everyone in the village works hard to preserve nature's gift. The fish is cut into thin, skin-on strips, brined, and smoked over gentle heat for as long as two weeks. The process desiccates the salmon and coats it with a thick layer of smoke, providing a natural curing agent. Sometimes this smoked salmon is cut into smaller strips and packed into glass jars with oil or rendered salmon fat and heat processed.

Salmon is a fish like no other. As it swims toward us and into our experience, inhabiting familiar corners of our terrestrial territory, through rivers, streams, creeks, and brooks, it swims not just as a passing creature segregated in its watery avenue—it is a fish upon which entire ecosystems have evolved over millennium as they bring nutrients from the oceans. When they die and are eaten by bears and eagles, these nutrients are endowed to the land. Over the course of ages, in this way salmon have transubstantiated into the soil, the trees, brush and grass, and all life that rely on these. It's a fish that has fed North American civilizations for 13,000 years. This fish asks us to be mindful, to acknowledge that we share this world with so many other noble beings, for just as they carry all the the richness of the oceans upstream, so downstream flows an effluent of our irresponsible behaviors. They are emissaries, reminding us that we are interrelated to the oceans, and by eating them, we remember and honor our culture and history here as a people.

Salmon have many relations swimming in the same waters, members of the salmonid family including the **Arctic Char** and **Dolly Varden**. These are two very similar species that are caught in small quantities in the wilds of Alaska and Canada. Mostly sport fish, the Arctic Char has gained international reputation as it has recently become widely farmed. Some of these fish are anadronomous, and others live only in freshwater, spending most of the winter under ice, and have a naturally lean and focused flavor that is esteemed for its finesse. In European cuisine, char is considered the finest of all fish (when caught from the wild), and the farmed variety has gained quite a reputation in our Continental cuisine. I refer to it as "Salmon Lite," as it has much of the flavor of salmon without the richness. Its thick skin, having tiny scales that do not need to be removed, crisps very nicely. I think this is the very best skin of any fish, as it chars nicely (no pun intended) and puffs up, giving some separation between skin and fillet, which helps it become crunchy. Dolly Varden share these same qualities. The name comes from after a character in Charles Dickens's *Barnaby Rudge*. The character Dolly Varden was known to wear a flowered skirt with a brightly colored petticoat, and such a moniker describes the colorful nature of these fish, first introduced to our cuisine around the time of the Gold Rush.

There is a relatively important **Lake Trout** fishery, with about 550 tons landed every year between Wisconsin and Michigan. These are a species of freshwater char and have the light orange to red-colored flesh typical to salmon as they feed on shrimp and other small fish. Also known as **Lake Char**, **Mackinaw**, and **Siscowet**, these were once a very important fishery in the Great Lakes, where they were considered one of the "big four," along with sturgeon, herring and white fish.

White Fish was once the most important Great Lakes fishery, where they were known as **Humpbacks**. These richly flavored white-fleshed fish have always had great cultural acceptance both in the immediate area of the fishery and beyond. They have long been a staple in Jewish delis, where they are sold in smoked form. Averaging four pounds, they are known for their delicate flavor and silky texture.

Similar to char and Dolly Varden in taste and texture is **Trout**, which was the subject of important commercial fisheries in rivers and the Great Lakes, though in recent decades, wild trout has been only a sport fishery. The **Brook Trout**, **Brown Trout**, and **Rainbow Trout** were the important species. Farmed Rainbow Trout recently has become very popular and is grown in large quantities in Idaho and other inland areas. Trout has been farmed in the United States since 1853 and some of the commercial farms have been around for 50 years or more and are often tight-knit family operations. Though the products can be very mild in flavor (a quality a lot of people prefer in seafood), some producers are putting out a world-class product with full fat and flavor, such as McFarland Springs in California and Sunburst Trout Farms

in North Carolina, whom I largely credit with reintroducing the Rainbow Trout to fine cuisine. Their version is orange fleshed, a result of the carotenoids in the fish's diet. They can grow to be enormous in the wild, but smaller specimens are preferred for the table. Their structure is nearly identical to that of a salmon, though their flesh is a bit more tense and firm to the bite. Their flavor is not as fatty or aromatic as salmon. Their small bones can be hard to remove and usually require "v cutting": cutting out and removing the strip of flesh surrounding the bones.

The **Steelhead Trout** was first described by Lewis and Clark, who encountered it at the Dalles. They called it "**Salmon Trout**" and described it as having "silvery white colour on the belly and sides, and a blueish light brown on the back head." These are **Sea-Run Rainbow Trout**, or trout that behave like salmon, and were historically classified as trout, though they have recently been promoted to the rank of salmon. As they behave in similar fashion, so too do they develop a similar flavor profile. Unlike Pacific salmon, these fish can spawn several times. Steelhead mature both in streams (stream-maturing) and in oceans (ocean-maturing). Stream-maturing trout enter freshwater while sexually immature during the summer and early autumn. Ocean-maturing, known as **Winter-Run Steelhead** in the Pacific Northwest and Northern California, enter freshwater between November and April. The coastal streams along Pacific shores tend to be dominated by these Winter-Run Steelhead, whereas the large rivers leading inland, such as the Columbia, are nearly exclusively **Summer-Run Steelhead**. Steelhead's taste is similar to that of salmon but brighter, with a firmer texture and leaner flesh. It doesn't have the harmonious flavor of salmon, as it tastes very muscular, and its meat is so dense as to sacrifice some of the silky mouthfeel. While their bone structure is similar, the pin bones are extremely difficult to remove and should be cut out in the manner of a trout.

The **Cisco**, also known as **Lake Herring**, **Chub**, or **Tullibee**, was once the highest-volume fishery in the Great Lakes. These grow up to five pounds but are usually caught weighing at a half pound to two pounds. They are most often sold smoked, salted, or pickled. When cured, this fish takes on a delicious blend of salty, smoky, and oily flavors and has long been popular in Jewish delis, as well as in kitchens around the country, both inland and on the coast. They are also well prized for their roe, which makes a wonderful pâté especially when lightly smoked. And they are also delicious when fried in butter and herbs.

SALMON - SOCKEYE SALMON JUMPING FALLS   BCF   151

OPPOSITE Hupa Indian dip-net fishing salmon on the Trinity River, California, 1923. ABOVE Sockeye hung for smoking.

Lewis Hine was well-known for documenting child labor practices in the late 1800s.

This photo is of the sardine canneries in Maine that frequently employed boys and girls on the production line.

Sardine

The **Sardine** ranks among America's more legendary fish tales. The name *sardine* was derived from the island of Sardinia in the Mediterranean, around which the "true" sardine schooled, but in our globalized world, it has come to be a common term used to refer to a silver fish of a certain size. Smaller herring were for many decades canned in America as sardines. Linked by their shared culinary qualities, more than 20 species can legally be marketed as sardines, some of them bearing no relation, and the single name helps consumers feel familiar with such diversity.

There are two species of sardines in the United States, both members of the herring family. The **Spanish Sardine**, caught exclusively on Florida's coast, has been and still is a bait fishery. However, with more than a million pounds landed yearly, there's a lot of curiosity growing about this fish's culinary qualities, and it has begun appearing on menus throughout the Gulf region. But a million pounds is a fraction of this fishery's potential. In 1957, a government research vessel documented a school of Spanish Sardines mixed with the closely related **Round Herring** that was calculated to be 50 miles long and 10 miles wide. It's hard to estimate how many fish swam in that single school, but suffice to say that it was an incredible number, and according to anecdotal accounts from Gulf fishermen, the same holds true today.

Much like their herring cousins, fresh sardines exhibit a rainbow iridescence, shiny and reflecting a precious silver color. At their peak of quality, they will be curved in rigor and their flesh tight. Like all herring relations, sardines do not age well due to their high oil content, and their thin, deciduous scales wash off easily, exposing the soft skin underneath, especially along the belly cavity, which tends to rip. Fresh sardines are fabulous threaded onto skewers and grilled over a searing wood fire. They can be filleted, boned, and diced for raw preparation. And I think that they are among the very best of the family for salt curing, smoking, and salt- or air-drying, as their sweet Southern flavors mature beautifully under such methods.

Though a million-plus pounds of Spanish Sardines is a lot of fish, it's decimal dust compared to the **Pacific Sardine**. During the 1930s, the Pacific Sardine fishery based out of Monterey, California, was the largest commercial fishery in the Western Hemisphere, accounting for one quarter of total fish landings in the United States. In the fishery's halcyon years between 1932 and 1936, landings reached 1.5 billion pounds annually. But such a "loaves and fishes" miracle was not destined to last. By 1939, landings had dropped by a third to just over 900 million pounds. By 1945, the catch was half that, and only 37 million pounds in 1947. By 1953, only 2,000 pounds were landed.

The seas surrounding the Monterey Peninsula provide perfect habitat for the sardines to thrive. Nutrient-rich, cold-water upwells along the continental shelf create an underwater Eden of unending plankton blooms upon which the fish feed. In the nineteenth century, the quiet seaside hamlets dotting the coast gave no indication of the boom about to be discovered and the riches to be mined from the sea. A lot of folks were chasing their golden dreams in Northern California while a much surer prospect swam just off the coast. The area was initially settled in 1851 by Chinese immigrants who founded regional fishing communities. In the subsequent decades, the area became home to a flow of immigrants hailing from the rich fishing cultures of the Mediterranean. In 1889 the first cannery was built in North Beach near San Francisco. The first two canneries opened in Monterey in 1902 initiating the advent of famed Cannery Row, since immortalized in literature.

At this point the story gets a bit more complicated. Late in the decade of 1910 and early in the 1920s, a multi-decadenal shift in ocean currents brought warmer water into the area, encouraging a significant increase in reproduction capacity and growth of the sardine population. This massively increased biomass coincided with global political events and advances in the farm economy to further spur the fishery to achieve its unprecedented level of growth. By the outbreak of World War I, more than 10 canneries were operating in this once sleepy community. Sardine oil was an important component of America's industrial capacity, as it lubricated the machines of war. In addition, these factories were churning out food to aid the war effort and meeting increasing demand for fish meal for the rapidly expanding chicken industry. Production continued to increase, and the fleet expanded its fishing capacity, fully modernizing by 1928. The next year the Great Depression hit, and the economic climate forced the industry to limit food

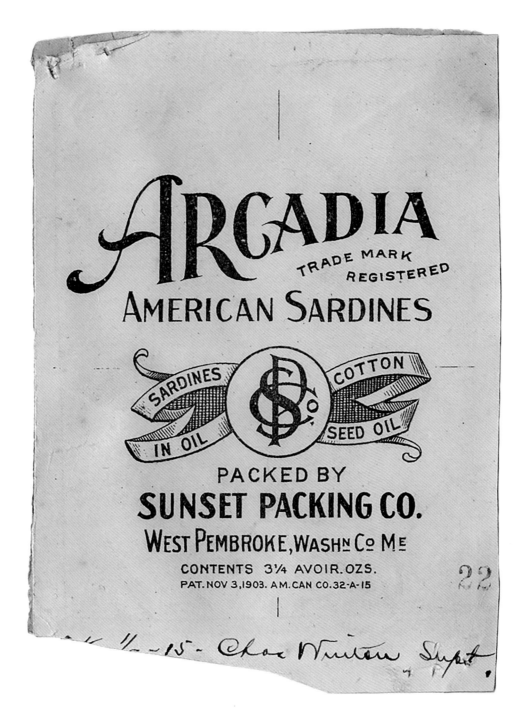

ARCADIA

TRADE MARK
REGISTERED

AMERICAN SARDINES

SARDINES
IN OIL

COTTON
SEED OIL

PACKED BY

SUNSET PACKING CO.

WEST PEMBROKE, WASHN Co ME

CONTENTS 3¼ AVOIR. OZS.

PAT. NOV 3, 1903. AM. CAN CO. 32-A-15

22

ABOVE Fresh sardines.
OPPOSITE Chinese fishery, Monterey, California, c. 1890.

canning operations. In order to save their industry and the jobs they provided, canneries had to increase their production of high-volume but low-value fish meal and oil. During these years, an average of 650 million pounds of sardines a year were processed into fertilizer or meal, and the intense economic pressure for increased volume led to increased fishing. But the inevitable and legendary collapse of the sardine fishery wasn't necessarily due to our greed alone. Examination of historic climatic influences, combined with data showing the percentage of the total sardine population we were then catching, suggest that this booming industry had long been locked into the crucible of decline.

The cycles that brought warmer waters to Monterey Bay continued to move. In their wake flowed the cooler waters more usual to the area, which restored the conditions supporting average levels of reproduction. By the mid 1940s, the changing environment had fully impacted the sardine population. Then World War II flipped the breaker on our nation's war industry, giving canneries a boost. Once again sardines were packed as "tight as sardines" in tin cans and headed overseas to fuel our soldiers. The humble sardine from the mighty Cannery Row produced 20 percent of canned seafood to feed our warring world. But just a few years later, with peace our reward, declining sardine populations and decreased consumer interest in canned sardines forced the collapse of the industry. The sardines were gone and Cannery Row was dead.

Canned sardines had long been popular as a staple of American cuisine and only gained in stature during the war as they became more widely available. But as the fortunes of Cannery Row waned, so too did our favor for canned sardines. The great geographer Edward Ackerman theorizes that "the adoption of Prohibition by the U.S. was the first blow which the sardine industry suffered. Like smoked herring, the consumption of sardines fell off sharply with the closing of the saloons." Sardines as beer munchies . . . mmmm.

Today, sardines are often used as an example of "the worst food someone could think of." Maybe we have just become so accustomed to more, let's say, innocuously flavored foods. Or maybe we suffer taboos relating to the "uncool" foods our grandparents ate. But everything old is cool again. We've been all too happy to rediscover the heirloom tomato varieties of

Monterey, Cal.

Chinese fishery Monterey cal C.H.T.
West Coast Scenery.

our grandmothers' gardens—why shouldn't we rediscover the heirloom flavors of our grandparents' pantries? Though Pacific Sardines have rebounded, and catches have recently been well over 100 million pounds, there is no longer a large-scale canning industry and nearly all fish are used for industrial purposes.

James Beard himself recommended canned sardines, writing, "Sardines are the perfect emergency food. If your shelves are stocked with these . . . you never need worry about feeding the unexpected guest." That's a pretty powerful recommendation from a very influential cook.

I'll leave you with a recommendation of my own. As a child, my father-in-law worked in a canning factory in Maine for a time, and he taught me a valuable lesson: the highest-quality fish were packed in oil. Second-tier fish got dressed up with tomato sauce. And the fish that no one wanted to eat, pulled from the bottom of the net? Well, those were packed in mustard. This industry is an important part of our heritage, and to reclaim it, we have to think outside the box, or if you will, rather think inside the can. For more on the East Coast canning industry, see the entry on herring (page 239).

Scallop

The **Scallop** is part of the lore and legend of New England seafood cooking, but to be honest, I never quite understood what all the fuss was about until one summer's day on Block Island, Rhode Island. There, my wife and I ate order after order of scallops, breaded and fried, served with nothing more than their own juices bursting forth from the crusty coating. The scallops were so ridiculously fresh from the sea, and it was in this form that I first understood the fleeting and beguiling beauty of Aphrodite's favorite shellfish.

In recent history, many claims of seafood fraud have been made against scallops. Skate and shark meat were said to be stamped out in rounds and sold as scallops to the consumer who didn't know any better. The coarseness of these two fish is not altogether different from a scallop badly mistreated, as so many were. In the 1980s legendary seafood house Browne Trading Company and its owner Rod Mitchell coined the term and introduced the world to the **Diver Scallop** and convinced a few divers to mine the depths of Maine's very cold waters. They picked only the most robust and largest scallops, and their meats, sometimes three to four ounces each—almost the same size as a cut of filet mignon—became all the rage on fine dining menus everywhere, but as this term had no market protection, *diver scallop* came to mean any scallop of significant size, 10 or fewer per pound.

Historically, scallops have been part of our coastal diet far longer than these shores have been called American. Middens in New England and the Gulf of Mexico offer evidence of large-scale consumption of these bivalves. They were never as important as clams or oysters or mussels, probably because, unlike those species, scallops are highly mobile. By snapping shut its shells rapidly, a scallop propels water through itself in a jet, which shoots the shells backward at a rapid rate. Around the frilly mantle of the scallop is a band of 64 primitive blue eyes. While these eyes cannot see in any detail, they can detect changes in light and some movement, alerting the scallop to a looming threat. Unlike oysters or clams, which have been exposed to tidal changes and have learned to shut their shells when out of water, scallop shells do not stay closed. Given this, scallops lose moisture and dry quickly and thus are shucked on the boat shortly after harvest. Only the very large and strong adductor muscle is saved, which in early American cookery was called the *heart*. The rest of the scallop is completely edible, depending on the quality of local waters, and though the scallop in its biology looks very much like a mussel or a clam, we don't eat whole scallops. Some farm-raised specimens are served in such a way. But because only the adductor has been prominently featured on our culinary landscape, most people would never think there was more to these creatures.

As they are filter feeders, siphoning out phytoplankton and other foods, scallops tend to accumulate small amounts of whatever is in the water. As with most shellfish, there are red tide concerns when algal blooms overwhelm the waters from which scallops are harvested. Some species of red algae contain powerful neurotoxins that are very dangerous for humans. Although clams, mussels, and oysters from the same waters could be deadly, scallops pose no danger to us because these toxins are stored in the viscera and digestive tract of the animal and we only eat the solid adductor muscle.

The **Sea Scallop** is the most commonly available scallop, which we simply refer to as a *scallop*. **Calico Scallops** also appear at market from time to time, though their small size makes them too tedious to shuck by hand. This job is done mechanically, assisted by steam, which further limits their culinary qualities. When truly fresh and well shucked, Calico Scallops can be beautiful when sautéed or as part of a sauce, but in their lesser form, they are totally appropriate for a fried "popcorn" scallop. Scallops are typically sold by the approximate number of pieces per pound, and so it is common to see them named U-10s, meaning there are under 10 per pound, or under whatever number follows the U. Larger scallops are certainly more impressive looking, but I'm not sold on the notion that they are always better eating. Smaller scallops at a cheaper price are a much better choice if making pasta with scallops folded into a rich tomato sauce. Medium-sized scallops are perfect for kebabs or as part of a seafood stew or chowder. There are multiple varieties of **Bay Scallops**, which are generally much smaller than the sea scallop, ranging up to 200 per pound. The **New England Bay Scallop**, also known as the **Nantucket Bay Scallop** or **Martha's Vineyard Bay Scallop**, command a price worthy of one of the most revered seafood items, and rightly so. This very small and limited season fishery runs from late autumn into the early months of the new year and is entirely

The **Weathervane Scallop** is on the other side of the spectrum in size, having monstrous-sized meats. And though a fishery exists for them in Alaska, the only place they are taken, it's relatively small, and its remoteness requires that almost all of the catch must be frozen at sea. This is not a bad thing, as they are often flash-frozen at such low temperatures as to lock in quality rather than diminish it. This fishery was started in 1968, when a bunch of New Bedford, Massachusetts, fishermen went to Cape Spencer in Kodiak, Alaska, to dredge for scallops. This previously untapped resource provided off-the-charts landings, with almost two million pounds harvested by just a few boats. But the fishery has remained limited in its production because it damages juvenile king crab populations, which is historically a very profitable and powerful fishing interest in the state.

There is some disagreement about the quality of scallops. "I find sea scallops to be boring. As an appetizer, indulging in one or two scallops is enough. After a few bites, they become bland and I am over them already! I always refer to sea scallops as the marshmallows of the sea," says chef Rick Moonen. Chef Chris Schlesinger describes scallops as "perhaps the most ethereal of all seafoods—delicately translucent, creamy, tender, with a nutty, sweet flavor." They can range from very mild to briny, depending on when and where they are harvested. As scallops typically spawn in spring, winter fisheries bring up the fattest, most "ripe" scallops at their peak of flavor. If you live along the coast or can afford true diver scallops, they can be recognized by their muscle, still so tense with life that when you touch it, its taut flesh recoils from the touch. Given that the quantity of true diver scallops is so small, they are difficult to come by. But this doesn't mean the rest of us can't find great-quality products. The key is to search for scallops that have been left untreated, often labeled at market as "dry pack" scallops. Fishermen and wholesalers have historically been allowed to soak scallops in a chemical brine of sodium-based preservatives that act as water-retention agents, causing the meat to absorb up to 15 percent excess moisture. Not only do treated scallops have a terrible chemical taste, akin to swallowing a vaporized cloud of spray-on deodorant, but as they cook swollen cell walls rupture and added liquid is released, causing the scallops to steam on the grill or in the pan. Trying to achieve any caramelization is futile, and the steam will give the meat an overpowering chemical flavor.

conducted by small boats running single-day trips. There are very tight regulations around this fishery and its sustainability. For instance, bay scallops cannot be fished before 10 a.m. or when the air temperature falls below 28 degrees, as air colder than the water would shock and kill the scallops, thus negating the ability to throw back alive any that are too small. These little morsels, as tall as they are wide, are more square or barrel-shaped than the flatter, disc-shaped sea scallops. Bay scallops can be served live, raw, or cooked, but, as with all scallops, I think their flavor is best developed when cooked to at least medium doneness, in much the same way that lamb's flavors are best revealed once put to the fire.

Dry pack, or untreated, scallops have none of this added crap, but deliver all the brine and clarity of flavor of the sea. Look for scallops that appear dry, almost matte, without sheen or any puddle of liquid beneath them. Look for a subtle variation in the color of the meats, from glowing pearly white to deeply rust-colored orange meats. Due to differences between the sexes, the deep orange meat, called *blushing scallops*, is due to excess pigments produced by female gonads. I generally prefer the pastel assortment of color, more so for the contrast they provide in presentation than any detectable preference in the flavor.

If you can find whole scallops, seek out the roe and milt. These are wonderful when poached and then ground to a silken paste with butter using a mortar and pestle, then dabbed on top of fresh-off-the-grill steaks or seafood or added to a pan sauce, before spooning around caramelized scallops. The meats themselves can be salted and left to air-dry, in much the same manner as salt cod, or they can be simply sun-dried, withering down to a tough leathery consistency. These become heavily punctuated in their flavor and are used to fortify broths or rehydrated into chowders, their flavor being very much different from fresh scallops, with a very umami-rich flavor and pulpy texture.

Scallops have been well imbued with a sense of romance from the very beginnings of Greek mythology when Aphrodite escaped the sea, skimming over the waves in a scallop shell. The scallop shell's graceful form and gentle curvature thus became identified as a symbol of sexual love and beauty.

Scallops' beauty runs from shell to plate, as the sweet nutlike meat, violet-scented like a freshening sea, is a delicacy in itself. Any culinary technique and almost every cuisine play well with scallops, as there is so much here to flatter. I prefer methods that add a contrast of flavor or texture, such as grilling or searing. I particularly like smoked scallops: a strong brine dries and tenses the meats, then a low gentle smoke for several hours allows them to fully absorb all the nuance and richness of the woodsy flavor before a hot treatment of smoke finishes the cooking, leaving a morsel the color of a toasted pecan and even more nutty and sweet.

Large scallops fished with a dredge. c. 1960.

Sea Bass

The *Serranidae* family consists of hundreds of fish worldwide. In the United States, this family includes the temperate basses, groupers, wreckfish, and other noncommercial species. I've separated many of these species into individual entries for subfamilies and grouped others by common culinary characteristics.

The sea basses are a somewhat complicated category, as the name *sea bass* is erroneously applied to so many different species, some related but more often not. The most important sea bass species in the mid-Atlantic and throughout the Gulf of Mexico are the **Black Sea Bass** and its nearly identical relations the **Bank Sea Bass** and **Rock Sea Bass**. Commercially, these fish are treated as equals and are sold under the same name. They differ only in where they swim and their coloration, which varies from deep black to verdigris to creamy yellow. For our purposes I, too, will treat them as equals.

The fisheries for these run from Maine south along the seaboard and throughout the Gulf of Mexico. They are caught by different methods, sometimes in traps or by hand lines, other times by troll or longline. As these are often caught in deep waters, their air bladder is sometimes distended from the change in pressure, and it protrudes from the mouth. Though this is certainly not attractive, it is not at all an indicator of lower quality. Generally, they are harvested at one to three pounds. Historically they averaged slightly larger, and a few giant fish weighing up to eight pounds may still be landed.

Black Sea Bass were once among the most popular and readily accessible fish along the coast of New York and New Jersey. Their abundance at market was due partly to the fact that they are resilient fish and, in the era before refrigeration, were able to be kept in live tanks, thus assuring quality.

Black Sea Bass are gorgeous fish, with patinated black flanks rippling with underlying bands of white flaunting a luminescent chevron pattern. And their flesh is no less distinguished. As they feed primarily on shrimp, crabs, and clams, their finely textured flesh is silken in its richness. Many chefs, including the legendary Jasper White, believe its intricate and elegant flavor has few rivals in the North Atlantic. While they are fabulous eating all year-round, it is in the late fall and winter their flavor and fat are proudest. Author and wildlife enthusiast A.J. McClane writes that its flesh "can be cooked by any method and is one of few fish that's difficult to ruin by a lack of culinary skill."

The skin is incredibly thin and subtly gelatinous. It crisps impressively well and recommends the fish to whole fried preparations. (However, when pan-frying fillets, which are very thin, the naturally moist flesh may parch before the skin crisps up.) The Black Sea Bass is wonderful when steamed whole or in fillets; the thin skin permits the flesh to absorb subtle aromas and flavors of any accompanying ingredient. And if that isn't enough, it is one of the most delicious fish served cold—its nuanced flavor persists charismatic and full. Serve chilled over salad or flaked into gazpacho. To prepare, I usually poach the fillets in water with a touch of white wine vinegar and a few slices of ginger, a particularly good partner as it draws out the sweeter, more floral character of the fish.

Just about the entirety of these fish is delicious. The roe, milt, and liver are all worth fighting over. I simply sauté the livers in butter with thyme and serve on toast. The roe and milt are ideal when beaten with warmed butter then cooled, a smooth paste to be used as compound butter melted over fillets. The head and bones are the very finest for making a clear, splendidly scented and clean, essence-like broth. If making fish consommé, this is the fish to use.

Other members of the sea bass family are not commercially targeted, though there are several species ranging along the Atlantic and Pacific coasts that are delicious eating. These are mostly caught as bycatch in fisheries or are popular in recreational fisheries. All members sport beautiful, sleek, snapper-shaped bodies and scarlet-red coloration with varying ornaments of yellow dappling and striation. In both oceans, these fish share cognate form, and in size they range from 10 to 18 inches in length. Often a long thread of bright coloration extends from their dorsal fin, such as with the **Longtail Bass** or the **Splittail Bass**. Others, like the **Yellowfin Bass,** boast anodyne tie-dye patterns. The **Spanish Flag** is uniquely distinguished by yellow bandeaux streaking across the ruddy skin. Together with these are the **Roughtongue Bass**, **Streamer Bass**, **Red Barbier**, **Hookthroat Bass**, and the **Threadfin Bass**. Though it is rare to find these fish at market you will be rewarded with pan-sized fillets. Their flesh is sweetly briny and very similar in texture and character to snapper though not quite as spirited—call them "Snapper-Lite."

There is a large group of fish, the hamlets, of which most are below food size. One species, the **Mutton Hamlet**, is sometimes landed as bycatch in snapper and grouper fisheries in Florida. They are about a foot long, and their grouper-like body shape portends the nature of its meat, which is by accounts identical to that of a small grouper.

On the West Coast, three species that were historically considered very fine food fish and and collectively known as **Cabrilla**, though they are not related to the Spotted Cabrilla, which is a grouper. These are now known as the **Kelp Bass**, **Barred Sand Bass**, and the **Spotted Sand Bass**. The Kelp Bass, historically known as **Kelp Salmon**, is found from the Columbia River delta through Southern California. It was very popular with Chinese populations and an important market fish in San Francisco. In the early 1900s, the Spotted Sand Bass, swimming in the waters of Monterey, California, and south, was acclaimed as among the finest food fish in California. According to David Starr Jordan they were so abundant in waters near San Diego he predicted they would become one of the most important fisheries of the West. The Barred Sand Bass, once known by the awesome '50s-rocker name "**Johnny Verde**," shares the same territory as the Spotted Sand Bass. Despite optimistic predictions and appreciation for these fish, they were never significantly targeted nor gained much value at market. They currently support very minor sport and commercial catches, but I wonder if this isn't a huge opportunity missed. They grow to good market size, between 1½ and 2½ feet long. Their meat is a perfect cross between the sinewy texture and vigorous flavor of Striped Bass and the large flake and sweet shellfish taste of grouper. Sounds like an ingredient worth investigating.

OPPOSITE Gloucester, Massachusetts, 1910.

Sea Chubs

The **Sea Chubs** as a group are fairly accurately advertised by their rather simple and oafish moniker. Individual species, however, are far more colorfully elaborated with names such as the **Opaleye**, **Zebra Perch**, **Halfmoon**, **Bermuda Chub**, and a host of _____ **Chubs** (preceded by varying color adjectives). The sea chub family has earned the nickname **Rudderfish** (the actual name of a jack species) for the fish's habit of following slowly in the wake of ships.

Though mostly sport fish in California and southern Florida, sea chubs are commercially fished in Hawaii and were fished in South Carolina until recently. The sea chubs that inhabit Hawaiian waters are considered excellent quality and are often prepared either raw or wrapped in leaves and steamed. The names of these species vary, but categorically the native name for this family is **Nenue** and refers to all the local species.

The edible qualities of Atlantic and Pacific species are hotly debated. In the Pacific, the Halfmoon and the Opeleye have both been historically considered an excellent food fish, while the other species are less highly regarded probably because they are not as abundant as the others. The **Bermuda Chub** and its close relation the **Yellow Chub** were once important food fish in addition to being popular game fish. But, as our taste preferences have changed over the years, the sea chubs have become less appreciated. All sea chubs share a similar culinary character. Their flesh is somewhat dark, often described as gray, and they have a considerable bloodline that needs to be removed, as it is quite strongly flavored. The texture is often cited as mushy, though its flavor is favorably related to that of weakfish. There are few mentions of these fish in modern cookery texts, so a professional culinary opinion is rare. However, one can find some very strong opinions scrolling through the chat threads on sportfishing blogs (a fun insomnia activity). One such site offered this gem: season fillets with salt and pepper, then throw them in the trash. Another recipe suggests serving the fish to someone you hate. Sport fishermen tend to be opinionated and, let's say, colorful. Having tried the fish myself, I find it to be fine if unmemorable, and would best describe it as Bluefish minus 90 percent of the flavor.

Sea Cucumber

Despite its rather benign name, the **Sea Cucumber** is not a vegetable, and it is a challenging ingredient to work with. There are thousands of species of sea cucumber and related species worldwide, the majority found in waters surrounding Asia. There have been successful export fisheries in the United States sporadically over the last century, but despite being profitable, none has endured. Currently, there is great interest in further developing the minor fishery operating in Alaska, but it is unlikely to become an important or high-volume operation. Although sea cucumbers are abundant along American coastlines, they have never been prominent in our cuisine except for small niche markets serving Asian communities.

To prepare sea cucumbers, they are often eviscerated, then boiled in saltwater for 45 minutes or more. The liquid is usually spiced with aromatics, as this helps to relieve the low-tide aroma for which the species is commonly known. In some preparations, it is preferred to boil them whole (with the viscera inside), as this intensifies the final product's flavor. After they are boiled, the rough skin is sloughed off and the body is split in half and spread to dry in the sun. They are sometimes smoked as part of the drying process. Once processed, sea cucumbers are referred to as *Trepang*. The salted, dried, and sometimes smoked product is simmered into broths and braised with vegetables. It may be rehydrated over several days, then sliced very thinly across its long granular muscle; the disks are then used to flavor stir-fries or soups.

When the sea cucumber is fresh from the water, its muscles are firm and taut, but as they have a chance to relax over time, they lose their rigidity, which makes the creature difficult to work with. Sea cucumbers eat through tongues attached to their feet, and their general appearance is far from attractive. The most flattering word to describe it would be *limp*. To clean them, cut off both ends, shaking loose whatever viscera may come out easily, then use a spoon to scrape out any remaining innards. Slice them open and lay them flat to expose their edible muscles—strips running the length of body that are easily peeled out. At this point they can be eaten raw, though I prefer their flavor and texture after a five-minute cure under a light dusting of salt. The meats can also be briefly blanched in heavily salted and preferably spiced water, which will remove any slime. The meats themselves can be braised and are said to resemble the meat of turtles. All in all, though this resource is right at our fingertips, it's not one that's likely to gain popularity in American cuisine any time soon.

Sea Urchin

The *Joy of Cooking* describes **Sea Urchins** as having "subtle, yet briny and complex flavor, something like an undiscovered species of oyster." An apt description but, like oysters, an urchin's flavor depends on the time of year and the locale in which it is caught. The **Green Sea Urchin** is the most important species caught on both the Atlantic and Pacific coasts, followed by the lesser **Brown** and **Purple Urchin** varieties. These unique-looking animals have the appearance of an overly used pincushion, with an abundance of sharp spines protruding from a dome-like shell. Though sea urchins have never been popular in America, there have been small pockets of fisheries spread throughout our waters, mostly to supply ethnic markets. A large industry in Maine employed divers to brave wintery waters and capture the Green Sea Urchin for export to Japan, where it is called *Uni* and is very popular in sushi. Only in the past few years has sea urchin, here known also as uni, found acceptance on fine dining menus in the United States.

They are best between late summer and the end of winter, their peak coinciding with Christmas. These odd denizens of the deep do not yield much in the way of edible content, as only the roe or gonads are eaten. There are five segments of these, generally arranged in a star pattern, in each urchin. To access these, the urchin is held upside down and scissors are used to cut a wide circle in the bottom portion of the shell. The juices and brown tissues are poured off, leaving just the desired parts. The roe and gonads can range in color from off-white to deep orange or dark red in hue, and the color relates to flavor: the darker it is, the more pronounced its flavor.

The flavors range from potently briny and oceanic to a moderate cucumber-melon-seaweed flavor. It has been described by the *New York Times* as a "cross between an oyster and sweetbreads, though hints of chocolate and cinnamon are not uncommon." In general, they have a marked taste of iodine, which when the urchin is overripe can be quite unpleasant. Urchins are

Green Sea Urchin.

measured in quality by color and texture. Bright yellow, firm, and sweet ones are the highest grade, muted yellow and softer texture the middle grade, and the lowest being dark in color, very soft, and often bitter. The female roes have a texture that is more granular, as it is a concentration of individual eggs, whereas the males have a finer texture that is more creamy and consistent. The texture is fatty, sometimes described as slippery. Though most often eaten raw, with simply a few drops of lemon, there is a small industry of salting urchins, which is done by adding salt at 25 percent of the weight of the urchin, then wrapping them in cheesecloth and draining overnight. The salt-dried urchin is most often grated over dishes as a seasoning. In more traditional American cuisine, raw urchin is pounded with butter and herbs to make compound butters or to finish soups and sauces.

Shad

The Latin name of **American Shad** is *sapidissima,* which means "most delicious," a description that has been debated since before the American Revolution. Of the several species of these herring relatives, the American Shad and **Hickory Shad** are the most common and important. The American Shad of the north is the highest quality and the fish upon which great culinary traditions were founded. The Hickory Shad is slightly smaller and more southerly in its range. The other species, **Gizzard Shad** and **Alabama Shad**, are decent eating, but the flesh is less flavorful and the roes tend to be smaller.

Like salmon, shad are anadromous, spending several years at sea before swimming back into rivers to spawn in the spring. The spawning runs begin in Florida in early January and continue up the coast with each river home to a different population that spawn according to the warming waters. The northern populations reach New England waters around June or July. As such, shad has always been celebrated as a harbinger of spring.

The rust-colored flesh is oily and extremely delicious, with a distinct sweet flavor considered to be among the best of any fish. Its major drawback is its complex bone structure. Shad have not only the typical pin bones running through the fillet but a second "floating" row of bones. Shad's high number of bones has limited its market appeal and caused it to be dismissed by

many. As James Beard writes: "A stuffed, baked shad, however, offers so much pure eating joy that the task of extracting all the bones is worth the effort."

Once boned, the shad fillet is very good cooked on planks and takes well to smoke. Some cooks recommend dealing with the bones by wrapping the shad in a parchment or foil and cooking it in a low oven for five to six hours, claiming that the bones simply disappear with heat and time. I have not found that this actually works, and the resulting fish is not pleasant. There's also a French custom that claims the addition of the herb sorrel will soften the texture of the bones, thus giving you a better eating fillet. I think the best workaround is to slowly roast the fish, then mash it with butter and pass the mixture through a sieve to remove the bones. The remaining purée is then potted and covered with a layer of coriander-scented butter and served as a spread.

There is great lore surrounding shad's excess boniness. My favorite tale is a Mi'kmaq Indian legend about a porcupine that was discontented with his life and asked the great spirit Manitu to change him into something else. In response, Manitu seized the animal, turned him inside out and tossed him into the river to begin his new existence as a shad. Fortunately it's still tasty, even if it's a pain in the ass.

But when it comes to shad, it is the roe that is really desired. The most popular part of the fish, shad roe is sold in pairs or "sets" and is a true delicacy. Because of this, the female fish are sought after, whereas the males are often discarded. The color of the roes can vary quite a bit from a beige-ish yellow to deep red or maroon, though many chefs say, and I agree, that color is not representative of flavor or quality. As the eggs, or berries, are quite rich, you must be picky when buying them. Overripe roes, with large, bead-like eggs that seem to be bursting from their thin membrane, are likely going to overcook quickly and be greasy. Ripe eggs will appear plump and firmly packed in their skein—this is the roe that you want. Underripe roes, called *green roes*, have very small beads that appear to be more of a single mass than individual berries; at this stage they can be quite bitter and lacking in the velvety richness for which they are prized. However, most fish are caught at their peak, when they begin their run upstream, and the quality of their roes should correspond accordingly.

Preparing shad roe is an art. Again from Beard: "It seems to be a dish that has but two extremes—wonderful and horrible." Great care should be taken not to overcook the roe, as they will dry out and become very grainy and unpleasant in texture. Neither the roe nor the flesh responds well to high heat, so keep it low and gentle. I prefer to cook the roe to medium rare, meaning a band of pink remains in the center. Others prefer it medium, when just a shade of pink tinges the inside.

Some folks say to parboil it, blanching it for just a few minutes before sautéing it. Beard summarily dismisses this method, as it renders the delicate roe "unfit for human consumption." Prior to cooking, I like to soak it in a weak vinegar and salt brine to tighten up the texture a little bit and purge any blood. This also helps to ensure even cooking. I pat the roe dry before sautéing them very slowly in butter (or bacon fat!), adding hard herbs such as thyme, bay, or rosemary to lend a sultry perfume. I always finish with a shot of vinegar or a good squeeze of lemon, as acid is vital to bringing the best out of the dish. A slug of Madeira or an Amontillado Sherry is also a wonderful flavor pairing. The resulting richly textured roe is melting on the palate punctuated with the briny tang of the sea.

Shad was rejected by early settlers as a fish unfit for a cultured table, partially because it was so abundant. In the now-weird thinking of that time, anything too common was exactly that— too common to be esteemed. I also suspect that there was a nasty racial bias at play here—because the "savage" Indians were so fond of the fish it mustn't be fit for the God-fearing. Eventually we did stop thumbing our noses at shad, and ironically enough,

the shad planking festivals that became quite popular springtime celebrations were an appropriation of the cooking method taught by the Indians. These parties, often thrown along the banks of a river, are a ritual of spring still practiced to some extent today. The flayed fish, split from the belly toward the backbone, are spiked to planks set adjacent to a smoldering open fire of orchard wood and oak. The slow heat permeates the fish for several hours until the oily flesh and rustic smoke meld perfectly.

The shad and its annual return were once one of the most important food sources on the East Coast. The fish, streaming, in untold numbers, back upriver to reach their spawning grounds, were easily caught in traditional weirs and nets strung across the length of rivers. The spawning ritual itself was something to see (and hear), as the vigorous fish and their spasmodic movements riled the water and produced splashing that could be plainly heard at some distance. But this abundance was not to last.

The impact of industrial dams along many major spawning rivers blocked the fishes' passage. Continued fishing led to further declines in populations until river systems such as the Connecticut, once the most prolific of all the shad runs, no longer had any fish return. According to Thomas F. DeVoe, in 1867, "This shad fishery has been gradually decreasing since the year 1824, so that now it is scarcely worth attending to. The fish now taken (1,838) for the whole season, does not exceed the number taken in a single day, as stated in 1817. All the fisheries in New York Harbor are nearly destroyed, and the fish which now supply the markets of that city are brought from the distance of 60, 80 and even 100 miles." To this day, the shad have not rebounded to anywhere near the levels of their historic abundance, and this "fish that fed the founding fathers," and nearly every other American at the time, is now a luxury item.

In another curious chapter in shad's history, the fish were introduced into the Sacramento River in 1871 as part of a government fishery development program. From there, they spread north, proliferating in the Columbia River system and now reside as far north as Alaska. Despite their success in their new environment, they never became the subject of major fisheries, likely because the salmon, which dominated the same rivers, have been far more valuable and culturally relevant.

FOLLOWING PAGES Southern fish vendor, Augusta, Georgia, c. 1900.

Shark

The release of the movie *Jaws* and its sequels emboldened negative attitudes toward sharks and forever altered our relationship with these majestic creatures. After the film came out, sharks were universally feared, and for many, the only good shark was a dead one. There are more than 70 species of shark swimming in our waters; some are highly migratory, others are more regional citizens. There have been numerous directed shark fisheries throughout our history, but shark has never stayed in vogue for long. The commercial worth of various shark species has waxed and waned due to complex factors ranging from wartime rationing to discovery of new energy sources and nutrition campaigns. Rarely has the shark been simply judged on its culinary merits, for if it were, it would be quite popular.

Sharks have a long and storied presence in our cuisine and economy. Shark oil was initially used as a cheaper substitute for whale oil, both to fuel gas lamps and to grease industrial machinery. Soon enough, the rendered oil was replaced by cheap coal. The shark meat, left over from the oil fisheries, was not considered a desirable product and was traditionally used as bait. And for good reason: rendering the oil left the flesh coarse, dry, and pretty much inedible. A medium shark yields two to three gallons of oil from its liver and fatty stomach coating alone. Very large sharks, such as a **Great White** or large **Mako**, rendered up to 10 gallons from the liver alone. Sharkskin has long been used to make very fancy boots typically worn by very fancy people.

In 1916, as a way to alleviate food shortages and contribute to the war effort, the government began a campaign promoting **Spiny Dogfish**, a small coastal shark historically known by many names including **Gray Shark** or **Gray Fish**, as a cheap source of protein. Though a substantial market was created, demand for the product declined significantly after the war ended. In 1937, an intensive fishery began to target the sharks for their livers, from which a nutritional supplement oil high in vitamin A was extracted. This renewed interest lasted until 1941, when synthetic vitamin A was developed. When the fishery was targeting the livers, the meat became a very inexpensive by-product. Once the livers lost their value, the fish were no longer worth catching. **Dogfish**, which has a history deep and strange enough to warrant its own entry (see page 186), is a category unto itself.

In the 1970s, the U.S. government again encouraged the development of shark fisheries, this time targeting larger species using gill nets and longlines in the Pacific. And this time it worked, and shark suddenly became quite a popular menu item. The fishermen engaged in these fisheries began to see that both tuna and Swordfish were very common as bycatch, enough so that they began to principally target these more valuable species. In an odd twist, once the shark lost prominence, the Swordfish and tuna fisheries of the 1980s and 1990s came under fire for their high bycatch of sharks. Due to their spawning habits, sharks are particularly vulnerable to fishing pressure, as these large predators require several years to reach sexual maturity, mate in lengthy cycles, have long gestation periods, and only give birth to small litters of "pups." They are one of the few fish to give live birth to their young. Thus it seems shark fisheries are fated to a cyclical love-hate/exploit-protect ebb and flow.

In the 1980s, China began increasing its imports of shark fins for the luxury dish shark fin soup, a symbol of wealth and hospitality that has continued to increase in its popularity as the country's middle class and wealth has grown. This massive appetite for fins led to some truly deplorable practices in international fisheries—the shark fins are worth so much that they are cut from living animals and the unwanted bodies dumped overboard, left to die a horrific death. The fins are sun-dried until they are fully desiccated. Given their size and light weight, the dried fins are easily concealed and have became a heavily traded item in the black market. Shark populations all over the globe have suffered from illegal and unregulated fisheries, as the animals are particularly susceptible to fishing pressure while they migrate far beyond the controlled waters of

Mako Shark, c. 1920.

nearby nations. But the worldwide shark population shouldn't be threatened—and individual animals shouldn't have to suffer—for no more than a bowl of soup. There are now many regulations and trade bans that have significantly diminished the shark fin trade. One of the most effective rules simply requires that the bodies of sharks be landed with their fins, thus ensuring that fishermen following the law are able to gain the rightful profit from each fish, while the sharks themselves are protected by the regulations of a limited fishery. As in most instances of unsustainable fishing, there's never a problem with the fish, only in how much of the fish we want. Sourced properly, shark fin soup is delicious and should be celebrated for its unique texture and subtle flavor.

All sharks, like skate, are cartilaginous fish with a semisoft skeleton. And like skate, they too lack a urinary tract and thus excrete urea through their skin. There is no ill effect of this on the quality or wholesomeness of the meat *if* the sharks are carefully and immediately bled and iced after capture. If they are not well cared for, rigor sets in and the meat becomes heavily tainted with an ammonia scent and sharp flavor that renders it completely inedible. There is some claim made in early cookbooks that soaking in milk or acidulated brine can rid tainted flesh of its funk, but I've never found this to be this effective. Shark meat with anything resembling ammoniation should be outright rejected. Don't try to fix broken fish.

Most of the commercially important species are found in both oceans, and thus when I write of their qualities, I am considering Atlantic and Pacific sharks of the same species to be interchangeable. Most large sharks are at their best culinary quality from late summer throughout early fall. Among the 20-plus species commercially caught, and many others landed incidentally in both recreational and commercial fisheries, a huge range of culinary qualities is displayed. The Mako and **Thresher**, two very large species, are often considered the highest in quality. They can grow up to 1,500 pounds, though a more modest 125 pounds is average. And when at their best, I find them equal, if not better, in my opinion (and that of many others), to Swordfish.

The **Hammerhead Shark**, **Leopard Shark**, and **Blacktip Shark** are all considered second-tier quality, as their meat is more coarse, less fatty, and somewhat muted in flavor, though they are still a perfectly great food fish. **Angel Shark**, which by its look and flavor seems to be a cross between a ray and a shark, has a fine consistency of flesh, similar to monkfish, and is fairly unique among the sharks. Its texture is particularly tender and smooth with a resilient structure. It gained great popularity in the 1980s when it was highly marketed, thanks to its availability as bycatch of the halibut industry. Angel Shark quickly became a darling of the restaurant world, though increased fishing pressure forced the fishery to take action to protect the fish, and the shark has been absent from menus and the market ever since.

Larger sharks are similar to Swordfish and tunas in that they have a band of bloodline tissue running along their cartilaginous skeletal structures. To get a sense of the freshness of these species, observe how tenacious this ribbon of cherry red muscle is. When fresh, it is neatly delineated from the pale grayish to peachy pink-colored flesh. As it ages, the bloodline loses density, and its structure becomes limp, sagging as its color fades into the surrounding meat, rather than standing out in stark contrast.

Looking back through two centuries' worth of cookbooks, shark is mentioned with far greater regularity than Swordfish or tuna, those species having come into vogue only within the past two generations. Ruth Spear comments upon shark's appeal: "Moister than swordfish after cooking, it loses the fishy edge that swordfish can have." It is also frequently compared to halibut and suggested as a substitute. In New England cuisine, **Blue Sharks** and **Bull Sharks** were often known as **Harbor Halibut** because their flavor was similar to the ever-popular fish.

When shark meat is perfectly fresh, it is as good under the broiler or on the grill as any species. The rich marbling of fat appearing like conduits running throughout the flesh bastes the meat as it cooks, preserving moisture and absorbing the flavor of live flame. Shark is as good served cold as it is hot off the grill. This is especially true when the meat is poached and left to chill in its cooking liquid. The next day, reduce the cooking liquid then mix it into a vinaigrette for dressing the fish. Nearly every species of shark is fabulous in chowders and stews, as its gelatinous flesh adds body and depth to the broth and remains firm even after long simmering. Some of the second-tier species such as **Porbeagle** are best when allowed to marry with other flavors as in stews or chowders.

Before chefs promoted fresh shark by relating it to Swordfish, it was very common to claim its quality by comparing it to chicken, as I found in many culinary texts from the turn of the twentieth century through World War II. Prior to that period, shark was most commonly mentioned as a salted product. Salt shark is made in the same manner as salt cod, with the loins cut into strips and packed in salt to dry on racks. Though the texture is significantly more fibrous than that of salt cod, salt shark can be substituted in almost any recipe calling for salted cod, halibut, and other types of white fish. Given the meatiness of the shark flavor, it can take on a slightly musty, cardboard aroma when salted, which can be reduced by the addition of wine or cider vinegar to the soaking water. The acid revives the fresh character of the meat, accentuates its flavor, and softens the overall robustness of the flesh.

OPPOSITE Pink Shrimp in Petersburg, Alaska, c. 1933.
FOLLOWING PAGES Coonstripe Shrimp.

Shrimp

"Shrimp is the fruit of the sea."

—BUBBA LECTURING FORREST GUMP

Shrimp has been America's favorite seafood for decades now, but its ascendency has been very recent in terms of fisheries history. In America there are both cold-water and warm-water shrimp fisheries, though warm-water shrimp is the vast majority of the catch, representing 90 percent or more of the ex-vessel price (the price fishermen are paid for the product). The first record of a commercial warm-water shrimp fishery comes from the mid-1800s in the Barataria Bay area of Louisiana, though there were sustenance fisheries throughout the Gulf and southern Atlantic region prior to that. Initially only **White Shrimp** were caught, as they were found near to shore and abundant. Men worked the bayou by hand with cast nets, a picturesque method that involves throwing a weighted circular net on top of visible schools of shrimp. It was a very labor-intensive, low-volume fishery. The first statistics for catch come from 1889, where it was estimated that 8.3 million pounds were caught. In 1913, a Massachusetts captain named Billy Corkum introduced the otter trawl, used in northern finfish fisheries, to Florida. Described as an "ungainly contraption of ropes, cables, wooden doors and nets," it was modified from its northern design to drag a cable along the bottom, while the net was positioned just above the ocean floor. The cable would "tickle" the shrimp, forcing them upwards and into the mouth of the net. This allowed fisheries to expand beyond the bayous and nearshore waters, ranging dozens of miles into the Gulf, where it was reported by the Louisiana Conservation Committee that fishermen found "an immense fishing ground where boundless supply of adult shrimp always exist, with endless possibilities for the future of the shrimp industry." Catches rapidly grew, and in 1918 almost 30 million pounds were landed.

Shrimp of all varieties are particularly perishable, especially in the hot weather of the South, which precluded them from being traded far past their immediate local market until the 1870s when shrimp canning was refined. This advance, coupled

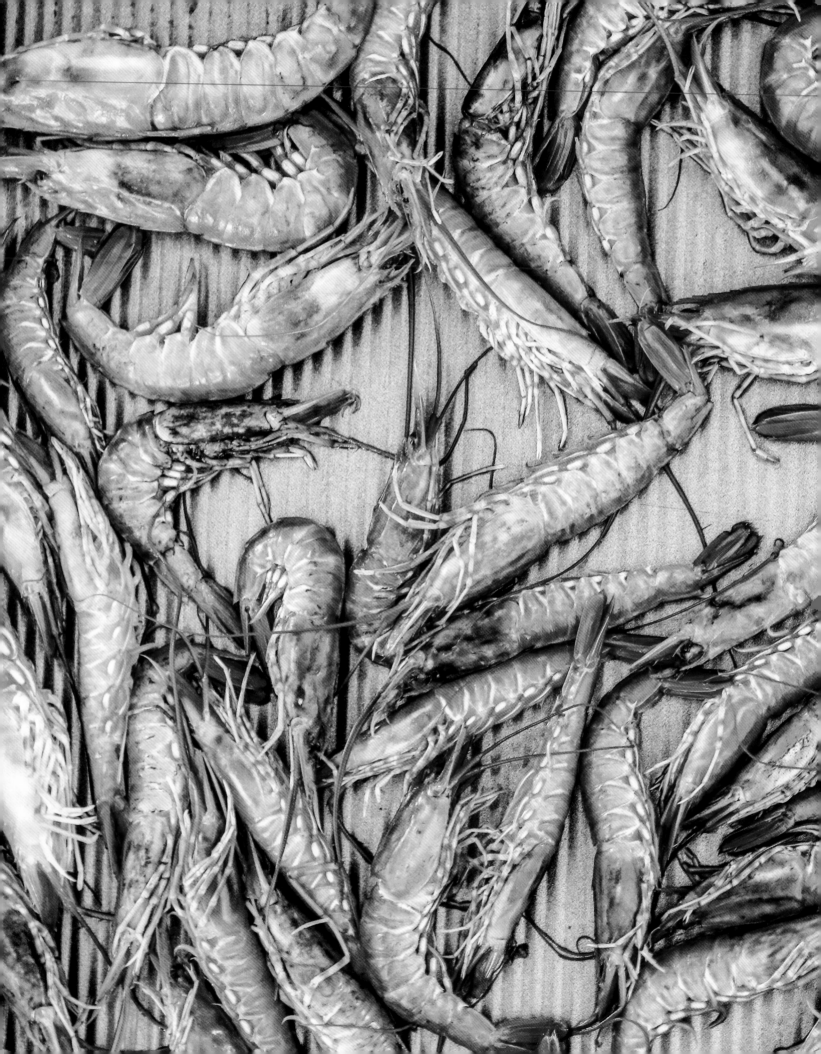

with the expansion of the railroads, created opportunity for shrimp to enter into the broader scope of American cuisine. By the 1920s, the industry was using newly available freezing techniques and crushed ice as a means to preserve the shrimp during offshore fishing trips. This capacity allowed fishermen to further implement the new trawling technology, and within the decade the catch reached 79 million pounds per year. In 1943, a teenager named J.M. Lapeyre from Houma, Louisiana, invented a shrimp-peeling machine after noting how easily shrimp meat slid out of its shell when stepped on with a rubber boot. The machine could process more than a thousand pounds per hour and radically expanded market access by reducing the cost of labor and thereby the cost of shrimp.

In 1937, the U.S. Bureau of Fisheries finished a shrimp census documenting populations throughout the Gulf, which brought immediate attention to the fishery from large-scale boats, and they quickly moved to take advantage of the newly discovered abundant fishing areas. That year the catch jumped 16 million pounds. White shrimp are diurnal, and fishing operations were therefore conducted only during the day, which obscured the existence of **Pink Shrimp** and **Brown Shrimp**, both offshore-dwelling nocturnal creatures, until 1947 when "**Browns**" were discovered off Texas and "Pinks" off the Florida Keys in 1949. By 1950, with the fleet targeting three species, U.S. shrimpers were catching more than 190 million pounds. This huge fishing effort, coupled with a pervasive drought in the late 1940s and early 1950s, brought about the first collapse in the shrimp fisheries; the White Shrimp were decimated as the brackish bayous in which they spawned became increasingly salty. On the other hand, Brown Shrimp, which spawn better in higher-salinity waters, thrived. And the total catches didn't show much decline as the fleet largely switched to nighttime operations, fishing on "Pinks" and "Browns." According to *National Geographic* in 1957, "Greater riches are being brought up than all the gold ever sunk off the Spanish Main."

The shrimp industry has long been centered around Louisiana, and increasingly so in the western waters of Florida. Fannie Farmer considered the shrimp from Lake Pontchartrain to be the very highest in quality. Along the East Coast, White and Brown shrimp are caught from Pamlico Sound, North Carolina, throughout the eastern waters of Florida, where the Pink Shrimp begins to flourish. Since the early 1800s there is record of small-scale fisheries all along the coast serving local markets. They were particularly popular in Charleston, South Carolina.

The three species, denoted by the color of their shells when raw, are subtle in their differences. When cooked, Brown Shrimp will turn a sunset orange color, Pink Shrimp a dark shade of pink, and White Shrimp a light pink. Brown Shrimp are caught mostly in Texas, and they are the largest of the three species in terms of size. The waters in which they are predominantly caught are highly saline, and their flavor is correspondingly iodine. Waters with salt concentrations between 15 and 30 parts per thousand allow for the buildup of an iodine flavor in the organisms on which shrimp feed, whereas those caught in brackish water, less than 15 parts per thousand, do not exhibit such flavor, as organisms do not accumulate iodine at these concentrations. This distinctive tang, along with a taste generally described as murky, make Brown Shrimp the most robustly flavored of the three major species. The White Shrimp, caught mostly from Louisiana into the waters of Florida, are considered the highest quality, with the cleanest flavor and a snappy texture. Pink Shrimp, caught mostly in Florida, are considered nearly equal in quality to the White Shrimp.

The **Seabob Shrimp**, mostly caught off Cameron Parish in Louisiana, are available mostly in the winter, when they "run" near shore on muddy bottoms. These smaller shrimp are noted for their delicate meat and sweet taste, similar to that of the crawfish.

Shrimp fisheries have long been inefficient in terms of the amount of bycatch they take in. Since shrimp swim alongside many species of juvenile fish, there has been some sustainability outcry against the common fishing methods. In some global shrimp industries the amount of bycatch has been as high as 10 pounds of sealife to one pound of shrimp. For a long time, shrimp fisheries were also taking sea turtles, an unfortunate bycatch that stopped with the invention of the TED (turtle excluder device). According to a wonderful story related by Paul Johnson in his great book *Fish Forever*, the TED was first named the "Georgia Jumper" and implemented by a fisherman named Sinkey; it was quickly adopted by the industry and regulators. It not only allowed the turtles to swim out of the net, it excluded the Cannonball Jellyfish and Horseshoe Crabs that fouled the nets.

In the United States, bycatch is down significantly, and fishermen are beginning to take that bycatch to market rather than tossing it overboard. Before being brought to market, shrimp are often soaked in a very strong brine solution of solar salt and seawater that causes all the small bycatch—small fish, starfish, and whatever else comes to the net—to float to the top and be easily removed. This doesn't affect the shrimp's quality or culinary appeal.

Other important warm-water species include the **Rock Shrimp**, a deepwater species harvested in Florida and so named for its extremely hard shell. Though these were long known about, an extensive fishery did not begin until 1970, when a peeling machine that could handle the hard exoskeleton was developed. The meat is small and tightly concentric. This is the species commonly known as **Popcorn Shrimp** when battered and deep-fried.

The **Apple Shrimp**, also known as the **Spotted Pink Shrimp**, are a small bycatch in the White Shrimp fishery. Gulf seafood guru Jim Gossen writes that these are "noticeably sweeter than White or Brown. If one wanted to eat raw Gulf shrimp one could choose no shrimp better than the apple. The subtlest, most complex tasting of the Gulf shrimp."

The **Royal Red Shrimp** are considered the best of all of the warm-water Atlantic shrimp, with a texture that is more delicate than any other. They are caught in extremely deep waters along the east coast of Florida, with minor landings in western Florida and Alabama. These were first discovered in 1957 at a depth of 1,000 feet. They are deep crimson and have a noted salty, sweet, and buttery taste likened to lobster.

The **Mantis Shrimp**, called **Sea Lights** or **Sea Lice**, are caught throughout the Atlantic coast and into the Gulf. This very small fishery lands only two tons, largely as bycatch of White Shrimp. These have a wonderful taste, considered similar to lobster. The five species that live in the Gulf are quite detested by shrimpers, because they can strike surprisingly fast and leave bites that are surprisingly painful.

A.J. McClane describes finding a freshwater shrimp called **Macrobrachium** in Lake Okeechobee. These strange creatures reach up to 30 inches long and are most distinguished by their well-developed front legs, which are muscular and thick-shelled and extend far past the heads in a claw-like fashion. Various species of macrobrachium are farmed, and very minor amounts are wild caught in the United States, but there is opportunity for this species to make inroads in the market.

Other U.S. fisheries target the cold-water shrimp. One of these is for the small, pink-colored shrimp marketed as **Northern Shrimp** (formerly and confusingly known as **Pink Shrimp**) and typically called **Salad Shrimp** or **Bay Shrimp**. Though there are multiple species that swim in the Gulf of Maine and along the Pacific coast, aside from their state of origin, they are not often segregated in the market. Their texture, as is that of all cold-water shrimp, is quite a bit softer than warm-water shrimp, and they take better to dry cooking methods, such as sautéing or roasting. They can become mushy when cooked in liquid or steamed. The first recorded harvest of **Maine Pink Shrimp** was in 1883, but it was not until 1934 that a trawl fishery began. These are fished near shore from December through May, when female shrimp migrate toward shore to lay their eggs. Initially, this industry was directed to local markets, but canning and quick-freezing applications expanded the market inland. Northern Shrimp landings represent but a small fraction of those of the Gulf and southern Atlantic shrimp fisheries and have traditionally been very low priced. In the mid-1970s, the fishing fleet from Gloucester began targeting these shrimp once large aggregations of them were discovered farther offshore. These populations were both male and female, and heavy fishing pressure decimated the stocks, which peaked at 22 million pounds per year. At the time of writing, shrimp simply haven't returned to the Gulf of Maine, and the fishery has been closed for several years. This is likely due to warmer waters causing the shrimp to remain offshore, as well as decreased populations from both natural decline and fisheries' pressure.

The Pacific Northwest **Pink/Northern Shrimp** fishery was targeted by a small fleet in earlier decades and became an important industry in 1956 with the introduction of an otter trawl similar to those used in the Gulf of Mexico. This was the result of exploratory fishing by the government, which revealed large populations during a 1955 survey. The fishery spread throughout the West Coast shortly thereafter. While Maine fisheries are closed, those on the West Coast continue,

with the vast majority landed in Oregon, slightly less in Washington state, and very small landings in California. Much of this type of shrimp is still canned or frozen, as the shrimp are particularly perishable and should be eaten or processed within a day of capture.

Smaller fisheries along the West Coast target a number of closely related larger species that are highly sought after. The best known of these fisheries are for **Spot Shrimp**, often labeled **Spot Prawns**; the largest fishery is in Alaska, where they are mostly caught in deepwater traps. As the fisheries extend farther south, they become known by their provenance, such as **Monterey Prawn** or **Santa Barbara Prawn**. Two other very closely related species, which for all purposes are the same in the kitchen, are the **Coonstripe** (inclusive of three species: **Dock**, **Humpy**, and **Humpback Shrimp**) and **Sidestripe Shrimp**. These are beautiful species that range from scarlet-orange to pink with stark white markings. As these shrimp are caught in traps and are gently handled, there has been a growing demand for them as a live product, particularly in Asian markets along the West Coast. They are similar in flavor to the Royal Red Shrimp and have a very sweet taste with a nutty, buttery finish. Like all cold-water shrimp, they are best cooked very quickly via dry-heat-methods as they can dry out easily.

The **Pacific Rock Shrimp**, found in California waters, are nearly identical to the Atlantic Rock Shrimp of Florida. These are also known as **Ridgeback Shrimp**, or **Ridgeback Prawns**, so named for the noticeable ridge running along the back of its hard shell. These very sweet shrimp have rich, red meat and a snappy texture.

Prawn and *shrimp* are interchangeable terms, typically used to designate size. Though there are biological differences, you'd be very hard pressed to tell them apart on a taste basis. The term *prawn* is most commonly used in foreign countries and in the South, where it has some cultural caché.

While all of these delicious shrimp are available to us and should be sought out, they only account for 10 percent of the shrimp that we eat. Well over 90 percent of the raw shrimp sold in the United States is farmed in foreign countries, the vast majority of those in Asia and Latin America. A small amount are farmed in the United States, many of those in

ABOVE AND RIGHT Shrimp fishermen in Delcambre, Louisiana

ABOVE Dried shrimp, California, 1889.

FOLLOWING PAGES Next-generation shrimp fisherman in Cameron, Louisiana.

indoor recirculating systems. The shrimp farming industry has broadly been guilty of environmentally unsustainable practices, though many producers have been pursuing more sustainable methods and decreasing the environmental impact of shrimp farming. Some outlier producers have even been found guilty of slavery and other human rights abuses in their processing. This is by no means a blanket verdict on all farmed shrimp—as in all things, there are great producers as well as bad—but from a culinary standpoint, wild American shrimp win out every time even before ethics are considered.

Shrimp consumption has risen dramatically since the 1970s, with the majority of that growth coming in low-income households, where consumption has risen by 45 percent. In middle- and high-income households, consumption has increased by 15 percent. Though shrimp has always been a staple in the Gulf and Southeast, it was considered a treat in inland markets. Landings of wild American shrimp have held steady at an average of about a half pound per capita, with aquaculture imports growing from just about a half pound to more than 3½ pounds per person since 1980.

A very small amount of the shrimp we eat are fresh; the rest are frozen or canned. This is one of the factors that limit the ability of American shrimp to compete with extremely low-priced imports, as markets are necessarily far from their source. Fresh shrimp are prone to black shell, or melanosis, in which the head, if left on, begins to show small black spots as an indication of age. However, fresh (never frozen) shrimp are a true delight—their flavor is acute and aromatic. And while the texture of frozen is certainly not bad, it can lack the crispness of fresh. When buying shrimp, they are available in every possible format: head on, head off, shell on, shell off, breaded and frozen, butterflied. When buying them raw, they are typically labeled by the number of shrimp per pound—U10s, 16/20s, and so on up to 70 (U meaning under __ per pound) for salad shrimp, and some that range over 150 per pound. Cocktail shrimp are typically 12 to 15 or larger.

Shrimp are also marketed smoked, semi-preserved in vinegar, and in fermented paste form. The general yield of shrimp is about 50 percent edible meat for head-on, shell-on shrimp. The heads are my favorite part of the shrimp, and when cooked, they develop an incredibly opulent flavor with all the aoma of the sea. They are useful for making stocks and soups, especially a bisque, in which seared shrimp heads can be puréed into the liquid to both thicken and flavor it. It's always best to cook the shrimp with their shells on, as they add flavor to the meat and help keep its texture crisp. This is especially true when preparing whole shrimp to be grilled, seared, or broiled—these methods maintain the texture of the meat, while the singed shells adds a subtle and nuanced flavor. The shells become edible when they crisp up.

Dried shrimp has long been a specialty in Asian cuisines. These were first produced in America in 1873 when a Cantonese fisherman named Lee Yuen built a shrimp-drying platform in Louisiana. The shrimp were laid out in the hot summer sun and flipped periodically, allowing them to ferment as they dried over the period of a couple of days. Most of this product was shipped to China, until the local Creole and Cajun cooks discovered these flavorful shrimp with an indefinite shelf life and found them perfect for making gumbo. Cajun dried shrimp, often made from Seabob Shrimp, became a specialty of the region, though made by a slightly different method. The shrimp are cooked in heavily salted water, then spread out

and left to dry in the sun for three days. The fully dried shrimp are shaken in a colander to remove the brittle shells, which are ground to a powder and can be used as seasoning. These dried shrimp are used to flavor just about anything and when rehydrated have a wonderful texture, similar to fresh shrimp, which they retain even after long cooking times.

Shrimp are very common throughout the world, and therefore you will find them popular among nearly every ethnicity and cuisine. Shrimp consumption continues to rise in the United States, and that growth shows no signs of slowing down anytime soon. Shrimp's popularity is due to its incredible versatility—its flavor melds into dishes better than just about any other seafood. But all shrimp are not created equal. And though there is great farmed product available, wild American shrimp—from the cold waters of our northern states to those from the warm waters of Louisiana and the Gulf, where they are steeped in that region's traditions of hospitality—are truly worth seeking out.

Gumbo

Part French-inspired bouillabaisse, part West African mafé, made with local ingredients and sprinkled with filé powder (a powder of dried sassafras leaves) from the Choctaw Indians and a dash of voodoo mystery—perhaps no dish better represents the diversity and history of our southern coast than gumbo. The name *gumbo* is derived from a West African word for okra, a food brought to the New World through the slave trade. Given the multiculturalism of New Orleans due to its positioning as a trade hub, there have been many evolutions of the dish in both the kitchens of fine restaurants and the home kitchens of rich and poor alike. In *The Creole Cookery Book*, published in 1885, the making of gumbo was called an "occult science" that "should be allowed its proper place in the gastronomical world."

There is generous, friendly debate over the particulars of the dish, specifically about the use of okra or filé as a thickener with or without the addition of roux, a foundation of French cuisine brought to the melting pot by the Acadians. The best-known gumbos are those that feature shrimp, chicken, and sausage, but whatever meat is available from the swamp, forest, or tides is fair game. No matter the combination of ingredients you use as your base or the color of your roux (another hot-button issue), the only thing everyone seems to agree on is that a proper gumbo must be served over rice.

I prefer a gumbo made with a light brown roux and okra, flavored with filé, and of course full of shrimp, oysters, and soft-shell or hard-shell Blue Crabs. This version is one aggregated and adapted from many old church association cookery books.

¼ pound Cajun shrimp (dried)

1½ quarts simmering water

½ pound butter

½ cup flour

½ pound bacon, diced

1 pound okra, thinly sliced crosswise

1 large onion, diced

1 large green bell pepper, diced

4 stalks celery, thinly sliced

4 cloves garlic, minced

2 teaspoons crushed red pepper flakes

2 teaspoons smoked sweet paprika

1 teaspoon cayenne pepper

1 teaspoon dried thyme

2 bay leaves

1 tablespoon gumbo filé powder

8 Blue Crabs, cut for gumbo

1 pint shucked oysters

Steamed white rice, for serving

Put the shrimp in a large bowl and pour 1½ quarts simmering water over them. Let sit for one hour. Strain and reserve shrimp and water separately.

In a large, heavy pot, brown the butter over medium-high heat and stir in the flour. Cook, stirring, until the flour is golden brown, about five minutes. Remove from the pot and reserve.

Add the bacon to the pot, and render over medium heat. Add the okra, onion, pepper, celery, and garlic, and cook for 10 minutes. Add the spices and crab pieces, and cook for two minutes. Add the reserved roux, stir to combine, then add the reserved shrimp broth and simmer for one hour. Add the shrimp and oysters, and simmer another 10 minutes. Let the gumbo sit for at least 20 minutes before serving over steamed white rice.

Shrimp Boil

A close relation to the Southern crawfish boil, the shrimp boil is a time-honored social affair that requires the "polite classes" to shed their airs of propriety and dig into a messy, spicy pile of steamed shrimp. Steaming in beer with copious amounts of "boil spice" adds complex layers of bitterness and heat to the fresh, candy-sweet shrimp. This iconic dish is known by various regional appellations that extend from Galveston Bay through the parish bayous of Louisiana and around the coast into the Carolinas. Tidewater Boil, Beaufort Boil, Frogmore Stew . . . these are all names that fall under the general heading of Low Lountry cuisine, which encompasses the unique geography and cultural influences of the Georgia and South Carolina coasts. These events often include corn, sausage, crabs, and a more mild seasoning.

Shrimp Cocktail

The combination of shellfish and spicy sauces has a long history. But the uniquely American tradition of ketchup-based sauces spiked with various piquant and savory additions began sometime in the 1860s with the introduction of a dish of shucked oysters served in a bowl and topped with ketchup. This pairing evolved through the years to include any combination of horseradish, Tabasco®, Worcestershire sauce, sherry wine, whiskey, and so on. Early twentieth-century cookbooks feature variations of the seafood cocktail that use lobster, oysters, crab, and leftover seafood from previously cooked dishes. The seafood cocktail was particularly popular during Prohibition, when these appetizers were served in place of traditional cocktails but using the same glassware, thus the name. It took a while for shrimp to become widely available outside of the southern coastal regions, but once fishing technology increased catches and cold-storage technology enabled long-range transport, shrimp quickly became the darling of the gourmet class. The shrimp, preferably the largest available, are cooked shell-on in a flavored court bouillon and then chilled, peeled, and hooked over the rim of a large coupe-type glass, which also holds cocktail sauce atop a bed of shredded iceberg lettuce.

Shrimp cocktail's popularity rose beginning in the 1920s and, according to a survey of New York City restaurant menus, was prominent on tables into the 1980s—the Plaza, Delmonico's, the Quilted Giraffe, Rainbow Room, the Russian Tea Room, and more. But its top billing was soon to end. In 1987, Marian Burros, writing in the *New York Times* declared that shrimp cocktail "may be an endangered species," having been relegated to the steakhouse culture of restaurants and banquet halls.

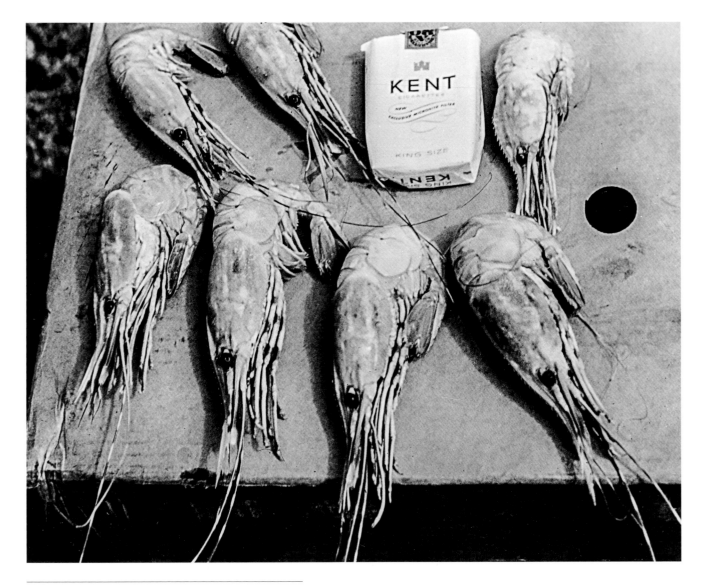

ABOVE Sidestripe Shrimp, 1959.

OPPOSITE Shrimp boat captain in Delcambre, Louisiana.

Poached skate wing.

Skate and Ray

I first knew **Skate** by their eggpods—rectangular discs with thorn-like edges that float up from the sea and collect in the wrackline at ebb tide. Though skate have long been abundant and caught in considerable quantity in our waters, American consumers were largely unaware of this culinary treasure hidden in plain sight. The rise of high-profile French restaurants and cuisine led the way in introducing us to an ingredient that much of the world has long enjoyed. But we still held fast to our prejudices. In his seafood treatise, James Beard wrote that skate are "regarded by most people as something odd and uneatable that floats in on the tide. Children are fascinated by them and dogs like to roll on top of them, apparently preferring them to other types of dead fish."

Commonly found along all coasts, the many different varieties are mostly interchangeable when it comes to culinary use. On the West Coast, the **Big Skate**, **Longnose Skate**, and the **California Skate** are considered the choicest species. In other waters, the **Roundel** of the Gulf and the **Winter Skate**, **Smooth Skate**, and **Thornyback Skate** in the Atlantic all take top honors. These bottom-dwelling fish feed on a variety of seasonal prey, the commonalities being mostly mollusks, crabs, and small fish. And, as with all seafood, you are what you eat (or rather, they are), and these delicious flavors carry through into their flesh. Skate are typically long lived, slow to mature sexually, and produce, at most, only a few dozen offspring per year, thus making them susceptible to fishing pressure.

Like sharks, skate are cartilaginous fish, meaning they have no hard bone. Their semisoft skeletons have a unique set of culinary uses that are quite desirable. Like other cartilaginous fish, skate lack a urinary tract system and excrete the uric acid through their skin. Improper handling after death can lead to a buildup of urea in their flesh, which can significantly taint the flavor with a powerful ammonia scent. When caught, they must be bled immediately, and the edible portions removed from the body in order to protect their wonderful flavor and quality. It is said that an "ammoniated" skate can be relieved by soaking in milk or acidulated water, but I have never found this to be successful enough to warrant serving. This biting aroma may completely ruin not only the flavor of your dinner but also the smell of your house. Properly treated skate is worth picking out of a crowd at the fish market. Despite the necessity of immediately and correctly processing the whole fish, skate is among few fish fillets that benefit from some aging before its full potential is realized. As the coarse and fibrous flesh ages, its terse and taut texture softens and relaxes into silken strands of uniquely flavored meat. I find skate best after they age two to three days, tightly covered in the refrigerator.

The Atlantic skates have long been appreciated in Europe, where they are an important part of seafood cookery; they are particularly well established and esteemed in France. However in the United States, skate have long been underappreciated, though they have been available, either as a bycatch from cod and shrimp fisheries or more recently as product of targeted fisheries. When sold at market it is most always in a form known as *wings*. These diamond-shaped cuts are the entire pectoral fins of the animal and are equivalent to what we consider fillets. Skate skin is covered with a thick layer of mucilaginous slime, which is not only unattractive but makes filleting them hard. These scaleless fish are imbedded with many very sharp, hair-like thorns, which make working with them a challenging if not painful process. The skin of the skate is never served, so the slime is no more than an inconvenience, but it can be removed if desired. Two methods work equally well: soaking the entire wing in acidulated water for 20 minutes or by scrubbing with salt and a stiff brush. I prefer the salt-brushing method, as it is quicker and does not alter the flavor in any way. The skin can be removed with a pair of staunch pliers. Grab the skin at the thickest part of the wing and, with a good firm grip, peel toward the lip of the wing. The skin should come off in one piece with an entirely satisfying ripping sound. This is not an easy task and it takes practice to gain proficiency. The skin can also be removed by gently working a knife underneath it and shearing the skin off in strips to reveal the meat beneath. The easiest method is simply to cook it with the skin on and then peel it off with a spoon when it is ready to eat. In all preparations of skate, I recommend brining the meat prior to cooking; this conditioning process helps to maintain the structure of the fillet without sacrificing the tender and melting quality of the flesh.

I find that poaching is the very best way to prepare any skate, and cooking with the skin on lends the poaching liquid an incredible depth of flavor and richness. It also adds texture, giving the broth a silken and gelatinous mouthfeel, which augments the texture of the fillets. Like flounder, skate have both a top and a bottom fillet (four fillets per animal). The top fillets on larger animals are about one and a half times as thick as the underside fillets. On smaller skate, the top fillets can sometimes be three times as thick as are the bottom fillets.

The cheeks of skate are worth asking after. These small bits have a very different texture than the fillets—being a whole muscle, they are more akin to scallops in their texture. The skate liver is another delicacy that should not be overlooked. Though there is not much history of its use in American cooking, the French cuisine authority Larousse mentions both fried livers and fritters made with it. My favorite preparation is to poach the livers in hard cider, then pound them with butter, lemon juice, and salt, and serve as a sauce for the skate itself or as a chilled potted spread with warm, butter-toasted crostini.

The "bones," or the thin fanlike cartilage separating top and bottom fillets, are delightful eating from smaller skate. Described as "unviscious bone" by Grigson, the fan of ribs

are separated from the meat, soaked in strong brine, and then deep-fried until crisp. This addictive crunchy snack reminds me of cracklins, as they're similarly porous, absorbing oil and salt that accentuate the surprisingly bright taste. The cartilage and skin make one of the very nicest of all fish stocks, more neutral in its character than not, but full of fresh, clean flavors, with a hint of saline and great gelatin content. It's a perfect way to add both flavor and body to chowders or seafood stews such as bourride or bouillabaisse. Skate meat, especially that of very large **Barndoor Skate**, was said to be used by unethical fishmongers as a substitute for scallops—the meat was punched out into rounds and sold to unsuspecting or ignorant consumers. I've not ever seen any proof of this nor had any validation of this practice by fishmongers I've known.

Skin-on skate wing.

ABOVE Fisherman's Wharf, San Francisco, California, 1943.
OPPOSITE Shrimp boat in Brunswick, Georgia, c. 1965.

The meat, much like the cartilage, is structured in long bands running perpendicular to the animal along its spine. The pencil-thin strands are thickest where the wing connects to the body, tapering down to a whisper-thin point at the edge of the fin. When poached, it retains its beautiful and uniquely striated texture, meltingly tender yet meaty in flavor. The fillets are uniquely beautiful in both form and flavor. It leaves a lingering and slight tackiness on the palate from the natural gelatin gleaned from the cartilage. I've always found skate best served with acid to punctuate both the richness of the flavor and cut through its mouthfeel.

While classically served with browned or blackened butter, skate also takes nicely to olive oil, especially one with a strong bite, which adds a very nice, piquant counterpoint to the flesh and draws out a bit more of its sweetness and herbal character.

Skate and **Rays** are closely related, though they can be very different from a culinary standpoint. Some rays have a very distinctive texture—much firmer of flesh and meatier in flavor. Some of them, like the **Cow Nose Ray**, are near equal to veal in texture and flavor, so much so that I think it is actually a mammal posing as a fish. But in most cases, treating a ray as you would skate will yield delicious results.

Skate and Rays are at their peak of flavor in winter, when they are not spawning, and they naturally pair well with the heartier foods of the season. Delicious with everything from "warm" spices like cinnamon to sweet winter squashes to plucky whole-grain mustard vinaigrettes, skate are very versatile, being as good served hot as cooked, then chilled and simply served under a vinaigrette or mayonnaise. Skate can be smoked with a gentle-flavored wood until pale straw colored, usually no more than four to eight hours. This is mostly as a flavoring rather than a preservative method. And there are few things more delicate and delicious than skate smoked and sautéed in butter and finished with a squeeze of fresh lemon juice.

Smelt

Of all the fish that can be lumped into the category of small silver fish, **Smelt** is the most accessible from a culinary and flavor standpoint. On the East Coast, the **Rainbow Smelt** is the most important species, and this northern fish has a particular culture associated with it. In my home state of Maine, I watch snowmobiles pull fully decked-out sheds across thick ice. Once the sheds are set up in the middle of a lake, fishermen will sit inside and dangle a line through a hole drilled in the ice, hoping to catch handfuls of these beauties. But it's not just about the fish, it's one of winter's few reasons to celebrate being outside—they are the first animal to bravely make its way back into our northern climes every year. In January and February, these anadronomous fish begin to swim up rivers to spawn in the estuaries, streams, and lakes before returning to the sea. It's so cold during smelt fishing season that there is a term to describe smelt that have not frozen: *Green Smelt*. Unless your shack is kept warm, it's almost impossible not to freeze them, having pulled the fish from their aqueous world into −10°F air (or colder).

Not only is ice fishing a chance to watch the New England Patriots game, because they always make the playoffs, on a handheld black-and-white TV (or smartphone), and drink a bunch of beer, the delicious smelt themselves are worth eating. Although they grow up to 14 inches, the average Rainbow Smelt is rarely more than six inches long and less than four ounces in weight. Smelt have a micro sheath of super-thin scales that do not need to be removed prior to cooking, though they might slough off onto your fingers. The skin of this fish is beautifully pearlescent, with a rainbow-color streaking down its sides. This coloration dims rather quickly once the fish is out of water, but in a winter landscape, the ethereal colors of a fading fish are enough to brighten the day. The name *smelt* derives from the Anglo-Saxon term *smoelt,* meaning "smooth" or "shining," which is an apt description of their beautiful appearance. The smaller fish have relatively soft bones, which are edible. To clean the fish, simply snip right at the base of the head from the back to sever the backbone; then grasp the head and pull toward the belly to remove it, and with it will come all of the viscera.

One of the great joys of smelt are the roes. They are incredibly clean tasting—fresh but briny—with a creamy-rich texture. When cooking a lot of smelt, there is likely to be enough roe to make a little side dish. I like to toss the roe in cornmeal and fry it very quickly in butter. If I have only a handful of fish, I leave the roe inside the fish; as it cooks, it adds a wonderful floral aroma to the flesh and a beautiful creamy texture when eating.

The conditions necessary to fish for smelt are harsh, but the fish themselves are really quite tame in terms of their culinary profile—that is, they don't challenge with an overly robust flavor the way anchovies do, but they are chockful of a personality all their own. Fresh smelt broadcasts a very strong and pleasant aroma of watermelon and cucumber, all backed by the elegant scent of violet. When my friend first described that scent to me, I didn't believe him until I had fresh smelt for the first time. It is truly something to celebrate. These aromas, though ebullient, fade relatively quickly, leaving just the gentle, mildly sweet flavor of the flesh. Smelt take very well to pickling with strong spices such as nutmeg and star anise, whose floral aspects revive the charisma of the fish. My favorite pickling recipe calls for cleaning and gutting the smelt, then packing them tightly together and covering each layer with a mixture of nutmeg, mace, salt, brown sugar, and a copious amount of bay leaves. I let the fish sit for one day before bringing equal parts vinegar and water to a boil and pouring it over the fish to marinate for another two days. Though these pickled smelt will keep for two weeks or more, their flavors peak between days 3 and 5, yielding a wonderfully snappy and crisp texture.

The smelt caught along the Eastern Seaboard are mostly part of a recreational catch. The commercial fisheries are based in Wisconsin, with small outposts in other Great Lakes states. Though smelt are originally a marine species, a small population of landlocked smelt from a lake in Maine were transferred to the Great Lakes system as part of an effort to introduce landlocked salmon to that ecosystem. The smelt was to be dinner for the salmon, but nearly a century later the salmon are long gone, never having gained a foothold, while the smelt have thrived.

A close relation to the smelt is the **Capelin**, a very economically and environmentally important species. It is one of the primary food sources for the North Atlantic groundfish, especially the cod. The same species swim in the Pacific, and the fisheries for Capelin are directed toward reduction and industrial purposes, as the fish is not as high in quality as the smelt. Additionally, it is caught in deep offshore waters, making delivery of high-quality product of these little fish difficult. The roe of the Capelin, known as *masago*, is a very important aspect of that fishery. We are likely most familiar with it as a topping on a sushi roll. It is often mixed with wasabi and green food coloring and is very similar to *tobiko*, the roe of flying fish.

On our Pacific coast there are a great number of species of the smelt family and many closely related fish that for all culinary purposes are herein treated equally. California is home to the largest smelt fishery. Pacific smelt tend to be larger than those of the Atlantic: the largest, the **Whitebait Smelt** and **Surf Smelt**, can grow up to 18 inches; the **Pacific Rainbow** and the **Longfin Smelt** are slightly smaller. All Pacific varieties share the same distinct personality as their Atlantic counterpart.

The cook's main concern when using any of these species is simply their size, which determines the rigidity of the bones. Smaller fish can be grilled, broiled, fried, or sautéed whole, whereas larger fish must have their backbones removed, which requires simply heading and gutting the fish. Then lay the fish belly side down, and apply gentle pressure with your thumb as you slide it down the backbone. This pushes the fillets away from the bone structure, completely freeing one side and allowing you to grab the tail and easily peel the remaining bones off the second fillet.

One species in the Pacific smelt group stands out above all the rest—the **Eulachon**, which Lewis and Clark thought to be "superior to any fish they had ever tasted." These fish, also known as **Candlefish** and **Hooligan** (a colloquial pronounciation), have for centuries been prized foodstuff for First Nations tribes along the Northwest coast and into Alaska. *Eulachon* is a Chinook word, and the fish were particularly important to this tribe. What sets Eulachon apart from other fish is their extremely high oil content, so high, in fact, that Native Americans dried the fish, then threaded a wick or twig though it to burn the fish as a candle, hence the name *Candlefish*. This high fat content should not be a put-off to the eater, as it is easily digestible and also allows for some very interesting cooking applications. The oil in these fish can be gently rendered by poaching them in water. The fat is then skimmed from the top, and the poached fish are finished by frying in their own fat until crisp. Another preparation I particularly

ABOVE Dressed smelt.

OPPOSITE An excerpt from the diaries of Lewis and Clark detailing the Eulachon.

exceeds the upper; and the mouth opens

great extent, folding like that of the herring.

has no teeth. the abdomen is obtuse

smooth; in this differing from the herring,

anchovey &c of the Malacapterygious

and Class Clupea, to which

ever I think it more nearly

than to any other altho' it

their accute and serrate

and the under jaw exceed-

upper. the scales of this

are so small and thin

minute inspection

suppose they had

filled with roes

colour and have

-able alimentary

best when cooked

is by roasting

then on a wooden

-vious prepar-

so fat that

sauces, and

to

it

a-

sh

ord-

hou-

ally

has n

abdom

-ing th

little fir

that witho

you woul

none. they a

of a pure what

scarcely any pere-

duch. I found the

in Indian stile, whi

a number of them toge

spit without any pre

-ation whatever. they a

they require no aditinal

I think them superior to an

like is to save the oil of rendered Eulachon and submerge raw fish in it to cook confit style with a small knob of ginger and a few slices of lemon, which results in an unbelievably flavorful, tender-textured dish.

Native Americans also use this rendered fat as a condiment to drizzle over pemican (a dried fish jerky) or smoked salmon. The fish's fat is solid at room temperature, making Eulachon, despite its modest size (10 inches or smaller), the very best smoking fish there is, in my opinion. All smelt and their relations are wonderful smoked, but the Eulachon absorbs and softens the rustic flavors of woodsmoke, and the density and texture of its fat gives the fish a mouthfeel not unlike foie gras.

David Starr Jordan in his treatise on the fish of the Pacific coast minced no words in his proclamation that Eulachon is "the finest food fish in the world—tender, fragrant, digestible." I always thought that was such a practical ending to that statement.

The fisheries for Eulachon have declined significantly over the past 20 years or more. The fishery has always been centered around the Columbia River, and the great James Beard described the return of Eulachon to the river's tributaries as "resembling a great orgy." Landings peaked in Washington State at just under four million pounds in the late 1980s, but the more recent landings have been under 20,000 pounds for the entire nation.

The **Night Smelt** of the Pacific coast, however, is a curious one due to its downright awesome mating rituals. In this manner, it is just like the **California Grunion**. Both fish typically live in nearshore waters and are relatively nondescript—except for their werewolf-like condition. Three to four days after each full moon between March and June, like clockwork, these fish lunge from the water onto the beach and energetically burrow down shallow holes in order to deposit their eggs or sperm in the sand. This is quite a sight to see, as James Beard describes them being "amusing fish" whose "floundering antics have always reminded me of a disorderly, unrehearsed ballet." This is one of the only, if not the only, fish mating ritual, to be referenced in popular culture, having been featured in the 1990s cult-comedy movie *Don't Tell Mom the Babysitter's Dead.* Such an event also makes for a very easily gathered dinner, a fact not lost on local residents. Indeed, the grunion moon always shines on an eager and waiting audience, most holding coolers.

The Grunion is one of the Pacific species of silversides. These culinary doppelgangers, found in both the Atlantic and the Pacific, include the **Topsmelt**, **Jacksmelt**, and are commonly known as **Smelt**, **Green Smelt**, **Shiner**, **Spearing**, or **Sperling**. The Atlantic silversides also have a charming mating ritual that has been simply is best described as joyous. Around late spring, huge schools head into the shallows, where they find protection among beds of eelgrass to splash around and jump from the water. The water becomes frothy, and the air fills with the cackling sound of tails slapping the water. McClane calls them "cheerful, fecund little creatures." He also bestows high praise on them, calling them fishes fit for a king and ranking them tops among all of the smelt-type fish.

From a culinary use, smelt and all its relations are most often sold in a dish called whitebait. In the eastern Atlantic, Whitebait is in fact a species of fish, but in America it refers to a dish comprised of any number of different small silver fish species, all roughly the same size, that have been eviscerated, tossed in flour or cornmeal, and deep-fried. They are traditionally served with tartar sauce. If you have particularly small fish, I recommend leaving the head on but scraping out the belly cavity, resulting in a dish known as "fries with eyes." Beard offers a very curious recipe for whitebait pancakes, describing a batter just thick enough to bind together a pound of fish with grated garlic and Parmesan.

I like to celebrate the way the remarkable smelt endure freezing temperatures as they swim toward our barren winter world, offering themselves up at a time of the year when anything new is a welcome discovery. And so I often play this out to its extreme. I thread the smelt onto balsam fir skewers at a 45-degree angle so that they create an arrow-shaped chevron pattern. I then use the snowblower to find my grill, fire it up, pour glasses of hot brandy-spiked mulled cider, and toast my hands as I sear the succulent and aromatic fish. Winter doesn't usually offer much in the way of scents, so the billowing puffs of orchard wood smoke carrying the sweet cucumber and violet perfume of the fish, now basting in their own sizzling fat, are a welcome relief from the particular gravity of subzero air.

Snakehead

Northern Snakehead, commonly known as **Snakehead** have a broad diaspera. These are a scary fish but a delight on the plate. Their cylindrical bodies and rippling musculature give them the appearance of a snake crossed with a body builder. They are an invasive species first discovered in Maryland in 2002 and can walk out from its aquatic confines and travel moderate distances across land to reach another body of water. These top predators are voracious, outcompeting—or just outeating—native fish populations in both fresh and brackish water ecosystems. They are similar in appearance to, and are often mistaken for, two native freshwater species: the **Burbot**, a freshwater cod, and the **Bowfin**. And while these native species are not quite as tasty or as densely textured as the Snakehead, they are, for almost every purpose, completely interchangeable. The flesh is dull white with a somewhat elastic texture when raw. It has very little aroma, and when cooked, the flavor is focused and of moderate impact, lacking the tang found in saltwater fish. It is perfect for sautéing or adding to chowders, and it is quite excellent when smoked. The skin should be removed, as it is not attractive, and I find it to be rather bitter in flavor.

The Northern Snakehead originates from Asia and has long been popular as an aquarium fish. The fish was first introduced into U.S. waterways when a family released one into a pond in Crofton, Maryland, as part of a prayer ceremony. They have been captured in waters from California throughout the southern and eastern states. They are a menace and a threat anywhere they are found. It is in the Chesapeake watershed region that they have gained their strongest foothold and established breeding populations. In retaliation, a small but growing fishery for Northern snakehead has been developed, and landings in Virginia and Maryland have been increasing steadily since 2005. This opportunity to help restore balance to the ecosystems as well as create a profitable market for these delicious fish is owed to the work of many people in the region, but none more so than Steve Vilnit and John Rorapaugh. As fish distributors in the Washington, D.C., area they have tirelessly campaigned for and lobbied chefs to put this fish on menus—a placement its firm, clean-tasting, and meaty flesh deserves. And consumers are responding. We inadvertently play God when we blend elements of different ecosystems, which can lead to such invasions. But we can also reverse some of this damage by playing God in the kitchen!

Snapper

Worldwide, there are hundreds of snapper species from many families, but just over 20 grace our waters. Of all the charismatic species to swim along our southern coasts, perhaps the most identifiable and widely loved is the **Red Snapper**. This single species is so esteemed that it has come to represent the entire family, and though it is the (disputed) king of the family, there are many rivals to its crown. The *New York Times* described this fraternal competition simply as one of aesthetics: "the visual feast of red against snow-white flesh." One of the benchmark cooking fish, snapper are versatile and consistent—nearly every variety is firm in texture, white-colored in flesh, simple in bone structure, and sharp, sweet, and meaty in flavor. Despite being quite lean, they are resilient to high heat and retain their moisture as well as fattier fish do.

These fish must be eviscerated and iced very quickly after capture, as they are quick to spoil. My good friend Buddy Guindon, a legendary fisherman out of Galveston, Texas, taught me that icing also preserves the spirited saturation of their fresh-from-the-water complexion. The fish should be completely covered in ice, as any slight temperature difference, even from one fish touching another fish, causes the beautiful coloration to develop silver splashes. Though the tarnish regains a red hue, the fish never reclaim their brilliance. A still-vivid fish is a mark of quality and an equal mark of pride for the fisherman. The snapper family color swatch ranges from brilliant reds, pinks, and violets through all the other colors of the rainbow. As most creatures are camouflaged in some manner, such conspicuous glitz and glamour seems to befit but equally betray such aggressive predators. But most snapper are caught in moderately to deep water, where red wavelength light is absorbed by the water and makes the fish appear gray or black, camouflaging their otherwise raucous complexion. Within a single species there can be incredible variety and intensity of color, based on the location of its catch and the depth of the water. My favorite non-scientific description of this fish comes from *National Geographic* in 1923: "As food fishes, the snapper are perhaps the most important Southern family. A snapper is an all-around, up-to-date fish, an evolutionary product of the keenest of all competition in the fish world."

FOLLOWING PAGE Early snapper fishery in Florida, c. 1910.

As commercial fisheries in the United States go, the snapper fishery is considered young. Until the early 1850s, but for a few small local fisheries, there was no extensive effort to catch them. Around this time, a few enterprising New England cod boat captains sailed their schooners south to the Gulf, quickly coming upon a great abundance of snapper off the west coast of Florida. In following years more New England captains resolved to trade in the nor'easter gales of winter for the friendlier Gulf waters and developed a profitable and important fishery selling most of their catch into the regional markets of New Orleans and Mobile, Alabama. This trade continued until the early 1870s, when a few Southern companies took it upon themselves to expand markets. As the fishery centered in Florida, the Pensacola Ice Company, in the very new business of artificially producing ice, established an export market that soon began to ship snapper all over the country. One retailer, according to Goode, remarked that "any man who is willing to buy a red snapper has not lacked opportunity." The advent of ice production, as opposed to harvesting blocks from frozen northern ponds, enabled schooners to fish ever more remote areas of the Gulf. By 1900, more than 40 regionally based vessels were involved in the fishery, with much of the catch being sold in the very lucrative Havana, Cuba, market.

Despite this early history in the Gulf, the snapper family was not described by science until 1878. At that time, some quantity of the fish were being caught off the coast of New Jersey and Rhode Island and were somewhat common in New York markets. Curiously though, snapper did not find great favor and was slow to be adopted into the canon of American cuisine.

Snapper fisheries now are vital to marine economies around the country, especially in the southeastern states, the Gulf, and Hawaii. Snapper live in a variety of environments from rocky bottoms to reefs, concentrating around coral or submerged human-made structures, the most notable of which are the thousands of oil rigs peppered throughout the Gulf of Mexico. (This is a display of how the oil and fishing industries are unexpectedly entwined) These incredibly voracious and famously aggressive fish strike quickly, bite hard, and will test anyone's strength as they are reeled up from fathoms below. Though an incredible diversity of species commonly swim near or around snapper, you wouldn't know it because they don't get the chance to bite. Snapper are bullies, and other fish have to wait their turn.

The snapper fishery (often using by longline) has been a difficult one to manage, as the myriad species of snapper are often taken along with grouper and dozens of other species. Regulation cannot simply focus on one fish, as so many species are integrated and each must be managed. Historically, management created difficult economic and safety situations, as snapper were allowed to be caught only on specific days, regardless of market demand or the weather. These "derby" fisheries compelled fishermen to fish in sometimes dangerous conditions, and then the market would be flooded with fish and drive prices down. This encouraged high-volume fisheries, as there was no incentive to reward quality over quantity. Now, fishermen are granted individual quotas that allow them to decide when they want to fish in response to market demand and weather, a system that has led to a steady availability of consistently higher quality fish.

To the cook, there are far greater similarities than differences among the snapper brethren. The bones of all snapper make for a good stock when very gently simmered. If allowed to boil, it can become heavy flavored, but nothing that cannot be brightened by a dash of lemon juice or the addition of aromatic fennel or ginger. Snapper should be scaled soon after capture, as the scales dry out quickly and become difficult to remove. Snapper livers are a delicacy sautéed or pounded to a paste with butter and used to thicken soups or sauces. The roe and milt are also worth seeking out. The roes are delightful when gently sautéed in butter, like those of shad, or salted and dried into a bottarga-like product. The milt can be sautéed or poached, and I like it best served with a simple vinaigrette. As many snapper species come to market weighing just a pound or two, they are perfect for panfish preparations, single-portion fillets or for cooking whole, either grilled, oven roasted, or baked in salt. A classic Southern preparation known as "on the half shell" calls for slowly grilling the fillets from a 5- to 10-pound scale-on fish over the embers of a leisurely fire. The scales char, perfuming the meat with a unique flavor and preserving moisture in the flesh. Snapper are also great for braising, as in the famed Veracruz preparation from Mexico, as well as for chowders and stews.

Red Snapper, the most popular member of the family, is an admirably gorgeous fish with its stalwart body, gently tapered head, striking red eyes, fins, and scales that obscure the skin

OPPOSITE Mangrove Snapper. ABOVE Vermilion Snapper.

with a mottled silver pattern. The Red Snapper is the most important and valuable of all the snapper fisheries, and there are quite a few fish, some related and others not, that try to plagiarize its glory. There is a **Pacific Red Snapper** that rarely appears in the most southerly waters off San Diego and is not caught in a significant quantity. No other snapper can be called Red Snapper, but there are a few other fish that use the moniker, including several Pacific rockfish commonly sold as "Pacific Red Snapper," though they bear no relation and are not of equal quality. True Red Snapper range in size up to 35 pounds, with three to eight pounds as the market average. They are one of the most popular fillet fish, especially because the delicious skin crisps beautifully and, unlike that of many other snapper, does not curl when cooked. While they can be expensive, due to the girth of their fillets, they give a good yield of edible meat to bones.

Black Snapper is an excellent food fish and, despite its name, is really more a mixture of violet and brown coloration. At their biggest, they are just a few pounds and are not common in commercial fisheries. Small quantities are taken in the Florida Keys and around Galveston, Texas.

Other lesser known snapper include the **Dog Snapper**, which has canine-like teeth. Its meat is denser than most other snapper, though it is still flaky and delicate when cooked. The **Schoolmaster Snapper** is one of the smaller and rarer among the family. It is brilliantly colored, with white and red bands running along its body and beautiful yellow eyes and golden fins. Taken in a very small quantity commercially, they are considered good panfish or for whole-fish preparations. The **Blackfin Snapper**, colorfully known by the nickname **Hambone Snapper**, looks like the red snapper but is distinguished by yellow eyes. The rose hue of its body appears slightly faded next to that of the red snapper, and it's marked just above the pectoral fan by a black spot in the shape of a hambone. Considered a very fine eating fish, it's good raw or marinated as ceviche and is among the sweetest flavored of the snapper. The **Cubera Snapper** is the largest of the family, growing to over a hundred pounds. Despite their enormous size, these faded red-gray fish swim in relatively shallow waters but are seldom taken commercially. McClane recommends Cuberas under 20 pounds; he says at that size they are delightful eating, but as they grow larger the flesh becomes tense and coarse and is best used in chowders.

The **Gray Snapper**, also known as **Mangrove Snapper**, **Bastard Snapper**, or **Pensacola Snapper**, is commonly found swimming among the roots of mangrove forests when young and migrating offshore as they grow. This is the most common snapper throughout the western Atlantic and Caribbean. The fish are often caught near shore, ranging in size between one and three pounds, though they can get as big as 10 pounds. When just plucked from the water they glow purple-gray, but within a few hours they turn an alluring greenish, rusty bronze. Underneath the stubborn scales lies golden-tinged skin that will curl when cooked, even if scored. Their flesh is rather pink when raw, though it cooks to pearly white, and their flavor is as bright, clear, vivid, and oceanic as I've ever tasted. The aroma is mellow but shrimp-like, foreshadowing its sweetness. It has a broad bloodline and moderate fat content, and its soft, thin flake retains moisture well. Many consider the Mangrove Snapper to be equal, if not better, in quality to the Red Snapper. In my opinion, it is by far the best of the bunch.

The **Lane Snapper**, and its rarely caught Pacific equivalent, the **Spotted Rose Snapper**, are typically one to three pounds. On the plate they are distinguished by their delicate flesh; otherwise, they are as tasty as any relative and are particularly well suited to poaching or stewing. Both fish are pale pink and mostly silver, though the Lane Snapper has dramatic yellow stripes running from the eye through the tail, and each is marked by a black blotch beneath the dorsal fin. Lane Snapper was not commonly caught until the late 1970s, and since then it has been consistently more available in markets.

The **Mutton Snapper** is considered one of the better-tasting though not most beautiful of the snapper. It is olive green, with a deep reddish tinge marked by white bands running the length of its side. Beautiful blue lines running just under its eyes create an impression of aquamarine mascara. Also known as **Muttonfish**, these fish average 5 to 10 pounds, though they grow up to 20, and have one of the finer textures of all snapper.

The **Queen Snapper** is the most beautiful of all the family. Forsaking the box-like contours of its kin, it is elongated, sleek, and handsomely marked, with a tail that elegantly forks into trailing threads. Queen Snapper are scarlet red above the lateral line, which shifts to a silver-pink below. Growing up to three feet, these are the deepest-dwelling snapper and may be

Red Snapper, Venice, Louisiana.

found as far down as 1,500 feet or more. They are most often taken as bycatch of grouper and tilefish longline fisheries. Their fillets are lithe and velvet-textured, perfect for raw preparation such as crudo. They are very clean in flavor, with a bright sea-breeze aroma and white color to the flesh when cooked.

The **Silk Snapper** and **Vermilion Snapper**, also known as the **B-Liner Snapper**, are two different species that in flavor and quality are often considered equal to the Red Snapper. These fish are very similar to Red Snapper and are often passed off as such, though they can be distinguished by the yellow tinge in their fins and eyes. Vermilions are the second most important snapper fishery and average two to four pounds in size; Silks are slightly larger. They both have thin skin that crisps tidily, though it must be scored so as not to curl. The Vermilion is thought to be one of the most abundant of the East Coast snapper.

Yellowtail Snapper is a favorite in Key West and still swims along the Eastern Seaboard and throughout the Gulf. This unique snapper casts a gray-bluish color with dusky spots and dandelion-yellow stripes. McClane states that it has a significantly shorter shelf life than other snapper, but I don't know why this would be true. It was once common as a breakfast food in the Keys; perhaps because yesterday's catch wouldn't last till dinner? Goode complained that vendors hawking these in early morning made a habit of walking down the street, "just at the hour when one most desires to sleep," yelling, "Yallertail! Yallertail!" It has a delicate white flesh and is by all accounts a very good eating fish.

There are other snapper species in both the Atlantic and Pacific that are rarely caught or are not marketed at all. These include the **Wenchman** and **Mahogany Snapper** of the Atlantic, and the **Colorado Snapper** and **Amarillo Snapper** in the Pacific. Though some of these are highly esteeemed as food fish, their absence at market warrants no further description of them.

There are several species of snapper important in the cuisine and fisheries of Hawaii. The **Long-Tailed Red Snapper** is also known as **'Ula'ula Koa'e** in Hawaii. It is traditionally served raw as sashimi and thus is perhaps best known by its Japanese name: *Onaga*. Like all the Hawaiian snappers, they have light pink flesh and are best in the winter when they are at their fattiest. Consistent with family character, Hawaiian snappers are similar in taste to those swimming along our other shores and can be prepared like those fish, including being roasted or steamed whole, poached and baked. One departure from the norm is that their delicate and tender flake makes them more difficult to grill than other snapper.

Pink Snapper, or **Opakapaka**, is considered one of Hawaii's premier fish. It has a delicate flavor, and its moist flake laminated with streaks of fat is perfect for sashimi. **Jobfish**, relatives of snapper, are well represented in the Pacific. The **Green Jobfish**, known locally in Hawaii as **Uku**, is the most important commercial species, with a wonderfully firm flake and dense texture on par with that of Striped Bass. Their taste is consistent with the sweetness of snapper but reveals a deeper and meatier flavor.

FOLLOWING PAGES Queen Snapper.

The skin is the best indicator of freshness—it is a deep mottled purple to almost black when very fresh, shifting to light purple-pink with shades of brown as it grows stale. This skin can be the very best part of fresh squid, as its depth of flavor intensifies that of the meat, while pairing up with flavors of char and smoke perfectly. Another benefit of using fresh squid is that often frozen product has been glazed in a protective sheathing of ice when processed. Though this protects the quality of product, it sometimes brings with it a treatment of sodium preservative. This treatment acts to retain moisture, which is then exuded in the cooking process, thus ruining any hope of char or adhesion of breading. It also leaves a chemical taste in the back of one's mouth.

In addition to fresh and frozen squid, there is a long history of canned squid and semi-preserved squid that has been lightly salted and pickled, as well as sun-dried and salted squid, which are fully preserved for overseas trade. Most of us are introduced to squid through its alternate name, borrowed from an Italian cuisine, *calamari*. When cooking squid, regardless of the cuisine, there is a definite rule that must be followed: cook them for less than 2 minutes or more than 20 but never anything in between, as they will toughen significantly. Lengthier cooking allows squid to relax into a delightfully porous yet firm texture. For a very rustic dish, fishermen put them directly on the boat's muffler or exhaust pipe to crisp them up for a snack while heading home.

Typically squid range from 3 to 10 inches in tube length, and their tentacles are oftentimes as long as, if not a few inches longer than, their body. **Giant Squid** can grow to more than 40 feet in length but are not served at the table at this size. When smaller, their tubes can be cut into thick steaks and, when scored multiple times in a nice cross-hatch pattern, can be grilled or seared to a thick golden crust, best if flattened with a bacon press or similar weight.

Like other cephalopods, squid use ink for deception and defense. As they spray the ink, it binds with mucus to form a murky cloud, roughly the size and shape of the squid, which distracts predators as the animal uses its jet propulsion to dart away. If you purchase an intact squid, the ink sac can be carefully removed from the viscera and expressed into a small bowl of liquid, such as white wine. Only a very small amount of ink is needed to deeply stain and flavor any dish, and this additional liquid simply makes it easier to incorporate into a recipe. This ink has an acutely concentrated briny flavor and mushroom-like scent, with a richness of color that saturates anything it touches with its deep midnight purple color (including your teeth). It is especially potent in dishes from risottos to pastas to sauces. Most often you'll find squid ink in small packets salted and frozen, as it is exceedingly perishable.

Squid have been prized in Mediterranean and Asian cuisines throughout history and held a minor role as a food species in colonial America. Unfortunately, it is most often used in this country as bait, as it is the favored food of some of our most esteemed fish species, such as Striped Bass, known in northern New England as "Squid Hound." Jasper White recalls that in the not-too-distant past he regularly saw fishermen throwing incidentally caught squid on the dock to rot as their principal catch of cod and bass were unloaded.

Squid's creamy-white flesh has an earthy sweetness like that of a carrot and a meaty flavor, though as it ages it turns slightly opaque and yellowish and creamier in its flavor, with a metallic hint. Old squid smells musty and oily, with a flat aroma of cabbage or sulfur that is immediately recognizable; squid with this characteristic should always be rejected.

Squid take particularly well to the fruity flavors of red wine and stand up to hearty ingredients such as garlic, celery, allspice, cumin, Worcestershire sauce, and tomato paste—in fact, that sounds like a pretty good stew in itself! The salted and sun-dried forms are best when soaked in red or white wine for about a day, allowing them to rehydrate before chopping them finely and stewing them into mixed shellfish dishes such as cioppino.

In New England, the Portuguese fishing community has a long and storied culinary history with squid, braising them or stuffing them with linguiça sausage, garlic, and kale before sewing them back up to cook in red wine. The classic "Rhode Island style" preparation calls for dredging squid in cracker crumbs and then crisply frying it before tossing with pickled hot pepper, garlic, and a dousing of olive oil.

FOLLOWING PAGES Tagging Striped Bass in Maryland.

Striped Bass and White Perch

The temperate basses are another sub-family of the *Serranidae (grouper, sea bass)*. There are only two species, one of them being among the most important of all species in the United States. The **Striped Bass** has been a part of this continent's food culture and fisheries long before Europeans and other colonizers set foot on this land. According to Roger Williams, the Indian term for Striped Bass was **Missuckeke-kequock**, meaning "much" or "great fish." These fish grew so large that tribes such as the Melicita of New Brunswick easily took them with harpoons when they gathered at the head of a river.

In his accounts of early explorations of the Chesapeake Bay, Captain John Smith described the abundance of Striped Bass as being dense enough that one might walk across their backs "drishod." In North Carolina only the largest fish were eaten, with those under four feet in length tilled into the ground. An early American chronicler by the name of William Wood observed that "though men are soone wearied with other fish, yet are they never with basse." Settlers in the Plymouth Colony found this fish so abundant and were able to catch them in such great numbers that they used them as fertilizer as well as for food. When they were running plentifully, tons of these anadromous fish would be netted from the rivers, the heads eaten immediately, and the bodies salted and left to store for winter. A roasted or boiled Striped Bass head is filled with bits of meat in the chin, cheeks, and tongue, as well as a spoonful of marrow in the head cavity. This was one of the true delicacies in early American cuisine and was perhaps the first great American dish.

The Dutch settlers in Manhattan call this fish *twalft (twelfth)*, and being that they called the shad *elft (eleventh)*, it leads one to believe that prior to their settlements they had only known ten fish, each new fish discovered being so named by its number in order. Though Striped Bass is the official name, there are many regional colloquial and commercial names for this fish. In Maryland, one would be hard pressed to get a waterman to call it anything but **Rockfish**. In the northern stretches of New England, it goes by **Striper**, **Greenhead**, or **Squid Hound**. Adding to the trouble are names such as **Linesider**, **Pimpfish** (the origin of this name I cannot divine), and simply **Rock**.

These fish range from the St. Lawrence River in Québec down to the mouth of the Mississippi River. There are accounts that these were once caught in profusion everywhere along the Atlantic coast, including every major river system, each having its own breeding stock. There's even record of Striped Bass being caught as far north in the Mississippi River as St. Louis.

The Striped Bass's tolerance for both fresh and salt water has allowed it to be introduced into landlocked bodies of water for the purposes of sportfishing, as well as to control populations of invasive species such as the Gizzard Shad. This popular table fish was introduced to the West Coast in 1879 when the government shipped 133 fish caught in New Jersey by train to California, where they were released into the San Francisco Bay. This advance platoon took hold, and now there is a permanent population swimming a wide territory from California into Washington State, with the bulk of the population being in the San Francisco Bay and around Coos Bay, Oregon. Though they are abundant on the West Coast, they are not the subject of an important commercial fishery but are popular as recreational catch. McClane theorizes that they never gained popularity there because of the monolithic cultural position of another anadronomous fish: the salmon.

Today, the Striped Bass breeding grounds are centered in four locations, though numerous other spots make small contributions. The Chesapeake Bay alone accounts for 70 to 90 percent of the population of coastal migratory Striped Bass. The Delaware Bay, Hudson River, and areas of Cape Cod are the other major breeding centers. Juvenile fish tend to stay in the fresh or brackish water where are they were born for two to four years before migrating out into the full-salt ocean waters along the Eastern Seaboard. That said, the larger Striped Bass females tend to go far asea while, by some accounts, about 90 percent of the male population remains in the Chesapeake.

Historically, not only were striped bass caught in gigantic numbers, the fish themselves were gigantic. David Starr Jordan recounts one trip in which fishermen took 38,000 pounds of fish, hundreds of them being 60 pounds or larger, and several being over 105 pounds each. The roe of one of these fish was measured at weighing 44 pounds alone. The largest Striped Bass on record, though there's some disparity about this, was a 125-pound fish taken off the coast of North

Carolina in 1891. Such a fish would have been well over six feet in length. Nowadays, a 50-pound Striped Bass is newsworthy, with most fish averaging just over 28 inches and weighing 12 pounds.

The Striped Bass is an anadromous fish, one that spends its life in salt water and breeds in brackish or freshwater, thus making it particularly susceptible to the impacts of human settlement. Dams erected throughout the country destroyed or blocked much of the habitat in which these mighty fish once bred, and their aggregation and proximity to settlements made them easy targets for overfishing. As their populations declined, early efforts were taken to restore them. One of the earliest efforts of artificial propagation was undertaken in 1873 by the U.S. Fish Commission. A second, more successful attempt saw 400,000 juvenile fish released into Salmon Creek in North Carolina in 1879.

In 1639 the General Court of the Massachusetts Bay Colony ordered that neither Striped Bass nor cod could be used as fertilizer. Just a few years later the court declared limits to how many boats could fish for them. These are likely the first fisheries conservation efforts enacted on this continent. The fish was so valued and important that in 1670 the Plymouth Colony opened the first public school funded by income from the Striped Bass fisheries. In 1758 New York passed a law prohibiting the sale of Striped Bass during the winter in response to "a great decrease of that kind of fish." But the demand for Striped Bass at the table only grew, and populations continued to decline over several centuries until they reached a critically low point in the 1980s. Given that the majority of Striped Bass are caught in state waters, conservation efforts required collaboration among every state on the Eastern Seaboard in order to bring these fish back to healthy levels. These efforts, unprecedented in their scope and diplomatic difficulty, resulted in one of the greatest sustainability success stories there is. By 2007, populations had rebounded to levels considered historic (I don't believe we actually know how abundant these fish once were), and moratoriums on fishing have since been lifted. Once again, this king of fish has regained its place at our tables. Since the recovery of these populations, the percentage of fish caught in commercial fisheries has declined, as 75 to 80 percent of all fish currently landed are taken in recreational fisheries.

But during that period of scarcity, the Striped Bass was never far from our minds and hybridized fish filled the market gap. In 1967 the wild Striped Bass was crossed with the freshwater **White Bass**, and the resulting fish has been an aquaculture success story. Grown mostly in indoor tanks in freshwater, often times in hydroponic systems that also produce vegetables, these fish are sold as **Hybrid Bass**, **Hybrid Striped Bass**, and the very gaily named **Sunshine Bass**. These gained ever greater prominence in the market with large-scale production beginning in 1986.

But these farmed fish are a far cry from the beauty and majesty of the Striped Bass. According to Amanda Hesser, "You can taste its story in its succulent flesh: it takes on the sweetness of the fresh river waters where it's spawned, salinity from the ocean and meatiness from muscling its way down the eastern coastline." She goes on to say, "The farmed version is about as close to the wild as a dog is to a wolf."

Hybrid Bass are a good fish and worthy of merit, but do not compare to their wild relations. The two can be easily identified, as the wild has seven or eight unbroken olive-brown bands running along its flank while the Hybrid Bass has the same bands but near the belly they begin to break into a jagged path. The aquacultured fish are the perfect size for roasting or frying whole. Their fillets are moderately thick, with a small flake and white flesh tinged gray. The skin is clean flavored and crisps nicely, and both the meat and skin are very well flattered by cooking in butter. It is a really great all-purpose fish in that it performs well in any method, takes on other flavors with ease, is easy to fillet, and it is always available fresh at market. That said, I do have a few issues. The texture can be difficult. Depending on the producer and what the fish is fed, the texture can range from an unappetizing mush (rarely) to quite firm and pleasant. On average I'd say that in most cases the texture leans toward firmer. This can be improved by brining the fillets in a low-density salt/sugar solution. This not only firms up the meat to a taut and even snappy bite, but it can also ameliorate the sometimes muddy flavor common to these fish. As these fish are mostly sold "in the round," meaning just as they came from the water, their bellies are often stuffed full of feed. I have two problems with this. The first is that I'm paying the same price for fish as I am for

fish feed. My second gripe is that the feed doesn't taste good. If the fish are not allowed to purge freshly eaten feed from their system before they die, the flavor of the feed permeates the entire fish. However, this is can be ameliorated rather easily. If you have a fish that gives a slight stale or cardboard odor, add a little vinegar or lemon juice to the brine, as this will help to balance out and mask that character.

The great James Beard commented that the Striped Bass is "certainly one of the two or three greatest fish." He also adds that cold Striped Bass was among the "most popular dishes in the great French restaurants of New York." These fish are strong, their musculature seen rippling with a beautiful purplish-blue shimmer when fresh from the water. Their large scales are sturdy and lend a verdant olivaceous tone. When very fresh, the skin is pure silver striated with midnight black bands running along the flanks. As the fish age, the skin becomes reddish and finally dull gray when past its prime. Its flesh is uniquely flavored with the rich combination of influences from its diet, including clams, mussels, crabs, menhaden, herring, and its favorite food, squid. It has a firm and oily flake that is at once fatty enough to self-baste in cooking and retain moisture, but the mouthfeel is that of a leaner fish and has a slight mouth-drying quality. The flavor is of moderate intensity, with a unique sweet-sour character, and the meat has a fresh and pleasantly gamey aroma. Though it adapts to nearly any cooking method, I think moderate heat best flatters its texture and best draws out its aroma and flavor. It can be served skin on, though one fault of the Striped Bass is that it takes on not only the flavor of its diet but also of the waters in which it swims. Fish caught in less-than-pristine waters can present accents and flavors such as petroleum and other unpleasant vestiges of human populations. As such, I prefer to remove the skin, generally before cooking, though for whole roasting or grilling it is best to leave on until serving.

Though these fish can grow to a truly impressive size, it is the smaller fish that most impress on the plate. For a time, fish weighing six to eight pounds were the preferred size. Though they vary by state, regulations now require fish to be at least 28 inches in length, which is about a 12-pound fish. Fish larger than 30 pounds can develop a sinewy texture, and I think these are best for braising and are especially good for chowder.

Thomas F. DeVoe, writing in the late 1800s of the New York markets, praised Striped Bass of any size as among the great fish, though those weighing one half to one pound were considered the ultimate quality. Such preferences were precisely part of the species' decimation. They are at their peak of flavor in late September and October, having spent the summer in vigorous pursuit of prey and growing ever fatter as the leaner fortunes of winter approach.

Despite this fish's wild populararity, it receives oddly insignificant attention in many classic culinary texts. Most recipes are simple instructions for broiling steaks, and the sauces recommended are on the lower order of creativity, typically drawn butter or anchovy butter being enough to suffice. I believe that the general public was so familiar with Striped Bass that it did not warrant inclusion. And as far as creative license, Striped Bass's charismatic flavor generally dissuades impulsive additions by cooks. In the recipes I have encountered, it's clear that the abundance of this fish called for preservation, and it was very popular both salted and pickled, and the variations in such recipes are quite diverse.

I think that the luscious and juicy meat of Striped Bass is at its very best when poached. And I'm particularly partial to McClane's reminiscence of his grandmother's preparation: thick fillets poached in water with a copious measure of black pepper and handfuls of bay leaf. I substitute wine for half the water, actually preferring red to white. The full-bodied flavors and spices draw out a surprisingly gentle personality in the vigorous fish. If grilling, broiling, or sautéing, I will first marinate the fish in red wine vinegar, grated garlic, salt, and thyme. For all preparations, the flesh benefits from pre-seasoning with salt or brine for half an hour to an hour prior to cooking. Not only does this help to retain moisture, but it also allows the seasoning to penetrate better through the dense flesh and enhances the flavor throughout. I do not think frying is a good application for this fish as it is already so charismatic that adding so much richness only diminishes its robust personality.

The head and body make for a very rich flavored stock, but care must be taken to simmer as gently as possible to avoid a cloudy and murky flavored liquid. I've found it's best to

Beer truck driver stops and looks at fish in DeMartino's market window, New York City, 1943.

slowly simmer the bones and head in butter in a large pot with the top on so that they gently steam through prior to the addition of water and wine. Though I rarely add celery to stock made of any other fish, here it helps to retain Striped Bass's crispness of flavor, though only half a stalk is needed to do so.

As mentioned above, historically the heads were regarded as the finest eating of the fish. My absolute favorite preparation is to roast them in a wood oven on a bed of thyme and onions. The smoking woodsy scent of the herb makes true magic of this dish. But since a wood oven is a rare luxury, I often replicate the same over a charcoal grill or simply by roasting the fish in an oven. Simmering the head in a broth rich with fresh herbs like parsley draws out an entirely different character. A nice presentation is to serve the head split down the middle so that the rich marrow is easily spooned out. The cheeks, tongue, and meat around the collar can be picked off with a fork. As these bits of meat are so rich in themselves, I like to serve them with a simple vinaigrette alongside for dipping.

The **White Perch**, while related to Striped Bass, is a wholly different culinary animal. Growing rarely larger than a foot, these dense, round fish are perfect for roasting or frying whole. Their small fillets are moderately firm in flake, with grayish-white meat and a tamer flavor than that of Striped Bass. They originate in the same waters and often overwinter in deep offshore waters. Unlike Striped Bass, the White Perch do not migrate along the coast and are mostly caught in fresh and brackish waters. As such they do not develop the same robust musculature and flavor associated with ocean fish. Their diet is mostly insects and, seasonally, baby eels and the spawn of Alewives. Their skin is considered by some to take on a bitter quality in the summer months, though it's my preference to remove the skin any time of year.

The White Perch was once the most important and popular panfish in the mid-Atlantic region, where its fisheries were quite important and valuable. The majority of fish came from the upper reaches of the Chesapeake, whose proximity to Baltimore allowed for easy transport by rail throughout the country. Despite this Northern popularity, in the South

they have been historically maligned and thought only fit for chowder or fertilizer. They have always been very popular in the Midwest, where significant quantities have been fished in rivers and the Great Lakes system. These populations are the result of fish trapped upstream after a spawning migration or by a shift in the course of a waterway. Over time, they have grown very abundant throughout the eastern and midwestern states and are considered, along with the unrelated freshwater **Yellow Perch**, to be *the* fish to be used in a Midwest fish fry. A classic preparation found in early culinary texts calls for roasting them directly over a fire, basted with an acidic sauce of lemon juice or vinegar. Another calls for stewing them in vinegar, lemon juice, or other sour sauce. They take particularly well to the flavors of fresh herbs, especially chervil and parsley. My favorite dish is to stew fillets in a mixture of sherry and wine that has been flavored with nutmeg, anchovy, and parsley. As the eating qualities of both White Perch and Yellow Perch are similar, such recipes work equally well for both. Today the majority of the White Perch still come from Maryland, with Ohio landing about half the volume. With the Yellow Perch, it is Ohio that leads the pack, with landings that are double those in Maryland.

While their culinary history is modest, White Perch is credited by many sources as the fish that sparked the genesis of sportfishing in America. With time to pursue leisurely activities, a coterie of early-American elite, including honorary member George Washington, formed the Schuylkill Fishing Company in Pennsylvania in 1732. Their flag bore the image of the White Perch. To gain membership, it is said that prospective fishermen had to fry six White Perch in butter, then flip them in a pan at once. Thus began our country's history of recreational fishing and culinary showmanship.

PREVIOUS PAGES Striped Bass gill-net fishing in Rock Hall, Maryland. OPPOSITE White Perch.

Sturgeon

Sturgeon are living fossils of the Triassic period. It is considered to be "a primitive fish," whose general biological character has remained unchanged in its 245 million years of existence. Sturgeon also look the part. These monster-like fish grow to a truly massive size, with long, shovel-shaped snouts and bodies covered with thick, leathery skin and an armor of bony plates (aka "scutes").

Sturgeon are present in many areas of the world and have long been esteemed as food fish in many cultures. They are most noted as the source of caviar. Though the word is misapplied to the roe of other species, true caviar comes just from sturgeon. It is only relatively recently that caviar became the near unattainable luxury it is today. Though the roe has always been used in different ways—salted, eaten fresh, and even processed into oil for gas lamps—it wasn't until the advent of refrigeration that caviar found an export market first centered around the Caspian Sea, where the finest caviars are made. Despite its historic market value being that of a regular foodstuff, caviar has long been associated with people of discerning taste and wealth. Shakespeare employs this sentiment in *Hamlet*, when the title character describes it in a speech as "'twas caviary to the general," meaning too nuanced or sophisticated for the masses to understand. Though I disagree with this Platonic elitism, caviar—though appreciable on all levels—is indeed a product that further reveals its beauty and charm once your palate is trained to understand it.

Sturgeon are an anadromous species, swimming into freshwater to spawn, though most of their lives are spent in brackish or tidal areas of river deltas or estuaries. Some sturgeon are exclusively freshwater fish, living in rivers and large lakes. In America, there are several commercially relevant species of this fish and related species that are similar enough in culinary terms and history so as to include them in this entry. On the West Coast, the **Green Sturgeon** and the **White Sturgeon** have long supported fisheries and were an important food source for Native Americans. Though far from the largest of the sturgeon, the White Sturgeon can grow to 700 pounds and live more than 100 years. On the East Coast, the **Short-Nosed Sturgeon** and the **Atlantic Sturgeon** were once important commercial species, but are now protected,

ABOVE Postcards showing early sturgeon fisheries, c. 1890.
OPPOSITE Italian fishermen, 1929.

as these nearshore and river-dwelling species fell victim to rampant overfishing, habitat alteration, and even campaigns to cull the population. In the West, the Sacramento, Fraser, and Columbia rivers were at a time astonishingly thick-set with these giants. Such substantial populations were also common in the powerful rivers of the East Coast, particularly in the Damariscotta and Hudson rivers and in the Delaware Bay. As these fisheries predated refrigeration, isolated regional communities developed unique and colorful vernacular to characterize this fish. In the Hudson fishery, where sturgeon meat was particularly popular to the north, it came to be known as **Albany Beef**. In keeping with the hyperbolic descriptions of early America's bounty, it was said that a man could walk dry-shod across the river on the backs of the sturgeon. Lingering colonial loyalty along the James River in Virginia inspired the local nickname **Charles City Bacon**. One commonality of these regional names is that they all describe the meat-like qualities of sturgeon. While the flesh of these fish was extremely popular in some areas, in others it was considered fit for nothing but fertilizer. In southern rivers near Savannah and Charleston, the fish were packed and sent to New York, where there was a market for the meat and a center for processing roes. In cosmopolitan New York, one of the most famous chefs of the late nineteenth century, Charles Ranhofer of Delmonico's restaurant, wrote menus featuring sturgeon. However, in other cities, the fish was shunned from cuisine. Despite this historical dichotomy, sturgeon is mentioned far more often in early Southern cookbooks than in Northern ones.

In Maine, when sturgeon were eaten, there was a particular preference for fish weighing less than 18 pounds, which were locally known as **Pegging Awls**. From the body only the top portion was eaten. Caviar and sturgeon's richly fat belly were considered unfit for consumption and were largely used for the production of high-quality oil.

Another industrial use for sturgeon was for their sounds, or air bladders, which, as in most fish, are very high in gelatin; they were used to make glue. Sturgeon were so important in the New England economy that in the 1880s it was the region's second most valuable fishery.

Human actions all but destroyed the habitat of these fish in North America, and the pressure of overfishing further compounded their near extirpation. Even as sturgeon populations dwindled, we erected dams on the mighty Sacramento, Fraser, and Columbia rivers (in addition to those long standing in the East). As conservation measures were passed, the fish's presence at market waned, and eventually, for lack of familiarity, sturgeon fell from good graces in our culinary culture.

Given the massive size of wild sturgeon, they have almost always been delivered to market in "bullet form"—head, tail, and viscera removed. These trimmed fish were far easier to pack and ship. Somewhat unique for the era, sturgeon was sold mostly as a fresh product, with a small portion of the harvest being salted. This was partly due to the fisheries' locations in the river systems, which also served as shipping routes between population centers, allowing the product to be distributed quickly.

In 1989, a major breakthrough was made when the first captive-born female sturgeon reached sexual maturity. Since this achievement, the farming of sturgeon has come to be a sustainable market replacement for struggling wild-caught fish. Sturgeon farms—usually indoor ponds known as recirculating aquaculture systems—now operate in many regions all over North America.

Almost all sturgeon found in market are farm raised, and due to the economics of these farms, the fish are grown only to 15 to 30 pounds, at which size their roes have developed and the meat is at its peak quality. As the fish are extremely slow growing, reaching even this small size requires 15 to 20 years. It is widely considered that young sturgeon have a better flavor. Regardless of the size of the sturgeon, its skin is not edible and conceals beneath it a thick layer of subcutaneous fat. To remove some fat, the fillets can be deep-skinned, meaning a thin layer of flesh and fat is taken off with the skin when sheared from the fillet. The flesh is very dense, with thick, yellow bands of fat coursing through it. The meat is finely grained, and its fillets are ivory, sometimes leaning to pink, in color. If smaller, the fish can be cut into steaks but are more typically found as fillets. As the bones are few and easily removed, the edible yield is very high.

Wild-caught sturgeon can sometimes exibit a brackish or muddy aroma, though this does not carry through to the flavor. The fillets often have a slight whiff of cucumber, or a pleasantly "green" or herbal scent. Pressure bleeding, a technique used at harvest in which high-pressure water is flushed through the veins to remove all the blood, helps to maintain a very clean flavor. Wild sturgeon feed on small crustaceans, mollusks, insects, and plant matter. Farmed fish feed contains a range of ingredients that keep the flavor mildly sweet, expansive on the palate, and generally slight and gentle in impact.

Green Sturgeon meat is considered lesser quality compared to White Sturgeon. Green Sturgeon flesh retains a slate/reddish color and a more muted taste and is considered best for canning and smoking. Though White Sturgeon is equally good for smoking, it is preferred for fresh uses.

The fat in the flesh self-bastes, the meat when cooking and helps to retain moisture, but it can also be overwhelming and make cooking difficult. Despite this richness, the meat has a tendancy to dry out. It is so dense that the heat may not evenly penetrate it without overcooking the outer areas. Slow-cooking methods are often the most effective and also flatter sturgeon's mild flavor and aptly soften its meaty, veal-like texture. Sturgeon benefits from a brief cure, perhaps 15 to 20 minutes under a light sprinkling of salt, which is washed off before cooking.

Another approach, one that greatly benefits sturgeon's texture and flavor, is to twice-cook the meat. Older cookery texts sometimes suggest to pre-blanch sturgeon in salted water or milk to render the fat before proceeding with the recipe. Some call for the fish to be poached for a significant time (up to an hour) before further braising in an aromatic broth. Gently poaching the fish in a heavily salted solution of equal parts vinegar and water for a brief 10 minutes is best, especially for grill or broil preparations when excess fat can drip into the fire and cause flareups, which can leave an acrid taste. After such a rendering method, the flesh more effectively takes a brine or marinade.

I've also come across recipes advising to hang the sturgeon in a cool place for two to three days to allow its flavor to develop as its fats oxidize. The meat is then immersed in a strongly flavored marinade for 24 hours. After such treatment it is now

Stalls at the Fulton Fish Market, New York City, c. 1930s.

textured like Swordfish and can be used in a similar manner. This process of aging and tenderizing tough meats is indeed fairly common in global cuisines, though mostly applied to land animals. A similar technique is used with shark in the classic Spanish dish *cazón en adobo.*

Sturgeon is wonderful confited in a neutral fat such as vegetable oil or mild olive oil, as it contributes so much of its own fat and flavor. The fish proves itself to be among the very best fish for slow braising. I especially admire the result of braising in the method of *en barigoule*—fish, fennel, carrots, celery, lemon, and spices submerged in wine and olive oil.

Thick cuts can sieze up and become coarse and dry if exposed to high heat. If sautéeing or grilling, I cut the fillet thinly on the bias, producing portions with a larger surface area. This counteracts the textural density of the fish and evens the cooking process. I also recommend starting any cooking process with the fish at room temperature to ease the penetration of heat.

Sturgeon found enduring fame in the delis of New York, when prepared either in the salt-cured gravlax style and cold-smoked or brined and gently hot-smoked. Because of its fat content, sturgeon absorbs smoke well and integrates its flavor fluently. Sturgeon makes among the finest of all smoked fish.

Sturgeon's semisoft cartilaginous "bones" make an excellent stock—rich, gelatinous, and well textured. Behind caviar, the soft, cartilaginous notochord, or spinal cord, is one of the most desirable parts of the fish. One method for removing the spine is unique: at the tail end, use a knife to sever and expose enough bone to gain a good grip, then, using a hook for leverage, pull the entire cord straight from the fish, leaving the flesh entirely intact.

Long considered a delicacy in Russian and Chinese communities, the rich marrow is a wonderfully unique ingredient that can be adapted to any cuisine. The cord is typically two to four feet long and encased in white connecting links best described as vertebrae, though that term is not technically correct, as they are not hard bone. Inside these "vertebrae" is the rich marrow, a soft jelly-like substance that makes a perfect last-minute addition to sauces or soups. Mixed with butter, it makes a particularly silken compound butter imbued with compelling flavor. The spinal cord itself is a very elastic yellow band that

resembles a piece of home gym equipment. This interior cord can be dried and powdered and then used to flavor or thicken soups and sauces. The marrow can be used in a similar manner.

Russians that emigrated to the United States brought with them a tradition of a preserved product called *balyk*. The belly is cured by traditional methods, as with cod, though the dense meat along the dorsal section requires a special technique. Strips of flesh are first buried in a mixture of salt, allspice, cloves, bay leaf, and mace for 12 to 15 days. They are then soaked in water for two days to soften before air-drying for four to six weeks. When the cure has properly "struck," the exterior blooms in a sheer layer of mold similar to certain types of charcuterie (another commonality between sturgeon and land animals). This lengthy process results in a product that is almost as silky as cured salmon, translucent when sliced, and redolent of cucumber and herbs, with the sultry flavor of the included spices.

In addition to the sturgeon species, there are other fish that are used for caviar production and whose flesh is similar in character and quality. The **American Paddlefish**, also known as **Spoonbill Catfish**, are native to Mississippi and Missouri river systems, ranging as far north as the Dakotas. They were once common in some of the Great Lakes and throughout the Chesapeake watershed areas of Pennsylvania, New York, and Maryland. Overfishing and habitat destruction or blockage ended these populations. They are caught by gill nets or pound nets, and Paddlefish roe is comparable to that of sturgeon and has earned a good reputation. The meat is less flavorful, with a touch of the murky flavor inherent to many river fish. A quick soak in buttermilk or acidulated salt brine remedies this muddy note, and the Paddlefish can then be prepared in any manner appropriate to sturgeon. Like sturgeon, Paddlefish were erroneously considered to be a problem fish, as it was thought they ate the eggs of more valuable species like pike. There were efforts to destroy these fish, a concept completely foreign to modern management principles.

The **Hackelback** is another species that lives in the mighty river systems of the middle states. Also known as the **Shovelnose Sturgeon**, **Sand Sturgeon**, and **Switchtail**, it is very well regarded for its roe; caviar from Hacklebacks is now considered on par with top-quality sturgeon caviar.

Surgeonfish, Tang, and Unicornfish

The surgeonfish moniker is applied to a large number of species that inhabit warm waters all over the globe. The three families include the **Tangs**, **Unicornfishes**, and **Surgeonfishes**. These are some of the most colorful and charismatic fish anywhere. The vast majority of the catch is directed to the aquarium industry, where they command top dollar, especially the **Blue Tang**, which was the avatar of Dory, a main character in the movie *Finding Nemo*.

A small amount of these fish are used for food. The **Kole Tang** is particularly popular in Hawaii for use in traditional luaus. Across all species, these small fish tend to be strongly flavored and firm fleshed, and though sometimes served raw, they are most commonly fried whole.

Swordfish

Much lore and legend swirls around **Swordfish**. There are tales of the fish ramming so forcefully into ships that the sword penetrated two timbers deep. Baird said that "Sword strike with velocity and accumulated force as dangerous in its effects as heavy artillery projectile." The fish hunts by the savage method of slashing through schools of bait, its razor-sharp bill tearing to pieces anything in its path. Of their brute nature, Oppian stated this couplet: "Nature her bounty to his mouth confined, / gave him a sword, that left unarmed his mind."

Historically, harpoon was the only major commercial means of taking Swordfish. In New England and the North Pacific, in late summer and early fall, these fish are prone to becoming numb with cold and are found swimming at the water's surface, warming their blood for the night, when hunting resumes in deep waters. Small boats, never far from shore, used tall, narrow lookout towers, which Grigson described as "ladder like in their silhouette and long metal platforms that jettied out over the sea like a murderous arm." This fishery took mostly female specimens, which were more apt to frequent the surface waters. The earliest record of its use for food comes from a local Barnstable, Massachusetts, newspaper in 1841, mentioning that they were pickled and salted in Martha's Vineyard. Though they were well known to fishermen prior to that date, no effort

was made to capture them. "Previous to 1862, fresh swordfish was limited to Cape Cod and the south shore. Salted product was shipped to the West Indies and southern states," wrote Goode. In 1864 South Shore Swordfish were sent to Boston for a trial market, and fresh consumption has grown ever since. At the same time as it became very popular in Boston, it was not popular in New York, and in 1874 less than 2,000 pounds were consumed there.

In the 1980s, as it was discovered that smaller females and males swam deeper and could be taken by gill net and longline, these methods took over as the principal catch method. Technological advancements furthered this shift: the development of single-strand monofilament in conjunction with the use of chemical light sticks attached to baited hooks greatly expanded the effectiveness of longline gear. Bycatch issues, especially of sharks and turtles among other species, have long plagued gill-net and longline methods. Gill nets, originally used in shark fisheries, had begun to take Swordfish as bycatch, and so fishermen began using them to target Swordfish. And in the late 1980s, Hawaiian tuna fishermen began to find Swordfish on their longlines, and thus that fishery expanded to target Swordfish as well as tuna, increasing the catch to the point where the Hawaiian catch was three times the total catch of all other U.S. waters combined.

Unloading Swordfish, 1947.

OPPOSITE Handling the Swordfish catch, 1947.

Swordfish are most often found in frontal zones where warm-water currents meet with deep cold-water upwellings. These areas provide the ideal conditions for plankton blooms and are factories for unbelievable production of marine life. Longliners are most successful in their efforts around the full moon, when the nights are brightest and the Swordfish can see the baited hooks. For gill-net fisheries, it's the opposite, as darker nights obscure the mesh of the nets and make it easier to ensnare fish. Harpoon harvests occur exclusively during the day and often deliver the highest-quality fish, as the fishing is done on single day trips, and boats return to market that same afternoon. Harpooning also decreases a fish's struggle, which can increase its overall quality. As a hooked fish struggles against the line, sometimes for 20 hours or more, it builds up body heat and lactic acid. Overheating can change the chemistry of a fish's flesh, causing oils to separate; the muscles themselves can get so hot from exertion that they actually "cook." These actions degrade the quality of flesh, causing it to begin breaking down in ways not necessarily obvious during a casual perusal of the seafood case.

That said, I am not diminishing the potential quality of a longline or gill-net caught fish. It's widely recognized that, when done right and in the right season, long-lining yields fish of good quality. The fattest fish are taken in the North Pacific waters in the late summer and early fall, when their migrations from Mexico hit their northernmost peak in Alaska. In the Atlantic, they peak in flavor by middle to late October; in Hawaii, the peak season is April to July. This may make it seem as if the fishery were just as simple as following a calendar. It's not. An entire ocean's worth of variables—from feed fish availability and abundance to water temperatures, currents, global weather patterns like El Niño, and even lunar cycles—have a say in the timing. Next time you eat Swordfish, appreciate how much intelligence it took to get that fish to your plate.

These ocean giants feed principally on squid, menhaden, and mackerel, and their flesh in turn reflects an equally rich, fatty character and lustrous quality. Because of this fat, Swordfish taken at their peak freeze well. The density of their muscle fibrils and fat can withstand the pressures of freezing, maintaining its high moisture content and full fat flavor and aroma. In fact, it can be preferable to use a properly frozen fish caught at the peak of its flavor rather than a fresh but flabby and insipid specimen taken in early spring after a lean winter.

The color of Swordfish varies greatly. Smaller fish tend toward paler ivory color with little dots, like stitching, running through the meat. As they grow, they can gain a pinkish-orange or peach-like color, depending upon their diet. This variation makes shopping fun, but most experienced tasters and fishermen claim color does not indicate much difference in the flavor. The major factor affecting quality is the fat content, and the highest-quality fish will have a very fine marbling of translucent fat, which gives it much of its flavor. The most important thing to look for when buying Swordfish is the vibrancy and compactness of the red-tissue bloodline. When fresh, it is brilliant red with a brownish hue. As it ages, its color fades to a limp brown and leeches this color into the surrounding flesh. Whether buying steaks or loins, look for this ribbon of flesh to be bright cherry red.

Swordfish is a particularly well-designed fish—its battle-ready and strongly protruding sword leads the powerful barrel-body as it tapers into a curved half-moon tail. It's not a slender fish, yet its sleek shape, made for swimming distances long and fast, is elegant nonetheless. The coarse flesh radiates from the spine in ever-larger concentric circles. Larger fish are trimmed of bone and cut down into four equally sized loins. Smaller fish will be cut into sides, with a prominently Y-shaped or fountain contour of blood line dividing the two circles of flesh before spreading outward just under the skin.

A one-inch-thick slice of loin is preferred if one cooks on the grill. For braising, ask for the trim pieces—usually the fatty belly and miscut steaks they can't retail due to awkward shape or weight. There's no reason to start with a perfectly butchered loin if you're going to cut it into chunks anyway, plus the best part is the belly. And for sautéing or broiling, use loin or side cuts that are about 1/2-inch thick; this thickness allows for the cooking medium to lend its unique flavor to the dish while also maintaining the meat's moisture and quality. The texture is naturally somewhat oily and rugged, but the fleshy muscular layers give it a fine and moist consistency. It is always best to cook Swordfish from room temperature to allow even heat penetration.

ABOVE Tractors on the wharf, Boston, Massachusetts, 1947.

The meat is somewhat broad in its flavor, with a moderate intensity and aroma. The bloodline has a notably sour component to its flavor. On young and particularly fresh fish, I like to leave a small amount of the bloodline in, providing contrast of texture and flavor. This fatty red tissue contains much of the toxin that consumers are warned against in Swordfish, which can be largely negated by removing it. Some cooks claim that the bloodline is good for basting the fillet, and I agree with this to some extent. I'll leave it in when using a method in which the fish's fat helps to cook and moisten the fish, such as sautéing or broiling. But for a method such as grilling, where the fat mostly drips into the flame, I find that it only starts grease fires rather than impassioning the taste buds.

Swordfish, and to a large extent tuna and shark, have gained great popularity in our beef-centric culture, which values many of the same textural components and mouthfeel qualities prized in these fish. It also cooks like beef—easy to broil, sautés well, doesn't stick to a grill, makes for easy kebabs, and so forth—and thus we are very comfortable with it. But just as beef has many different and greatly varying textures, so too does Swordfish: from the coarsely textured large grain of the cut below the collar ranging down to the very finely flaked and sinewy section inches before the tail. My favorite part is the rich belly section. As with tuna, this is where the greatest proportion of fat is stored, and thus this area is the most flavorful and interesting in character to me. I particularly like it braised, especially with aromatics such as fennel, bay leaf, and peppercorns, or cooked in a mixture of half olive oil and red or white wine, and maybe some water. After two hours of very low, gentle cooking, a hefty two- to three-pound belly portion will be meltingly tender and silken. It is still relatively easy to handle, but you'll see it flakes apart with no more than the gentle push of a spoon. Its own rich, mouth-coating fat combines with the olive oil to make an intense base for vinaigrette. This oil and fat mixture can be frozen and used to cook other fish. I especially like to freeze it in cubes, then pull it out as needed to make a simple sauce to serve over nearly any grilled, broiled, or sautéed fish.

The loin muscles of Swordfish also braise well, though the texture is similar to that of chicken breast and can dry out quickly. The most important rule of Swordfish is to never overcook it, as its musculature firms and becomes chewy and unappetizingly cotton-like, even sandy, in texture. Though often cooked with its skin on, the skin is never eaten. These fish have scales when they are young, though they lose them as they age, making the skin quite tough; it does not break down or have a nice palatability to it.

According to Marian Burros, writing in the *New York Times*, "In the early part of the [twentieth] century, the average weight of a swordfish when caught was about 300 pounds; by 1960 it was 266 pounds; and by 1999 it was 90 pounds." When Swordfish was heavily overfished in the 1990s, sharks such as the Thresher and Mako, which are very similar to Swordfish in taste and texture, were dishonestly substituted on the plates of unknowing customers. And though we hold deception as the greatest of culinary sins, I've found that Mako shark can be a delightful, sometimes even preferred, stand-in for Swordfish. And I'm not alone. Jasper White, one of the greatest seafood chefs in our culinary history, states that "mako is equal to, if not better than swordfish and more consistent as the swordfish can change its quality characteristics so incredibly between various seasons."

Whether Swordfish or shark, the dense meat takes very well to a marinade, particularly ones including any booze such as sherry or Pernod, as the alcohol begins to denature and break down muscle tissue, giving the meat a soft, velvety texture and allowing the flavors to penetrate. Thick marinades, such as a chunky paste of mashed shallots and garlic with plenty of herbs, are especially good when grilling or broiling Swordfish. A lengthy cooking time, generally about 10 minutes per inch of thickness, gives these ingredients time to char and form a nicely textured crust.

A small amount of Swordfish was traditionally cured in salt, treated by the same Mediterranean methods used with tuna (see page 59). I particularly like salted loins shaved thin and doused in olive oil. The liver and roe of Swordfish are the unknown treasures that you have to ask your fishmonger for days ahead, as Swordfish is almost always landed without head, guts, or tail. These I salt and dry for a few weeks before using them grated fresh over pasta or thinly shaved over salad. According to Davidson, very thinly sliced smoked Swordfish rivals smoked salmon in quality, although it is stronger and saltier in taste. Swordfish is traditionally brined

in a weak salt-and-sugar solution for up to a week, after which it is smoked for several days. The low heat and sweet perfumed smoke of applewood permeate deeply into the flesh and soften the coarseness of the muscle into a silken smooth loin. I will agree with Davidson that when the fish is sliced thinly and simply drizzled with lemon juice and olive oil, it is as beautiful a preparation as can be. It's perfect for a carpaccio, the sliced fish layered with thinly shaved zucchini just plucked from the vine. I once ran a menu item in which a few slices of smoked Swordfish were thrown on top of a white pizza at the last minute, along with an arugula and shaved fennel salad.

These suggestions may be a lot more exciting than what you are likely used to, the blue-plate catch-of-the-day of broiled Swordfish, rice pilaf, and vegetable of the day brought to your table by Doris who then pulls your napkin-swaddled silverware from her back pocket before pointing out the location of the ketchup bottle on your table, just in case. It's my opinion that if we are to take such a majestic animal for our purposes, it is only right and good that we praise it properly, upping our game to make the most of this truly special ingredient.

FOLLOWING PAGE, LEFT Unloading fish in snowstorm, Gloucester, Massachusetts, 1960.

ABOVE Tautog.

FOLLOWING PAGES Crab traps at Ponchatrain Blues, Slidell, Louisiana.

Tautog

Since before the European settlement of this country, **Tautog** has been an important food fish. Its name, originating with the Algonquin Indians, is the most appropriate one among the many historical names used for this fish throughout many different regions. Other regionally important names include the North Carolina vernacular **Oyster Fish** and the common New York term, **Blackfish**. This moniker alludes to the fish's most common appearance: a thick mottled skin that is mostly black, though it can range from gray to a dark brownish green, depending on its habitat. They live along the coast around rock jetties, reefs, and pilings and feed upon all sorts of mollusks, such as clams, oysters, and barnacles. Tautog has a large, circular gill plate ending in fully formed teeth. Inside the mouth, its palate is a hard, bony plate used to crush the hard shells of its prey.

Tautog's diet is directly mirrored in the flavor of its flesh—delicate and nuanced, with the brine of an oyster and the sweetness of crab, its texture firm and snappy. It is sometimes called **Chowder Fish** because it works so well in that preparation. In this regard, it's somewhat similar to eel, as it stews well and integrates with other flavors easily. Because it lives on rocky bottoms and around wrecks, it has a very thick skin with heavy scales to protect it from abrasion and injury. The scales are quite difficult to remove, including a strip of them running along the lateral line that is quite stubbornly attached, and so I do not serve the skin. However, cooking with the skin on adds to the flavor of the fish and protects it from drying out. The flesh runs far into the head, extending nearly over the eyes. This is all usable meat; unlike the collar sections of most fish this flesh has very little connective tissue and is consistent in texture with the rest of the fillet. The cheeks are small, but on larger fish they are certainly worth carving out. The meat of the fillet itself is a glowing pearly white with a faint hint of purple. Though the fish is quite lean, it has a richness of flavor and silken texture. The bones are among the very best of any species for making a stock that is clear and bright in flavor. To capture the full essence, I first simmer the split head and bones in butter, keeping the pan lid on, to gently steam them in their own juice before adding wine, peppercorns, and fennel to round out the concentrated essence. Tautog does not take well to smoking, as the flavors contrast in a tinny and unflattering way.

They are a very resilient and vigorous fish, which enabled them to be transported live to important markets in the early smacks or wellboats. They can still be found in live tanks, particularly in Asian markets. It has always been an immensely popular recreational fishery, and although anglers made the majority of landings in recent years, commercial landings have been increasing in response to its growing market value.

A close relative of the Tautog is the smaller and brightly colored **Cunner**. This dusky orange fish, growing to about a foot and a half in length, shares the same canine-like teeth and feeds on similar species. Averaging about 1.5 pounds, it is similar in flavor, texture, and cooking qualities to its larger cousin, though it is not as esteemed. It is not currently an important market species, though historically it was regularly on the dinner plates of people in northern New England. Records show immense quantities of this fish marketed in Massachusetts and Maine. Curiously, reports from 1905 show that more than 280,000 pounds were landed in Maine alone, yet just two years later the fish found no buyers and was given away or sold to the poor. There is record of declining catches after 1905 but none that point to any mass depletion of the species. We just simply decided we didn't like it anymore, I guess. The Algonquin name of this fish is **Chogset**, though it is also known as **Nipper** or **Bergall**. It is said that its current name, Cunner, was earned by the fish's reputation of skillfully stealing bait from hooks, to the great annoyance of fishermen.

Ten-Pounder

These explosively vigorous and highly prized gamefish, with interchangeable names mostly known as **Ten-Pounder**, are in fact multiple species caught throughout the eastern Gulf, Florida Keys, and Hawaii: **Ladyfish**, **Machete**, and **Hawaiian Ladyfish**, aka **Hawaiian Tarpon**, and in local dialect **Awu'awu**. These are very bony fish both that thrill anglers but disappoint cooks with their inconspicuous flavor, complex skeletal structure, and uninspiring texture. Though there are statistics relating to the annual landings of both fish, much of that is taken by the recreational sector, and the dockside value of these fish is paltry.

In Hawaii, the Awu'awu has a long and storied role in local cuisine. They were traditionally captured and reared in ponds to ensure a supply of a chief's favorite fish (for more on Hawaiian fish ponds, see Milkfish, page 293). The fish no longer enjoys the honor or popularity that accompanies royal custom, but it is still commonly used for making the ever-popular fish cakes. Regarding Hawaiian Tarpon, there is little reference to any associated culinary traditions, but many sportfishing websites take a cue from Hawaiian cuisine and suggest a similar fish cake preparation.

Given the great percentage of bone to flesh and the labor required to catch them, these species are not likely to become commercially important and will probably remain regional curiosities to be found at the charter docks when the boats come in.

Tilapia

Tilapia living in both salt and fresh water are commonly found throughout waterways of Florida, where several million pounds are harvested annually. All four species found in American waters are non-native and have been introduced into ecosystems by the aquarium and aquaculture trades. The first species was introduced into the wild in 1961 when specimens were brought in by Auburn University for experiments in aquatic plant control. Escapes from this project as well as subsequent escapes from other farms led to the establishment of these fish on both coasts of Florida but predominately in the inland lakes. Fisheries catch data begins in 1973, with no mention of the fish prior to that time. Landings in Florida peaked at nearly six million pounds, and they have recently been found in small quantities in Hawaiian waters.

The meat is tinged pinkish-white and has a very mild flavor that is distinctive, depending upon its environment. The quality of this fish is wholly a reflection of the water quality from which it comes. Those from brackish or clear waters will have a far more distinguished and clean flavor than those coming from muddy waters. The texture is clean, and the flake is firm and small. These fish have little fat and are a good gateway fish, as they are rich in flavor and readily available. The vast majority of the tilapia consumed in America is a farmed product, mostly imported, and it is one of this nation's most popular seafood items. The wild capture represents a very small volume but is an important sport and commercial catch.

Tilefish

As an executive chef, the first fish I typed onto my inaugural menu was **Tilefish**. I have always been charmed by its tender but firm meat, resembling that of a Striped Bass but having a wholly unique flavor. Its aroma is savory, admitting a buttermilk sour-sweetness that foreshadows a complex but playful flavor that is as rich as a scallop and is often compared to lobster.

Tilefishes have a very curious tale, even as fish tales go. The species were not known to science, let alone diners, until May 1879 when a Captain Kirby was trawling for cod in the waters southwest of Nantucket and was greatly surprised when he hauled aboard 5,000 pounds of an unknown and somewhat strange-looking fish. With haste, a fine specimen was sent below deck to the galley and prepared for a taste trial. All who ate the fish that day agreed that it had one of the finest constitutions and flavor of any fish they had previously had. Tilefish presently became abundant in East Coast markets as captains learned to fish them, setting their nets deeper than they did for cod. In the following years, it quickly became the darling of cuisine, in much the same way, more recent decades have witnessed Chilean Sea Bass and Orange Roughy suddenly positioned atop every menu.

And here's where the story gets even more peculiar and mysterious. Not three years after its discovery, the fish completely disappeared. In March 1882 merchant vessels crossing the Atlantic reported passing through vast shoals of dead tilefishes obscuring the surface over areas ranging many square miles. Ships arriving to Boston, Philadelphia, and Washington, D.C., validated that this calamity spanned the entire Northeast and mid-Atlantic coasts. The cause of this mass mortality was unknown, though it is now speculated that shifting currents trapped the fish in an inversion of cold water, extirpating them *en masse*. It wasn't until 1892 that we find a record that another tilefish was caught, and a few years again before its presence returned at market. By the time it was again available, consumers had forgotten, lost interest, or had discovered a new favorite, and tilefish has never again been as dominantly popular as it briefly was. In the decades following this disaster until modern time the tilefish population has steadily increased, with a few major dips along the way, and now it is once again subject of increasing culinary curiosity.

There are six species of tilefishes swimming the Eastern Seaboard and throughout the Gulf. Five of them, ranging in size from one to four feet are, for culinary purposes, equal. Tilefish, often referred to as **Golden Tilefish**, is the largest species in the family and the most commonly found at market, as it is both a targeted species in longline fisheries as well as an incidental catch in the grouper fishery. The **Goldface Tilefish** is slightly smaller, growing to just under two feet but packing all the charisma of its larger kin. Three other tilefish species that make for fine fare are **Blackline Tilefish**, **Anchor Tilefish**, and **Blueline Tilefish**, all rarely growing past a foot and intermittently seen at market. The sixth, the **Sand Tilefish**, is not well esteemed, as it has a slightly bitter flavor and is usually quite small. The **Pacific Golden-Eyed Tilefish** and the **Ocean Whitefish** (a true tilefish) are found in the Pacific. Both species support commercial fisheries and are considered culinary equivalents to the Atlantic species.

All of the tilefish species are unique and beautiful in their appearance. Though being somewhat oafish of face, they are sleek and well built. They are sometimes known as the **Clown of the Sea** due to their colorful spotting and exaggerated, worried-looking eyes. This deepwater species displays casts of cerulean blue and olive green that can deviate into yellow, rose, sepia, and purple along their midline down onto their belly.

All tilefishes claim a fine-grained, smooth texture and delicate flavor, reminiscent of the best characteristics of halibut, but with the gamey moxie of a Striped Bass. Evelene Spencer, a great cookbook author of the early twentieth century, states boldly: "Tilefish is a superior food in every way that is best when boiled or baked like cod." Its unique firmness makes it a good choice for stews and braises. This taut texture makes it a wonderful candidate for salt-curing like cod. I find tilefishes at their zenith when bathed in a dense brine before being slowly hot-smoked and sliced very thin. The flavors of highly aromatic wood with a hint of spice, such as alder or cherry, provide the fish a perfect point of flattery. The skin is very thick, and, though edible, the high heat needed to give it a pleasant texture is not in the best interest of the flesh. Tilefish's predominantly crustacean-based diet gives it a confident and charismatic flavor, and its personality pairs well with many cuisines. It has a relatively thick band of red muscle tissue, or bloodline, though this is soft in flavor and contrasts well with the ashen-white flesh.

Goldface Tilefish.

Triggerfish

Triggerfish is distinguished by its incredibly tough skin and zealously adherent scales. When I got my first delivery of these fish, I was put off by how difficult it was to access the fillets beneath what seemed like a full metal jacket. I have come to prefer peeling the skin off the whole fish (with the help of a very sharp knife), resulting in a fish that looks more flayed more than filleted. The effort is rewarded generously: hiding beneath that Kevlar-like skin is flesh that is sweet and tender, with a wonderfully buttery aroma.

There are many triggerfish species widely distributed in many waters, but few are marketable. The **Gray Triggerfish**, **Queen Triggerfish**, and **Ocean Triggerfish** of the Atlantic, all culinary peers and rarely distinguished as more than triggerfish, are the only species caught in any significant quantity, and largely as bycatch of the snapper fishery. Given their rarity on any coast, they are always well received by any cook lucky enough to find them. The Queen Triggerfish, also known by the unflattering names **Old Wife** and **Old Wench**, is a specimen colorfully painted with a happy blend of green and bluish-grays patterned onto a yellow canvas. In addition to her colorful outfit, the fish's rear dorsal fin has a long wisp-like thread trailing behind.

The name *triggerfish* is in reference to the first spine of the fish's dorsal fin. When touched, the bone-hard spike springs into vertical position like something out of a James Bond movie. The family Latin name roughly translates to "similar to a crossbow."

Once the skin has been removed, triggerfish are easily filleted like any other round fish and the well-shaped fillets possess few bones. When cooked, the flesh is off-white and glisteningly moist, with a high fat content and a tender, beautiful flake running head to tail (more lateral than vertical). The relatively thin fillets sear well, taking on color without drying out. Triggerfish feed on crabs, mussels, and sea urchins and take on flavors characteristic of those species. The very fatty flesh is self-basting in preparations such as broiling or grilling. Butter intensifies the fish's sweetness, adding a nutty characteristic and balance; when cooked in butter it smells like roasted pecans and an ocean breeze. Olive oil highlights milder oceanic and herbal flavors in the fish. It also is one of the very best candidates for braising, as its fillets maintain their structure, and the flavor is agreeable with almost anything you pair it with. On very large fish, the cheeks and tongue are worth the effort to remove them.

Another bycatch of the snapper fisheries and very similar to triggerfish in their culinary qualities, **Filefish** are more oblong and slender. Of the filefishes, three grow large enough to be considered for the table: the **Unicorn Filefish**, **Orange Filefish**, and **Scrawled Filefish**, which all grow to two feet or more. I've tasted a filefish only once, and I know why. They are so delicious that when one is landed you can be sure it will go home with the captain.

Tripletail

Atlantic Tripletail has recently become a darling of Southern chefs, and rightfully so. I remember the first time I saw this fish when a vendor showed me a shipment of cool "new" fish that he was peddling. The **Tripletail** stuck out—rather unattractive but impressively built, with a body of pronounced heft. They are compact fish, looking as if they'd swum into a wall too many times. The fish appears to have three tail fins, but it's simply an illusion made by the anal and dorsal fins extending nearly as far back as the tail fin.

Fished commercially in southern waters mostly around Georgia and Florida, these fish are found as far north as Nova Scotia and throughout the mid-Atlantic and Southeast, where they are known by regional names such as **Black Perch** in the Charleston area and, quite inexplicably, **Flasher** in New York and surrounding areas. Its West Coast twin, the **Pacific Tripletail**, swims at the very southern edge of our coast and does not appear to support any fishery. It is identical to the Atlantic Tripletail for every purpose other than scientific description. It's unlikely you'll find it at market but, should you be so lucky, any culinary reference to the Atlantic Tripletail will tell you all you need to know.

Young tripletails are found mostly inshore in estuaries and bays, where they exhibit the bizarre habit of floating on the surface on their sides. Their coloration—a mix of reds, yellows, and browns—gives them the appearance of a floating leaf, disguising it from predators. Older fish, which grow over three feet though most often caught at half that size, head to open water, where they are found near sunken wrecks, buoys, or floating debris.

If the fish's cruel countenance doesn't turn you off, you'll be amply rewarded by its thick pearly white fillets and smooth, lustrous flakes. The thickness of the fillets is similar to that of a prime cut of grouper or halibut, although the tripletail texture is softer and its flavor is more brackish with a lingering sweet aftertaste. It is such an excellent food fish that it is best served simply, flattered with nothing more than a lemon wedge. Long underappreciated by chefs, Atlantic Tripletail is finding new champions in its home waters.

LEFT Queen Triggerfish.
OPPOSITE A good day for the seagulls, Provincetown, Massachusetts, 1937.

12654-E

Albacore Tuna.

Tuna

"All the sea is their native country. They are wandering fish"

—FRAY MARTIN SARMIENTO

And wander they do. Tuna are among the most beautiful and perfectly designed of all fish. They are meant to swim long distances at incredible speeds, their bullet-shaped bodies gliding as gracefully through the water as a bird does through the sky. Their bodies are painted with spirited colors radiating across mirror-like skin. Tunas range greatly in size from the diminutive **Bonito** to the giant **Bluefin Tuna**. Many tunas have a corselet of large scales running under their pectoral fins, whereas others do not have any scales, but all are decorated with dramatic fins perfectly engineered to slice through water.

Though tuna has long been part of the cuisine of native Hawaiians, in most other parts of the country these fish were relatively unknown and unexploited until the beginning of the twentieth century. Partially this is because most tunas swim far from shore, and the technologies to catch them efficiently had not yet been developed. Additionally, traditional fisheries offered such bounty that there was little need to look past them, either for dinner or economic opportunity.

At the beginning of the twentieth century, the seafood canning industry in California was beginning to find footing. Sardines and salmon were the main products, and the canning of tuna came about through the failure of another effort. A company in Southern California had built a factory for processing and canning sardines, but when the sardines failed to appear in the area, it was forced to innovate alternatives. Experiments in canning tuna began in 1903, and in 1909 the first successful packing of **Albacore Tuna** was shipped to market. Its creators were delighted by the discovery that canned tuna tasted much like chicken. This was further supported by an 1880 government pamphlet entitled "Cattle of the Sea," which proclaimed the virtues of canned tuna and stated that its delicate flavor was like that of chicken breast and that "in fact, it has been called 'sea chicken.' " (I was not aware that chicken had been used as the common denominator so far back in history. At least we Americans are consistent.) By 1917, in addition to Albacore Tuna, **Yellowfin Tuna**, **Skipjack**, and

Bluefin tunas were all in regular production on the canning line. This burgeoning industry was made possible by the introduction of gasoline engines, which powered deepwater boats employing purse seines to capture the schooling tunas.

Canned tuna found a ready and eager market, and the businesses thrived, becoming incredibly profitable. Annual consumption increased from a half pound of canned tuna per person in 1937 to two pounds per person by 1960. Between the years of 1960 and 1973 annual consumption grew even more, from two pounds to more than three pounds per person. Coupled with population increases during that period, the total volume growth in the industry was over 80 percent. But by 1970, this lucrative industry was facing competition from foreign processors supplying tuna from abundant fisheries produced by cheap labor. American companies soon relocated their operations farther west into the Pacific, where the industry is still centered today.

Tuna are often found swimming in the company of dolphins, and a commonly employed fishing method was to locate a pod of dolphins and set a giant purse seine net around them, knowing the tuna were close at hand. This led to horrific rates of dolphin mortality. As our environmental conscience grew at pace with the increasing volume of tuna fisheries, this issue came into public view. In 1972 the Marine Mammal Protection Act was enacted to reduce bycatch of dolphins and other marine mammals through improvement of fishing gear and methods. With the collaboration of the tuna industry, modifications to the fishing gear were made, and by the late 1970s dolphin deaths had been reduced from a half million per year to approximately 20,000. About the same time, the United States was facing increasing international competition from fishing fleets that were not governed by American law. In an unfortunate turn, dolphin mortality actually rose in international waters due to increased fishing by these international fleets. In response, the "Dolphin Safe" labeling campaign started in the late 1980s as a way to ensure that tuna imported into the United States had been caught in ways that were consistent with the laws followed by our own fisheries. Not only did this create an economic enforcement mechanism that protected the dolphins, it also protected our domestic fisheries from being placed at a disadvantage for doing the right thing. "Dolphin Safe" on a label simply communicates that the fishery that captured the tuna "did not use the dolphin-set method, and that the tuna was caught on a trip on which no dolphins were chased, encircled or were killed."

ABOVE RIGHT Schooling Yellowfin. OPPOSITE Harpooning Bluefin Tuna.

Efforts to create markets for tuna outside of the can stumbled through a couple of different decades. A rather notable attempt, first mentioned in 1949, was to introduce America to Tuna Franks, known as "Sea Dogs," "Tunies," or "Ham of the Sea." Described as the "20th century's novelty meat" (not a good slogan!), this niche product targeted observant Catholics by offering a meatless option for Fridays to replace the family-favorite hot dog. By all accounts the numbers made sense. Consumption of hot dogs averaged 3.5 million pounds per day but dropped to only 500,000 pounds on Fridays, making a pretty good case for the meatless hot dog. But these "Friday Franks" never caught on. The idea resurfaced several times, about once every decade, until the late 1980s, when a failed line of assorted cold cuts, including tuna luncheon loaf, tuna bologna, and tuna breakfast sausage, finally put the idea to bed (maybe?).

Attempts to introduce Americans to fresh tuna also met with some difficulty. Part of the problem was that fishermen did not know how to deliver high-quality tuna to market, leading one prominent detractor, James Beard, to claim, "This is a fish that I think is better canned than fresh." Jane Grigson mused that American cooks were simply "put off by the bloody look" that is common to most tuna. But nonetheless a bold attempt was made by none other than Julia Child, who included a recipe for tuna à la Provençal in her classic book *Mastering the Art of French Cooking*. She relates tuna steaks to Swordfish and in her introduction waxes about the Provençal appreciation of fresh tuna, a product that her readership likely had little experience with and even less access to.

Despite tuna being incredibly abundant off our Atlantic shores, commercial fishermen never targeted them until the 1960s. The U.S. government sponsored a few exploratory fishing trips for Bluefin Tuna in the Gulf of Maine between 1951 in 1953 and found great abundance of tuna but no market demand for fresh product. Another factor limiting fishing interest was the absence of canneries like those in California that would readily buy up excess catch. Furthermore, tuna can be monstrous in size, and they are not easy or necessarily safe to catch and were not financially worth the effort it took to transport them or the space and time it took to ice and dress them. The result was that tuna was simply not regarded as a food fish. When it was caught and it didn't end up at the cat-food factory, it was likely left to rot on the beach.

The ascension of fresh tuna to the ranks of the most valued fish in the world is the story of the rise in popularity of sushi, the global culinary phenomenon that has become a principal driver of many economic aspects of the fishing industry. The Japanese fishing fleet, operating at maximum capacity in their local waters, started looking abroad for new sources for their favorite piscatorial pleasure. In 1971, Japanese buyers showed up on the docks of Gloucester, Massachusetts, offering $1 per pound for the few Bluefin Tuna were brought in, a major leap from the going rate of 5 cents. And thus the boom began. By the mid-1970s, freezer ships were docked in Maine and Massachusetts to purchase and freeze Bluefin Tuna to be shipped to the Tsukiji Market in Tokyo.

In return for the increasingly exorbitant prices they were paying, the Japanese demanded fish of the very highest quality. Tuna's quality is determined by the individual fish's genetics, but even more so by how long it takes to land, kill, bleed, and ice the fish. These large and powerful animals can swim at extreme speeds and increase their body temperature during a prolonged battle against a rod and reel. They not only build their body temperature but can increase to the point of overheating. Lactic acid softens the flesh and gives it an unpleasant tang. Overheating can literally cook the fish in what's known as *burned tuna syndrome*. This is especially true of the warm-blooded Bluefin Tuna, which, if engaged for a prolonged fight, can cook itself from the inside out—its flesh becoming grainy and losing its vibrant red color or even turning ash-gray in the center of the loins.

Color is very important to the value of tuna, and experienced buyers look for consistently colored flesh throughout the animal, with no gray or discolored spots along the bloodline. The color of the flesh should be matte, absent of any rainbow swirl or oily sheen that may be a sign that the fish's temperature had risen high enough to have separated some of the fat from the muscle. In all sushi-grade tunas, the color must be brilliant red, the highest grade having a vibrant and translucent quality. Fish that meet this highest criterion are judged Number 1 Quality and command a significant price premium. Those whose flesh is slightly duller in color, more opaque in their luster, still bold and beautiful but not quite stunning, are judged Number 2+ or Number 2. Typically, only fish above 60 pounds are graded. These rankings, however, are not bound by any legal definition

but rather are based on a traditional agreement, subjective in nature, between the buyer and the seller, who agree that there is a difference in quality and that the difference is worth paying for. But this only matters if you're serving the fish raw, for once cooked, fresh tuna of any grading will be indistinguishable from another.

Tuna generally falls into two categories: the rich, deep red–fleshed species and those with lighter or more variable coloration. Within the second group, quality is still discerned in part by color, though the optimal characteristics depend more upon size, species, and season, thus making the judgment of quality even more variable. The single best way to detect the freshness and quality of any tuna is to inspect the dark red bloodline tissue that cross-sects the four loins and runs along the spine and rib bones. In very fresh fish, this tissue is firm and compact and its color even and full. As any tuna ages, this tissue will leach its color into the lighter flesh of the loin. As the fish begins to fade, the bloodline's own color will become more brown than red. You have likely encountered the bright super-pink and perfectly consistently colored frozen tuna steaks at your local retailer or strip mall sushi joint. This unnatural color indicates that the fish has been treated by a process called "tasteless smoke." Also known as carbon monoxide, this harmless gas acts as a color preservative and enhancer. While treated fish is typically not the highest-quality product, it is perfectly safe to eat. The bigger issue is that this hyper-colored fish has trained a generation of diners, newly introduced to sushi, that tuna should be bright pink, and thus, when presented with a gorgeous top-quality piece of true sushi-grade tuna, they likely won't recognize its quality.

ABOVE Tuna and Wahoo in market, Hawaii. FOLLOWING PAGES Yellowfin Tuna hanging on the board, Empire, Louisiana.

The assimilation of sushi into American culture happened very quickly. Though there is debate over the exact date, by the late 1960s a pioneering sushi restaurant in Los Angeles had attracted national attention. Soon enough, every fashionable cosmopolitan hub had its roster of sushi bars. By the mid-1970s Americans placed our stamp on this Japanese tradition with the introduction of the California Roll. (But hey, tradition has never stopped us, and that's what makes food so much fun here.) Most diners don't realize that *sushi* refers primarily to the seasoned rice and does not automatically include fish. *Sashimi* is bite-size portions of raw fish, usually eaten with wasabi and soy sauce. Given the prevailing culture and cuisine of America, the acceptance of eating raw fish is an astounding shift and represents an expansion of our comfort zone and reflects our general expectation of safe food. But we have certainly adopted sushi as our own. Between 1988 and 1998, the number of sushi bars in America increased fivefold. We love it as both a luxury and a convenience food, and it is considered both fine dining and health food. The other day, I found sushi for sale next to Gatorade™ at the gas station.

The Yellowfin Tuna, **Bigeye Tuna**, and Bluefin Tuna are chief among the species commonly used for sushi and sashimi preparations. While they all share common characteristics of deep red flesh and luxurious fat, there is great distinction to be made among the species and even between different fish of the same species.

Bluefin Tuna is an incredible species represented in both the Pacific and Atlantic oceans. These highly migratory fish swim tens of thousands of miles in any given year, which has made management of this most highly prized of all fish species very difficult. In a single year, a fish can pass through the Mediterranean, North Atlantic, Gulf of Mexico, and back. These warm-blooded fish are forever on the move, swimming at speeds of up to 55 miles per hour, and they need to feed constantly to maintain their efforts and body temperature.

Such incredible physical feats require a Bluefin to eat as much as 10 percent of its body weight every day. Off the coast of New England, the **Atlantic Bluefin** reach their culinary pinnacle in the summer, having spent a season feeding on mackerel, herring, and squid. The vast majority of Bluefin historically has been landed in California, where much of the product was destined for canneries. Recent records show catches peaked in 1966 at just below 35 million pounds, compared to nearly two million pounds in Massachusetts the same year. Much of the Bluefin that is brought to market is known as **School Bluefin**, individual fish weighing from 50 to 200 pounds. Fish weighing 400 to 600 pounds were common into the 1980s, and trophy fish of more than 1,000 pounds were not unheard of. Large tunas are rare these days, and when such a creature is landed, it is treated with utmost respect, as is can command an astronomical price. In 2013, one fish weighing nearly 500 pounds was sold for just under $1.8 million. While part of this price represents a publicity stunt, it exemplifies the gold-rush mentality that has led to the decimation of these fish in oceans worldwide.

Part of what makes the Bluefin so unique is that it has several different kinds of meat, each prized for its own unique character and texture. The deep crimson loins lighten in color toward the belly as incredible amounts of fat begin to course through the flesh. The belly itself, know as *ventresca* or *toro*, is as fatty as any cut of any animal could be. It is richly textured, more fat than not, with wispy streaks of red muscle separating the white marbling. This is the choicest of cuts for sashimi, and the toro, or tuna belly, commands a very hefty price. The lighter and fattier upper belly portions have an incredible almost foie gras–like richness and a wonderful iodine and sweet flavor. Cooking can mute the flavor of some tunas, such as Albacore and Yellowfin, but the opposite is true for Bluefin. Its flavor is most diminutive when raw, though the subtle complexities of the fish are stunning. As it cooks, the flavor begins to intensify as the fat renders out, giving the taste a completely different balance of flavors with heavy iron notes and acidic tang. In this way it is not unlike lamb. When Bluefin is raw, it's flavor is unlike any other seafood, nearly betraying its saltwater origins, and its texture is springy, resembling that of finely grained beef. This singular and unique texture becomes very firm and dry when the fish is fully cooked. Older cookbooks often preface any recipe for cooking Bluefin by calling for a lengthy soak in brine.

Unloading Catch of Tuna Fish, Long Beach Island, N. J.

Howard Mitcham suggests soaking 1½-inch-thick steaks in brine to leach some of the blood and then curing them for two to three days in a ¼-inch layer of salt. This Portuguese method firms and bleaches the tuna, making it perfect for accepting marinades.

The Bigeye Tuna is very similar to the Yellowfin. In Hawaii, both species are known as **Ahi**, meaning "fire," which represents the striking coloration of these fish. While Bigeye Tuna is not nearly as deeply scarlet as Bluefin, its red, somewhat pinkish color intensifies as the fish get older. Fish are landed from 20 to well over 200 pounds. The larger fish are caught in deeper cold waters and have a higher fat content than Yellowfin, earning the Bigeye Tuna consideration as the better of the two for sashimi. Given its high fat content, Bigeye is considered the best of all tuna species for grilling, as it stays moist and does not cook quite as firm as does Yellowfin. Bigeye and Yellowfin are easily distinguished in their whole form: Bigeye is more plump, with a stout head and unusually large eyes, whereas Yellowfin are more sleek. I've always thought the Bigeye resembles a Maurice Sendak creature. In most culinary applications these species are interchangeable. A high-quality Yellowfin may very well be better eating than a lesser-quality Bigeye because, as with all tunas, quality depends on the fish itself and the care in capture. Both the Yellowfin and Bigeye are extremely fast-growing fish; Yellowfin can add up to 60 pounds of weight in a single year. Yellowfin are caught worldwide and represent the second-most-important species in terms of volume, accounting for about 27 percent of the global catch. Like Bigeye and Bluefin, larger Yellowfins—those ranging 70 to 200 pounds—are graded. The significant landings of smaller Yellowfins, known by the market term **Footballs**, or **Shibi** in Hawaii, and weighing 30 to 70 pounds, are typically not graded. This is a very important species in the Gulf of Mexico, with the deepwater fishery based out of Empire and Venice, Louisiana, located at the very southern tip of the land that sheaths the Mississippi River as it courses into the Gulf. The fish has a bit of confusing history. In 1920, a Yellowfin was caught off the coast of southern Florida. This highly migratory species had been regularly caught in the Pacific for centuries but was unknown in those Florida waters and thought to be unknown to science. Thinking it a new discovery, it was named **Allison Tuna** (*Thunnus allisoni*), after the director of a local aquarium. This is but another example of how fish common in many regions end up with multiple colloquial identities, which creates confusion in the scientific literature but also tells a story and offers a sense of the regional history of fisheries in any given area. Most Yellowfin is caught by purse seine, though there is a high-quality hook-and-line fishery. The Yellowfin and the Albacore are somewhat unique in that they are both very important in both canning and fresh markets. Yellowfin and Bigeye are very versatile; both are great for salt curing and drying, sashimi, and, I think, are particularly charming in their complexity when lightly cured and cold-smoked.

Another of the deep red–fleshed tunas is the underappreciated **Blackfin Tuna**. These fish are very abundant worldwide, especially in the Gulf of Mexico, where they range from 5 to 50 pounds, averaging around 15 pounds. They are rarely commercially targeted in relation to the more valuable and larger species. I think this is the most interesting of all the red-fleshed tunas, as it has very high concentrations of iron and its flesh is very lean with a sharp flavor. The bright, clean acidity and dense, lean flake make them perfect for preserving in oil or curing in salt and sugar. When Blackfin is cooked fresh, just a brief salting prior to cooking is all that's needed to firm its somewhat soft texture. Despite its deep red color when raw, when cooked it becomes light gray, the same as Bigeye and Yellowfin (Bluefin Tuna takes on a deep gray color).

The most abundant of the tuna caught worldwide, representing an average of 55 percent of the global catch, is the Skipjack. Skipjack are found in both the Atlantic and Pacific, and on the West Coast the **Black Skipjack** is a near identical species. Though the vast majority of the catch is destined for canning, I think it is one of the most underappreciated and most versatile species in terms of preserving. Skipjack are very well suited for smoked, salted and dried, or oil-preserved preparations. This is the fish used in Japanese cuisine for the production of *katsuobushi*, a smoked, dried, and fermented product that is then shaved razor thin into wispy flakes and used to garnish dishes or to make flavored broths. Skipjack is commonly called **Oceanic Bonito**, which is why *katsuobushi* is often referred to as "Bonito flakes." Though Skipjack is not much esteemed in the Gulf or Atlantic waters, it has long been an important food fish on the Pacific coast and especially in Hawaii, where it is known as **Aku** and sometimes by the odd regional moniker **Watermelon**. Most often these fish are

landed around 10 pounds, though they range up to 40. Its light to dark-pink flesh, growing darker as the fish ages, has a pronounced and elegant flavor somewhat comparable to that of a young Yellowfin. It's a great species for sashimi and is the preferred fish used in the Hawaiian dish *poke*. In older American cookbooks, Skipjack recipes often recommended a long soak in brine to tame its flavor, but I feel that this robs it of its nuanced character and beautiful sea breeze aromatics. The roe is particularly prized and makes a wonderful bottarga, and its bones are commonly grilled or fried in Hawaiian cuisine.

Bonito, found in both the Atlantic and Pacific oceans, are very common and are often much smaller than other tunas, usually weighing two to six pounds but sometimes much more. This fish is not to be confused with the **Little Tunny**, also known as the **Bonita**. The name *Bonito*, Spanish for "beautiful," aptly describes these lovely, bullet-shaped fish with mirror-like silver skin and radiating blue lines. Their flesh is very fatty and similar to mackerel or a jack in texture and appearance. These are a great grilling fish, and their light- to medium-pink flesh is well flattered when smoked or marinated in dishes such as escabeche. Its stronger flavor and naturally salty taste has earned it a host of detractors, who say it's not worth eating. In the other camp are those, myself included, who believe that when prepared correctly it is among the most interesting of the family. That said, it's not legally allowed to be labeled as "tuna" and must be sold as "Bonito." On larger fish, there is a section of meat in the head just behind the eyes that I consider the best part of the fish. This section can be cut into slices and marinated with herbs and wine for grilling or broiling. Bonito have thick gill plates, and the collars, cut from just behind the gill plates, are great for the grill or deep-frying. Bonito have a significant amount of blood and must be carefully bled immediately after capture, or their flesh can become mushy and will deteriorate quickly. Though these are not much considered or respected as a food fish in today's market, a writer in New England in 1871 remarked that it was "the salmon of the sea. It is as nourishing as beef, and Bonito is the worthy rival of the Spanish Mackerel and the Sheepshead." Alas, this high praise did not win the Bonito an enduring fanbase, and it has never since enjoyed great popularity.

The Albacore Tuna, found worldwide, is an important species in the canning industry. And though traditionally it has not been much respected as a fresh fish, that taboo is waning as more and more high-quality pole-caught fish are making their way to market. They can grow up to 50 pounds, though they average about half that. When under five years old, the young fish migrate and are caught in large shoals. As they get older, mature Albacore settle into more solitary patterns in deeper waters farther out to sea. The flesh of young Albacore is pale beige, becoming pink as it matures. Its taste is the most delicate of all the tunas, and its fine texture and small flake are silky, like that of the Yellowfin. Unlike other tunas, Albacore is fattiest and considered best flavored when young. Paul Johnson writes of their unique scent as a "mineral like smell that can only be described as the odor of steel." The roe is particularly good for curing. James Beard writes: "Since albacore has the lightest meat, it is, of course, the best of the various tunas for poaching." Albacore has long been highly esteemed in southern Europe and the Mediterranean, though when they were first caught here in America, they were considered to be inedible. I imagine this was partially due to fishermen not knowing how to care for them, but as Goode surmises, "perhaps it was due to the fact that we do not know how to cook them." Albacore is not as firm or dense in texture as other tunas, making it a secondary species in quality for sashimi. Helen Brown mentions that Albacore was popular in California cooking until 1926, when it was said to have disappeared from those waters and did not return for 12 years. When it did come back, she says it returned not only into California waters, but for the first time swam into those of Oregon and Washington, where significant fresh fisheries are conducted today. In Hawaii, Albacore is known as **Tombo Ahi** and has long been considered a great eating fish. *Tombo* means "dragonfly" in Japanese and likely refers to its very long pectoral fins. Albacore caught in the waters surrounding Hawaii are often quite large, ranging from 40 to 80 pounds. Albacore are among the oiliest of all tunas, thus making them great for the grill, for confit, and for serving cold or marinated.

The Little Tunny of the Atlantic coast is commonly known as **False Albacore** and the aforementioned Bonita. These are not a targeted species, though a fair number of fish are landed as bycatch, particularly in the Gulf, where they often weigh three to seven pounds, though they can grow up to 30 pounds. Their meat is very dark red, reminding some of the color of liver, and has a very pronounced taste. The bloodline is larger than on most tunas, and trimming this leads to a low edible yield. Many recipes recommend soaking the meat in a brine of salt and milk prior to cooking to help bleach the flesh and somewhat mute its flavor. Unlike other tunas, the flesh retains its color after cooking. In Hawaii, a very similar fish that is rarely caught but is quite esteemed is known as **Kawakawa**, or **Mackerel Tuna**. It has a similarly dark, rich flavor, heavy with umami and iron and balanced by a quick acidity. This depth of personality makes it especially good, in my opinion, for smoking, as its meaty character is well flattered by the sultriness of the smoke.

Bullet Mackerel, also known as **Bullet Tuna**, and its close relation the **Frigate Mackerel**, also known as the **Frigate Tuna**, are nearly identical but for slight taxonomic distinctions. In common reference, Bullet Mackerel is used to describe both of these species of small fish, rarely larger than five pounds. Though called "mackerels" in the kitchen they are more similar to Bonito—their strongly flavored, darkly colored meat and concentrically ringed flesh makes them better suited to tuna recipes, and I recommend a light brine, acidulated with a bit of white wine, before marinating with garlic, herbs, and oil. These are great for grilling, pan-frying, or poaching and marinating as escabeche.

There are a number of parts of various tunas that, though not traditionally served, can be as enticing as the finest sashimi. Tuna buckroe, or testes, is delicious when poached, cooled, sliced thinly, and served with sliced chile peppers, sweet onions, vinegar, and olive oil. The roe of the female are traditionally made into bottarga—salted, pressed, and hung to air-dry for several months until hard. The parched outer layer reveals a smoothly textured orange center, all of which can be finely grated as a seasoning for salads, risottos, or pastas or sliced and moistened with olive oil and eaten as is. My favorite preparation is to finely grate the bottarga and mix it with sherry vinegar, chopped parsley, shallot, and olive oil to make a potent vinaigrette for serving atop grilled tuna steaks. Tuna intestines can be cured under salt for a couple of days. You need to ensure that the gallbladder was not punctured, or the entire effort will be tainted with an unruly flavor. The salted intestines are then rinsed before stewing into tomato sauces, soups, or beans to add a deeply rich flavor. The strip of meat and connective tissue joining the dorsal fin to the body can also be salted and used in a similar fashion.

The liver and other pieces of fatty trim can be very gently rendered in water to yield a clear and clean-tasting oil that I like to use drizzled over grilled or seared tuna portions. It also can be used to finish soups or in vinaigrettes to add a huge boost of flavor. The oil will go rancid quickly, so it is best to use this within two to three days of preparation. And one of my very favorite parts of the tuna is the spine, prepared in a dish taught to me by chef Chris Cosentino. I trim the rib bones from the spine, then season it heavily with salt. I fry the bones in a half inch of olive oil until any bits of meat are crisped and the bones start to release liquid from between the vertebrae. I then add a couple of spoonfuls of capers, lots of sliced garlic, a couple of chile peppers, and two large handfuls of picked mint leaves. When the capers are crisp and the mint leaves shattering, the dish is done. Serve the bones with all the crispy garnish and a good bit of the oil. Sever the vertebrae and spoon out the warm, custard-like marrow hidden inside to spread over toast. Top with the garnishes and oil, and you'll have a hard time convincing me that any other part of the tuna can compare!

ABOVE Bluefin left to rot on the beach, 1891.

FOLLOWING PAGES, LEFT Folk art in the Atchafalsya, Louisiana.

FOLLOWING PAGES, RIGHT Happy hour, 1937.

To prepare a fresh turtle, scrub the shell and wash away any collected mud and dirt. Cut off the head, then either hang it, allowing it to bleed out, or plunge the body and head into a bucket of salted water and let those parts soak for half an hour. They should then be blanched for 15 minutes in enough unsalted water to cover them. Rub off the skin from the head, legs, and feet, and pull out the toenails. Remove the bottom and top shells by separating them from the meat, using a very sharp knife. The liver and any eggs should be set aside for use in finishing the soup. Carefully remove the remaining viscera and gallbladder, taking care not to puncture it, and discard. Cut off the meat from the bones and make stock by slowly simmering the shells, bones, and head for two to three hours. Once the stock is done, add the meat, seasonings, and vegetables, and braise for 45 to 90 minutes until tender. Turtle meat can also be purchased as a prepared product.

Mock Turtle soup has long been a stand-in for the involved preparation of the original dish. Made from calves heads and other trimmings in place of turtle, it is well-regarded but considered a second-tier substitute. Lewis Carroll comically includes a character named Mock Turtle in his epic tale *Alice's Adventures in Wonderland*. The animal was made up of a collection of the ingredients in a mock turtle soup. Upon seeing the Mock Turtle, Alice asks her companion the Gryphon, "What is his sorrow?" "'Once,' said Mock Turtle at last, with a deep sigh, 'I was a real Turtle.'" Given the difficulty of preparing soup from a live animal and the fact that many of the species upon which the classic recipes are based are no longer appropriate to catch, maybe Mock Turtle is a good idea.

Turtle Soup

Commander's Palace in New Orleans is the place to experience this gem in the legacy of American cuisine, which they now make with Snapping Turtle. This recipe is adapted from their classic version.

- 1½ sticks butter
- 2½ pounds turtle meat, diced
- Salt and freshly cracked black pepper
- 6 stalks celery, diced
- 3 bell peppers, diced
- 2 medium onions, diced
- 30 cloves garlic, minced
- 1 tablespoon dried thyme
- 1 tablespoon dried oregano
- 4 bay leaves
- 2 quarts veal stock
- 1 cup all-purpose flour
- 1 (750-ml) bottle dry sherry
- 1 tablespoon hot pepper sauce
- ¼ cup Worcestershire sauce
- 2 large lemons, juiced
- 3 cups tomatoes, peeled, seeded, and chopped
- 10 ounces fresh spinach (stems removed), roughly chopped
- 6 hard-boiled eggs, chopped

In a large soup pot over medium-high heat, melt ½ stick butter. Add turtle meat and brown. Season to taste with salt and pepper, and continue to cook until liquid is almost dry, 18 to 20 minutes. Stir in the celery, bell peppers, onions, and garlic, then add thyme, oregano, and bay leaves, and sauté, stirring frequently, for about 20 minutes. Add stock, bring to a boil, and simmer for 30 minutes. Skim any fat that comes to the top.

While stock is simmering, make the roux. In a small saucepan, melt the remaining 1 stick butter over medium heat. Slowly add the flour, stirring constantly with a wooden spoon. Take care not to burn the mixture. After all of the flour has been added, cook until roux smells nutty, is pale in color, and has a consistency of wet sand, about three minutes. Set aside to cool until soup is ready (roux should be cool when adding to hot soup).

Using a whisk, stir the roux into the stock vigorously, adding a little at a time to prevent lumping. Simmer for about 25 minutes, stirring often to prevent sticking on bottom. Add sherry, and bring to a boil. Add hot sauce and Worcestershire sauce. Simmer and skim any fat or foam that comes to top. Add lemon juice and tomatoes, and return to a simmer. Stir in spinach and eggs, return to a simmer, and adjust seasoning. Serve hot.

Wahoo

I was first introduced to **Wahoo** as "**White Tuna**," not a legal name but nonetheless an apt description of its flesh. Though wahoo is not tuna, it is a member of the tuna/mackerel family and is, in fact, the largest of the mackerels. This deepwater open-ocean fish is well known in the cuisines of the Caribbean and Hawaii. It's available year-round as bycatch of the tuna industry but is better known in the summer, when it comes nearer to shore and is caught in a number of fisheries. While a few of these fish end up in market, the vast majority of those landed are caught recreationally. It is an important fish in Hawaiian cuisine, where it is known as **Ono**, meaning "sweet." European explorers, when first mapping the Hawaiian Islands, found Ono to be plentiful off the island of Oahu. Earlier maps indicate that a very common spelling of the word *Oahu* was "Wahoo," and this is believed to be the origin of the fish's continental name.

These mirror-bright silver fish with azure bands are on average landed between 10 and 50 pounds, though they grow significantly larger. They are as fast a fish as one can imagine, both in speed and in looks. Their long, slender bodies are clearly designed to cut through the water, and their deep, carved musculature is as strong and beautiful as that of any fish. In this way, the Wahoo is every bit equal to its relatives, but its meat is nothing like you'd expect from mackerel or tuna, as its flesh is very white and fairly dry (though it radiates out in concentric bands in the same manner as tuna). When cut, Wahoo has a sea-green opalescence. The bloodline, when fresh, is bright cherry red, though as the fish ages it takes on a browner hue. It is best when cooked rare or medium, much the way most tuna is. It's very good steamed, as its dense but porous meat absorbs flavors very well, especially highly aromatic spices such as star anise, clove, and cinnamon, and vegetables such as fennel and celery. Its skin is edible, though it can be very chewy on fish larger than 20 pounds. It has very fine scales are easily removed. Its liver—very dense and fatty—makes a fine meal served on its own, poached or even grilled then sliced thinly and topped with an herb salad.

Wahoo roe is especially good. In my opinion, it's one of the very finest of the tuna/mackerel family and is as good preserved in a bottarga fashion as it is sautéed like shad roe when taken from smaller fish. Though they won't add much body or depth of texture, its bones make for a good stock if cooked very briefly, lending a quick, easy burst of flavor.

Instead of being cut into two fillets, as is common with mackerel, Wahoo is often cut into four cigar-shaped loins, four on each fish. It takes well to marinades and is great on the grill or under a broiler. The texture is best when sliced across the grain and on a bias in order to give the finest mouthfeel.

Wahoo may also be prepared by many long- and short-term preservation methods. It makes a perfect stand-in for salmon when prepared as gravlax, especially with the addition of cool-flavored herbs such as dill or fennel. It also makes a very good smoked product, either dry-cured and cold-smoked as you would a salmon, or hot-smoked as you would mackerel. It does particularly well with pastrami flavors in the cure. And when cold-smoked and sliced thinly on a bias, it reveals its concentric flakes beautifully, and its oil remains embedded in the flesh, giving it a silken mouthfeel. For longer preservation, Wahoo can be brine pickled (though a quick pickle for flavoring is wonderful) or salted in whole loin form. Salt Wahoo is a pretty nice homemade stand-in for Bonito flakes. And while Wahoo is often introduced to us through sushi, as the actually nonexistent "White Tuna," it's worth celebrating as its own species. Raw, cooked, or preserved, Wahoo is its own character even among the strong personalities of its more famous relatives.

OPPOSITE Spotted Seatrout.

Weakfish

I've always been fascinated by **Weakfish**, perhaps because every time I got a delivery of it, it seemed noticeably different. The nomenclature describing this species is entirely confounding, as it a catchall name covering four individual species, including the **Sand Seatrout**, also known as the **Sand Weakfish**; the **Spotted Seatrout**, also known as the **Spotted Weakfish**; the **Silver Seatrout**, also known as the **Silver Weakfish**; and the **Weakfish**, also known as **Gray Trout**. But none of these fish is related to trout. Got that?

As Goode comments: "the history of American fisheries contains very little respecting the habits of these species, although it is so important an element of food to the inhabitants of the southern coast." He laments not only a lack of scientific understanding but a lack of regional folklore or attention to the details of regionally available species. To further complicate things, the term *Sea Trout* (two words) refers to the anadromous Sea-Run Trout that spend part of their life cycle in the sea while **Seatrout** (all one word) refers broadly to the four species mentioned above. The Weakfish and kin are members of the drum family, so named for their ability to vibrate a muscle against their air bladder, creating and amplifying a soft droning sound that is the family's distinguishing feature.

Weakfish did not earn their name due to a lack of moxie or endurance; in fact, they are a rather robust fish. Many believe that the name refers to the weak condition of the cartilage on the sides of the fish's mouth, which rips easily away from the fisherman's hook. Another origin story derives from a poem written by Jacob Steendam about the New Netherlands (Manhattan) in which he references the fish by its Dutch name *weekvis*, which means "soft flesh." In early American texts, any of the weakfish kin are generally referred to by their original name **Squeteague**, an Algonquin Indian word meaning "very handsome fish."

These are indeed handsome, slender fish, each displaying shades of iridescent silver and grayish tones highlighted with blue accents and blushes of multicolor red and brown spots. Each species is patterned uniquely, depending on where along the Atlantic and Gulf coasts they were caught. The Sand

Seatrout and Silver Seatrout reach a maximum size of 1 ½ feet, whereas the Spotted Seatrout and the Weakfish grow to double that size, though most fish average 1½ to 2 feet. These popular sport fish are caught in shallow waters and estuaries along the coast, where they feed on crustaceans and small fish. Only the Spotted Seatrout seeks out habitat in eelgrass and rocky areas, whereas the others prefer muddy or sandy bottoms.

These fish all share more or less similar qualities in cooking and at the table, though some exceed others in certain traits. However, they all must be properly handled after catch—gutted and iced immediately—as their flavor and vibrancy fade far quicker than most fishes. When freshly caught, weakfish are very distinctive and well flavored yet delicate. They suffer a very short shelf life, fading after as little as a day or two, losing vitality and integrity, exuding moisture and thus flavor in cooking.

Their gray-white flesh can often be tinged roseate, and it is appreciated for its soft flake and a meaty and somewhat gamey flavor that is complex and unique with a crisp aftertaste. The fillets are lean and have little connective tissue, giving them their signature soft and yielding bite that is still firm enough to hold up to cooking and plating. Even the freshest fish doesn't smell particularly "fresh" or bright, but is rather muted—a seaweed aroma, weak with ocean brine. Their thin edible skin is very tasty and easily scaled. Smaller fish are perfect for grilling whole, or the fillets may be pan-fried or broiled. The weakfish's mild but pleasant aroma, easy flavor, and economical price make this an attractive choice for home cooks looking to try something new. Its flavor is such that a strong sauce is not needed. Chopped fresh herbs, such as basil, mixed with butter or olive oil is a perfect way to charm the fish, regardless of its preparation.

When the fish is poached, the flesh can become dull gray in color but is otherwise wonderful, as it absorbs flavors well. The heads of all of these species are among of my favorites for making stock, as they have a very complex and savory flavor profile. The roe, particularly of the Weakfish and Speckled Trout are highly regarded, being thought equal in quality to the roe of mullet or shad. They are best when either cured or sautéed, and it's said that the delicious, sweet roe was the favorite meal of our first president. The weakfish "sounds," a commercial term for the

air bladders, have long had a valuable market of their own, as they are used in the production of isinglass (a fining agent used in beer and wine production) and glue. In North Carolina, where significant quantities of weakfish have historically been landed, the fish were most often shipped north to market in their whole form. In this manner, the fishermen lost the value of the sounds, until in 1878, a young entrepreneur invented a machine called the Trout Sounder. This simple tool allowed for the sound to be removed through the gill opening without damaging or otherwise altering the look of a whole fish likely destined for fresh trade.

According to cookbook author Ruth Spear, "Weakfish were so prolific in Atlantic Coast waters in the 1860s that they were netted like herring. By the turn of the century, they were unknown and appeared only occasionally during the next five decades, [and] one finds no references to them in cookbooks before the mid-1970s." Despite this historic and continuing trend of periods of both abundance and scarcity, all four species remain popular recreational and food fish, from the northern reaches of the Weakfish (Gray Trout) in Nova Scotia to the western border of Campeche Bay, which marks the end of common territory shared by the other three species. Fishermen in Cape Cod refer to weakfish by yet another name, **Drummer**, because of the low grinding sound it makes while traveling in schools. Like a lot of things fishermen do, this name seems pretty practical. As the weakfish are indeed members of the drum family and being so related by this shared behavior, they are able to voice their displeasure at being hooked just as anglers are known to employ colorful invective when these tasty fish rip themselves free from the line.

Wolffish

This nightmare-inducing fish is likely the source of some ages-old yarn of sea monsters emerging from the infinite blue to invade a bored sailor's daydreams. **Wolffish** is hands-down my favorite white-fleshed fish species. Unfortunately, a lot of other people have shared this opinion. Thus, it is no longer commercially fished in the United States at this time, though wolffish imported from Iceland can sometimes be found at market. There are two closely related Atlantic species, the **Spotted Wolffish** and **Atlantic Wolffish**, both equal in culinary quality. The only difference between them is varying degrees of ugliness. In the North Pacific, the **Wolf-Eel** grows several feet longer than its Atlantic relatives, reaching up to eight feet in length. A second Pacific species, the **Bering Wolffish**, is more modest and grows only up to four feet, like its Atlantic cousins. Admittedly, I have not tasted all of these species, but given reports from trusted friends and a few shared basic biological traits between the fish, I will hazard to state that they are all equal in character and qualities, and equally fabulous as food fishes. These deepwater species are solitary and truly peculiar-looking creatures, colored shades of black, gray, brown, and beige. With a head that is composed mostly of a ferociously powerful jaw full of sharp canine teeth, wolffish bear no small resemblance to bulldogs. But these strong jaws are precisely what make them such tasty fish, as they are built to crush thick-shelled oysters, clams, crabs, and lobsters—a labor-intensive diet that elucidates a fairly complete idea of what the wolffish clan tastes like.

Historically, they were caught as bycatch of the cod fishery, and the meat was usually salted and sold as salt cod. When fresh fillets gained foothold as the preferred market form of fish, wolffish were common in our markets, oftentimes sold as **Ocean Catfish** or **Seawolf**. Average specimens range two to three feet and are most often found in skin-off fillet form; however, a fishmonger proud of his or her product will often display the head—not only as a conversation starter but also because the cheeks are exceptional eating. Its flesh is moderately dense like monkfish, though it has a silken-rich texture like Sablefish. It flakes easily with the back of a fork when cooked, and its brilliant white flesh remains very moist and is resilient to most cooking methods. In a raw state, the flesh should be only moderately firm to the touch with a slight elasticity. As it cooks, it tenses up, resulting in a perfect textural cross between silk and substance. The color when fresh, is consistently luminously white with no evidence of graying or yellowing, which is a marker of age. The delicate and unchallenging shellfish flavor of this fish responds equally well to butter as to olive oil, and it pairs particularly well with woodsy and robust herbs such as bay, thyme, and rosemary.

Broiling on a bed of such herbs is my favorite way to prepare wolffish, though the cheeks are at their peak when braised in a sherry-spiked court bouillon flavored with mace and peppercorn, which yields a unique texture and experience in fish cookery. As the dense and stringy meat of the fist-sized cheeks slowly succumbs to the temptations of the slow simmering braise, the meat disrobes its oceanic identity and presents an unctuousness and texture similar to pork belly—fatty and fork tender—all rounded out by the resulting palate-coating gelatinous sauce.

A wolffish's large and bulbous head is matched in girth by its collar for a few inches before the body begins to taper significantly toward the tail, like a large, flattened eel. The thicker portion, cut closer to the head, does well in nearly any cooking method, especially as steaks under the broiler or cubed as for kebabs. The raw meat's somewhat porous texture allows marinades to deeply penetrate. Even a quick dousing with a bit of vinegar, thyme, and citrus zest will provide all the accent needed; no sauce required. I don't recommend slow-roasting this fish, as I think it needs a little singe to mature its flavor and provide some taste contrast. Grilling is a sure bet, though care must be taken, as callous handling of the fillets can feed more fish to the fire than to your family.

Wrasse

The **Wrasse** family is well represented in our waters, with most species swimming in the Atlantic. These fish range greatly in size—smaller species grow but a few inches, while the largest can stretch three feet and beyond. The **Tautog** and **Cunner** are favorite sons of the wrasse family and have a significant enough history to warrant a separate entry (see page 464). According to Alan Davidson, Revolutionary War veteran General Pinckney so favored the flavor of Tautog he ordered a live-well ship laden with the fish delivered to Charleston harbor, where they were released in hopes of settling a new population. It is claimed that relatives of these fish were still to be found in those southerly waters some 50 years later. No such attention was paid to other species in the family. Most wrasses find their most northern territory in North Carolina and proliferate through the South and the temperate waters of the Gulf.

This colorful group of fish looks like a merry band of pop-art pranksters on their way to a party at Warhol's Factory. To match, many come with equally interesting names. In markets

along the Atlantic coast one might find the **Spanish Hogfish**, one of the most conspicuous of all fish. Much of its body is golden yellow, but its dorsal ridge—from the eye down half its length—vibrates with a mottled blue and purple stamp laced with red-edged scales. It's also considered the choicest eating fish in the family. Others include the **Creole Wrasse**, its ornamentation epitomizing a Mardi Gras krewe strutting down Tchoupitoulas. The **Puddingwife**, my favorite wrasse name, is dappled with all the Easter colors in the pastel crayon box. **Hogfish** is the largest wrasse, averaging 6 to 10 pounds, though some fish can grow as large as 45 pounds and 3½ feet or more. They are erroneously called **Hog Snapper** (they have no relation to snapper). To add to the confusion, Hogfish is sometimes suggested in historical accounts as an alternate name of the Pigfish, a member of the unrelated grunt family.

The Hogfish has never been common at market for a good reason. It is such a famously great-eating fish—firm-fleshed with resilient texture, and sweet crab flavor—that it rarely makes it beyond the fisherman's own table.

Of the Pacific wrasse species, the **California Sheephead**, (unrelated to the Sheepshead of the Atlantic) also known simply as **Goat**, is the only commercially targeted species on the continental coastline. These can grow upwards of 30 pounds, though their average is five to six pounds.

All wrasse have heavy scales and thick pharyngeal, bony throat teeth used to crush their prey. Their diet is composed predominantly of mollusks, crustaceans, lobsters, and other such tasty things, and as a result, their flavor is to be admired—assertive and robust, but not strong. They are among the most aromatic fish, smelling richly of butter, shellfish, and a slight iodine and brine tang. They present a firm, snappy texture nearly crisp to the bite and have a moist, moderately sized flake. The skin of wrasse species is thick and it can require a fair amount of force to remove the scales, an effort that can damage the integrity of the fillet. The skin is often slightly bitter, but even so it can enhance the fish's flavor and preserve its moisture, so I usually cook the fillets with the scales and skin on and simply peel them off before serving. Moderately sized fish are wonderful roasted whole, as they present beautifully and are easy to serve due to their simple bone structure. I especially like roasting wrasse over a bed of sturdy herbs such as rosemary or thyme, then adding a shot or two of brandy and igniting it just as I carry the dish to the table. The liquor flames off and mixes with the juices and fat of the fish to create a seductive sauce.

Wreckfish

I first came across **Wreckfish** when I was searching for a sustainable substitute for grouper. At the time, I believe only a single boat, maybe two, was fishing for this species. I got into a bit of a bidding war with a couple of other chefs, which made the fishermen very happy. Any time I was lucky enough to be the winning chef, I could say without much doubt that we were the only restaurant in America serving Wreckfish that night. Also known as **Stone Bass**, this relation of the sea bass family, is closely related to the **Hawaiian Sea Bass**, or **Hapuʻupuʻu**, and along the Pacific coast to the **Giant Sea Bass**, also known as **Black Sea Bass**, a critically endangered fish. I have not eaten the Giant Sea Bass, but the Wreckfish and the Hawaiian Sea Bass are interchangeable in the kitchen, though they do differ significantly in size. Hawaiian Sea Bass average 5 to 10 pounds, and Wreckfish usually tip in around 40 pounds. Hapuʻupuʻu is very well-suited for steamed preparations, especially the smaller and more tender fish. Often seasoned, then wrapped in a banana leaf, the entire packet is placed over a pot of aromatized water or very slowly grilled; the leaf traps moisture and steams the fillet in its own juices.

They are quite plump and full in their shape and can grow up to six feet or more. Juveniles are found at the top of the water column, aggregating around floating objects, whereas adults live on rocky bottoms and other habitats such as shipwrecks, from which they derive their shared common name, Wreckfish. The east coast fishery began in 1987, when they were discovered in an area known as the Charleston Bump off the shores of South Carolina and Georgia. Due to the deepwater nature of the fishery, it required specialized gear to haul these large fish up from as deep as 2,500 feet. The gear was prohibitively costly, and thus there was not a very large fleet that targeted them, though there was a maximum of eight boats allowed at any time to engage in the fishery. Wreckfish feed mostly on small fish and crustaceans, lending them a sweet, crablike flavor and to flatter their somewhat fibrous yet tender texture. I'm not aware of any fishery for the juveniles, and thus the larger adult fish, averaging around 30 to 40 pounds, is about the only form in which the fish will be found in market.

In the kitchen, its flesh is tinged pink and gray, becoming bone white in color when cooked, and its raw, slightly fibrous texture eases into a much more moist and tender one. The richness of flavor is due more to its sweetness than fattiness. Its skin is far too tough to serve, though it is helpful in preparation to maintain moisture. The bones of the Wreckfish, especially the head, are intensely flavored and gelatinous, making a clean, brightly flavored stock, but it's quite rare that you'll buy a whole fish. I prefer the fattier belly sections, as they are thick enough to yield attractive portions and have less of the dense connective tissue than the top fillets. The herbaceous qualities of olive oil pair perfectly with Wreckfish, heightening its flavor. The fish are at their peak in the late fall and early winter, which is fortunate, as these fish lend themselves perfectly to the layered flavors of stewed preparations. I will often stew it with large chunks of autumn squash and walnuts. The squash breaks down and thickens the braising liquid, while the walnuts offer a textural counterpoint. These woodsy and hearty flavors accentuate an entirely different side of this fish's personality.

OPPOSITE Hogfish.

FOLLOWING PAGES Gazing out at sea, Gloucester Massachusetts, 1943.

BIBLIOGRAPHY

Bittman, Mark. *Fish: The Complete Guide to Buying and Cooking.* New York: Wiley Publishing, Inc., 1994.

Brown, Helen. *West Coast Cook Book.* New York: Alfred A. Knopf, 1991. (Originally published in different form in 1952 by Little, Brown and Company, Boston.)

Carson, Rachel L. *The Sea Around Us.* New York: Oxford University Press, 1951.

——. *The Edge of the Sea.* Boston: Houghton Mifflin Company, 1955.

Clark, Eleanor. *The Oysters of Locmariaquer.* New York: Harper Perennial Modern Classics, 2006. (First published New York: Pantheon Books, 1964.)

Deutsch, Hermann B. *Brennan's New Orleans Cookbook.* New Orleans: Robert L. Crager & Company, 1961.

Hersey, John. *Blues.* New York: Alfred A. Knopf, 1987.

Horton, Tom, and William M. Eichbaum. *Turning the Tide: Saving the Chesapeake Bay.* Washington, D.C.: Island Press, 1991.

Jacobson, Rowan. *A Geography of Oysters: The Connoisseur's Guide to Oyster Eating in North America.* New York: Bloomsbury USA, 2008.

Johnson, Paul. *Fish Forever:. The Definitive Guide to Understanding, Selecting, and Preparing Healthy, Delicious, and Environmentally Sustainable Seafood.* Hoboken, New Jersey: John Wiley & Sons, Inc., 2007.

Kurlansky, Mark. *Cod: A Biography of the Fish That Changed the World.* 1997.

——. *The Big Oyster: History on the Half Shell.* New York: Random House Trade Paperbacks, 2006.

——. *The Last Fish Tale: The Fate of the Atlantic and Survival in Gloucester, America's Oldest Fishing Port and Most Original Town.* New York: Ballantine Books, 2008.

Love, R. Malcolm. *The Food Fishes: Their Intrinsic Variation and Practical Implications.* New York: Van Nostrand Reinhold Company, 1988.

Mitcham, James Howard. *Clams, Mussels, Oysters, Scallops & Snails.* Orleans, Massachusetts: Parnassus Imprints, 1990.

Mitchell, Joseph. *The Bottom of the Harbor.* New York: Pantheon Books, 2008. (Originally published in slightly different form by Little, Brown in 1959.)

Oliver, Sandra L. Saltwater Foodways: New Englanders and Their Food, at Sea and Ashore, in the Nineteenth Century. Mystic, Connecticut: Mystic Seaport Museum, Inc., 1995.

Peterson, James. *Fish & Shellfish*. New York: William Morrow and Company, Inc., 1996.

Rodger, Robin W. A. *The Fisheries of North America: An Illustrated Guide to Commercial Species*. Halifax, Nova Scotia, Canada: Canadian Marine Publications, 2006.

Shapiro, Sidney, ed. *Our Changing Fisheries*. Washington, D.C.: United States Government Printing Office, 1971.

Spencer, Evelene, and John N. Cobb. *Fish cookery, Six hundred recipes for the preparation of fish, shellfish and other aquatic animals, including fish soups, salads and entrées, with accompanying sauces, seasonings, dressings and forcemeats.* Boston: Little, Brown, and Company, 1925.

Thoreau, Henry David. *Cape Cod*. New York: Thomas Y. Crowell Company, 1961.

Titcomb, Margaret. *Native Use of Fish in Hawaii*. Honolulu: University of Hawaii Press, 1972. (Originally published in 1952 as Memoir 29 of the Polynesian Society, Wellington, New Zealand.)

Trenor, Casson. *Sustainable Sushi: A Guide to Saving the Oceans One Bite and a Time*. Berkeley, California: North Atlantic Books, 2008.

Warner, William W. *Beautiful Swimmers: Watermen, Crabs and the Chesapeake Bay*. New York: Penguin Books, 1979. (Orignally published by Little, Brown and Company, 1976.)

Wennersten, John R. *The Oyster Wars of Chesapeake Bay*. Centreville, Maryland: Tidewater Publishers, 1981.

Wisdom, Mrs. John Minor, Miss Elise Meyer, and Mrs. John E. Hurley. *New Orleans: Carnival Cook Book*. New Orleans: Women's Republican Publications, Inc., 1951.

Woodard, Colin. *The Lobster Coast: Rebels, Rusticators, and the Struggle for a Forgotten Frontier*. New York: Viking, 2004.

Wright, Anneka. *Neptune's Table: A View of America's Ocean Fisheries*. Seattle, Washington: National Marine Fisheries Service, 2002.

IMAGE CREDITS

© Alexandra Daley-Clark: 259, 303.

© Ben Weiner: 475.

© Jay Fleming: i, ii, 4, 22, 34, 36, 39, 40, 51, 80, 99, 106, 117, 124, 168, 170, 175, 182, 197, 218, 284, 292, 298, 300, 320, 324, 325, 334, 400, 438, 446, 448, 495, 500.

Alaska State Library, U.S. Arctic Health Research Center Collection, P220-048: 361.

Barton Seaver: 53, 54, 57, 64, 65, 77 (bottom), 89, 92, 101, 113, 155, 163, 167, 176, 185, 186 (top), 189, 191, 194, 200, 205, 212, 229, 232 (top), 248, 250, 251, 254, 260, 266, 278, 283, 287, 290, 296, 301, 313, 318, 331, 338, 339, 340, 341, 343, 344, 350, 358, 366, 374, 387, 396, 414, 415, 420, 426, 427, 433, 434, 464, 469, 470, 493.

Chesapeake Bay Maritime Museum, Photograph by Robert de Gast: 98, 132.

Courtesy of Don Lindgren, Rabelais Fine Cookbooks: 87, 130, 145, 152, 153, 280, 281, 329 (both images).

Courtesy of DPLA; Gloucester Lyceum & Sawyer Free Library (right): 12.

Courtesy of John F. Kennedy Presidential Library and Museum: 103.

Courtesy of Maine Historical Society: 258.

Courtesy of Maine State Archives: 257, 271.

Courtesy of Missouri History Museum, St. Louis, 421.

Courtesy of Monroe County Public Library: 18, 264, 491.

Courtesy of National Archives, 192.

Courtesy of National Oceanic and Atmospheric Administration, 13, 14, 24 (right), 25, 31, 45, 60, 63, 67, 68, 71, 77 (top), 79, 86 (all images), 90 (top), 115, 133, 143, 148, 156, 167, 187, 188, 198, 211, 228, 234, 232 (bottom), 240, 288, 314, 319, 369 (both images), 375, 379, 395, 402, 406, 407, 412, 417, 450, 453, 458, 462, 474 (both images), 478, 487.

Courtesy of Oregon State Archives: 348 (all images), 349.

Courtesy of The Scarborough Historical Society: 123.

Courtesy of the Tide Institute: 372, 373.

Digital Commonwealth: 61, 73, 482.

Getty Images: 24 (left).

Government Printing Office: 135, 354 (both images).

iStock: 88, 178, 279, 346, 389.

Ken Berg: 94.

Leslie Jones : 3, 12 (left), 17 (right), 20, 21, 43, 136, 140, 141, 160, 236, 237, 276, 311, 451, 455, 456, 457, 460.

Library of Congress: 1, 6, 8, 11, 17 (left), 26, 28, 29, 30, 33, 42, 46, 90 (bottom), 109 (bottom right), 144, 146, 150, 238, 256, 261, 272, 273, 274, 277, 328 (bottom), 351, 352 (all images), 355, 357 (all images), 368, 370, 383, 390, 393, 416, 445, 471, 484, 489, 502, 503, 504.

Mark Boughton: 7, 10, 74 (top), 84, 110, 120, 121, 164, 173, 177, 184 (both images), 199, 202, 203, 208, 210, 214, 215, 221, 222, 230, 231, 294, 295, 323, 333 (both images), 384, 402, 404, 405, 408, 411, 413, 429, 467, 477, 481, 488, 498, 507.

Courtesy of Maryland Biodiversity: 109 (bottom left).

Michael Piazza: v, 19, 48, 58, 82, 125 (top right, bottom left, bottom right), 126, 128, 129, 174, 195, 209, 243, 255, 268, 304, 309, 310, 312, 321, 376, 378, 380, 398, 436, 442, 443, 472, 509.

Neal Parent: 225, 306, 458, 463.

Penobscot Marine Museum, J. E. Perkins Collection, 363; National Fisherman Collection 104, 262, 289, 360.

Photograph © 2017 Museum of Fine Arts, Boston, viii.

Image Scans from Author's Private Collection of collectibles: iv, 241, 317 (both images), 326.

Steve McCutcheon, McCutcheon Prints; Anchorage Museum, B2003.011.4: 361.

The Art Institute Chicago / Art Resource, NY: 244.

University of Washington no. 564, PH Coll 1294: 364.

UWF Historic Trust collection: 246, 424, 430, 431.

ACKNOWLEDGMENTS

A very special thanks to my wife, Carrie, for her brilliant design of this, our fourth book together. She has joined me in this incredible journey, along the way learning her own fluency in the exceedingly diverse language of seafood and its culture. Without her elegant and engaging design, this book wouldn't be half of what it is.

Thanks to Katy Kennedy Rivera for her leadership organizing this enormous task and for her constant support of my need to write for sleepless days at a time.

To Kate Winslow for her intelligent and enthusiastic collaboration in tackling this massive rodeo of a project and her essential guidance when the path forward was not clear.

And now that I've thanked these three incredible women, allow me to now ask for their forgiveness. I apologize for asking all of you to be a part of this crazy endeavor. Thank you for your patience, empathy and belief in me.

Jeff and Sandy Witherly for lovingly caring for our newborn son, allowing us to have actual work days to finish this book.

This book would not have been possible without the countless experts who have been with me on my decades-long journey into the world of seafood. Many of these colleagues and friends provided vital assistance in accessing to hard-to-find seafood and connecting me to the people and stories behind them.

I am very proud that this book is a showcase for the incredible visual storytelling of the photographers who worked along side me, and those whose portfolios I was allowed to mine for the exceptional photographs that complete this book. Jay Fleming for his soulful portraits of the Chesapeake Bay and its watermen. Michael Piazza for his contributions and partnership on this, now our fourth book together. Mark Boughton for his generous spirit, companionship, and ability to capture the character and characters of our southern coast. Brendan Bullock for undertaking the editing of work from diverse sources. Ken Berg for generously sharing images of the Pacific Northwest. Neal Parent for sharing his keen eye for the subtle spirit of Maine's coast. The family of Leslie Jones for allowing me to celebrate their father's brilliant work. Maine Historical, Monroe County Public Libraries, Penobscot Marine Museum.

Thank you especially to the individuals and companies who provided in-kind and financial support for the extensive travel required to pull off this book. A special thank-you to Karen Profita and the Louisiana Seafood Marketing Board for arranging and enabling what was truly an epic tour of our southern coast.

Thanks to Fortune Fish, Future of Fish, High Liner Foods, Highliner Fish Company, Hog Island Oyster Co., Howard Fisher, Island Creek Oyster Co., JJ McDonnell & Co., Louisiana Seafood Marketing Board, Northern Divine Caviar, ProFish, Rappahannock River Oyster Co., Red's Best, Samuels and Son, Sea to Table, Seattle, and Taylor Shellfish

Many thanks to Marilyn Kretzer for her friendship and guidance and to the entire Sterling team for their vision to bring this idea to fruition and their talents in making it a book I will forever be proud of.

I am grateful to Don Lindgren of Rabelais Fine Books on Food & Drink for being so generous with his time and lending his one-of-a-kind expertise to helping me research classic texts and image collections.

Jack Montgomery, for guidance on photography, thank you.

Thank you to those who took time to read early drafts and provide critical feedback and editing:

Jared Auerback, Eliza Barclay, Ari Bernstein, Nick Branchina, Rachel Caggiano, Barry Costa-Pierce, Adam St. Gelais, Paul Greenberg, Tom Griffiths, Jim Griffin, Kathy Gunst, Elizabeth Herendeen, Michael Leviton, Ben Martens, Harlan Pearce, John Rorapaugh, Christine Burns Rudalevige, Tj Tate, Steve Vilnit, Jamie Wright.

Additionally there are countless people who have helped me in this effort. Forgive me if I've left anyone off:

Gary Bauer, Peter Battisti, Sonny Beal, Kenny Belov, Ned Bell, Sebastian Belle, David Bertrand, The Bosarge Family, Nancy Civetta, Corky Clark, Mayor Sherbin Collette, Ryan Cope, Karen and Jerry Cushman, Lauren D'Angelo, Cheryl Dahle, The Dimin Family, John Fallon, Tenney Flynn, Albert P. "Rusty" Gaude III, Pete Gerica, Amy Grondin, Jim Gossen, Buddy Guindon, Raz Halili, Chris Hanson, Matt Jacobson, Jill Jenson, Paul Johnson, Kate Masury, Brad Matthews, Matt and Gary Moretti, Nick Muto, Lance Nacio, John Pappalardo, Coltus Pearson, Willy Rich, Travis Riggs, Ashford Rosenberg, Jon Rowley, Darren Saletta, Jeremy Sewall, Bren Smith, Richard Stavis, Steve Train, Wendell Verret, Jasper White, Josh Whigham, Zack Yates, and the Harbor Fish Team.

ABOUT THE AUTHOR

Barton Seaver has spent more than two decades pursuing his passion for seafood, both in the kitchen and on the water. As an award-winning chef, he ran highly acclaimed restaurants in Washington, DC. Following a successful culinary career, he turned his focus toward fisheries and conservation as an Explorer for the National Geographic Society. He is the author of several books on the topic of sustainable seafood and cookery, including *For Cod and Country*, *Two If By Sea*, and *Where There's Smoke*. He has crewed on fishing boats and despite his best efforts is not a very good angler.

From his childhood memories of time on the Chesapeake to his far-flung voyages, the salty brine of sea air evokes the closest written chapters of his life. He now lives in Maine on a working waterfront, among the fishermen he so admires and honors with this book.

INDEX

Davis Codfish is *Absolutely Boneless!*

"Notice the thick, glistening Codfish the man is holding. Only steaks like these can give you Codfish suitable for an old-fashioned New England Codfish dinner. Look for the recipe on page seven of my cook book Now!"

EVERY day of the year I go to my codfish room. How interesting it is to watch my fisher folks skinning the large codfish steaks. Then to watch clever girls pulling the bones from steaks— to provide good eating Codfish for you—without bones.

As visitors stroll through my Codfish Room, they ask, "What do you do with those small bits of codfish trimmed from the steaks?" Those are what we call Codlets. They are every bit as good as the steaks themselves, delicious for creamed Codfish. Then another, "How many bones are in those steaks, and how do the girls know when they get them all?" That's easy to explain, for as you stand there, these very accurate girls will feel the bones with their left thumb and pull the bones the same instant with pincers in their right hand—AND THEY'LL COUNT THEM. When they have seventeen—they have them all— for that's all there are on each side of the codfish.

So you know when you get your Codfish from Davis that it's *free from bones*. Wouldn't you like to have a box of these *different* fish NOW?

Frank E. Davis   The Gloucester Fisherman

Sweet, Tender Codfish Steaks

Firm, meaty codfish are carefully cut into steaks, as illustrated below, and then packed just as you want them. Notice below, a 10 lb. box has just been packed. When the parchment paper is folded over the steaks, they are kept clean, fresh and moist. Try a box Now and learn why Davis Codfish is the favorite with "lovers of good codfish."

Price, delivered free:

20 lb. box	$7.60
10 lb. box	3.90
5 lb. box	2.00
1 lb. box	.40

Codlets

These are the small, dainty pieces that are trimmed from the codfish as it is cut into steaks. Absolutely free from bones and every morsel pure, wholesome codfish. Economical as well as healthful. Price, delivered free:

20 lb. box	$4.60
10 lb. box	2.40
5 lb. box	1.25
1 lb. box	.25

Fresh Codfish

Choice, clean, white pieces of FRESH CODFISH are especially packed in parchment lined tins for Davis Customers. Just try it as a salad dish, with diced onions, and plenty of mayonnaise. Our cook book gives many wonderful recipes for preparing this delicacy. Price, delivered free:

	No. ½	No. 1
Per dozen	$2.90	$4.75
Per tin	.25	.40

Fresh Halibut

Large, steak-like pieces of sweet, tender halibut, carefully packed in parchment-lined tins. Its delicious flavor keeps it in constant demand. I hope I'll have enough for all my customers. Send for some now. Price, delivered free:

Per dozen tins, $4.75   Per tin, $.40

Breakfast in a hurry?
Ready-Mixed Codfish Cakes

When you want a "quick" breakfast—have some Codfish Cakes. Choice salt codfish smoothly blended with boiled potatoes and the proper seasoning. Just open the package—roll the contents into small balls —and fry a delicious brown. My, don't they "hit the spot" these snappy, cool mornings. Try some!

Price, delivered free:

Per dozen tins, $2.60   Per tin, $.22

Codfish Fluff

Pure codfish, shredded by machinery into a light fluffy form. Free from skin and bones. No soaking— all ready for your favorite fish ball recipe.

Price, delivered free:

10 lb. box	5 lb. box	1 lb. box
$3.30	$1.70	$.35

Sliced Codfish
In Glass

Just hold one of these jars up before you. The glistening white slices will amaze you. For tender steaks are carefully sliced to wafer thinness and then conveniently packed in air-tight jars. Keep a few jars always on hand. Will keep perfectly in any climate. Price, delivered free:

Per dozen jars, $4.75   Per jar, $.40

Codfish Fluff
In Glass

I wish you could see my clever codfish workers shred small pieces of codfish into this light, fluffy form. And then to show its pureness and bright, white color, it is packed in special glass jars—airtight. Just freshen it a minute in cold water and it is ready to use. Price, delivered free:

Per dozen jars, $3.20   Per jar, $.27

Frank E. Davis Fish Company, Gloucester, Mass.